Laws & Regulations for California LMFTs and LPCCs

Laws & Regulations for California LMFTs and LPCCs

A Desk Reference for Licensed Clinicians, Associates and Trainee's

by:

Daniel Stewart, Ph.D.

Ashlee Fisher, M.A.

DISCLAIMER: Nothing contained in this book is intended or meant to constitute ethical or legal advice. The information in this book does not create a client-therapist relationship, or any other relationship with the authors. At the time of publication, information and laws presented may have changed or be outdated. The authors and publisher are not responsible for errors, omissions or for any consequences from application of the information in this book and make no guarantee, express or implied, with respect to the contents of the publication. Readers are responsible for obtaining such advice and guidance from their professions regulatory board, professional organization or contact an attorney as appropriate.

ISBN-10: 0578544083
ISBN-13: 978-0578544083

Contents

This page is intentionally left blank

Introduction

While being familiar with counseling theories and techniques is important as a psychotherapist, knowing the laws and regulations that surround mental health is just as important, if not even more. Knowledge of relevant laws and regulations is a necessary part of progressing through counseling graduate programs, passing the California Law & Ethics Exam as well as protecting your license and assets. Paramount to this is the protection of the client in clinical practice.

It is our hope that this book is a valuable resource for licensed professionals, associates, and trainees. As professional clinical counselors and marriage and family therapists, there are a number of regulatory and statutory laws that apply to the practice and application of psychotherapy. While it would be an accomplishment to memorize all laws relating to the practice of psychotherapy, we know that this is neither feasible nor possible. As counselor educators, trainers and mentors to students and those currently in the field, we have seen time and time again how easy it is to overlook our legal obligation, let alone know what our legal obligations are.

For graduate students and associates, it is our hope that you utilize the book as it is intended, to learn about how laws protect your client, your license, and protects the integrity of the profession. At first, the material may seem overwhelming. Yes – IT'S A LOT. However, we kept this in mind when developing the book. Whether you are using this book in a graduate course, studying for the California Law & Ethics Exam, or simply brushing up on the "shoulds" and musts" of your obligations, let each page, section and chapter simmer within you. Make connections to the ethical codes produced by ACA & CAMFT. Look for similarities, look for places of divergence and watch as the pieces to appropriate and lawful practice fall into place.

For licensed professional clinical counselors and marriage and family therapists, we hope that this book serves as a whetstone to sharpen your responses to act legally and ethically for the benefit of your client and to protect and safeguard your own welfare and license. Like any professional occupation working with the general public, you must continue to ask yourself "Am I acting in the best interest of my client?" "What laws and regulations apply to this situation?" "How can I meet the needs of my client while complying with legal mandates?" While this book focuses exclusively on the California regulatory and statuary laws that govern psychotherapeutic practice, we argue that ethics is just as important and provides an important and needed frame to view these questions from.

When we use the following terms in the book "counselor", "clinician", "therapist" or "psychotherapist", we are referring to the same group of individuals, those that are practicing professional clinical counseling and marriage and family therapy. When we first decided to proceed with the development of this book we decided to reflect on our own experiences in our professional law and ethics courses as students.

We also reflected on the comments and reviews of students that we have taught in those same courses as counselor educators. We came to the conclusion that it was important to provide not only our own commentary regarding the laws, but actually provide you the sections and codes as they are presented by California Statues and Regulatory Boards. We believe this is an important difference between being told what the law 'is' and knowing and accessing it for yourself. By being informed this way, you might better understand the letter of the law.

This book provides a compilation of statutory laws, codes, and regulations that govern professional clinical counseling and marriage and family therapy and is suggested to be used as a companion reference along with ethical standards. Preceding each section of the letter of the law, we have highlighted what we believe to be some important areas to take note of. We do not go into depth on each specific law, as we believe that many of these laws while having many nuances, are straightforward, and easy to understand. Note that we are not interpreting the law, as we are not practicing lawyers.

The laws and regulations presented in this book are for informational purposes only. This book does not cover all laws and regulations that a therapist in practice may encounter, however, it covers essential content required for graduate courses, licensing exams, as well as day to day requirements for lawful practice as therapists in the State of California. This book is not intended or meant to constitute ethical or legal advice. For such advice, therapists are advised to refer such questions to professional organizations, California State Licensing Board (BBS) or contact an attorney.

This page is intentionally left blank

CHAPTER 1
Counseling & Psychotherapy

This chapter provides an overview of the administration and regulation of the practice of Professional Clinical Counseling and Marriage and Family Therapy by the Board of Behavioral Sciences (BBS). This chapter covers definitions that you need to be aware of to navigate through educational requirements, supervision requirements and post license requirements discussed further in later chapters. Some other laws cited here are requirements for displaying your license as well as who is an "approved supervisor".

SO WHAT DO I NEED TO KNOW?

The simple answer...everything! Since this is not feasible, we have teased out a few items that we have noticed in our courses and practice that either are confusing or seem to be a continuous area of concern. To practice psychotherapy, you either have to be a student enrolled and progressing through a graduate program, have earned the graduate degree and registered as an Associate, or have completed all licensure requirements and have been issued a license to practice. The extent to which each of these individuals can practice (student – trainee, associate & licensed) is regulated by laws.

The law is explicit in that students, currently in a graduate program, are given the title "Trainee". Whether studying PCC or MFT, the word "Trainee" applies to those students who have completed at least 12 semester or 18 quarter units in their approved program (BPC 4999.12g & 4980.03c). The term "Associate" is reserved for those that have completed their degree program and have registered with the Board of Behavioral Sciences to work towards their required supervision hours (4999.12f & 4980.03b). While in the graduate program, students are required to complete a certain amount of clinical hours, sometimes these courses are called "field experience", "fieldwork" or "internship". The latter term is what usually causes confusion.

Students in their "internship" are still "Trainee's" by law. While you may be "interning" at your local Department of Behavioral Health, it is important to clarify to your clients that you are unlicensed and are enrolled in a program and completing your hours as part of the degree requirements. To identify yourself as an Intern causes confusion and potentially misleads your client. The word "Licensed" preceding PCC for MFT (whether spelled out or abbreviated) identifies that you are approved by the Board of Behavioral

Sciences to practice lawfully as a fully licensed therapist. For those not licensed, identifying yourself as anything other than provided by law is both unethical and illegal. This can result in civil and criminal consequences for unprofessional conduct.

Approved Supervisors are those that are licensed as an LPCC, LMFT, LCSW, Psychologist or Psychiatrist who have had their licensed for at least 2 years and have completed supervision training (4999.12h & 4980.03g). There are other requirements that supervisors need to comply with to lawfully supervise, such as ensuring the license is valid and ensuring they meet the education requirement to supervise those registered under a different license than the one the supervisor possesses, amongst others. Associate's gaining their post degree hours are encouraged to verify their supervisor's license through the website: www.bbs.ca.gov. This can be done independently, free of charge and all you need is their first and last name.

What is Scope of Practice?

A question that we frequently hear is, "What is the different between a LMFT and LPCC"? Simple, their titles. Well, actually there's more to it than that. The difference lies in the scope of practice. This is, "What they are trained to do" "Who they are allowed to work with" and "How they go about doing what they do". BPC 4999.20 defines the scope of practice for Licensed Professional Clinical Counselors and BPC 4980.02 defines Licensed Marriage and Family Therapy scope of practice.

SO WHAT DO I NEED TO KNOW?

What you will notice is that both licenses allow for the use of psychotherapeutic techniques to assist their clients. Note: When we use the terms "psychotherapeutic techniques" or "counseling techniques" we are using them to express the same services. Traditionally, PCC's are trained to work with individuals and groups and develop interventions to assist them in living a more fulfilled life, or at least, "remediate" issues they are dealing with. The focus is usually on the individual, how they are coping with problems, what behavioral issues they would like to address and what goals they have to solve these issues.

Unlike PCC's, MFT's are trained not only to work with individuals and groups, but also with couples and families. This is probably one of the most important distinctions in that PCC's cannot do so without additional training (BPC 4999.20 a3). MFT's also traditionally work within the systems frame of viewing these problems being situated within interpersonal relationships. With families, MFT's specifically look at how problems develop, cultivate and are perpetuated within the family system. While this may be an over simplification, this is essentially the difference. Therein, scope of practice is not only embedded in law, but it is seeded in graduate courses and in training.

Marriage and Family Therapy programs are specifically designed to teach students how to examine family systems, address dysfunctionality and provide appropriate treatment and recommendations. Counseling Theories that are family systems oriented are a central focus in these programs. *Does this mean that if a client has a problem but it does not affect the family nor interpersonal relationships an MFT cannot work with them?* Some have argued that with the addition of the LPCC license, MFT's should not work with these individuals because it is outside of their scope. It can also be argued that all problems affect interpersonal relationships and therefore falls within the scope.

Coursework and counseling theories in a PCC graduate program typically focus on the individual. Usually this means having no contact with the family or significant other (marital or couple counseling). Because working with children frequently requires speaking with parents or guardians, consulting with them may be necessary. Nothing in the law currently, specifically prohibits consultation or collaboration with parents or guardians for the well-fair of your client, the minor child. It should be made clear however, that the parents/guardians are not your client. Typical consultation and collaboration elicits information on the problem (from parent/guardian point of view), changes or improvement in behavior, as well as valuable reports that may help in charting progress. PCC's are eligible to work with couples and families if they meet additional education requirements identified by BPC 4999.20(a) and discussed in chapter 2.

There are other professions and occupations that provide counseling that are specifically exempt from being licensed. Physicians, religious leaders and those who work for governmental or non-profit organization (to name a few) whose position situates them to counsel are exempt from needing to be licensed. Yet, they by law cannot claim to be licensed, and this therefore protects the field (BPC 2908). Note also that Hypnotherapist, Life Coaches and Life Consultants are not regulated by the BBS and are not required to meet licensing standards. However, there are other laws (not included in this book) that provides restrictions on terminology and application used when advertising and providing services to avoid general public confusion. For example: those that are unlicensed but provide hypnotherapy specifically must provide their clients with a document stating they are unlicensed.

Scope of practice is found directly within the laws, for professional clinical counselor this is found under Business and Professions Code 4999.20 and for marriage and family therapists Business and Professions Code 4980.02. When we talk about the scope of practice, this is specific to each license.

When we say "each license," we mean the three distinct master level professions that perform psychotherapy in the State of California, which are professional clinical counselors, Marriage and Family Therapist and clinical social workers. While there are distinctions between these licenses, there is overlap as well. Therapists with different licenses may see the clients with very similar issues, however, how they approach those issues may be different depending on their education, experience, skills and scope of practice. The assessments and the tools that we utilize to develop interventions may be different. And the training that you receive as a result of your education and your scope of practice is a driving force in how you work with the client.

When we talk about the scope of practice, we're talking about what you legally can do as defined by the Board of Behavioral Sciences according to the license or registration you possess. There are restrictions, and then there are expanded opportunities for what you can do. When we talk about the scope of practice, we are also looking at what types of assessments you may be able to utilize, the kinds of interventions you may be able to implement, and again, which clinical issues you might be able to use those interventions with. What must be considered is whether any restrictions prohibit you from working with specific groups or particular populations. There is a restriction under the LPCC license as part of the initial scope of practice, and then it broadens a bit more once additional training.

Specifically under Business and Professions Code 4999.20 it states the following in regards to scope of practice, " Professional clinical counseling" means the application of counseling interventions and psychotherapeutic techniques to identify and remediate cognitive, mental, and emotional issues, including personal growth, adjustment to disability, crisis intervention, and psychosocial and environmental problems, and the use, application, and integration of the coursework and training required by Sections 4999.32 and 4999.33.

 It also states that "Professional clinical counseling" includes conducting assessments for the purpose of establishing counseling goals and objectives to empower individuals to deal adequately with life situations, reduce stress, experience growth, change behavior, and make well informed, rational decisions. So, as you can see in this particular section, it indicates that professional clinical counselors can use assessments, these are psychological tests that they can utilize as part of the scope of practice. We will see a little bit later that there are some limitations on the type of psychological tests that they can use. Furthermore, "Professional clinical counseling" is focused exclusively on the application of counseling interventions and psychotherapeutic techniques for the purposes of improving mental health, and is not intended to capture other, nonclinical forms of counseling for the purposes of licensure. For purposes of this paragraph, "nonclinical" means "nonmental health."

This clarification provides some information and guidance that PCC's are not providing nonmental health counseling. The law goes on to say that "professional clinical counseling does not include the assessment or treatment of couples or families unless the professional clinical counselor has completed all of the following training and education:" Remember we stated earlier that there was a restriction on potentially the type of clients or the population and the groups that PCC can work with? This limitation is one of them. While there is a restriction, according to the law, there is also an exception.

You are allowed to work with these populations so long as you complete the following:
    (i)   Six-semester units or nine quarter units specifically focused on the theory and application of marriage and family therapy.
    (ii)   (ii) A named specialization or emphasis area on the qualifying degree in marriage and family therapy; marital and family therapy; marriage, family, and child counseling; or couple and family therapy. Then you would also need to complete no "less than 500 hours of documented supervised experience working directly with couples, families, or children." Those 500 can be part of the 3,000-post-degree supervised hours discussed in this book and the law. Once licensed, you will need to complete "a minimum of six hours of continuing education specific to marriage and family therapy, completed in each license renewal cycle."

For MFT, the law states the following: "For the purposes of this chapter, the practice of marriage and family therapy shall mean that service performed with individuals, couples, or groups wherein interpersonal relationships are examined for the purpose of achieving more adequate, satisfying, and productive marriage and family adjustments. This practice includes relationship and pre-marriage counseling. The application of marriage and family therapy principles and methods includes, but is not limited to, the use of applied psychotherapeutic techniques, to enable individuals to mature and grow within marriage and the family, the provision of explanations and interpretations of the psychosexual and psychosocial aspects of relationships, and the use, application, and integration of the coursework and training required by Sections 4980.36, 4980.37, and 4980.41." You will notice that there is no apparent restriction listed in the law when it comes to population or assessment.

Testing: Listed in the scope of practice for both PCC's and MFT's are the use of testing and assessment. However note that the PCC's are not allowed to use the following tests: projective tests, personality, intelligence, neuropsychological or three or more tests to determine the psychosis, dementia, amnesia, cognitive impairment or criminal behavior (BPC 4999.20). These assessments are considered to be out of the scope of practice for a PCC. MFT's are allowed to utilize the aforementioned tests as established by the California Attorney General Opinion Number 83 – 810, by Attorney General John K. Van de Kamp in 1984. Here it is clarified that MFT's are allowed to construct, administer and interpret psychological tests as long as:

(1) The individual that they are utilizing the test on is an actual client in psychotherapy

(2) The use of the test is within the MFT's scope, including education and training

(3) The MFT does not hold him or herself out as a psychologist.

Additionally it should be noted that the Attorney General's opinion clarified that the use of these psychological test are solely to "be used to examine an interpersonal relationship between spouses or members of a family for the purpose of achieving more adequate, satisfying and productive marriage and family adjustments". While the opinion actually uses terms like "marriage counselors" or "marriage, family and child counselors", this is meant to refer to today's Marriage and Family Therapist. Remember that LPCC's that do complete the six semester units or nine quarter units specifically focused on the theory and application of marriage and family therapy can assess and treat couples and families and may use assessments, however, because the licensee is a PCC, the restrictions found in 4999.20(c) still apply.

However, regardless of the breadth of scope available to the licensee or registrant, it is expected that they will refer clients to other licensed healthcare professionals when client issues are outside their scope of education, training, and experience. You are not likely to know how to treat every problem found in the DSM 5. This refers not just scope of practice (again the legal aspects of this that we were talking about) but the scope of competence. The question you must always ask is, "Am I competent enough to help this client? Can I provide the appropriate level of services that is adequate for their mental, emotional, and psychological need?" When we talk about the scope of competence, we are talking about what you know and what you can do as informed by your education, training, and experience. There is no expectation that you will be able to treat every client issue that you come across, that's probably just not possible for any psychotherapist. With cultural considerations, family dynamics, interpersonal dynamics, and psychological wellness concerns, there may be issues and situations that you are unfamiliar with. If you have no experience or no relevant training, it would be inappropriate for you to continue to provide services. Here the scope of practice might allow you to work with the client, but your scope of competence is lacking, and therefore, it would be inappropriate.

It is quite possible that some therapist has a scope of competence that exceeds others because of their education, their own experience, and their professional training, while another therapist may not be as competent in some areas although they both may have very similar educational backgrounds. The great thing about scope of competence is that you can expand it so you can become more competent in a clinical area. So, let's say you want to be more competent in working with clients that have severe and persistent mental illness specific to schizophrenia, you can go and obtain additional training. You can take classes, attend workshops, read up on that particular diagnosis, and received supervision as you learn to become competent in working with this diagnosis. Note: You cannot expand your scope of practice unless identified explicitly in the law or you obtain an additional license that has that expanded scope. An example would be obtaining licensure as a Psychologist.

PCC Definitions

Business & Professions Code
4999.12. Definitions
For purposes of this chapter, the following terms have the following meanings:
(a) "Board" means the Board of Behavioral Sciences.

(b) "Accredited" means a school, college, or university accredited by a regional or national institutional accrediting agency that is recognized by the United States Department of Education.

(c) "Approved" means a school, college, or university that possessed unconditional approval by the Bureau for
Private Postsecondary Education at the time of the applicant's graduation from the school, college, or
university.

(d) "Applicant for licensure" means an unlicensed person who has completed the required education and required hours of supervised experience for licensure.

(e) "Licensed professional clinical counselor" or "LPCC" means a person licensed under this chapter to practice professional clinical counseling, as defined in Section 4999.20.

(f) "Associate" means an unlicensed person who meets the requirements of Section 4999.42 and is registered with the board.

(g) "Clinical counselor trainee" means an unlicensed person who is currently enrolled in a master's or doctoral degree program, as specified in Section 4999.32 or 4999.33, that is designed to qualify him or her for licensure and who has completed no less than 12 semester units or 18 quarter units of coursework in any qualifying degree program.

(h) "Supervisor" means an individual who meets all of the following requirements:

> (1) Has held an active license for at least two years within the five-year period immediately preceding any supervision as either:
>
> > (A) A licensed professional clinical counselor, licensed marriage and family therapist, psychologist licensed pursuant to Chapter 6.6 (commencing with Section 2900), licensed clinical social worker, or equivalent out-of-state license.
> > (B) A physician and surgeon who is certified in psychiatry by the American Board of Psychiatry and Neurology, or an out-of-state licensed physician and surgeon who is certified in psychiatry by the American Board of Psychiatry and Neurology.

(2) If the individual is a licensed professional clinical counselor seeking to supervise an associate marriage and family therapist, a marriage and family therapist trainee, or an associate professional clinical counselor or licensee seeking experience to treat couples and families pursuant to subparagraph (B) of paragraph (3) of subdivision (a) of Section 4999.20, he or she shall meet the additional training and education requirements in subparagraphs (A) to (C), inclusive, of paragraph (3) of subdivision (a) of Section 4999.20.

(3) For at least two years within the five-year period immediately preceding any supervision, has either practiced psychotherapy or provided direct clinical supervision of psychotherapy performed by marriage and family therapist trainees, associate marriage and family therapists, associate professional clinical counselors, or associate clinical social workers. Supervision of psychotherapy performed by a social work intern or a professional clinical counselor trainee shall be accepted if the supervision provided is substantially equivalent to the supervision required for registrants.

(4) Has received training in supervision as specified in this chapter and by regulation.

(5) Has not provided therapeutic services to the supervisee.

(6) Has and maintains a current and active license that is not under suspension or probation as one of the following:

(A) A marriage and family therapist, professional clinical counselor, or clinical social worker, issued by the board.
(B) A psychologist licensed pursuant to Chapter 6.6 (commencing with Section 2900).
(C) A physician and surgeon who is certified in psychiatry by the American Board of Psychiatry and Neurology.

(7) Is not a spouse, domestic partner, or relative of the supervisee.

(8) Does not currently have or previously had a personal, professional, or business relationship with the supervisee that undermines the authority or effectiveness of the supervision.

(i) "Client centered advocacy" includes, but is not limited to, researching, identifying, and accessing resources, or other activities, related to obtaining or providing services and supports for clients or groups of clients receiving psychotherapy or counseling services.

(j) "Advertising" or "advertise" includes, but is not limited to, the issuance of any card, sign, or device to any person, or the causing, permitting, or allowing of any sign or marking on, or in, any building or structure, or in any newspaper or magazine or in any directory, or any printed matter whatsoever, with or without any limiting qualification. It also includes business solicitations communicated by radio or television broadcasting. Signs within church buildings or notices in church bulletins mailed to a congregation shall not be construed as advertising within the meaning of this chapter.

(k) "Referral" means evaluating and identifying the needs of a client to determine whether it is advisable to refer the client to other specialists, informing the client of that judgment, and communicating that determination as requested or deemed appropriate to referral sources.

(l) "Research" means a systematic effort to collect, analyze, and interpret quantitative and qualitative data that describes how social characteristics, behavior, emotion, cognitions, disabilities, mental disorders, and interpersonal transactions among individuals and organizations interact.

(m) "Supervision" means responsibility for, and control of, the quality of mental health and related services provided by the supervisee.

Consultation or peer discussion shall not be considered supervision and shall not qualify as supervised experience. Supervision includes, but is not limited to, all of the following:

(1) Ensuring the extent, kind, and quality of counseling performed is consistent with the education, training, and experience of the supervisee.

(2) Monitoring and evaluating the supervisee's assessment, diagnosis, and treatment decisions and providing regular feedback.

(3) Monitoring and evaluating the supervisee's ability to provide services at the site or sites where he or she is practicing and to the particular clientele being served.

(4) Monitoring and addressing clinical dynamics, including, but not limited to, countertransference-,intrapsychic-, interpersonal-, or trauma-related issues that may affect the supervisory or the practitioner patient relationship.

(5) Ensuring the supervisee's compliance with laws and regulations governing the practice of licensed professional clinical counseling.

(6) Reviewing the supervisee's progress notes, process notes, and other patient treatment records, as deemed appropriate by the supervisor.

(7) With the client's written consent, providing direct observation or review of audio or video recordings of the supervisee's counseling or therapy, as deemed appropriate by the supervisor.

(n) "Clinical setting" means any setting that meets both of the following requirements:

(1) Lawfully and regularly provides mental health counseling or psychotherapy.

(2) Provides oversight to ensure that the associate's work meets the experience and supervision requirements set forth in this chapter and in regulation and is within the scope of practice of the profession.

(o) "Community mental health setting," means a clinical setting that meets all of the following requirements:

(1) Lawfully and regularly provides mental health counseling or psychotherapy.

(2) Clients routinely receive psychopharmacological interventions in

conjunction with psychotherapy, counseling, or other psycho-social interventions.

(3) Clients receive coordinated care that includes the collaboration of mental health providers.

(4) Is not a private practice.

4999.12.5. Registrant title name change

(a) (1) The title "professional clinical counselor intern" or "professional clinical counselor registered intern" is hereby renamed "associate professional clinical counselor" or "registered associate professional clinical counselor," respectively. Any reference in any statute or regulation to a "professional clinical counselor intern" or "professional clinical counselor registered intern" shall be deemed a reference to an "associate professional clinical counselor" or "registered associate professional clinical counselor."

(2) Any reference in this chapter to the term "intern" means "associate."

(b) Nothing in this section shall be construed to expand or constrict the scope of practice of a person licensed or registered pursuant to this chapter.

MFT Definitions

4980. Definitions

(a) "Board," as used in this chapter, means the Board of Behavioral Sciences.

(b) "Associate," as used in this chapter, means an unlicensed person who has earned his or her master's or doctoral degree qualifying him or her for licensure and is registered with the board as an associate.

(c) "Trainee," as used in this chapter, means an unlicensed person who is currently enrolled in a master's or doctoral degree program, as specified in Sections 4980.36 and 4980.37, that is designed to qualify him or her for licensure under this chapter, and who has completed no less than 12 semester units or 18 quarter units of coursework in any qualifying degree program.

(d) "Applicant for licensure," as used in this chapter, means an unlicensed person who has completed the required education and required hours of supervised experience for licensure.

(e) "Advertise," as used in this chapter, includes, but is not limited to, any public communication, as defined in subdivision (a) of Section 651, the issuance of any card, sign, or device to any person, or the causing, permitting, or allowing of any sign or marking on, or in, any building or structure, or in any newspaper or magazine or in any directory, or any printed matter whatsoever, with or without any limiting qualification. Signs within religious buildings or notices in church bulletins mailed to a congregation shall not be construed as advertising within the meaning of this chapter.

(f) "Experience," as used in this chapter, means experience in interpersonal relationships, psychotherapy, marriage and family therapy, direct clinical counseling, and nonclinical practice that satisfies the requirements for licensure as a marriage and family therapist.

4980.09. Registrant title name change
(a) (1) The title "marriage and family therapist intern" or "marriage and family therapist registered intern" is
hereby renamed "associate marriage and family therapist" or "registered associate marriage and family
therapist," respectively. Any reference in statute or regulation to a "marriage and family therapist intern"
or "marriage and family therapist registered intern" shall be deemed a reference to an "associate
marriage and family therapist" or "registered associate marriage and family therapist."
(2) Any reference in this chapter to the term "intern" means "associate." Any reference in statute or
regulation to the abbreviation "MFTI" means an "AMFT."
(b) This section shall not be construed to expand or constrict the scope of practice of a person licensed or
registered pursuant to this chapter.

PCC Scope of Practice

Business & Professions Code
4999.20. Professional Clinical Counseling – Scope of Practice
(a) (1) "Professional clinical counseling" means the application of counseling interventions and psychotherapeutic techniques to identify and remediate cognitive, mental, and emotional issues, including personal growth, adjustment to disability, crisis intervention, and psychosocial and environmental problems, and the use, application, and integration of the coursework and training required by Sections 4999.32 and 4999.33.

"Professional clinical counseling" includes conducting assessments for the purpose of establishing counseling goals and objectives to empower individuals to deal adequately with life situations, reduce stress, experience growth, change behavior, and make well-informed, rational decisions.

(2) "Professional clinical counseling" is focused exclusively on the application of counseling interventions and psychotherapeutic techniques for the purposes of improving mental health, and is not intended to capture other, nonclinical forms of counseling for the purposes of licensure. For purposes of this paragraph, "nonclinical" means nonmental health.

(3) "Professional clinical counseling" does not include the assessment or treatment of couples or families unless the professional clinical counselor has completed all of the following training and education:

(A) One of the following:

(i) Six semester units or nine quarter units specifically focused on the theory and application of marriage and family therapy.

(ii) A named specialization or emphasis area on the qualifying degree in marriage and family therapy; marital and family therapy; marriage, family, and child counseling; or couple and family therapy.

(B) No less than 500 hours of documented supervised experience working directly with couples, families, or children.

(C) A minimum of six hours of continuing education specific to marriage and family therapy, completed in each license renewal cycle.

(4) "Professional clinical counseling" does not include the provision of clinical social work services.

(b) "Counseling interventions and psychotherapeutic techniques" means the application of cognitive, affective, verbal or nonverbal, systemic or holistic counseling strategies that include principles of development, wellness, and maladjustment that reflect a pluralistic society. These interventions and techniques are specifically implemented in the context of a professional clinical counseling relationship and use a variety of counseling theories and approaches.

(c) "Assessment" means selecting, administering, scoring, and interpreting tests, instruments, and other tools and methods designed to measure an individual's attitudes, abilities, aptitudes, achievements, interests, personal characteristics, disabilities, and mental, emotional, and behavioral concerns and development and the use of methods and techniques for understanding human behavior in relation to coping with, adapting to, or ameliorating changing life situations, as part of the counseling process.

"Assessment" shall not include the use of projective techniques in the assessment of personality, individually administered intelligence tests, neuropsychological testing, or utilization of a battery of three or more tests to determine the presence of psychosis, dementia, amnesia, cognitive impairment, or criminal behavior.

(d) Professional clinical counselors shall refer clients to other licensed health care professionals when they identify issues beyond their own scope of education, training, and experience.

4999.22.Use of Term " Licensed Professional Clinical Counselor," Exceptions

(a) Nothing in this chapter shall prevent qualified persons from doing work of a psychosocial nature consistent with the standards and ethics of their respective professions. However, these qualified persons shall not hold themselves out to the public by any title or description of services incorporating the words "licensed professional clinical counselor" and shall not state that they are licensed to practice professional clinical counseling, unless they are otherwise licensed to provide professional clinical counseling services.

(b) Nothing in this chapter shall be construed to constrict, limit, or withdraw provisions of the Medical Practice Act, the Clinical Social Worker Practice Act, the Nursing Practice Act, the Psychology Licensing Law, or the Licensed Marriage and Family Therapist Act.

(c) This chapter shall not apply to any priest, rabbi, or minister of the gospel of any religious denomination who performs counseling services as part of his or her pastoral or professional duties, or to any person who is admitted to practice law in this state, or who is licensed to practice medicine, who provides counseling services as part of his or her professional practice.

(d) This chapter shall not apply to an employee of a governmental entity or a school, college, or university, or of an institution both nonprofit and charitable, if his or her practice is performed solely under the supervision of the entity, school, college, university, or institution by which he or she is employed, and if he or she performs those functions as part of the position for which he or she is employed.

(e) All persons registered as associates or licensed under this chapter shall not be exempt from this chapter or the jurisdiction of the board.

4999.24.Course of Study Activities Not Limited by LPCC Act

Nothing in this chapter shall restrict or prevent activities of a psychotherapeutic or counseling nature on the part of persons employed by accredited or state-approved academic institutions, public schools, government agencies, or nonprofit institutions engaged in the training of graduate students or clinical counselor trainees pursuing a course of study leading to a degree that qualifies for professional clinical counselor licensure at an accredited or state-approved college or university, or working in a recognized training program, provided that these activities and services constitute a part of a supervised course of study and that those persons are designated by a title such as "clinical counselor trainee" or other title clearly indicating the training status appropriate to the level of training.

MFT Scope of Practice

4980.02. Practice of Marriage, Family and Child Counseling; Application of Principles and Methods

For the purposes of this chapter, the practice of marriage and family therapy shall mean that service performed with individuals, couples, or groups wherein interpersonal relationships are examined for the purpose of achieving more adequate, satisfying, and productive marriage and family adjustments. This practice includes relationship and premarriage counseling.

The application of marriage and family therapy principles and methods includes, but is not limited to, the use of applied psychotherapeutic techniques, to enable individuals to mature and grow within marriage and the family, the provision of explanations and interpretations of the psychosexual and psychosocial aspects of relationships, and the use, application, and integration of the coursework and training required by Sections 4980.36, 4980.37, and 4980.41, as applicable.

CHAPTER 2
Education & Licensure Requirements

There are specific requirements that must be met in California in order to register as an associate, accumulate supervised hours, sit for testing and finally be fully licensed to practice psychotherapy as an LPCC or LMFT. The laws vary to some degree for each license category, however the requirements are established by law and are enforceable by the BBS. Generally, to be licensed as an LPCC, you need a doctorate or master's degree that focused on counseling or psychotherapy. If the degree was obtained in California, the institution had to be either accredited or state approved by the Bureau for Private Secondary Education (BPC 4999.12). For those looking to be licensed as an MFT, the board has established several degree titles that the individual can possess, as long as the emphasis is in marriage and family therapy or marriage, family, and child counseling. The MFT degrees need to be from institutions that are regionally accredited, state approved or nationally accredited by the Commission on Accreditation for Marriage and Family Therapy Education (COAMFTE).

Degree Program Entry & Completion

While it may be the responsibility of each institution to ensure that they are complying with the regulations set forth for degree programs, each student or perspective student should be aware of the institutions accreditation or approval and ensure that they meet the BBS requirements to offer such a degree that allows them to be license eligible. This is called a qualifying degree. This can be verified on the Board of Behavioral Sciences website. The degree requirements shift for two specific entry and completion dates for both MFT's and LPCC applicants. Those that begin their academic study before August 1, 2012 and complete their degree program by December 31, 2018 must meet specific requirements. The content requirements have been established by the Board of Behavioral Sciences and are then implemented by the institution.

There are some major changes for those seeking to be *licensed as a professional clinical counselor in the State of California.* Two statutes exist under the Business and Professions Code that describes approved degrees towards licensure. The first is BPC 4999.32, and this would be identified as previous or older counseling degrees. Specifically, these are for individuals who began their master's degree program before August 1, 2012, and they finished their degree before December 31, 2018. These degrees were somewhere between 48-semester units or 72 quarter units and had a variety of courses that met at least many of the core content requirements by the State of California according to the Business of Professions Code. The newer degree, the one that was established by the Business of Professions Code for those that either did not finish their degree by December 31, 2018, and/or they began their degree after August 1, 2012. If you are currently in an LPCC Degree Program, your degree likely will meet Business and Professions Code 4999.33, which in summary requires applicants to possess a master's or doctoral degree that is in counseling or psychotherapy in content and meets the requirements as required by the BBS. These are called 'In-State' degrees, and of the 13-core content courses required, the degree must contain at least 10 of them along with practicum/fieldwork/internship courses, and additional advanced coursework. The degree must also contain "no less than 60 graduate semester units or 90 graduate quarter units of instruction."

To graduate from your program with the degree, you are required to complete a minimum of 280 hours of face-to-face counseling clinical experience that is supervised working with individuals' families or groups. Note that the 280 hours that you are required to complete as part of your degree requirement it is merely part of finishing your degree to graduate, those 280 hours do not count towards post-degree supervised experience.

The degree title may vary amongst counseling programs across the state. Some might call it a Master of Art or Master of Science in Counseling. Another program my title it a Masters in Counseling Psychology, while others a Masters in Clinical Mental Health Counseling. Regardless of the specific degree title, they all have to meet specific standards whether it has to do with semester or quarter units and the course content that is provided.

There are also changes for those seeking to be _licensed as a marriage and family therapist in the State of California_. Two statutes exist under the Business and Professions Code that describes approved degrees towards licensure. The first is BPC 4980.37, and this would be identified as previous or older counseling degrees. Specifically, these are for individuals who began their master's degree program before August 1, 2012, and they finished their degree before December 31, 2018. These degrees were somewhere between 48-semester units or 72 quarter units and had a variety of courses that met at least many of the core content requirements by the State of California according to the Business of Professions Code. The newer degree, the one that was established by the Business of Professions Code for those that either did not finish their degree by December 31, 2018, and/or they began their degree after August 1, 2012. If you are currently in an MFT Degree Program, your degree likely will meet Business and Professions Code 4990.36, which in summary requires applicants to possess a master's or doctoral degree that is in marital therapy, family therapy, couples therapy, or child counseling or psychotherapy in content and that meets the requirements as required by the BBS. These are called 'In-State' degrees, and requires additional coursework and advanced topics to be included in the degree curriculum. The degree must also contain "no less than 60 graduate semester units or 90 graduate quarter units of instruction."

To graduate from your program with the degree, you are required to complete a minimum of 150 hours of face-to-face counseling clinical experience that is supervised working with individuals' families or groups. Note that the 150 hours that you are required to complete as part of your degree requirement it is merely part of finishing your degree to graduate, however they can count towards post-degree supervised experience.

MFT students can earn up to 1300 hours within the degree program that can count towards post-degree hours. According to BPC 4980.43 up to 750 is direct clinical experience (face to face counseling), and the other 550 is non-clinical experience.

Out of State/Out of Country: When individuals come from Out of State, they are still held to the same educational requirements that students that are trained and educated in California have, however, there are some differences. The Board does allow individuals that have out-of-state degrees to remediate coursework (meaning to complete those additional coursework after they've obtained their degree so they would apply to the Board they typically would receive something called a "deficiency letter." That deficiency letter would outline what additional items need to be completed (as long as the degree used to apply for the registration/license met the minimum requirements to begin with).

Individuals trained outside the United States may be eligible to obtain a registration and a license as well. They would need to request their institution to send their educational transcripts and other required documents to the National Association of Credential Evaluation Services (NACES). Their members review all out of the country education (international education) and provide a report that would describe if the degree is equivalent to a regionally accredited master's degree in the United States. The document would identify the title of that degree and then they would go on and provide a comprehensive evaluation of the coursework and education and compare it to education and training that would be typically obtained in the United States. The evaluation document from NACES would then be sent to the Board of Behavioral Sciences to determine if they would deem it to be equivalent as well and what deficiencies might exist. Remember, the Board has full authority over determining if a degree meets requirements.

Hours Towards Licensure

So now you have completed your master's degree, and you are looking to apply for your registration number. Some things need to be kept in mind. California Business and Professions Code 4999.42 / 4980.40 requires the applicant shall have meet the educational requirements as specified either through section 4999.32 / 4980.37 or the newer degree 4999.33 / 4980.36 and also states that the applicant shall not have committed acts or crimes constituting grounds for denial of licensure under BPC 480. Business and Professions Code 4999.42 / 4980.40 additionally it says that the Board shall not issue a registration to any person who has been convicted of a crime in this or another state or in a territory of the United States that involves sexual abuse of children or who is required to register pursuant to Section 290 of the Penal Code or the equivalent in another state or territory.

When you graduate with your degree, you can immediately start counting counseling and psychotherapy hours before you receive your registration number. This is found under Business and Professions Code 4999.46 and 4980.43 and essentially what it says is that as long as you apply to the Board of Behavioral Sciences within 90 days of receiving your degree (when it is conferred on your transcript), you can count hours towards 3,000 post-degree hours. Essentially it states that when you graduate from your program, you need to apply, and the Board needs to receive your application within 90 days. The evaluators will look at the postmarked date on the envelope and look at the date that you graduated so the sooner you apply, the better, and again your degree can either be the masters or the doctoral degree that is the qualifying masters or doctoral degree. For those who graduate on or after January 1, 2020, that individual needs to obtain their supervised work experience at a workplace that requires that they complete a live scan (fingerprinting) and provide the Board a copy of the live scan.

You cannot work in a private practice either as an employee or volunteer until your registration number has been approved. Again, if you graduated from school and received an excellent offer to work in a private practice, you cannot work in that private practice until you have a registration number. You can, however, work in other settings such as a school or government organization or nonprofit agency that's not a private practice, you just cannot work in a private practice during that 90-day window.

Supervised Professional Experiences – For both MFT's and PCC's, you will need to complete a minimum of 3,000 hours of Supervised Professional Experience in no less than two years, also known as 104 weeks. You can count no more than 40 hours in any seven consecutive days. Many therapists work 40 hours a week if working full-time, but you cannot claim more than 40 hours a week, even if you work two jobs. The maximum amount of time that you can claim in a week is 40 hours. Remember there's going to be downtime, there's going to be times where clients cancel, there's going to be times where you are not necessarily doing counseling or writing clinical notes, but you might be doing something completely different, so obviously that number is going to vary based upon your own work experience.

The 3,000 hours have specific requirements that need to be met. The Board has decided that no less than 1750 hours needs to be direct clinical counseling with individuals, groups, couples, or families using a variety of psychotherapeutic techniques and recognized counseling interventions. A maximum of 1,250 can be identified as non-clinical practice which can be direct supervisor contact (supervision), administering and evaluating psychological tests, writing clinical reports, writing progress, client-centered advocacy, attending workshops, attending seminars, attending trainings or conferences that are directly related to professional clinical counseling or marriage and family therapy that have been pre-approved by your supervisor.

For those seeking the LPCC, you must complete 150 hours in a community mental health setting or hospital (BPC 4999.12). There is some history regarding this, in fact, this was something that was required to remove any resistance and opposition against the development of the LPCC. The law states that no less than 150 hours need needs to be completed that (1) lawfully and regularly provide mental health counseling or psychotherapy to clients they are routinely receiving (2) psychopharmacological interventions in conjunction with psychotherapy, counseling or other psychosocial interventions, (3) those clients receive coordinated care that includes the collaboration of mental health providers and (4) the site is not a private practice.

For those seeking the LMFT, you must complete no less than 500 total hours of experience in diagnosing and treating couples, families, and Children (BPC 4080.43).

It is important to remember that wherever you go to be employed or to volunteer, it may mean that if it is not one of these settings already that you are going to have to go volunteer or be employed for at least 150 hours in another setting to meet the requirement.

You have a total of six years to complete your hours under the initial registration. The first year you receive your registration number is identified as your initial registration as an APCC of AMFT, and then you have five more renewals after that for a total of six years. Note that these hours cannot be more than six years old. This happens when someone does not finish their hours in the six-year time frame and require another application and registration.

So, let's look a little bit at what supervision looks like and how to obtain supervision. You will need a supervisor that has been licensed for at least two years. You can verify the timeframe by going to the Board of Behavioral Sciences website, click on verify license, enter the name and verify that the supervisor has had their license for at least two years. There are also some additional requirements that supervisors will need to follow as part of their responsibilities.

Business and Professions Code 4999.46.2 & 4980.43.2 says except for experience gained by attending workshops seminars training sessions or conferences direct supervisor contact shall occur as follows: So what that means is that you do not have to have direct supervisor contact for attending workshops, seminars training sessions or conferences, you do need their approval so that they can identify that as hours that they will count, but you do not need direct supervisor contact just for those activities. However, the section further states "(1) Supervision shall include at least one hour of direct supervisor contact in each week for which experience is credited in each work setting. (2) A trainee shall receive an average of at least one hour of direct supervisor contact for every five hours of direct clinical counseling performed each week in each setting. For experience gained after January 1, 2009, no more than six hours of supervision, whether individual, triadic, or group, shall be credited during any single week (3) An associate gaining experience who performs more than 10 hours of direct clinical counseling in a week in any setting shall receive at least one additional hour of direct supervisor contact for that setting. For experience gained after January 1, 2009, no more than six hours of supervision, whether individual supervision, triadic supervision, or group supervision, shall be credited during any single week. (4) Of the 104 weeks of required supervision, 52 weeks shall be individual supervision, triadic supervision, or a combination of both."

Furthermore, "one hour of direct supervisor contact" means any of the following: (1) Individual supervision, which means one hour of face-to-face contact between one supervisor and one supervisee. (2) Triadic supervision, which means one hour of face-to-face contact between one supervisor and two supervisees. (3) Group supervision, which means two hours of face-to-face contact between one supervisor and no more than eight supervisees. Segments of group supervision may be split into no less than one continuous hour. A supervisor shall ensure that the amount and degree of supervision is appropriate for each supervisee".

Examination: Effective January 1, 2016 examinations have been restructured for both the PCC and MFT license. The first examination has been restructured in that both applicants must take a California Law and Ethics exam within the first year of their initial registration. Passing this exam is required to move on to the second and final examination. For MFT's, the second examination is the Clinical Exam, for PCC's the second examination is the National Clinical Mental Health Counseling Examination (NCMHCE). The second exam for both licensees cannot be taken until the individual has completed all education requirements, supervised hours and have successfully passed the first exam.

OTHER THINGS TO KNOW

Trainees for both PCC and MFT licensure are not allowed to work in private practice. Associates are allowed to work in private practice, but only as employees supervised by a fully licensed approved supervisor or as volunteers supervised by a fully licensed approved supervisor. Approved supervisors in private practice can supervise no more than three associates. And associates in private practice cannot be contracted, nor can associates open up his or her own private practice and provide services independently. The initial registration to obtain an associate number is for 1 year, renewable for total of six years.

PCC Education and Licensure Requirements

4999.32.Qualifications for Examination; Degree Requirements
(a) This section shall apply to applicants for licensure or registration who began graduate study before August 1, 2012, and completed that study on or before December 31, 2018. Those applicants may alternatively qualify under paragraph (2) of subdivision (a) of Section 4999.33.

(b) To qualify for licensure or registration, applicants shall possess a master's or doctoral degree that is counseling or psychotherapy in content and that meets the requirements of this section, obtained from an accredited or approved institution, as defined in Section 4999.12. For purposes of this subdivision, a degree is "counseling or psychotherapy in content" if it contains the supervised practicum or field study experience described in paragraph (3) of subdivision (c) and, except as provided in subdivision (d), the coursework in the core content areas listed in subparagraphs (A) to (I), inclusive, of paragraph (1) of subdivision (c).

(c) The degree described in subdivision (b) shall contain not less than 48 graduate semester units or 72 graduate quarter units of instruction, which shall, except as provided in subdivision (d), include all of the following:

(1) The equivalent of at least three semester units or four quarter units of graduate study in each of the following core content areas:

(A) Counseling and psychotherapeutic theories and techniques, including the counseling process in a multicultural society, an orientation to wellness and prevention, counseling theories to assist in selection of appropriate counseling interventions, models of counseling consistent with current professional research and practice, development of a personal model of counseling, and multidisciplinary responses to crises, emergencies, and disasters.

(B) Human growth and development across the lifespan, including normal and abnormal behavior and an understanding of developmental crises, disability, psychopathology, and situational and environmental factors that affect both normal and abnormal behavior.

(C) Career development theories and techniques, including career development decisionmaking models and interrelationships among and between work, family, and other life roles and factors, including the role of multicultural issues in career development.

(D) Group counseling theories and techniques, including principles of group dynamics, group process components, developmental stage theories, therapeutic factors of group work, group leadership styles and approaches, pertinent research and literature, group counseling methods, and evaluation of effectiveness.

(E) Assessment, appraisal, and testing of individuals, including basic concepts of standardized and nonstandardized testing and other assessment techniques, norm-referenced and criterion-referenced assessment, statistical concepts, social and cultural factors related to assessment and evaluation of individuals and groups, and ethical strategies for selecting, administering, and interpreting assessment instruments and techniques in counseling.

(F) Multicultural counseling theories and techniques, including counselors' roles in developing cultural selfawareness, identity development, promoting cultural social justice, individual and community strategies for working with and advocating for diverse populations, and counselors' roles in eliminating biases and prejudices, and processes of intentional and unintentional oppression and discrimination.

(G) Principles of the diagnostic process, including differential diagnosis, and the use of current diagnostic tools, such as the current edition of the Diagnostic and Statistical Manual of Mental Disorders, the impact of cooccurring substance use disorders or medical psychological disorders, established diagnostic criteria for mental or emotional disorders, and the treatment modalities and placement criteria within the continuum of care.

(H) Research and evaluation, including studies that provide an understanding of research methods, statistical analysis, the use of research to inform evidence-based practice, the importance of research in advancing the profession of counseling, and statistical methods used in conducting research, needs assessment, and program evaluation.

(I) Professional orientation, ethics, and law in counseling, including professional ethical standards and legal considerations, licensing law and process, regulatory laws that delineate the profession's scope of practice, counselor-client privilege, confidentiality, the client dangerous to self or others, treatment of minors with or without parental consent, relationship between practitioner's sense of self and human values, functions and relationships with other human service providers, strategies for collaboration, and advocacy processes needed to address institutional and social barriers that impede access, equity, and success for clients.

(2) In addition to the course requirements described in paragraph (1), a minimum of 12 semester units or 18 quarter units of advanced coursework to develop knowledge of specific treatment issues, special populations, application of counseling constructs, assessment and treatment planning, clinical interventions, therapeutic relationships, psychopathology, or other clinical topics.

(3) Not less than six semester units or nine quarter units of supervised practicum or field study experience that involves direct client contact in a clinical setting that provides a range of professional clinical counseling experience, including the following:

(A) Applied psychotherapeutic techniques.
(B) Assessment.
(C) Diagnosis.
(D) Prognosis.
(E) Treatment.
(F) Issues of development, adjustment, and maladjustment.
(G) Health and wellness promotion.
(H) Other recognized counseling interventions.

(I) A minimum of 150 hours of face-to-face supervised clinical experience counseling individuals, families, or groups.

(d) (1) (A) An applicant whose degree is deficient in no more than two of the required areas of study listed in subparagraphs (A) to (I), inclusive, of paragraph (1) of subdivision (c) may satisfy those deficiencies by successfully completing postmaster's or postdoctoral degree coursework at an accredited or approved institution, as defined in Section 4999.12.

(B) Notwithstanding subparagraph (A), an applicant shall not be deficient in the required areas of study specified in subparagraph (E) or (G) of paragraph (1) of subdivision (c) unless the applicant meets one of the following criteria and remediates the deficiency:

(i) The application for licensure was received by the board on or before August 31, 2020.

(ii) The application for registration was received by the board on or before August 31, 2020, and the registration was subsequently issued by the board.

(2) Coursework taken to meet deficiencies in the required areas of study listed in subparagraphs (A) to (I), inclusive, of paragraph (1) of subdivision (c) shall be the equivalent of three semester units or four quarter units of study.

(3) The board shall make the final determination as to whether a degree meets all requirements, including, but not limited to, course requirements, regardless of accreditation.

(e) In addition to the degree described in this section, or as part of that degree, an applicant shall complete the following coursework or training prior to registration as an associate:

(1) A minimum of 15 contact hours of instruction in alcoholism and other chemical substance abuse dependency, as specified by regulation.

(2) A minimum of 10 contact hours of training or coursework in human sexuality as specified in Section 25, and any regulations promulgated thereunder.

(3) A two semester unit or three quarter unit survey course in psychopharmacology. (4) A minimum of 15 contact hours of instruction in spousal or partner abuse assessment, detection, and intervention strategies, including knowledge of community resources, cultural factors, and same gender abuse dynamics.

(5) A minimum of seven contact hours of training or coursework in child abuse assessment and reporting as specified in Section 28 and any regulations adopted thereunder.

(6) A minimum of 18 contact hours of instruction in California law and professional ethics for professional clinical counselors that includes, but is

not limited to, instruction in advertising, scope of practice, scope of competence, treatment of minors, confidentiality, dangerous clients, psychotherapist-client privilege, recordkeeping, client access to records, dual relationships, child abuse, elder and dependent adult abuse, online therapy, insurance reimbursement, civil liability, disciplinary actions and unprofessional conduct, ethics complaints and ethical standards, termination of therapy, standards of care, relevant family law, therapist disclosures to clients, and state and federal laws related to confidentiality of patient health information. When coursework in a master's or doctoral degree program is acquired to satisfy this requirement, it shall be considered as part of the 48 semester unit or 72 quarter unit requirement in subdivision (c).

(7) A minimum of 10 contact hours of instruction in aging and long-term care, which may include, but is not limited to, the biological, social, and psychological aspects of aging. On and after January 1, 2012, this coursework shall include instruction on the assessment and reporting of, as well as treatment related to, elder and dependent adult abuse and neglect.

(8) A minimum of 15 contact hours of instruction in crisis or trauma counseling, including multidisciplinary responses to crises, emergencies, or disasters, and brief, intermediate, and long-term approaches.

4999.33. Alternative Qualification for Examination; Degree Requirements
(a) This section shall apply to the following:

(1) Applicants for licensure or registration who begin graduate study before August 1, 2012, and do not complete that study on or before December 31, 2018.

(2) Applicants for licensure or registration who begin graduate study before August 1, 2012, and who
graduate from a degree program that meets the requirements of this section.

(3) Applicants for licensure or registration who begin graduate study on or after August 1, 2012.

(b) To qualify for licensure or registration, applicants shall possess a master's or doctoral degree that is counseling or psychotherapy in content and that meets the requirements of this section, obtained from an accredited or approved institution, as defined in Section 4999.12. For purposes of this subdivision, a degree is "counseling or psychotherapy in content" if it contains the supervised practicum or field study experience described in paragraph (3) of subdivision (c) and, except as provided in subdivision (f), the coursework in the core content areas listed in subparagraphs (A) to (M), inclusive, of paragraph (1) of subdivision (c).

(c) The degree described in subdivision (b) shall contain not less than 60 graduate semester units or 90 graduate quarter units of instruction, which shall, except as provided in subdivision (f), include all of the following:

(1) The equivalent of at least three semester units or four quarter units of graduate study in all of the following core content areas:

(A) **Counseling and psychotherapeutic theories and techniques**, including the counseling process in a multicultural society, an orientation to wellness and prevention, counseling theories to assist in selection of appropriate counseling interventions, models of counseling consistent with current professional research and practice, development of a personal model of counseling, and multidisciplinary responses to crises, emergencies, and disasters.

(B) **Human growth and development across the lifespan**, including normal and abnormal behavior and an understanding of developmental crises, disability, psychopathology, and situational and environmental factors that affect both normal and abnormal behavior.

(C) **Career development theories and techniques**, including career development decisionmaking models and interrelationships among and between work, family, and other life roles and factors, including the role of multicultural issues in career development.

(D) **Group counseling theories and techniques**, including principles of group dynamics, group process components, group developmental stage theories, therapeutic factors of group work, group leadership styles and approaches, pertinent research and literature, group counseling methods, and evaluation of effectiveness.

(E) **Assessment, appraisal, and testing of individuals**, including basic concepts of standardized and nonstandardized testing and other assessment techniques, norm-referenced and criterion-referenced assessment, statistical concepts, social and cultural factors related to assessment and evaluation of individuals and groups, and ethical strategies for selecting, administering, and interpreting assessment instruments and techniques in counseling.

(F) **Multicultural counseling theories and techniques**, including counselors' roles in developing cultural self-awareness, identity development, promoting cultural social justice, individual and community strategies for working with and advocating for diverse populations, and counselors' roles in eliminating biases and prejudices, and processes of intentional and unintentional oppression and discrimination.

(G) **Principles of the diagnostic process**, including differential diagnosis, and the use of current diagnostic tools, such as the current edition of the Diagnostic and Statistical Manual, the impact of co-occurring substance use disorders or medical psychological disorders, established diagnostic criteria for mental or emotional disorders, and the treatment modalities and placement criteria within the continuum of care.

(H) **Research and evaluation**, including studies that provide an understanding of research methods, statistical analysis, the use of research to inform evidence-based practice, the importance of research in advancing the profession of counseling, and statistical methods used in conducting research, needs assessment, and program evaluation.

(I) **Professional orientation**, ethics, and law in counseling, including California law and professional ethics for professional clinical counselors, professional ethical standards and legal considerations, licensing law and process, regulatory laws that delineate the profession's scope of practice, counselor-client privilege, confidentiality, the client dangerous to self or others, treatment of minors with or without parental consent, relationship between practitioner's sense of self and human values, functions and relationships with other human service providers, strategies for collaboration, and advocacy processes needed to address institutional and social barriers that impede access, equity, and success for clients.

(J) **Psychopharmacology**, including the biological bases of behavior, basic classifications, indications, and contraindications of commonly prescribed psychopharmacological medications so that appropriate referrals can be made for medication evaluations and so that the side effects of those medications can be identified.

(K) **Addictions counseling**, including substance abuse, co-occurring disorders, and addiction, major approaches to identification, evaluation, treatment, and prevention of substance abuse and addiction, legal and medical aspects of substance abuse, populations at risk, the role of support persons, support systems, and community resources.

(L) **Crisis or trauma counseling**, including crisis theory; multidisciplinary responses to crises, emergencies, or disasters; cognitive, affective, behavioral, and neurological effects associated with trauma; brief, intermediate, and long-term approaches; and assessment strategies for clients in crisis and principles of intervention for individuals with mental or emotional disorders during times of crisis, emergency, or disaster.

(M) Advanced counseling and psychotherapeutic theories and techniques, including the application of counseling constructs, assessment and treatment planning, clinical interventions, therapeutic relationships, psychopathology, or other clinical topics.

(2) In addition to the course requirements described in paragraph (1), 15 semester units or 22.5 quarter units of advanced coursework to develop knowledge of specific treatment issues or special populations.

(3) Not less than six semester units or nine quarter units of supervised practicum or field study experience that involves direct client contact in a

clinical setting that provides a range of professional clinical counseling experience, including the following:

(A) Applied psychotherapeutic techniques.
(B) Assessment.
(C) Diagnosis.
(D) Prognosis.
(E) Treatment.
(F) Issues of development, adjustment, and maladjustment.
(G) Health and wellness promotion.
(H) Professional writing including documentation of services, treatment plans, and progress notes.
(I) How to find and use resources.
(J) Other recognized counseling interventions.
(K) A minimum of 280 hours of face-to-face supervised clinical experience counseling individuals, families, or groups.

(d) The 60 graduate semester units or 90 graduate quarter units of instruction required pursuant to subdivision

(c) shall, in addition to meeting the requirements of subdivision (c), include instruction in all of the following:

(1) The understanding of human behavior within the social context of socioeconomic status and other contextual issues affecting social position.

(2) The understanding of human behavior within the social context of a representative variety of the cultures found within California.

(3) Cultural competency and sensitivity, including a familiarity with the racial, cultural, linguistic, and ethnic backgrounds of persons living in California.

(4) An understanding of the effects of socioeconomic status on treatment and available resources.
(5) Multicultural development and cross-cultural interaction, including experiences of race, ethnicity, class, spirituality, sexual orientation, gender, and disability and their incorporation into the psychotherapeutic process.

(6) Case management, systems of care for the severely mentally ill, public and private services for the severely mentally ill, community resources for victims of abuse, disaster and trauma response, advocacy for the severely mentally ill, and collaborative treatment. The instruction required in this paragraph may be provided either in credit level coursework or through extension programs offered by the degree-granting institution.

(7) Human sexuality, including the study of the physiological, psychological, and social cultural variables associated with sexual behavior, gender identity, and the assessment and treatment of psychosexual dysfunction.

(8) Spousal or partner abuse assessment, detection, intervention strategies, and same gender abuse dynamics.

(9) A minimum of seven contact hours of training or coursework in child abuse assessment and reporting, as specified in Section 28, and any regulations promulgated thereunder.

(10) Aging and long-term care, including biological, social, cognitive, and psychological aspects of aging. This coursework shall include instruction on the assessment and reporting of, as well as treatment related to, elder and dependent adult abuse and neglect.

(e) A degree program that qualifies for licensure under this section shall do all of the following:

(1) Integrate the principles of mental health recovery-oriented care and methods of service delivery in recovery-oriented practice environments.
(2) Integrate an understanding of various cultures and the social and psychological implications of socioeconomic position.
(3) Provide the opportunity for students to meet with various consumers and family members of consumers of mental health services to enhance understanding of their experience of mental illness, treatment, and recovery.

(f) (1) (A) An applicant whose degree is deficient in no more than three of the required areas of study listed in subparagraphs (A) to (M), inclusive, of paragraph (1) of subdivision (c) may satisfy those deficiencies by successfully completing post-master's or postdoctoral degree coursework at an accredited or approved institution, as defined in Section 4999.12.
(B) Notwithstanding subparagraph (A), an applicant shall not be deficient in the required areas of study specified in subparagraphs (E) or (G) of paragraph (1) of subdivision (c) unless the applicant meets one of the following criteria and remediates the deficiency:

(i) The application for licensure was received by the board on or before August 31, 2020.

(ii) The application for registration was received by the board on or before August 31, 2020, and the registration was subsequently issued by the board.

(2) Coursework taken to meet deficiencies in the required areas of study

listed in subparagraphs (A) to (M), inclusive, of paragraph (1) of subdivision (c) shall be the equivalent of three semester units or four quarter units of study.

(3) The board shall make the final determination as to whether a degree meets all requirements, including, but not limited to, course requirements, regardless of accreditation.

4999.36. Trainee Activities and Services; Applicant and School Responsibilities

(a) A clinical counselor trainee may perform activities and services provided that the activities and services constitute part of the clinical counselor trainee's supervised course of study and that the person is designated by the title "clinical counselor trainee."

(b) All practicum and field study hours gained as a clinical counselor trainee shall be coordinated between the school and the site where hours are being accrued. The school shall approve each site and shall have a written agreement with each site that details each party's responsibilities, including the methods by which supervision shall be provided. The agreement shall provide for regular progress reports and evaluations of the student's performance at the site.

(c) If an applicant has gained practicum and field study hours while enrolled in an institution other than the one that confers the qualifying degree, it shall be the applicant's responsibility to provide to the board satisfactory evidence that those practicum and field study hours were gained in compliance with this section.

(d) A clinical counselor trainee shall inform each client or patient, prior to performing any professional services, that he or she is unlicensed and under supervision.

(e) No hours earned while a clinical counselor trainee may count toward the 3,000 hours of required postdegree supervised experience.

4999.40. Degree granting programs; Notification of qualifications to students; Equivalent Education and Training Gained Outside the United States

(a) Each educational institution preparing applicants to qualify for licensure shall notify each of its students by means of its public documents or otherwise in writing that its degree program is designed to meet the requirements of Section 4999.32 or 4999.33 and shall certify to the board that it has so notified its students.

(b) An applicant for registration or licensure shall submit to the board a certification by the applicant's educational institution that the institution's required curriculum for graduation and any associated coursework completed by the applicant does one of the following:

(1) Meets all of the requirements set forth in Section 4999.32.
(2) Meets all of the requirements set forth in Section 4999.33.

(c) An applicant trained at an educational institution outside the United States shall demonstrate to the satisfaction of the board that he or she possesses a qualifying degree that is equivalent to a degree earned from an institution of higher education that is accredited or approved. These applicants shall provide the board with a comprehensive evaluation of the degree performed by a foreign credential evaluation service that is a member of the National Association of Credential Evaluation Services and shall provide any other documentation the board deems necessary.

4999.42. Associate Registration; Qualification
(a) An applicant shall meet all of the following qualifications to qualify for registration as an associate:

(1) Earned a master's or doctoral degree as specified in Section 4999.32 or 4999.33, as applicable. An applicant whose education qualifies him or her under Section 4999.32 shall also have completed the coursework or training specified in subdivision (e) of Section 4999.32.
(2) Be at least 18 years of age.
(3) Not have committed acts or crimes constituting grounds for denial of licensure under Section 480.

(b) The board shall not issue a registration to any person who has been convicted of a crime in this or another state or in a territory of the United States that involves sexual abuse of children or who is required to register pursuant to Section 290 of the Penal Code or the equivalent in another state or territory.

4999.46. Supervised Post-Master's Experience
(a) Except as provided in subdivision (b), all applicants shall have an active associate registration with the board in order to gain postdegree hours of supervised experience.

(b) (1) Preregistered postdegree hours of experience shall be credited toward licensure if all of the following apply:

(A) The registration applicant applies for the associate registration and the board receives the application within 90 days of the granting of the qualifying master's degree or doctoral degree.
(B) For applicants completing graduate study on or after January 1, 2020,

the experience is obtained at a workplace that, prior to the registration applicant gaining supervised experience hours, requires completed Live Scan fingerprinting. The applicant shall provide the board with a copy of that completed State of California "Request for Live Scan Service" form with his or her application for licensure.

(C) The board subsequently grants the associate registration.

(2) The applicant shall not be employed or volunteer in a private practice until he or she has been issued an associate registration by the board.

(c) Supervised experience that is obtained for the purposes of qualifying for licensure shall be related to the practice of professional clinical counseling and comply with the following:

(1) A minimum of 3,000 postdegree hours performed over a period of not less than two years (104 weeks).

(2) Not more than 40 hours in any seven consecutive days.

(3) Not less than 1,750 hours of direct clinical counseling with individuals, groups, couples, or families using a variety of psychotherapeutic techniques and recognized counseling interventions.

(4) Not less than 150 hours of clinical experience in a hospital or community mental health setting, as defined in Section 4999.12.

A maximum of 1,250 hours of nonclinical practice, consisting of direct supervisor contact, administering and evaluating psychological tests, writing clinical reports, writing progress or process notes, client centered advocacy, and workshops, seminars, training sessions, or conferences directly related to professional clinical counseling that have been approved by the applicant's supervisor.

(d) An individual who submits an application for licensure between January 1, 2016, and December 31, 2020, may alternatively qualify under the experience requirements of this section that were in place on January 1, 2015.

(e) Experience hours shall not have been gained more than six years prior to the date the application for licensure was received by the board.

4999.46.1. Responsibilities of Supervisors and Associates
(a) An associate or applicant for licensure shall be under the supervision of a supervisor at all times.

(b) As used in this chapter, the term "supervision" means responsibility for, and control of, the quality of mental health and related services provided by the supervisee. Consultation or peer discussion shall not be considered supervision and shall not qualify as supervised experience. Supervision includes, but is not limited to, all of the following:

> (1) Ensuring the extent, kind, and quality of counseling performed is consistent with the education, training, and experience of the supervisee.
> (2) Monitoring and evaluating the supervisee's assessment, diagnosis, and treatment decisions and providing regular feedback.
> (3) Monitoring and evaluating the supervisee's ability to provide services at the site or sites where he or she is practicing and to the particular clientele being served.
> (4) Monitoring and addressing clinical dynamics, including, but not limited to, countertransference-,intrapsychic-, interpersonal-, or trauma-related issues that may affect the supervisory or practitioner patient relationship.
> (5) Ensuring the supervisee's compliance with laws and regulations governing the practice of licensed professional clinical counseling.
> (6) Reviewing the supervisee's progress notes, process notes, and other patient treatment records, as deemed appropriate by the supervisor.
> (7) With the client's written consent, providing direct observation or review of audio or video recordings of the supervisee's counseling or therapy, as deemed appropriate by the supervisor.

(c) An associate shall do both of the following:
(1) Inform each client, prior to performing any professional services, that he or she is unlicensed and under supervision.

(2) Renew the registration a maximum of five times. No registration shall be renewed or reinstated beyond six years from the last day of the month during which it was issued, regardless of whether it has been revoked.

(d) When no further renewals are possible, an applicant may apply for and obtain a subsequent associate registration number if the applicant meets the educational requirements for a subsequent associate registration number and has passed the California law and ethics examination. An applicant issued a subsequent associate registration number shall not be employed or volunteer in a private practice.

4999.46.2. Direct Supervisor Contact
(a) Except for experience gained by attending workshops, seminars, training sessions, or conferences, as described in paragraph (5) of subdivision (c) of Section 4999.46, direct supervisor contact shall occur as follows:

(1) Supervision shall include at least one hour of direct supervisor contact in each week for which experience is credited in each work setting.

(2) A trainee shall receive an average of at least one hour of direct supervisor contact for every five hours of direct clinical counseling performed each week in each setting. For experience gained after January 1, 2009, no more than six hours of supervision, whether individual, triadic, or group, shall be credited during any single week.

(3) An associate gaining experience who performs more than 10 hours of direct clinical counseling in a week in any setting shall receive at least one additional hour of direct supervisor contact for that setting.

For experience gained after January 1, 2009, no more than six hours of supervision, whether individual supervision, triadic supervision, or group supervision, shall be credited during any single week.

(4) Of the 104 weeks of required supervision, 52 weeks shall be individual supervision, triadic supervision, or a combination of both.

(b) For purposes of this chapter, "one hour of direct supervisor contact" means any of the following:

(1) Individual supervision, which means one hour of face-to-face contact between one supervisor and one supervisee.

(2) Triadic supervision, which means one hour of face-to-face contact between one supervisor and two supervisees.

(3) Group supervision, which means two hours of face-to-face contact between one supervisor and no more than eight supervisees. Segments of group supervision may be split into no less than one continuous hour. The supervisor shall ensure that the amount and degree of supervision is appropriate for each supervisee.

(c) Direct supervisor contact shall occur within the same week as the hours claimed.

(d) Notwithstanding subdivision (b), an associate working in a governmental entity, school, college, university, or institution that is both nonprofit and charitable may obtain the required weekly direct supervisor contact via two-way, real-time videoconferencing. The supervisor shall be responsible for ensuring compliance with federal and state laws relating to confidentiality of patient health information.

(e) Notwithstanding any other law, once the required number of experience hours are gained, associates and applicants for licensure shall receive a minimum of one hour of direct supervisor contact per week for each practice setting in which direct clinical counseling is performed. Once the required number of experience hours are gained, further supervision for nonclinical practice, as defined in paragraph (5) of subdivision (c) of Section 4999.46, shall be at the supervisor's discretion.

4999.46.3. Supervised Experience: Acceptable Settings; Acceptable Supervision Practices

(a) A clinical counselor trainee, associate, or applicant for licensure shall only perform mental health and related services as an employee or volunteer, and not as an independent contractor. The requirements of this chapter regarding hours of experience and supervision shall apply equally to employees and volunteers. A clinical counselor trainee, associate, or applicant for licensure shall not perform any services or gain any experience within the scope of practice of the profession, as defined in Section 4999.20, as an independent contractor. While an associate may be either a paid employee or a volunteer, employers are encouraged to provide fair remuneration.

(1) If employed, an associate shall provide the board, upon application for licensure, with copies of the corresponding W-2 tax forms for each year of experience claimed.

(2) If volunteering, an associate shall provide the board, upon application for licensure, with a letter from his or her employer verifying the associate's status as a volunteer during the dates the experience was gained.

(b) A clinical counselor trainee shall not perform services in a private practice.

(c) A trainee shall complete the required predegree supervised practicum or field study experience in a settingthat meets all of the following requirements:

(1) Is not a private practice.

(2) Lawfully and regularly provides mental health counseling or psychotherapy.

(3) Provides oversight to ensure that the clinical counselor trainee's work at the setting meets the experience and supervision requirements in this chapter and is within the scope of practice of the profession, as defined in Section 4999.20.

(4) Only experience gained in the position for which the clinical counselor trainee volunteers or is employed shall qualify as supervised practicum or field study experience.

(d) (1) An associate may be credited with supervised experience completed in any setting that meets both of the following:

(A) Lawfully and regularly provides mental health counseling or psychotherapy.

(B) Provides oversight to ensure that the associate's work at the setting meets the experience and supervision requirements in this chapter and is within the scope of practice for the profession, as defined in Section 4999.20.

(2) Only experience gained in the position for which the associate volunteers or is employed shall qualify as supervised experience.

(3) An applicant for registration as an associate shall not be employed or volunteer in a private practice until he or she has been issued an associate registration by the board.

Any experience obtained under the supervision of a spouse, relative, or domestic partner shall not be credited toward the required hours of supervised experience. Any experience obtained under the supervision of a supervisor with whom the applicant has had or currently has a personal, professional, or business relationship that undermines the authority or effectiveness of the supervision shall not be credited toward the required hours of supervised experience.

(f) A clinical counselor trainee, associate, or applicant for licensure shall not receive any remuneration from patients or clients and shall only be paid by his or her employer, if an employee.

(g) A clinical counselor trainee, associate, or applicant for licensure shall have no proprietary interest in his or her employer's business and shall not lease or rent space, pay for furnishings, equipment, or supplies, or in any other way pay for the obligations of his or her employer.

(h) A clinical counselor trainee, associate, or applicant for licensure who provides voluntary services in any lawful work setting other than a private practice and who only receives reimbursement for expenses actually incurred shall be considered an employee. The board may audit an applicant for licensure who receives reimbursement for expenses and the applicant for licensure shall have the burden of demonstrating that the payments received were for reimbursement of expenses actually incurred.

(i) A clinical counselor trainee, associate, or applicant for licensure who receives a stipend or educational loan repayment from a program designed to encourage demographically underrepresented groups to enter the profession or to improve recruitment and retention in underserved regions or settings shall be considered an employee. The board may audit an applicant who receives a stipend or educational loan repayment and the applicant shall have the burden of demonstrating that the payments were for the specified purposes.

(j) Each educational institution preparing applicants pursuant to this chapter shall consider requiring, and shall encourage, its students to undergo individual, marital, conjoint, family, or group counseling or psychotherapy, as appropriate. Each supervisor shall consider, advise, and encourage his or her associates and trainees regarding the advisability of undertaking individual, marital, conjoint, family, or group counseling or psychotherapy, as appropriate. Insofar as it is deemed appropriate and is desired by the applicant, educational institutions and supervisors are encouraged to assist the applicant to locate that counseling or psychotherapy at a reasonable cost.

4999.46.4. Supervisees; Location of Services; Maximum Registrants; Oversight Agreement

(a) A clinical counselor trainee, associate, or applicant for licensure shall only perform mental health and related services at the places where his or her employer regularly conducts business and services.

(b) An associate who is employed or volunteering in a private practice shall be supervised by an individual who is employed by, and shall practice at the same site as, the associate's employer. Alternatively, the supervisor may be an owner of the private practice. However, if the site is incorporated, the supervisor must be employed full-time at the site and be actively engaged in performing professional services at the site.

(c) A supervisor at a private practice or a corporation shall not supervise more than a total of three supervisees at any one time. A supervisee may be registered as an associate marriage and family therapist, an associate professional clinical counselor, or an associate clinical social worker.

(d) In a setting that is not a private practice:

A written oversight agreement, as specified in regulation, shall be executed between the supervisor and employer when the supervisor is not employed by the supervisee's employer or is a volunteer.

(2) A supervisor shall evaluate the site or sites where an associate will be gaining experience to determine that the site or sites provide experience

that is in compliance with the requirements set forth in this chapter.

(e) Alternative supervision may be arranged during a supervisor's vacation or sick leave if the alternative supervision meets the requirements in this chapter and regulation.

4999.46.5. Audit of Supervisors
The board may audit the records of any supervisor to verify the completion of the supervisor qualifications specified by this chapter and by regulation. A supervisor shall maintain records of completion of the required supervisor qualifications for seven years after termination of supervision and shall make these records available to the board for auditing purposes upon request.

4999.53. Required Examinations
(a) Effective January 1, 2016, a registrant or an applicant for licensure as a professional clinical counselor shall pass the following examinations as prescribed by the board:

(1) A California law and ethics examination.
(2) A clinical examination administered by the board, or
the National Clinical Mental Health Counselor Examination if the board finds that this examination meets the prevailing standards for validation and use of the licensing and certification tests in California.

(b) Upon registration with the board, an associate professional clinical counselor shall, within the first year of registration, take an examination on California law and ethics.

(c) A registrant or an applicant for licensure may take the clinical examination or the National Clinical Mental Health Counselor Examination, as established by the board through regulation, only upon meeting all of the following requirements:
(1) Completion of all required supervised work experience.
(2) Completion of all education requirements.
(3) Passage of the California law and ethics examination.
(d) This section shall become operative on January 1, 2016.

MFT Education & Licensure Requirements

4980.36. Qualifying Degree Program for Licensure or Registration; Beginning Graduate Study After August, 1, 2012 or Completing Graduate Study After December 31, 2018
(a) This section shall apply to the following:

(1) Applicants for licensure or registration who begin graduate study

before August 1, 2012, and do not complete that study on or before December 31, 2018.

(2) Applicants for licensure or registration who begin graduate study before August 1, 2012, and who graduate from a degree program that meets the requirements of this section.

(3) Applicants for licensure or registration who begin graduate study on or after August 1, 2012.

(b) To qualify for a license or registration, applicants shall possess a doctoral or master's degree meeting the requirements of this section in marriage, family, and child counseling, marriage and family therapy, couple and family therapy, psychology, clinical psychology, counseling psychology, or counseling with an emphasis in either marriage, family, and child counseling or marriage and family therapy, obtained from a school, college, or university approved by the Bureau for Private Postsecondary Education, or accredited by either the Commission on Accreditation for Marriage and Family Therapy Education, or a regional accrediting agency that is recognized by the United States Department of Education. The board has the authority to make the final determination as to whether a degree meets all requirements, including, but not limited to, course requirements, regardless of accreditation or approval.

(c) A doctoral or master's degree program that qualifies for licensure or registration shall do the following:
    (1) Integrate all of the following throughout its curriculum:

(A) Marriage and family therapy principles.

(B) The principles of mental health recovery-oriented care and methods of service delivery in recovery-oriented practice environments, among others.

(C) An understanding of various cultures and the social and psychological implications of socioeconomic position, and an understanding of how poverty and social stress impact an individual's mental health and recovery.

(2) Allow for innovation and individuality in the education of marriage and family therapists.

(3) Encourage students to develop the personal qualities that are intimately related to effective practice, including, but not limited to, integrity, sensitivity, flexibility, insight, compassion, and personal presence.

(4) Permit an emphasis or specialization that may address any one or more of the unique and complex array of human problems, symptoms, and needs of Californians served by marriage and family therapists.

(5) Provide students with the opportunity to meet with various consumers and family members of consumers of mental health services to enhance understanding of their experience of mental illness, treatment, and recovery.

(d) The degree described in subdivision (b) shall contain no less than 60 semester or 90 quarter units of instruction that includes, but is not limited to, the following requirements:

(1) Both of the following:
(A) No less than 12 semester or 18 quarter units of coursework in theories, principles, and methods of a variety of psychotherapeutic orientations directly related to marriage and family therapy and marital and family systems approaches to treatment and how these theories can be applied therapeutically with individuals, couples, families, adults, including elder adults, children, adolescents, and groups to improve, restore, or maintain healthy relationships.

(B) Practicum that involves direct client contact, as follows:
(i) A minimum of six semester or nine quarter units of practicum in a supervised clinical placement that provides supervised fieldwork experience.
(ii) A minimum of 150 hours of face-to-face experience counseling individuals, couples, families, or groups.
(iii) A student must be enrolled in a practicum course while counseling clients, except as specified in subdivision (c) of Section 4980.42.
(iv) The practicum shall provide training in all of the following areas:
(I) Applied use of theory and psychotherapeutic techniques.
(II) Assessment, diagnosis, and prognosis.
(III) Treatment of individuals and premarital, couple, family, and child relationships, including trauma and abuse, dysfunctions, healthy functioning, health promotion, illness prevention, and working with families.
(IV) Professional writing, including documentation of services, treatment plans, and progress notes.
(V) How to connect people with resources that deliver the quality of services and support needed in the community.
(v) Educational institutions are encouraged to design the practicum required by this subparagraph to include marriage and family therapy experience in low income and multicultural mental health settings.
(vi) In addition to the 150 hours required in clause (ii), 75 hours of either of the following, or a combination thereof:
(I) Client centered advocacy, as defined in Section 4980.03.

(II) Face-to-face experience counseling individuals, couples, families, or groups.

(2) Instruction in all of the following:
(A) Diagnosis, assessment, prognosis, and treatment of mental disorders, including severe mental disorders, evidence-based practices, psychological testing, psychopharmacology, and promising mental health practices that are evaluated in peer reviewed literature.

(B) Developmental issues from infancy to old age, including instruction in all of the following areas:
(i) The effects of developmental issues on individuals, couples, and family relationships.
(ii) The psychological, psychotherapeutic, and health implications of developmental issues and their effects.
(iii) Aging and its biological, social, cognitive, and psychological aspects. This coursework shall include instruction on the assessment and reporting of, as well as treatment related to, elder and dependent adult abuse and neglect.
(iv) A variety of cultural understandings of human development.
(v) The understanding of human behavior within the social context of socioeconomic status and other contextual issues affecting social position.
(vi) The understanding of human behavior within the social context of a representative variety of the cultures found within California.
(vii) The understanding of the impact that personal and social insecurity, social stress, low educational levels, inadequate housing, and malnutrition have on human development.

(C) The broad range of matters and life events that may arise within marriage and family relationships and within a variety of California cultures, including instruction in all of the following:
(i) A minimum of seven contact hours of training or coursework in child abuse assessment and reporting as specified in Section 28, and any regulations promulgated thereunder.
(ii) Spousal or partner abuse assessment, detection, intervention strategies, and same gender abuse dynamics.
(iii) Cultural factors relevant to abuse of partners and family members.
(iv) Childbirth, child rearing, parenting, and stepparenting.
(v) Marriage, divorce, and blended families.
(vi) Long-term care.
(vii) End of life and grief.
(viii) Poverty and deprivation.
(ix) Financial and social stress.
(x) Effects of trauma.
(xi) The psychological, psychotherapeutic, community, and health

implications of the matters and life events described in clauses (i) to (x), inclusive.

(D) Cultural competency and sensitivity, including a familiarity with the racial, cultural, linguistic, and ethnic backgrounds of persons living in California.

(E) Multicultural development and cross-cultural interaction, including experiences of race, ethnicity, class, spirituality, sexual orientation, gender, and disability, and their incorporation into the psychotherapeutic process.

(F) The effects of socioeconomic status on treatment and available resources.

(G) Resilience, including the personal and community qualities that enable persons to cope with adversity, trauma, tragedy, threats, or other stresses.

(H) Human sexuality, including the study of physiological, psychological, and social cultural variables associated with sexual behavior and gender identity, and the assessment and treatment of psychosexual dysfunction.

(I) Substance use disorders, co-occurring disorders, and addiction, including, but not limited to, instruction in all of the following:

(i) The definition of substance use disorders, co-occurring disorders, and addiction. For purposes of this subparagraph, "co-occurring disorders" means a mental illness and substance abuse diagnosis occurring simultaneously in an individual.
(ii) Medical aspects of substance use disorders and co-occurring disorders.
(iii) The effects of psychoactive drug use.
(iv) Current theories of the etiology of substance abuse and addiction.
(v) The role of persons and systems that support or compound substance abuse and addiction.
(vi) Major approaches to identification, evaluation, and treatment of substance use disorders, co-occurring disorders, and addiction, including, but not limited to, best practices.
(vii) Legal aspects of substance abuse.
(viii) Populations at risk with regard to substance use disorders and co-occurring disorders.
(ix) Community resources offering screening, assessment, treatment, and followup for the affected person and family.
(x) Recognition of substance use disorders, co-occurring disorders, and addiction, and appropriate referral.
(xi) The prevention of substance use disorders and addiction.

(J) California law and professional ethics for marriage and family therapists, including instruction in all of the following areas of study:

(i) Contemporary professional ethics and statutory, regulatory, and decisional laws that delineate the scope of practice of marriage and family therapy.

(ii) The therapeutic, clinical, and practical considerations involved in the legal and ethical practice of marriage and family therapy, including, but not limited to, family law.

(iii) The current legal patterns and trends in the mental health professions.

(iv) The psychotherapist-patient privilege, confidentiality, the patient dangerous to self or others, and the treatment of minors with and without parental consent.

(v) A recognition and exploration of the relationship between a practitioner's sense of self and human values and his or her professional behavior and ethics.

(vi) Differences in legal and ethical standards for different types of work settings.

(vii) Licensing law and licensing process.

(e) The degree described in subdivision (b) shall, in addition to meeting the requirements of subdivision (d), include instruction in case management, systems of care for the severely mentally ill, public and private services and supports available for the severely mentally ill, community resources for persons with mental illness and for victims of abuse, disaster and trauma response, advocacy for the severely mentally ill, and collaborative treatment. This instruction may be provided either in credit level coursework or through extension programs offered by the degree-granting institution.

(f) The changes made to law by this section are intended to improve the educational qualifications for licensure in order to better prepare future licentiates for practice, and are not intended to expand or restrict the scope of practice for marriage and family therapists.

4980.37. Qualifying Degree Program for Licensure or Registration; Beginning Graduate Study Before August, 1, 2012 or Completing Graduate Study Before December 31, 2018

(a) This section shall apply to applicants for licensure or registration who begin graduate study before August 1, 2012, and complete that study on or before December 31, 2018. Those applicants may alternatively qualify under paragraph (2) of subdivision (a) of Section 4980.36.

(b) To qualify for a license or registration, applicants shall possess a doctor's or master's degree in marriage, family, and child counseling, marriage and family therapy, couple and family therapy, psychology, clinical psychology, counseling psychology, or counseling with an emphasis in either marriage, family, and child counseling or marriage and family therapy, obtained from a school, college, or university accredited by a regional accrediting agency that is recognized by the United States Department of Education or approved by the Bureau for Private Postsecondary Education. The board has the authority to make the final determination as to whether a degree meets all requirements, including, but not limited to, course requirements, regardless of accreditation or approval. In order to qualify for licensure pursuant to this section, a doctor's or master's degree program shall be a single, integrated program primarily designed to train marriage and family therapists and shall contain no less than 48 semester or 72 quarter units of instruction. This instruction shall include no less than 12 semester units or 18 quarter units of coursework in the areas of marriage, family, and child counseling, and marital and family systems approaches to treatment. The coursework shall include all of the following areas:

(1) The salient theories of a variety of psychotherapeutic orientations directly related to marriage and family therapy, and marital and family systems approaches to treatment.

(2) Theories of marriage and family therapy and how they can be utilized in order to intervene therapeutically with couples, families, adults, children, and groups.

(3) Developmental issues and life events from infancy to old age and their effect on individuals, couples, and family relationships. This may include coursework that focuses on specific family life events and the psychological, psychotherapeutic, and health implications that arise within couples and families, including, but not limited to, childbirth, child rearing, childhood, adolescence, adulthood, marriage, divorce, blended families, stepparenting, abuse and neglect of older and dependent adults, and geropsychology.

(4) A variety of approaches to the treatment of children.

The board shall, by regulation, set forth the subjects of instruction required in this subdivision.

(c) (1) In addition to the 12 semester or 18 quarter units of coursework specified in subdivision (b), the doctor's or master's degree program shall contain not less than six semester or nine quarter units of supervised practicum in applied psychotherapeutic technique, assessments, diagnosis, prognosis, and treatment of premarital, couple, family, and child relationships, including dysfunctions, healthy functioning, health promotion, and illness prevention, in a supervised clinical placement that provides supervised fieldwork experience within the scope of practice of a marriage and family therapist.

(2) For applicants who enrolled in a degree program on or after January 1, 1995, the practicum shall include a minimum of 150 hours of face-to-face experience counseling individuals, couples, families, or groups.

(3) The practicum hours shall be considered as part of the 48 semester

or 72 quarter unit requirement.

(d) As an alternative to meeting the qualifications specified in subdivision (b), the board shall accept as equivalent degrees those master's or doctor's degrees granted by educational institutions whose degree program is approved by the Commission on Accreditation for Marriage and Family Therapy Education.

(e) In order to provide an integrated course of study and appropriate professional training, while allowing for innovation and individuality in the education of marriage and family therapists, a degree program that meets the educational qualifications for licensure or registration under this section shall do all of the following:

(1) Provide an integrated course of study that trains students generally in the diagnosis, assessment, prognosis, and treatment of mental disorders.

(2) Prepare students to be familiar with the broad range of matters that may arise within marriage and family relationships.

(3) Train students specifically in the application of marriage and family relationship counseling principles and methods.

(4) Encourage students to develop those personal qualities that are intimately related to the counseling situation such as integrity, sensitivity, flexibility, insight, compassion, and personal presence.

(5) Teach students a variety of effective psychotherapeutic techniques and modalities that may be utilized to improve, restore, or maintain healthy individual, couple, and family relationships.

(6) Permit an emphasis or specialization that may address any one or more of the unique and complex array of human problems, symptoms, and needs of Californians served by marriage and family therapists.

(7) Prepare students to be familiar with cross-cultural mores and values, including a familiarity with the wide range of racial and ethnic backgrounds common among California's population, including, but not limited to, Blacks, Hispanics, Asians, and Native Americans.

(f) Educational institutions are encouraged to design the practicum required by this section to include marriage and family therapy experience in low income and multicultural mental health settings.

4980.38. Notification to Students of Design of Degree Program; Certification of Fulfillment of Requirements

(a) Each educational institution preparing applicants to qualify for registration or licensure shall notify each of its students by means of its public documents or otherwise in writing that its degree program is designed to meet the requirements of Section 4980.36 or 4980.37, and shall certify to the board that it has so notified its students.

(b) An applicant for registration or licensure shall submit to the board a certification by the applicant's educational institution that the institution's required curriculum for graduation and any associated coursework completed by the applicant does one of the following:

(1) Meets all of the requirements set forth in Section 4980.36.

(2) Meets all of the requirements set forth in Section 4980.37 and paragraphs (4) and (5) of subdivision (a) of Section 4980.41.

4980.39. Additional Coursework; Inoperative January 1, 2019

(a) An applicant for licensure whose education qualifies him or her under Section 4980.37 shall complete, as a condition of licensure, a minimum of 10 contact hours of coursework in aging and long-term care, which may include, but is not limited to, the biological, social, and psychological aspects of aging. On and after January 1, 2012, this coursework shall include instruction on the assessment and reporting of, as well as treatment related to, elder and dependent adult abuse and neglect.

(b) Coursework taken in fulfillment of other educational requirements for licensure pursuant to this chapter, or in a separate course of study, may, at the discretion of the board, fulfill the requirements of this section.

(c) In order to satisfy the coursework requirement of this section, the applicant shall submit to the board a certification from the chief academic officer of the educational institution from which the applicant graduated stating that the coursework required by this section is included within the institution's required curriculum for graduation, or within the coursework, that was completed by the applicant.

(d) The board shall not issue a license to the applicant until the applicant has met the requirements of this section.

4980.395. Additional Continuing Education Requirement

(a) A licensee who began graduate study prior to January 1, 2004, shall complete a three-hour continuing education course in aging and long-term care during his or her first renewal period after the operative date of this section and shall submit to the board evidence, acceptable to the board, of the person's satisfactory completion of the course.

(b) The course shall include, but is not limited to, the biological, social, and psychological aspects of aging.

(c) A person seeking to meet the requirements of subdivision (a) of this section may submit to the board a certificate evidencing completion of equivalent courses in aging and long-term care taken prior to the operative date of this section, or proof of equivalent teaching or practice experience. The board, in its discretion, may accept that certification as meeting the requirements of this section.

(d) The board may not renew an applicant's license until the applicant has met the requirements of this section.

(e) Continuing education courses taken pursuant to this section shall be applied to the 36 hours of approved continuing education required in Section 4980.54.

(f) This section shall become operative on January 1, 2005.

4980.396. Required Coursework or Supervised Experience; Suicide Risk Assessment and Intervention

(a) On or after January 1, 2021, an applicant for licensure as a marriage and family therapist shall show, as part of the application, that he or she has completed a minimum of six hours of coursework or applied experience under supervision in suicide risk assessment and intervention. This requirement shall be met in one of the following ways:

(1) Obtained as part of his or her qualifying graduate degree program. To satisfy this requirement, the applicant shall submit to the board a written certification from the registrar or training director of the educational institution or program from which the applicant graduated stating that the coursework required by this section is included within the institution's curriculum required for graduation at the time the applicant graduated, or within the coursework that was completed by the applicant.

(2) Obtained as part of his or her applied experience. Applied experience can be met in any of the following settings: practicum or associateship that meets the requirement of this chapter, formal postdoctoral placement that meets the requirements of Section 2911, or other qualifying supervised experience. To satisfy this requirement, the applicant shall submit to the board a written certification from the director of training for the program or primary supervisor where the qualifying experience has occurred stating that the training required by this section is included within the applied experience.

(3) By taking a continuing education course that meets the requirements of Section 4980.54. To satisfy this requirement, the applicant shall submit to the board a certification of completion.

(b) As a one-time requirement, a licensee prior to the time of his or her first renewal after January 1, 2021, or an applicant for reactivation or reinstatement to an active license status on or after January 1, 2021, shall have completed a minimum of six hours of coursework or applied experience under supervision in suicide risk assessment and intervention, using one of the methods specified in subdivision (a).

(c) Proof of compliance with this section shall be certified under penalty of perjury that he or she is in compliance with this section and shall be retained for submission to the board upon request.

4980.397. Required Examinations; Effective January 1, 2016

(a) A registrar or an applicant for licensure as a marriage and family therapist shall pass the following two examinations as prescribed by the board:

(1) A California law and ethics examination.

(2) A clinical examination.

(b) Upon registration with the board, an associate marriage and family therapist shall, within the first year of registration, take an examination on California law and ethics.

(c) A registrant or an applicant for licensure may take the clinical examination only upon meeting all of the
following requirements:

(1) Completion of all required supervised work experience.

(2) Completion of all education requirements.

(3) Passage of the California law and ethics examination.

4980.40. Qualifications

An applicant for licensure shall satisfy all of the following qualifications:

(a) Meet the educational requirements of Section 4980.36 or both Sections 4980.37 and 4980.41, as applicable.

(b) Be at least 18 years of age.

(c) Have at least two years of supervised experience as specified in this chapter and its corresponding regulations.

(d) Successfully pass a California law and ethics examination and a clinical examination. An applicant who has successfully passed a previously administered written examination may be subsequently required to take and pass another written examination.

(e) Not have committed acts or crimes constituting grounds for denial of licensure under Section 480. The board shall not issue a registration or license to any person who has been convicted of a crime in this or
another state or in a territory of the United States that involves sexual abuse of children or who is required to register pursuant to Section 290 of the Penal Code or the equivalent in another state or territory.

4980.41. Eligibility to sit for Licensing Exams; Coursework or Training

(a) An applicant for licensure whose education qualifies him or her under Section 4980.37 shall complete the following coursework or training in order to be eligible to sit for the licensing examinations as specified in subdivision (d) of Section 4980.40:

(1) A two semester or three quarter unit course in California law and professional ethics for marriage and family therapists, which shall include, but not be limited to, the following areas of study:

(A) Contemporary professional ethics and statutory, regulatory, and decisional laws that delineate the profession's scope of practice.

(B) The therapeutic, clinical, and practical considerations involved in the legal and ethical practice of marriage and family therapy, including family law.

(C) The current legal patterns and trends in the mental health profession.

(D) The psychotherapist-patient privilege, confidentiality, the patient dangerous to self or others, and the treatment of minors with and without parental consent.

(E) A recognition and exploration of the relationship between a practitioner's sense of self and human values and his or her professional behavior and ethics.

This course may be considered as part of the 48 semester or 72 quarter unit requirements contained in Section 4980.37.

(2) A minimum of seven contact hours of training or coursework in child abuse assessment and reporting as specified in Section 28 and any regulations promulgated thereunder.

(3) A minimum of 10 contact hours of training or coursework in human sexuality as specified in Section 25, and any regulations promulgated thereunder. When coursework in a master's or doctor's degree program is acquired to satisfy this requirement, it shall be considered as part of the 48 semester or 72 quarter unit requirement contained in Section 4980.37.

(4) For persons who began graduate study on or after January 1, 1986, a master's or doctor's degree qualifying for licensure shall include specific instruction in alcoholism and other chemical substance dependency as specified by regulation. When coursework in a master's or doctor's degree program is acquired to satisfy this requirement, it shall be considered as part of the 48 semester or 72 quarter unit requirement contained in Section 4980.37. Coursework required under this paragraph may be satisfactory if taken either in fulfillment of other educational requirements for licensure or in a separate course. The applicant may satisfy this requirement by successfully completing this coursework from a master's or doctoral degree program at an accredited or approved institution, as described in subdivision (b) of Section 4980.37, or from a board-accepted provider of continuing education, as described in Section 4980.54.

(5) For persons who began graduate study during the period commencing on January 1, 1995, and ending on December 31, 2003, a master's or doctor's degree qualifying for licensure shall include coursework in spousal or partner abuse assessment, detection, and intervention. For persons who began graduate study on or after January 1, 2004, a master's or doctor's degree qualifying for licensure shall include a minimum of 15 contact hours of coursework in spousal or partner abuse assessment, detection, and intervention strategies, including knowledge of community resources, cultural factors, and

same gender abuse dynamics. Coursework required under this paragraph may be satisfactory if taken either in fulfillment of other educational requirements for licensure or in a separate course. The applicant may satisfy this requirement by successfully completing this coursework from a master's or doctoral degree program at an accredited or approved institution, as described in subdivision (b) of Section 4980.37, or from a board-accepted provider of continuing education, as described in Section 4980.54.

(6) For persons who began graduate study on or after January 1, 2001, an applicant shall complete a minimum of a two semester or three quarter unit survey course in psychological testing. When coursework in a master's or doctor's degree program is acquired to satisfy this requirement, it may be considered as part of the 48 semester or 72 quarter unit requirement of Section 4980.37.

(7) For persons who began graduate study on or after January 1, 2001, an applicant shall complete a minimum of a two semester or three quarter unit survey course in psychopharmacology. When coursework in a master's or doctor's degree program is acquired to satisfy this requirement, it may be considered as part of the 48 semester or 72 quarter unit requirement of Section 4980.37.

(8) The requirements added by paragraphs (6) and (7) are intended to improve the educational qualifications for licensure in order to better prepare future licentiates for practice and are not intended in any way to expand or restrict the scope of practice for licensed marriage and family therapists.

4980.42. Trainees Services

(a) Trainees performing services in any work setting specified in Section 4980.43.3 may perform those activities and services as a trainee, provided that the activities and services constitute part of the trainee's supervised course of study and that the person is designated by the title "trainee."

(b) Trainees subject to Section 4980.37 may gain hours of experience and counsel clients outside of the required practicum. This subdivision shall apply to hours of experience gained and client counseling provided on and after January 1, 2012.

(c) Trainees subject to Section 4980.36 may gain hours of experience outside of the required practicum but must be enrolled in a practicum course to counsel clients. Trainees subject to Section 4980.36 may counsel clients while not enrolled in a practicum course if the period of lapsed enrollment is less than 90 calendar days, and if that period is immediately preceded by enrollment in a practicum course and immediately followed by enrollment in a practicum course or completion of the degree program.

(d) All hours of experience gained pursuant to subdivisions (b) and (c) shall be subject to the other requirements of this chapter.

(e) All hours of experience gained as a trainee shall be coordinated between the school and the site where the hours are being accrued. The school shall approve each site and shall have a written agreement with each site that details each party's responsibilities, including the methods by which supervision shall be provided. The agreement shall provide for regular progress reports and evaluations of the student's performance at the site. If an applicant has gained hours of experience while enrolled in an institution other than the one that confers the qualifying degree, it shall be the applicant's responsibility to provide to the board satisfactory evidence that those hours of trainee experience were gained in compliance with this section.

4980.43. Professional Experience; Associates or Trainees
((a) Except as provided in subdivision (b), all applicants shall have an active associate registration with the board in order to gain postdegree hours of supervised experience.

(b) (1) Preregistered postdegree hours of experience shall be credited toward licensure if all of the following apply:

(A) The registration applicant applies for the associate registration and the board receives the application within 90 days of the granting of the qualifying master's degree or doctoral degree.

(B) For applicants completing graduate study on or after January 1, 2020, the experience is obtained at a workplace that, prior to the registration applicant gaining supervised experience hours, requires completed Live Scan fingerprinting. The applicant shall provide the board with a copy of that completed State of California "Request for Live Scan Service" form with his or her application for licensure.

(C) The board subsequently grants the associate registration.

(2) The applicant shall not be employed or volunteer in a private practice until he or she has been issued an associate registration by the board.

(c) Supervised experience that is obtained for purposes of qualifying for licensure shall be related to the practice of marriage and family therapy and comply with the following:

(1) A minimum of 3,000 hours completed during a period of at least 104 weeks.

(2) A maximum of 40 hours in any seven consecutive days.

(3) A minimum of 1,700 hours obtained after the qualifying master's or doctoral degree was awarded.

(4) A maximum of 1,300 hours obtained prior to the award date of the qualifying master's or doctoral degree.

(5) A maximum of 750 hours of counseling and direct supervisor contact prior to the award date of the qualifying master's or doctoral degree.

(6) Hours of experience shall not be gained prior to completing either 12 semester units or 18 quarter units of graduate instruction.

(7) Hours of experience shall not have been gained more than six years prior to the date the application for licensure was received by the board, except that up to 500 hours of clinical experience gained in the supervised practicum required by subdivision (c) of Section 4980.37 and subparagraph (B) of paragraph (1) of subdivision (d) of Section 4980.36 shall be exempt from this six-year requirement.

(8) A minimum of 1,750 hours of direct clinical counseling with individuals, groups, couples, or families, that includes not less than 500 total hours of experience in diagnosing and treating couples, families, and children.

(9) A maximum of 1,250 hours of nonclinical practice, consisting of direct supervisor contact, administering and evaluating psychological tests, writing clinical reports, writing progress or process notes, client centered advocacy, and workshops, seminars, training sessions, or conferences directly related to marriage and family therapy that have been approved by the applicant's supervisor.

(10) It is anticipated and encouraged that hours of experience will include working with elders and dependent adults who have physical or mental limitations that restrict their ability to carry out normal activities or protect their rights. This subdivision shall only apply to hours gained on and after January 1, 2010. (d) An individual who submits an application for licensure between January 1, 2016, and December 31, 2020, may alternatively qualify under the experience requirements of this section that were in place on January 1, 2015.

4980.43.1. Supervisor Responsibilities
(a) All trainees, associates, and applicants for licensure shall be under the supervision of a supervisor at all times.

(b) As used in this chapter, the term "supervision" means responsibility for, and control of, the quality of mental health and related services provided by the supervisee. Consultation or peer discussion shall not be considered supervision and shall not qualify as supervised experience. Supervision includes, but is not limited to, all of the following:

(1) Ensuring the extent, kind, and quality of counseling performed is consistent with the education, training, and experience of the supervisee.

(2) Monitoring and evaluating the supervisee's assessment, diagnosis, and treatment decisions and providing regular feedback.

(3) Monitoring and evaluating the supervisee's ability to provide services at the site or sites where he or she is practicing and to the particular clientele being served.

(4) Monitoring and addressing clinical dynamics, including, but not limited to, countertransference-, intrapsychic-, interpersonal-, or trauma-related issues that may affect the supervisory or practitioner patient relationship.

(5) Ensuring the supervisee's compliance with laws and regulations governing the practice of marriage and family therapy.

(6) Reviewing the supervisee's progress notes, process notes, and other patient treatment records, as deemed appropriate by the supervisor.
(7) With the client's written consent, providing direct observation or review of audio or video recordings of the supervisee's counseling or therapy, as deemed appropriate by the supervisor.

4980.43.2. Direct Supervisor Contact
(a) Except for experience gained by attending workshops, seminars, training sessions, or conferences, as described in paragraph (9) of subdivision (a) of Section 4980.43, direct supervisor contact shall occur as follows:

(1) Supervision shall include at least one hour of direct supervisor contact in each week for which experience is credited in each work setting.

(2) A trainee shall receive an average of at least one hour of direct supervisor contact for every five hours of direct clinical counseling performed each week in each setting. For experience gained on or after January 1, 2009, no more than six hours of supervision, whether individual, triadic, or group, shall be credited during any single week.

(3) An associate gaining experience who performs more than 10 hours of direct clinical counseling in a week in any setting shall receive at least one additional hour of direct supervisor contact for that setting. For experience gained on or after January 1, 2009, no more than six hours of supervision,

whether individual, triadic, or group, shall be credited during any single week.

(4) Of the 104 weeks of required supervision, 52 weeks shall be individual supervision, triadic supervision, or a combination of both.
(b) For purposes of this chapter, "one hour of direct supervisor contact" means any of the following:

(1) Individual supervision, which means one hour of face-to-face contact between one supervisor and one supervisee.

(2) Triadic supervision, which means one hour of face-to-face contact between one supervisor and two supervisees.

(3) Group supervision, which means two hours of face-to-face contact between one supervisor and no more than eight supervisees. Segments of group supervision may be split into no less than one continuous hour. A supervisor shall ensure that the amount and degree of supervision is appropriate for each supervisee.

(c) Direct supervisor contact shall occur within the same week as the hours claimed.

(d) Notwithstanding subdivision (b), an associate working in a governmental entity, school, college, university, or an institution that is nonprofit and charitable may obtain the required weekly direct supervisor contact via two-way, real-time videoconferencing. The supervisor shall be responsible for ensuring compliance with federal and state laws relating to confidentiality of patient health information.

(e) Notwithstanding any other law, once the required number of experience hours are gained, associates and applicants for licensure shall receive a minimum of one hour of direct supervisor contact per week for each practice setting in which direct clinical counseling is performed. Once the required number of experience hours are gained, further supervision for nonclinical practice, as defined in paragraph (9) of subdivision (a) of Section 4980.43, shall be at the supervisor's discretion.

4980.43.3. Supervised Experience: Acceptable Settings; Acceptable Supervision Practices
(a) A trainee, associate, or applicant for licensure shall only perform mental health and related services as an employee or volunteer, and not as an independent contractor. The requirements of this chapter regarding hours of experience and supervision shall apply equally to employees and volunteers. A trainee, associate, or applicant for licensure shall not perform any services or gain any experience within the scope of practice of the

profession, as defined in Section 4980.02, as an independent contractor. While an associate may be either a paid employee or a volunteer, employers are encouraged to provide fair remuneration.

(1) If employed, an associate shall provide the board, upon application for licensure, with copies of the W-2 tax forms for each year of experience claimed.

(2) If volunteering, an associate shall provide the board, upon application for licensure, with a letter from his or her employer verifying the associate's status as a volunteer during the dates the experience was gained.

(b) (1) A trainee shall not perform services in a private practice. A trainee may be credited with supervised experience completed in a setting that meets all of the following:

(A) Is not a private practice.

(B) Lawfully and regularly provides mental health counseling or psychotherapy.

(C) Provides oversight to ensure that the trainee's work at the setting meets the experience and supervision requirements in this chapter and is within the scope of practice for the profession, as defined in Section 4980.02.

(2) Only experience gained in the position for which the trainee volunteers or is employed shall qualify as supervised experience.

(c) An associate may be credited with supervised experience completed in any setting that meets both of the following:

(1) Lawfully and regularly provides mental health counseling or psychotherapy.

(2) Provides oversight to ensure that the associate's work at the setting meets the experience and supervision requirements in this chapter and is within the scope of practice for the profession, as defined in Section 4980.02.

(3) Only experience gained in the position for which the associate volunteers or is employed shall qualify as supervised experience.

(4) An applicant for registration as an associate shall not be employed or volunteer in a private practice until he or she has been issued an associate registration by the board.

(d) Any experience obtained under the supervision of a spouse, relative, or domestic partner shall not be credited toward the required hours of supervised experience. Any experience obtained under the supervision of a supervisor with whom the applicant has had or currently has a personal, professional, or business relationship that undermines the authority or effectiveness of the supervision shall not be credited toward the required hours of supervised experience.

(e) A trainee, associate, or applicant for licensure shall not receive any remuneration from patients or clients and shall only be paid by his or her employer, if an employee.

(f) A trainee, associate, or applicant for licensure shall have no proprietary interest in his or her employer's business and shall not lease or rent space, pay for furnishings, equipment, or supplies, or in any other way pay for the obligations of his or her employer.

(g) A trainee, associate, or applicant for licensure who provides voluntary services in any lawful work setting other than a private practice and who only receives reimbursement for expenses actually incurred shall be considered an employee. The board may audit an applicant for licensure who receives reimbursement for expenses and the applicant for licensure shall have the burden of demonstrating that the payment received was for reimbursement of expenses actually incurred.

(h) A trainee, associate, or applicant for licensure who receives a stipend or educational loan repayment from a program designed to encourage demographically underrepresented groups to enter the profession or to improve recruitment and retention in underserved regions or settings shall be considered an employee.

The board may audit an applicant who receives a stipend or educational loan repayment and the applicant shall have the burden of demonstrating that the payment received was for the specified purposes.

(i) An associate or a trainee may provide services via telehealth that are in the scope of practice outlined in this chapter.

(j) Each educational institution preparing applicants pursuant to this chapter shall consider requiring, and shall encourage, its students to undergo individual, marital, conjoint, family, or group counseling or psychotherapy, as appropriate. Each supervisor shall consider, advise, and encourage his or her associates and trainees regarding the advisability of undertaking individual, marital, conjoint, family, or group counseling or psychotherapy, as appropriate. Insofar as it is deemed appropriate and is desired by the applicant, educational institutions and supervisors are encouraged to assist the applicant to locate counseling or psychotherapy at a reasonable cost.

4980.43.4. Supervisees: Location of Services; Maximum Number of Supervisees; Oversight Agreement

(a)A trainee, associate, or applicant for licensure shall only perform mental health and related services at the places where his or her employer regularly conducts business and services.

(b) An associate who is employed or volunteering in a private practice shall be supervised by an individual who is employed by, and shall practice at the same site as, the associate's employer. Alternatively, the supervisor may be an owner of the private practice. However, if the site is incorporated, the supervisor must be employed full-time at the site and be actively engaged in performing professional services at the site.

(c) A supervisor at a private practice or a corporation shall not supervise more than a total of three supervisees at any one time. Supervisees may be registered as an associate marriage and family therapist, an associate professional clinical counselor, or an associate clinical social worker.

(d) In a setting that is not a private practice:

(1) A written oversight agreement, as specified by regulation, shall be executed between the supervisor and employer when the supervisor is not employed by the supervisee's employer or is a volunteer.

(2) A supervisor shall evaluate the site or sites where a trainee or associate will be gaining experience to determine that the site or sites comply with the requirements set forth in this chapter.

(e) Alternative supervision may be arranged during a supervisor's vacation or sick leave if the alternative supervision meets the requirements in this chapter and regulation.

4980.43.5. Audit of Supervisors

The board may audit the records of any supervisor to verify the completion of the supervisor qualifications specified by this chapter and by regulation. A supervisor shall maintain records of completion of the required supervisor qualifications for seven years after termination of the supervision and shall make these records available to the board for auditing purposes upon request.

4980.44. Associate Notice to Client or Patient; Advertisement

An associate marriage and family therapist employed under this chapter shall comply with the following requirements:

(a) Inform each client or patient prior to performing any mental health and related services that he or she is an unlicensed registered associate marriage and family therapist, provide his or her registration number and the name of his or her employer, and indicate whether he or she is under the supervision of a licensed marriage and family therapist, licensed clinical social worker, licensed professional clinical counselor, psychologist licensed pursuant to Chapter 6.6 (commencing with Section 2900), or a licensed physician and surgeon certified in psychiatry by the American Board of Psychiatry and Neurology.

(b) (1) Any advertisement by or on behalf of a registered associate marriage and family therapist shall include, at a minimum, all of the following information:

(A) That he or she is a registered associate marriage and family therapist.
(B) The associate's registration number.
(C) The name of his or her employer.
(D) That he or she is supervised by a licensed person.

(2) The abbreviation "AMFT" shall not be used in an advertisement unless the title "registered associate marriage and family therapist" appears in the advertisement.

4980.49. Client Records; Retention
(a) A marriage and family therapist shall retain a client's or patient's health service records for a minimum of seven years from the date therapy is terminated. If the client or patient is a minor, the client's or patient's health service records shall be retained for a minimum of seven years from the date the client or the patient reaches 18 years of age. Health service records may be retained in either a written or an electronic format.

(b) This section shall apply only to the records of a client or patient whose therapy is terminated on or after January 1, 2015.

4980.55. Disclosure of Counselors Qualification's
As a model for all therapeutic professions, and to acknowledge respect and regard for the consuming public, all licensed marriage and family therapists are encouraged to provide to each client, at an appropriate time and within the context of the psychotherapeutic relationship, an accurate and informative statement of the therapist's experience, education, specialities, professional orientation, and any other information deemed appropriate by the licensee.

4980.72. Applicants Licensed Out of State; Equivalent Requirements
(a) This section applies to a person who is licensed outside of California and

74

applies for licensure on or after January 1, 2016.

(b) The board may issue a license to a person who, at the time of submitting an application for a license pursuant to this chapter, holds a valid license in good standing issued by a board of marriage counselor examiners, board of marriage and family therapists, or corresponding authority, of any state or country, if all of the following conditions are satisfied:

(1) The applicant's education is substantially equivalent, as defined in Section 4980.79. The applicant's degree title need not be identical to that required by Section 4980.36 or 4980.37.

(2) The applicant complies with Section 4980.76, if applicable.

(3) (A) The applicant's supervised experience is substantially equivalent to that required for a license under this chapter.

(B) For persons who have held their license for less than four years immediately preceding the date of application, the board shall determine substantial equivalency by considering hours of experience obtained outside of California during the six-year period immediately preceding the date the applicant initially obtained the license described above. If the applicant has less than 3,000 hours of qualifying supervised experience, time actively licensed in the equivalent profession shall be accepted at a rate of 100 hours per month, up to a maximum of 1,200 hours, if the applicant's degree meets the practicum requirement described in subparagraph (C) of paragraph (1) of subdivision (b) of Section 4980.79 without exemptions or remediation.

(4) The applicant passes the California law and ethics examination.

(5) The applicant passes a clinical examination designated by the board. An applicant who obtained his or her license or registration under another jurisdiction may qualify for licensure with the board without taking the clinical examination if both of the following conditions are met:

(A) The applicant obtained a passing score on the clinical licensing examination set forth in regulation as accepted by the board.
(B) The applicant's license or registration in that jurisdiction is active, in good standing at the time of his or her application, and is not revoked, suspended, surrendered, denied, or otherwise restricted or encumbered.

4980.74. Education and Experience Gained outside of California; Effective January 1, 2016
(a) This section applies to persons who apply for licensure or registration on or after January 1, 2016, and who do not hold a license as described in

Section 4980.72.

(b) The board shall accept education gained while residing outside of California for purposes of satisfying licensure or registration requirements if the education is substantially equivalent, as defined in Section 4980.78, and the applicant complies with Section 4980.76, if applicable. The applicant's degree title need not be identical to that required by Section 4980.36 or 4980.37.

(c) The board shall accept experience gained outside of California for purposes of satisfying licensure or registration requirements if the experience is substantially equivalent to that required by this chapter.

4980.76. Degree obtained outside the United States

An applicant for licensure or registration with a degree obtained from an educational institution outside the United States shall provide the board with a comprehensive evaluation of the degree performed by a foreign credential evaluation service that is a member of the National Association of Credential Evaluation Services (NACES), and shall provide any other documentation the board deems necessary.

4980.78. Substantially Equivalent Education; coursework required of applicants Not License outside of California; Effective January 1, 2016

(a) This section applies to persons who apply for licensure or registration on or after January 1, 2016, and who do not hold a license as described in Section 4980.72.

(b) For purposes of Section 4980.74, education is substantially equivalent if all of the following requirements are met:

(1) The degree is obtained from a school, college, or university accredited by an accrediting agency that is recognized by the United States Department of Education and consists of, at a minimum, the following:

(A) (i) For an applicant who obtained his or her degree within the timeline prescribed by subdivision (a) of Section 4980.36, the degree shall contain no less than 60 semester or 90 quarter units of instruction.

(ii) Up to 12 semester or 18 quarter units of instruction may be remediated, if missing from the degree. The remediation may occur while the applicant is registered as an intern.

(B) For an applicant who obtained his or her degree within the timeline prescribed by subdivision (a) of Section 4980.37, the degree shall contain no less than 48 semester units or 72 quarter units of instruction.

(C) Six semester or nine quarter units of practicum, including, but not limited to, a minimum of 150 hours of face-to-face counseling, and an additional 75 hours of either face-to-face counseling or client-centered advocacy, or a combination of face-to-face counseling and client-centered advocacy.

(D) Twelve semester or 18 quarter units in the areas of marriage, family, and child counseling and marital and family systems approaches to treatment, as specified in subparagraph (A) of paragraph (1) of subdivision (d) of Section 4980.36.

(2) The applicant shall complete coursework in California law and ethics as follows:

(A) An applicant who completed a course in law and professional ethics for marriage and family therapists as specified in paragraph (7) of subdivision (a) of Section 4980.81, that did not contain instruction in California law and ethics, shall complete an 18-hour course in California law and professional ethics. The content of the course shall include, but not be limited to, advertising, scope of practice, scope of competence, treatment of minors, confidentiality, dangerous patients, psychotherapist-patient privilege, recordkeeping, patient access to records, state and federal laws relating to confidentiality of patient health information, dual relationships, child abuse, elder and dependent adult abuse, online therapy, insurance reimbursement, civil liability, disciplinary actions and unprofessional conduct, ethics complaints and ethical standards, termination of therapy, standards of care, relevant family law, therapist disclosures to patients, differences in legal and ethical standards in different types of work settings, and licensing law and licensing process. This coursework shall be completed prior to registration as an intern.

(B) An applicant who has not completed a course in law and professional ethics for marriage and family therapists as specified in paragraph (7) of subdivision (a) of Section 4980.81 shall complete this required coursework. The coursework shall contain content specific to California law and ethics. This coursework shall be completed prior to registration as an intern.

(3) The applicant completes the educational requirements specified in Section 4980.81 not already completed in his or her education. The coursework may be from an accredited school, college, or university as specified in paragraph (1), from an educational institution approved by the Bureau for Private Postsecondary Education, or from a continuing education provider that is acceptable to the board as defined in Section 4980.54. Undergraduate courses shall not satisfy this requirement.

(4) The applicant completes the following coursework not already completed in his or her education from an accredited school, college, or university as specified in paragraph (1) from an educational institution approved by the Bureau for Private Postsecondary Education, or from a continuing education provider that is acceptable

to the board as defined in Section 4980.54. Undergraduate courses shall not satisfy this requirement.

(A) At least three semester units, or 45 hours, of instruction regarding the principles of mental health recovery-oriented care and methods of service delivery in recovery-oriented practice environments, including structured meetings with various consumers and family members of consumers of mental health services to enhance understanding of their experience of mental illness, treatment, and recovery.

(B) At least one semester unit, or 15 hours, of instruction that includes an understanding of various California cultures and the social and psychological implications of socioeconomic position.

(5) An applicant may complete any units and course content requirements required under paragraphs (3) and (4) not already completed in his or her education while registered as an intern, unless otherwise specified.
(6) The applicant's degree title need not be identical to that required by subdivision (b) of Section 4980.36.

4980.79. Substantially Equivalent Education; Coursework Required of Applicants Licensed outside of California

(a) This section applies to persons who apply for licensure as defined in Section 4980.72.

(b) For purposes of Section 4980.72, education is substantially equivalent if all of the following requirements are met:
(1) The degree is obtained from a school, college, or university accredited by an accrediting agency recognized by the United States Department of Education and consists of, at a minimum, the following:

(A) (i) For an applicant who obtained his or her degree within the timeline prescribed by subdivision (a) of Section 4980.36, the degree shall contain no less than 60 semester or 90 quarter units of instruction.
(ii) Up to 12 semester or 18 quarter units of instruction may be remediated, if missing from the degree. The remediation may occur while the applicant is registered as an intern.

(B) For an applicant who obtained his or her degree within the timeline prescribed by subdivision (a) of Section 4980.37, the degree shall contain no less than 48 semester or 72 quarter units of instruction.

(C) Six semester or nine quarter units of practicum, including, but not limited to, a minimum of 150 hours of face-to-face counseling, and an additional 75 hours of either face-to-face counseling or client-centered advocacy, or

a combination of face-to-face counseling and client-centered advocacy.
(i) An out-of-state applicant who has been licensed for at least two years in clinical practice, as verified by the board, is exempt from this requirement.
(ii) An out-of-state applicant who has been licensed for less than two years in clinical practice, as verified by the board, who does not meet the practicum requirement, shall remediate it by obtaining 150 hours of face-to-face counseling, and an additional 75 hours of either face-to-face counseling or client-centered advocacy, or a combination of face-to-face counseling and client-centered advocacy. These hours are in addition to the 3,000 hours of experience required by this chapter, and shall be gained while registered as an intern.

(D) Twelve semester or 18 quarter units in the areas of marriage, family, and child counseling and marital and family systems approaches to treatment, as specified in subparagraph (A) of paragraph (1) of subdivision (d) of Section 4980.36.
   (2) An applicant shall complete coursework in California law and ethics as follows:

(A) An applicant who completed a course in law and professional ethics for marriage and family therapists as specified in paragraph (8) of subdivision (a) of Section 4980.81 that did not include instruction in California law and ethics, shall complete an 18-hour course in California law and professional ethics. The content of the course shall include, but not be limited to, advertising, scope of practice, scope of competence, treatment of minors, confidentiality, dangerous patients, psychotherapist-patient privilege, recordkeeping, patient access to records, state and federal laws relating to confidentiality of patient health information, dual relationships, child abuse, elder and dependent adult abuse, online therapy, insurance reimbursement, civil liability, disciplinary actions and unprofessional conduct, ethics complaints and ethical standards, termination of therapy, standards of care, relevant family law, therapist disclosures to patients, differences in legal and ethical standards in different types of work settings, and licensing law and licensing process. This coursework shall be completed prior to registration as an associate.

(B) An applicant who has not completed a course in law and professional ethics for marriage and family therapists as specified in paragraph (7) of subdivision (a) of Section 4980.81 shall complete this required coursework. The coursework shall include content specific to California law and ethics. An applicant shall complete this coursework prior to registration as an intern.
   (3) The applicant completes the educational requirements specified in Section 4980.81 not already completed in his or her education. The coursework may be from an accredited school, college, or university

as specified in paragraph (1), from an educational institution approved by the Bureau for Private Postsecondary Education, or from a continuing education provider that is acceptable to the board as defined in Section 4980.54. Undergraduate coursework shall not satisfy this requirement.

(4) The applicant completes the following coursework not already completed in his or her education from an accredited school, college, or university as specified in paragraph (1) above, from an educational institution approved by the Bureau for Private Postsecondary Education, or from a continuing education provider that is acceptable to the board as defined in Section 4980.54. Undergraduate coursework shall not satisfy this requirement.

(A) At least three semester units, or 45 hours, of instruction pertaining to the principles of mental health recovery-oriented care and methods of service delivery in recovery-oriented practice environments, including structured meetings with various consumers and family members of consumers of mental health services to enhance understanding of their experience of mental illness, treatment, and recovery.

(B) At least one semester unit, or 15 hours, of instruction that includes an understanding of various California cultures and the social and psychological implications of socioeconomic position.

(5) An applicant's degree title need not be identical to that required by subdivision (b) of Section 4980.36.

(6) An applicant may complete any units and course content requirements required under paragraphs (3)

and (4) not already completed in his or her education while registered as an associate, unless

otherwise specified.

4980.81. Additional Coursework Required for Out-Of-State Applicants

This section applies to persons subject to Section 4980.78 or 4980.79, who apply for licensure or registration on or after January 2016.

(a) For purposes of Sections 4980.78 and 4980.79, an applicant shall meet all of the following educational requirements:

(1) A minimum of two semester units of instruction in the diagnosis, assessment, prognosis, and treatment of mental disorders, including severe mental disorders, evidence-based practices, psychological testing, psychopharmacology, and promising mental health practices that are evaluated in peer reviewed literature. This shall include at least one semester unit or 15 hours of instruction in psychological testing and at least one semester unit or 15 hours of instruction in psychopharmacology.

(2) (A) Developmental issues from infancy to old age, including

demonstration of at least one semester unit, or 15 hours, of instruction that includes all of the following subjects:

(i) The effects of developmental issues on individuals, couples, and family relationships.
(ii) The psychological, psychotherapeutic, and health implications of developmental issues and their effects.
(iii) The understanding of the impact that personal and social insecurity, social stress, low educational levels, inadequate housing, and malnutrition have on human development.

(B) An applicant who is deficient in any of these subjects may remediate the coursework by completing three hours of instruction in each deficient subject.
    (3) (A) The broad range of matters and life events that may arise within marriage and family relationships and within a variety of California cultures, including instruction in all of the following:

(i) A minimum of seven contact hours of training or coursework in child abuse assessment and reporting as specified in Section 28 and any regulations promulgated under that section.

(ii) A minimum of 10 contact hours of coursework that includes all of the following:

    (I) The assessment and reporting of, as well as treatment related to, elder and dependent adult abuse and neglect.
    (II) Aging and its biological, social, cognitive, and psychological aspects.
    (III) Long-term care.
    (IV) End-of-life and grief.
    (iii) A minimum of 15 contact hours of coursework in spousal or partner abuse assessment, detection, intervention strategies, and same-gender abuse dynamics.
    (iv) Cultural factors relevant to abuse of partners and family members.
    (v) Childbirth, child rearing, parenting, and stepparenting.
    (vi) Marriage, divorce, and blended families.
    (vii) Poverty and deprivation.
    (viii) Financial and social stress.
    (ix) Effects of trauma.
    (x) The psychological, psychotherapeutic, community, and health implications of the matters and life events described in clauses (i) to (ix), inclusive.

(4) At least one semester unit, or 15 hours, of instruction in multicultural development and cross-cultural interaction, including experiences of

race, ethnicity, class, spirituality, sexual orientation, gender, and disability, and their incorporation into the psychotherapeutic process.

(5) A minimum of 10 contact hours of training or coursework in human sexuality, as specified in Section 25 and any regulations promulgated under that section, including the study of physiological, psychological, and social cultural variables associated with sexual behavior and gender identity, and the assessment and treatment of psychosexual dysfunction.

(6) A minimum of 15 contact hours of coursework in substance use disorders, and a minimum of 15 contact hours of coursework in co-occurring disorders and addiction. The following subjects shall be included in this coursework:

(A) The definition of substance use disorders, co-occurring disorders, and addiction. For purposes of this subparagraph "co-occurring disorders" means a mental illness and substance abuse diagnosis occurring simultaneously in an individual.

(B) Medical aspects of substance use disorders and co-occurring disorders.

(C) The effects of psychoactive drug use.

(D) Current theories of the etiology of substance abuse and addiction.

(E) The role of persons and systems that support or compound substance abuse and addiction.

(F) Major approaches to identification, evaluation, and treatment of substance use disorders, co-occurring disorders, and addiction, including, but not limited to, best practices.

(G) Legal aspects of substance abuse.

(H) Populations at risk with regard to substance use disorders and co-occurring disorders.

(I) Community resources offering screening, assessment, treatment, and followup for the affected person and family.

(J) Recognition of substance use disorders, co-occurring disorders, and addiction, and appropriate referral.

(K) The prevention of substance use disorders and addiction.
    (7) A minimum of a two semester or three quarter unit course in law and

professional ethics for marriage and family therapists, including instruction in all of the following subjects:

(A) Contemporary professional ethics and statutory, regulatory, and decisional laws that delineate the scope of practice of marriage and family therapy.

(B) The therapeutic, clinical, and practical considerations involved in the legal and ethical practice of marriage and family therapy, including, but not limited to, family law.

(C) The current legal patterns and trends in the mental health professions.

(D) The psychotherapist-patient privilege, confidentiality, the patient dangerous to self or others, and the treatment of minors with and without parental consent.

(E) A recognition and exploration of the relationship between a practitioner's sense of self and human values and his or her professional behavior and ethics.

(F) Differences in legal and ethical standards for different types of work settings.

(G) Licensing law and licensing process.

CHAPTER 3
Practice Requirements

The Board of Behavioral Sciences has practice requirements for both professional clinical counselors and marriage and family therapists. For this reason, we will start this chapter addressing *informed consent.* We decided to include informed consent in this chapter under practice requirements due to the fact that you will likely not find the term "informed consent" throughout the laws and regulations. Informed Consent is more of a concept and a practice and not necessarily a form or document, although most therapist have developed some type of document that expresses this. For this reason you won't find succinct information within the laws and regulations detailing the informed consent process. However the Cobbs v. Grant case of 1972 provided much-needed information on the necessity of obtaining informed consent to maintain standard of care. This section also address other practice requirement for which will be identified in brief.

Informed Consent

Informed consent this is a necessary and required part of a therapeutic relationship and part of your practice. When we talk about informed consent, we often think about this being done in writing. You go to your primary physician's office, typically you're handed a form, it is read to you or you read it and then you sign it. Many therapists have an Informed consent form that they have developed and provide to the client, however, there's nothing in the law that specifically states that informed consent has to be obtained in writing. In fact, this could be something that's done verbally, especially if there are some cultural considerations where it may be inappropriate to do so, or there is no ability to obtain informed consent in writing then the verbal informed consent would be appropriately obtained. For many therapists in practice, obtaining informed consent in writing is just standard in order to prove later (since the burden of proof is on you) that you did in fact at least provide the client the document that, you at least went over the document, and that the client signed acknowledging that they received the document and/or that the information was something discussed between the client and the therapist. It should be noted that in Cobbs V. Grant 1972, this court case identified some specific pieces of informed consent that were necessary to build the trusting relationship between a therapist and a client and essentially for the counseling profession. One of them is that the client obtains and is provided the information about the potential benefits and potential risks of the treatment that the therapist is going to be providing. This is important so that the client can make the best decision possible for themselves.

Additionally, it was established that clients need to be aware that they have the right to enter into therapeutic treatment, but they also have the right to withdraw their consent to therapeutic treatment. Therapists should clarify that they do not have the same scope of practice or the same scope of knowledge in comparison to other therapists (e.g., LMFT vs Psychologist). Meaning that we clarify what our job is as therapists, if you are master level therapist then you don't hold yourself out to be a psychologist or psychiatrist. Additionally the court case argued that we give clients all the information about therapy, about the therapeutic practice, the intervention that we are going to engage in, and do so in a way that's understandable to them. We want to make sure that this is in very plain and understandable language.

There are some legal pieces that are identified that we do want to make sure that we cover as part of informed consent. We need to cover fees and the basis on how we are going to determine the fees and how we are going to obtain and collect those fees. If we utilize something called a fictitious business name or doing business as a DBA, we want to make sure that we provide that information to our clients. So if my private practice is called The Best Counseling Services In The City, well that's a fictitious business name. Note that The Best Counseling Services In The City does not have a license to practice as an LPCC or LMFT. You will need to make sure to let clients know about the fictitious business and inform them of the name and the designation of the owners of the practice. A similar requirement is established when it comes to who is providing services. If a Trainee or Associate is providing services, they need to inform the client who the supervisor is and their status.

The Code of Ethics for many professional organizations may suggest that obtaining informed consent should be done both verbally and in writing. Now again as previously said, according to the Business and Professions Code, it does not specify how we obtain informed consent whether it is verbally or in writing but that we need to obtain it. The Code of Ethics that you may follow could be the California Association For Marriage and Family Therapist, American Counseling Association or even the National Association of Social Worker, and again, this codes may suggest that it be done both in writing and verbally, so it would be important to not only understand the legal requirements but also your ethical requirements according to your professional associations.

There are some additional considerations that we want to make sure that we are keeping in mind when we are providing this document or providing the information verbally, one is we want to make sure that the client has legal capacity and competence to provide consent, meaning that they don't have a cognitive or mental impairment that would reduce or eliminate their ability to actually give this consent. If the client is a self-consenting minor 12 years or older, we want to assure that the client is mature enough to be able to understand the information presented and again, that information needs to be presented in as much as possible in plain and understandable language. If the client has a diagnosis of an intellectual disability, then we want to ensure that the information being provided is appropriate to their level of understanding. With all clients we want to make sure that the they understand that they have the right to refuse and decline the treatment. This is a central responsibility of the therapist, to convey that just because they initially agreed to treatment it does not mean that they are "stuck" and there's no way out.

There are some instances when informed consent should be and must be obtained in writing and that's when specific acts are going to be engaged in. A common event is videotaping a therapy session, we want to make sure that the client has signed giving permission for the session to be videotaped. If we are going to audiotape a session, then we want to make sure that we provide a document to our client informing them and getting their permission to audiotape by signing. This is the same if we are going to have someone else observing the session, like a student in training (Trainee) that we do get a document signed by that client agreeing to and providing permission and informed consent for that session to be observed by that third party. This is essentially the same information that we want to provide and share with our clients who we are offering telehealth services to.

Under Business and Professions Code 2290.5 it indicates that prior to providing telehealth, we want to ensure that we provide to our clients either verbal or written informed consent, verify that telehealth is an acceptable mode of delivering the healthcare services and then we need to ensure that we document that in our files. Regardless of how we obtain informed consent, we always want to document that in our notes that we've obtained that information. A copy of the informed consent is even you even more support to show that we've completed that informed consent process. We want to ensure that we complete informed consent and we want to cover some things with them about the risks and benefits, the potential dangers of having mental health services via the internet in that it may not be the most secure mode.

When we are looking at obtaining informed consent from someone who probably can't provide informed consent such as perhaps someone that has a diagnosis of dementia or they have such a level of cognitive impairment that it would be difficult to really ascertain if the client understood and could really provide true informed consent, or if they are under conservatorship, then we actually want to obtain the informed consent from their conservator. Similarly, with minors under 12, they are typically unable to legally provide informed consent. We obtain informed consent from their parents/guardians or conservators. For the actual client receiving treatment, we want to obtain something called assent. Assent is the process in which we explain the procedures in easy to understand language and attempt to have the client respond with some understanding. We want the willing participation of the client that we're actually going to be working with regardless of who is providing consent. This is very important to establish a good working relationship and to provide effective therapy and counseling.

The Business and Professions Code does not really provide a lot of guidance on what should be included in informed consent besides those few specific pieces that are identified, but many ethical standards have provided us some guidelines on what should be included in order to ensure that our clients have as much information as possible to make well-informed decisions about the uses of our services. Here are some of those guidelines found through ethical standards of the profession: We should talk to them and provide them some information about the nature and the limits of confidentiality and what that looks like, we should discuss instances in which we may need to report child abuse or elder / dependent adult abuse, and any responsibilities that the therapist has to report if the client is a danger to themselves or to others and any other similar situation. We need to provide information to clients about when information might be released to a third party and perhaps why that might be released to a third party. When we are working with couples or working with families, we want to clarify who the client is and then clarify the type of treatment that we're going to utilize for each family member or for the family unit.

As previously mentioned, we want to talk about the risks and the benefits of therapy. What are the drawbacks? What are some alternative treatments that the individual may be able to engage? Or if there's no treatment that would be required at all right, we need to make sure that we inform our clients of that. We want to make sure that our client has enough information about who we are, about the process, the procedures, the treatment, and the interventions so that they can again, make meaningful decisions about whether to engage in therapy with us. We want to ensure that we discuss the responsibilities of our relationship with our client, that we are that therapist and that we have a professional role and that our goal is to help and support our client. We want to talk a little bit about perhaps our professional qualifications, our theoretical orientations, and perspectives, perhaps some of the specialties that we may engage in, our time in practice, our overall experiences and perhaps any other information that might be deemed appropriate.

We should talk about the expected length of therapy and the number of sessions that we may be engaging in with our client. It would be important to disclose whether you offer 45-minute sessions or 60-minute sessions. We want to talk about the right to mutually terminate therapy, therein, we have the right to terminate therapy with our clients under certain conditions and our client has full rights to terminate therapy as well. You may want to talk about the procedures that may follow that, so always remember appropriate termination as necessary. We want to talk about the procedures for collecting our fees from our client and any particular procedures and information that we need to provide to them regarding raising our fees. Would you give a 90-day fee increase notice?

We want to talk a little bit about if we are subpoenaed on behalf of our client to testify, that we provide them the information on what fees we are going to charge for that (we have the right to charge for those particular times in which we are subpoenaed to testify). We want to make sure that we provide information on fees charged for preparing, copying and/or mailing records. We want to talk about any cancellation fees/no show fee. We should discuss policies on the use of telephone and our availability between sessions and emergencies. We are on vacation; we want to name someone who is going to be able to cover our practice in our absence (this is going to be another therapist that's been designated that we can refer our clients to for that time period). If we are incapacitated or unable to work with our client (perhaps because of an accident) we want to make sure that we have informed them about who would be able to access their records if they needed a copy and who they could continue therapy with.

There are two specific times where you may need to consider modifying your informed consent process. One of them is when you're working with couples or families and the other is when you're working with groups in group therapy and counseling. When you are working with couples and families, you want to consider implementing a no secrets policy. This policy essentially states that information that one member of the family shares or the couple shares and if the other member is not there at that particular time, that you may choose to disclose that information at your discretion if you believe it is in the best interest of therapy. What happens often in family therapy and couples' therapy, one individual of that unit is not present, and then one of the members share something and often shares it in a way that expresses they do not want that information to be shared to the other group member. This puts us in a bit of a precarious situation because then it limits our ability to treat the unit as a whole. So, we may want to make sure that we say very clearly upfront that there are no secrets and that we may at our discretion share that information with the unit when the other member returns if we believe it is in the best interest of therapy. This is

no secrets policy

something that you may actually want to develop a written form that illustrates this and have all members of the unit sign.

If you find yourself in a situation where members of the unit are not agreeing to this, then you may need to decide on what your next steps are. It is important in these situations to consider your next steps wisely. Remember that what clients share in the confidence of therapy is confidential, however in these particular situations, generally again keyword is generally, that information that you may disclose to other members of the party in therapy (in your sessions) is typically not considered to be a violation of the clients confidentiality as long as you have clearly, very clearly discussed that there are no secrets, and refer to the signed document indicating that they have agreed to this policy. Note that as the therapist, even with such document signed, there may be times when information would be inappropriate to share with the unit.

When you are working with groups in group therapy, you want to as part of your informed consent process ensure that you have clients at least agree, not just with you, but also to each other in the group as part of your group policy and rules, that they are not going to share information that was obtained in the group session. Make clear that we cannot guarantee that clients in the group will maintain confidentiality (this is one of the risks that should be discussed), but we as therapist will. The hope is that by having this verbal and written agreement between them, this information will not be disclosed. The other item is that we want to discuss is the relationships with the group members outside of group therapy. You may want to have some guidelines about out of group relationships between the members, what your hopes and goals are for the group and perhaps any other guidelines regarding therapeutic boundaries within and between group members. Finally, we might have a requirement that discusses termination and that if members decide to terminate early, that they give us enough time to help them process the termination (the loss of the group) to make sure that termination is done appropriately.

Some practice requirements identified in the law
Many therapists and agencies that employ therapists have developed a document which includes aspects of informed consent that are required legally by law as well as other aspects that may be required or suggested by ethical standards. The following are legally required aspects of the informed consent process:

1. Whether as an associate or as a licensed professional, a licensee must display their license in a conspicuous place at their primary place of practice, this means in a place that can be observed and seen by clients.
2. Therapist must disclose fees that will be charged for services rendered.
3. If a fictitious business name is utilized in private practice, the therapist

must inform the client prior to providing services the name and the license designation of the owner(s) of the practice.

4. If it the therapist is a covered entity under HIPAA, the therapist must provide a copy of the Notice of Privacy Practices.

5. Trainees and interns need to ensure that when they perform therapy, they inform clients that they are unlicensed and provide the required information as listed in this chapter regarding their supervisor/employer.

6. If services are being rendered using Telehealth, it must be documented.

All informed consent should be provided to clients in reasonably understandable language and should be documented in their records. Clients should be aware of the limits of confidentiality as part of the informed consent process.

MAINTAIN RECORDS FOR 7 YEARS

Other items therapist should note:
Therapist need to ensure that they maintain client records for a minimum of 7 years from the date that therapy was terminated. When working with a minor, the client's record should be kept at a minimum of 7 years from the date that the client turned 18 years old. These records can be maintained either in hard copy or electronic format.

Licensed therapist in private practice that are approved as defined by the Business and Professions Code can supervise no more than 3 interns at a time. Professional Corporation shall employ no more than 15 interns.

LPCC Practice Requirements

Business and Professions Code
4999.70. Display of License
A licensee shall display his or her license in a conspicuous place in his or her primary place of practice.
(Added by Stats. 2009, Ch. 619, Sec. 3. Effective January 1, 2010.)

4999.72. Fictitious Business Name
Any licensed professional clinical counselor who conducts a private practice under a fictitious business name shall not use any name that is false, misleading, or deceptive, and shall inform the patient, prior to the commencement of treatment, of the name and license designation of the owner or owners of the practice.

4999.74. Counseling Relationship & Process; Disclosure Requirement
Licensed professional clinical counselors shall provide to each client accurate information about the counseling relationship and the counseling process.

4999.75. Client Records Retention

(a) A licensed professional clinical counselor shall retain a client's or patient's health service records for a minimum of seven years from the date therapy is terminated. If the client or patient is a minor, the client's or patient's health service records shall be retained for a minimum of seven years from the date the client or patient reaches 18 years of age. Health service records may be retained in either a written or an electronic format.
(b) This section shall apply only to the records of a client or patient whose therapy is terminated on or after January 1, 2015.

4999.76. License Renewal; Continuing Education Requirement

(a) Except as provided in subdivision (c), the board shall not renew any license pursuant to this chapter unless the applicant certifies to the board, on a form prescribed by the board, that he or she has completed not less than 36 hours of approved continuing education in or relevant to the field of professional clinical counseling in the preceding two years, as determined by the board.

(b) The board shall have the right to audit the records of any applicant to verify the completion of the continuing education requirement. Applicants shall maintain records of completed continuing education coursework for a minimum of two years and shall make these records available to the board for auditing purposes upon request.

(c) The board may establish exceptions from the continuing education requirement of this section for good cause, as defined by the board.

(d) The continuing education shall be obtained from one of the following sources:

(1) A school, college, or university that is accredited or approved, as defined in Section 4999.12. Nothing in this paragraph shall be construed as requiring coursework to be offered as part of a regular degree program.

(2) Other continuing education providers, including, but not limited to, a professional clinical counseling association, a licensed health facility, a governmental entity, a continuing education unit of a four-year institution of higher learning that is accredited or approved, or a mental health professional association, approved by the board.

(e) The board shall establish, by regulation, a procedure for approving providers of continuing education courses, and all providers of continuing education, as described in paragraphs (1) and (2) of subdivision (d), shall adhere to procedures established by the board. The board may revoke or deny the right of a provider to offer continuing education coursework pursuant to this section for failure to comply with the requirements of this section or any regulation adopted pursuant to this section.

(f) Training, education, and coursework by approved providers shall incorporate one or more of the following:

(1) Aspects of the discipline that are fundamental to the understanding or the practice of professional clinical counseling.
(2) Significant recent developments in the discipline of professional clinical counseling.
(3) Aspects of other disciplines that enhance the understanding or the practice of professional clinical counseling.

(g) A system of continuing education for licensed professional clinical counselors shall include courses directly related to the diagnosis, assessment, and treatment of the client population being served.

(h) The board shall, by regulation, fund the administration of this section through continuing education provider fees to be deposited in the Behavioral Sciences Fund. The fees related to the administration of this section shall be sufficient to meet, but shall not exceed, the costs of administering the corresponding provisions of this section. For the purposes of this subdivision, a provider of continuing education as described in paragraph (1) of subdivision (d) shall be deemed to be an approved provider.

(i) The continuing education requirements of this section shall fully comply with the guidelines for mandatory continuing education established by the Department of Consumer Affairs pursuant to Section 166.
(Amended by Stats. 2012, Ch. 799, Sec. 78. Effective January 1, 2013.)

MFT Practice Requirements

4980.44.   Unlicensed Intern; Qualifications; Notice to Client or Patient; Advertisements
An unlicensed marriage and family therapist intern employed under this chapter shall comply with the following requirements:
(a) Possess, at a minimum, a master's degree as specified in Section 4980.36 or 4980.37, as applicable.

(b) Register with the board prior to performing any duties, except as otherwise provided in subdivision (g) of Section 4980.43.

(c) Prior to performing any professional services, inform each client or patient that he or she is an unlicensed marriage and family therapist registered intern, provide his or her registration number and the name of his or her employer, and indicate whether he or she is under the supervision of a licensed marriage and family therapist, licensed clinical social worker, licensed professional clinical counselor, licensed psychologist, or a licensed physician and surgeon certified in psychiatry by the American Board of Psychiatry and Neurology.

(d) (1) Any advertisement by or on behalf of a marriage and family therapist registered intern shall include, at a minimum, all of the following information:

(A) That he or she is a marriage and family therapist registered intern.
(B) The intern's registration number.
(C) The name of his or her employer.
(D) That he or she is supervised by a licensed person.

   (2) The abbreviation "MFTI" shall not be used in an advertisement unless the title "marriage and family therapist registered intern" appears in the advertisement.

4980.45. Employment or Supervision of Registrants; Maximum Number of Registrants

(a) A licensed professional in private practice who has satisfied the requirements of subdivision (g) of Section 4980.03 may supervise or employ, at any one time, no more than a total of three individuals registered as a marriage and family therapist intern, clinical counselor intern, or associate clinical social worker in that private practice.

(b) A marriage and family therapy corporation may employ, at any one time, no more than a total of three individuals registered as a marriage and family therapist intern, clinical counselor intern, or associate clinical social worker for each employee or shareholder who has satisfied the requirements of subdivision (g) of Section 4980.03. In no event shall any marriage and family therapy corporation employ, at any one time, more than a total of 15 individuals registered as a marriage and family therapist intern, clinical counselor intern, or associate clinical social worker. In no event shall any supervisor supervise, at any one time, more than a total of three individuals registered as either a marriage and family therapist intern, clinical counselor intern, or associate clinical social worker. Persons who supervise individuals registered as either a marriage and family therapist intern, clinical counselor intern, or associate clinical social worker shall be employed full time by the marriage and family therapy corporation and shall be actively engaged in performing professional services at and for the marriage and family therapy corporation. Employment and supervision within a marriage and family therapy corporation shall be subject to all laws and regulations governing experience and supervision gained in a private practice setting.

4980.46. Fictitious Business Names

Any licensed marriage and family therapist who conducts a private practice under a fictitious business name shall not use any name that is false, misleading, or deceptive, and shall inform the patient, prior to the commencement of treatment, of the name and license designation of the owner or owners of the practice.

4980.48. Trainees; Notice to Clients of Unlicensed Status; Advertisements

(a) A trainee shall, prior to performing any professional services, inform each client or patient that he or she is an unlicensed marriage and family therapist trainee, provide the name of his or her employer, and indicate whether he or she is under the supervision of a licensed marriage and family therapist, a licensed clinical social worker, a licensed professional clinical counselor, a licensed psychologist, or a licensed physician certified in psychiatry by the American Board of Psychiatry and Neurology.

(b) Any person that advertises services performed by a trainee shall include the trainee's name, the supervisor's license designation or abbreviation, and the supervisor's license number.

(c) Any advertisement by or on behalf of a marriage and family therapist trainee shall include, at a minimum, all of the following information:

(1) That he or she is a marriage and family therapist trainee.
(2) The name of his or her employer.
(3) That he or she is supervised by a licensed person.

4980.49. Clients Records; Retention

(a) A marriage and family therapist shall retain a client's or patient's health service records for a minimum of seven years from the date therapy is terminated. If the client or patient is a minor, the client's or patient's health service records shall be retained for a minimum of seven years from the date the client or the patient reaches 18 years of age. Health service records may be retained in either a written or an electronic format.

(b) This section shall apply only to the records of a client or patient whose therapy is terminated on or after January 1, 2015.

4980.50. Examination; Issuance of License; Examination Record Retention; Seven Year Limitation On Clinical Examination; Effective January 1, 2016

(a) Every applicant who meets the educational and experience requirements and applies for a license as a marriage and family therapist shall be examined by the board. The examinations shall be as set forth in subdivision (d) of Section 4980.40. The examinations shall be given at least twice a year at a time and place and under supervision as the board may determine. The board shall examine the candidate with regard to his or her knowledge and professional skills and his or her judgment in the utilization of appropriate techniques and methods.

(b) The board shall not deny any applicant, who has submitted a complete application for examination, admission to the licensure examinations required by this section if the applicant meets the educational and experience requirements of this chapter, and has not committed any acts or engaged in any conduct that would constitute grounds to deny licensure.

(c) The board shall not deny any applicant, whose application for licensure is complete, admission to the standard written examination, nor shall the board postpone or delay any applicant's standard written examination or delay informing the candidate of the results of the standard written examination, solely upon the receipt by the board of a complaint alleging acts or conduct that would constitute grounds to deny licensure.

(d) If an applicant for examination who has passed the standard written examination is the subject of a complaint or is under board investigation for acts or conduct that, if proven to be true, would constitute grounds for the board to deny licensure, the board shall permit the applicant to take the clinical vignette written examination for licensure, but may withhold the results of the examination or notify the applicant that licensure will not be granted pending completion of the investigation.

(e) Notwithstanding Section 135, the board may deny any applicant who has previously failed either the standard written or clinical vignette written examination permission to retake either examination pending completion of the investigation of any complaints against the applicant. Nothing in this section shall prohibit the board from denying an applicant admission to any examination, withholding the results, or refusing to issue a license to any applicant when an accusation or statement of issues has been filed against the applicant pursuant to Sections 11503 and 11504 of the Government Code, respectively, or the applicant has been denied in accordance with subdivision (b) of Section 485.

(f) Notwithstanding any other provision of law, the board may destroy all examination materials two years following the date of an examination.

(g) On or after January 1, 2002, no applicant shall be eligible to participate in a clinical vignette written examination if his or her passing score on the standard written examination occurred more than seven years before.

(h) An applicant who has qualified pursuant to this chapter shall be issued a license as a marriage and family therapist in the form that the board may deem appropriate.

(i) This section shall remain in effect only until January 1, 2016, and as of that date is repealed, unless a later enacted statute, that is enacted before January 1, 2016, deletes or extends that date.

CHAPTER 4
Unprofessional Conduct

There are standard expectations for how you should conduct yourself, this includes the accountability of MFTs and PCCs both inside and outside the professional realm. In this chapter, you will find specific information about what is expected of you and how you should conduct yourself. Unprofessional Conduct are acts and behaviors that are identified by statutory. The Board has the authoring of engage in investigating and disciplinary action to protect the public from incompetent, unethical or unprofessional practitioners.

The Board receives complaints usually from consumers (your clients) but also from other individuals that are in the community as well. Once a complaint is received the Board typically will investigate by asking the complainant more questions, obtaining documentation from them, and then inform the individual who is being complained about (the licensee or registrant and also known as the respondent) by making phone contact and even mail them documentation to respond to.

Unprofessional conduct can lead to disciplinary action by the Board of Behavioral Sciences as well as a criminal and civil liability. Disciplinary action can take place for behavior that violated laws and statutes within the delivery of services (such as sexual contact with a client or violating confidentiality) or behavior outside of the profession but considered to be substantially related to the qualifications, functions or duties (such as a DUI or drug use).

Sex with clients

Sex with a client is never a good idea. As noted in the previous chapter specifically for PCC's and MFT's, unprofessional conduct and the enforcement of violations extends to all therapists, as well as other professionals that fall within the jurisdiction BPC. However, note that in this chapter the BBS also gives a definition of sexual contact. In this chapter it is defined as an act that fulfills "sexual arousal, gratification, or abuse". Regardless of the intention, reason or excuse, sexual contact with a client is never professional and can result in administrative, criminal and civil action.

A common action taken against the therapist is due to sexual misconduct. There are both legal and ethical requirements when it comes to sexual contact with a client. The law in California states that a therapist may have sexual relationships with clients two years after the termination of therapy. Any sexual contact or conduct prior to this time is unlawful. Therapist should be aware of their professions ethical requirement, and that these professional associations may have a standard that exceeds California requirements and may have additional stipulations.

Terminating a therapeutic relationship solely to begin a sexual relationship with a client is also unprofessional. Note that even if a client consents to a sexual relationship or sexual contact, this cannot occur until 2 years after the termination of the therapeutic relationship. Depending on the Counseling/Therapy Association you join, it may be ethical to wait even longer (American Counseling Association requires a 5 year waiting period). However, with all that said, even if you waited 2 years as required specifically by law to engage in sexual contact and/or a sexual relationship, the imbalance of power will always be an issue. Additionally, it would be quite difficult to challenge allegations of unprofessional conduct if this client ever decided to bring such allegations to the court. This is where clients can argue that they were manipulated into the relationship.

When clients come to you and discloses that they had sexual contact with their therapist, you absolutely cannot disclose this information to anyone! It may be tempting and seem like the right thing to do, but there are no provisions in the law that allow for an exception of confidentiality here. What the therapist who becomes aware of this incident(s) is required to do is provide the client with the "Professional Therapy Never Includes Sex" brochure produced by the State of California. The therapist must discuss the brochure with the individual. This in itself can be therapeutic for client to have someone not only to discuss the incident(s), but to also be provided with information on what course of action they can take.

Cover Your Assets

Penalties for unprofessional conduct can result in conviction, fines, revocation, suspension, and probation of license as well as other potential ramifications. Therapists are encouraged to follow the laws and regulations as defined not only to protect their license, but also as a measure to protect the public, their clients. Some of the best ways to do this is becoming familiar with the laws and regulations in this chapter. You might have heard the acronym "CYA". Well we agree that behaving appropriately and professionally can CYA...and what we mean by this is 'Cover Your Assets'. Again even if you are not criminally charged for unprofessional behavior, you may be civilly liable as well as find your license in jeopardy, and these are all considered part of your assets as a therapist.

Therapists are highly advised to continue to maintain professional liability insurance. This is one of the most important steps in ensuring that you have the ability to defend yourself should a complaint, whether valid or not has been filed. Most professional associations provide or have an agreement with organizations that provide professional liability insurance, sometimes at a cost reduced for members.

Maintaining confidentiality is one way to keep yourself out of trouble. We've gone over confidentiality in the previous chapter, but it never hurts to have a reminder. Be clear on what the exceptions of confidentiality are and follow those closely. If you are unsure about your responsibilities, it might be helpful to seek consultation. Some professional associations offer free legal consultation for members.

Good record-keeping is probably number one on the list of protective measures. Therapist should always maintain their records appropriately and accurately. Records can be subpoenaed or court ordered at any time and it is important that therapists document their communications with clients. The best way to maintain records is to write clinical and progress notes up as soon as physically possible and do so as accurately as possible.

As previously mentioned, ensure that you are following the law. And not just the laws that pertain to your license, but the laws that all Californians are governed under. So if you had a little too much to drink, don't drive. Be aware that what you do in your personal life can have direct consequences on your professional life.

Become familiar and comply with all requirements in this chapter.

General Requirements for All Therapists in Law

Business and Professions Code
726. Commission of act of sexual abuse or misconduct with patient or client

The commission of any act of sexual abuse, misconduct, or relations with a patient, client, or customer constitutes unprofessional conduct and grounds for disciplinary action for any person licensed under this division, under any initiative act referred to in this division and under Chapter 17 (commencing with Section 9000) of Division 3.

This section shall not apply to sexual contact between a physician and surgeon and his or her spouse or person in an equivalent domestic relationship when that physician and surgeon provides medical treatment, other than psychotherapeutic treatment, to his or her spouse or person in an equivalent domestic relationship.

727.Applicability of Evidence Code provisions

The provisions of subdivision (2) of Section 1103 of the Evidence Code shall apply in disciplinary proceedings brought against a licensee for acts in violation of Section 726.

728.Provision of brochure by psychotherapist to patient alleging sexual intercourse or contact with previous psychotherapist during course of prior treatment

(a) Any psychotherapist or employer of a psychotherapist who becomes aware through a client that the client had alleged sexual intercourse or alleged sexual behavior or sexual contact with a previous psychotherapist during the course of a prior treatment shall provide to the client a brochure developed pursuant to Section 337 that delineates the rights of, and remedies for, clients who have been involved sexually with their psychotherapists. Further, the psychotherapist or employer shall discuss the brochure with the client.

(b) Failure to comply with this section constitutes unprofessional conduct.

(c) For the purpose of this section, the following definitions apply:

(1) "Psychotherapist" means any of the following:

(A) A physician and surgeon specializing in the practice of psychiatry or practicing psychotherapy.

(B) A psychologist licensed pursuant to Chapter 6.6 (commencing with Section 2900).

(C) A psychological assistant.
(D) A registered psychologist.
(E) A trainee under the supervision of a licensed psychologist.
(F) A marriage and family therapist.
(G) An associate marriage and family therapist.
(H) A marriage and family therapist trainee.
(I) A licensed educational psychologist.
(J) A clinical social worker.
(K) An associate clinical social worker.
(L) A licensed professional clinical counselor.
(M) An associate professional clinical counselor, as specified in Chapter 16 (commencing with Section 4999.10).
(N) A clinical counselor trainee, as specified in Chapter 16 (commencing with Section 4999.10).

(2) "Sexual behavior" means inappropriate contact or communication of a sexual nature. "Sexual behavior" does not include the provision of appropriate therapeutic interventions relating to sexual issues.

(3) "Sexual contact" means the touching of an intimate part of another person.

(4) "Intimate part" and "touching" have the same meanings as defined in subdivisions (g) and (e), respectively, of Section 243.4 of the Penal Code.

(5) "The course of a prior treatment" means the period of time during which a client first commences treatment for services that a psychotherapist is authorized to provide under his or her scope of practice, or that the psychotherapist represents to the client as being within his or her scope of practice, until the psychotherapist-client relationship is terminated.

729.Sexual exploitation of patient or client by physician and surgeon, or psychotherapist

(a) Any physician and surgeon, psychotherapist, alcohol and drug abuse counselor or any person holding himself or herself out to be a physician and surgeon, psychotherapist, or alcohol and drug abuse counselor, who engages in an act of sexual intercourse, sodomy, oral copulation, or sexual contact with a patient or client, or with a former patient or client when the relationship was terminated primarily for the purpose of engaging in those acts, unless the physician and surgeon, psychotherapist, or alcohol and drug abuse counselor has referred the patient or client to an independent and objective physician and surgeon, psychotherapist, or alcohol and drug abuse counselor recommended by a third-party physician and surgeon, psychotherapist, or alcohol and drug abuse counselor for treatment, is guilty of sexual exploitation by a physician and surgeon, psychotherapist, or alcohol and drug abuse counselor.

(b) Sexual exploitation by a physician and surgeon, psychotherapist, or alcohol and drug abuse counselor is a public offense:

(1) An act in violation of subdivision (a) shall be punishable by imprisonment in a county jail for a period of not more than six months, or a fine not exceeding one thousand dollars ($1,000), or by both that imprisonment and fine.

(2) Multiple acts in violation of subdivision (a) with a single victim, when the offender has no prior conviction for sexual exploitation, shall be punishable by imprisonment in a county jail for a period of not more than six months, or a fine not exceeding one thousand dollars ($1,000), or by both that imprisonment and fine.

(3) An act or acts in violation of subdivision (a) with two or more victims shall be punishable by imprisonment pursuant to subdivision (h) of Section 1170 of the Penal Code for a period of 16 months, two years, or three years, and

a fine not exceeding ten thousand dollars ($10,000); or the act or acts shall be punishable by imprisonment in a county jail for a period of not more than one year, or a fine not exceeding one thousand dollars ($1,000), or by both that imprisonment and fine.

(4) Two or more acts in violation of subdivision (a) with a single victim, when the offender has at least one prior conviction for sexual exploitation, shall be punishable by imprisonment pursuant to subdivision (h) of Section 1170 of the Penal Code for a period of 16 months, two years, or three years, and a fine not exceeding ten thousand dollars ($10,000); or the act or acts shall be punishable by imprisonment in a county jail for a period of not more than one year, or a fine not exceeding one thousand dollars ($1,000), or by both that imprisonment and fine.

(5) An act or acts in violation of subdivision (a) with two or more victims, and the offender has at least one prior conviction for sexual exploitation, shall be punishable by imprisonment pursuant to subdivision (h) of Section 1170 of the Penal Code for a period of 16 months, two years, or three years, and a fine not exceeding ten thousand dollars ($10,000).
For purposes of subdivision (a), in no instance shall consent of the patient or client be a defense. However, physicians and surgeons shall not be guilty of sexual exploitation for touching any intimate part of a patient or client unless the touching is outside the scope of medical examination and treatment, or the touching is done for sexual gratification.

(c) For purposes of this section:
(1) "Psychotherapist" has the same meaning as defined in Section 728.
(2) "Alcohol and drug abuse counselor" means an individual who holds himself or herself out to be an alcohol or drug abuse professional or paraprofessional.
(3) "Sexual contact" means sexual intercourse or the touching of an intimate part of a patient for the purpose of sexual arousal, gratification, or abuse.
(4) "Intimate part" and "touching" have the same meanings as defined in Section 243.4 of the Penal Code.

(d) In the investigation and prosecution of a violation of this section, no person shall seek to obtain disclosure of any confidential files of other patients, clients, or former patients or clients of the physician and surgeon, psychotherapist, or alcohol and drug abuse counselor.

(e) This section does not apply to sexual contact between a physician and surgeon and his or her spouse or person in an equivalent domestic relationship when that physician and surgeon provides medical treatment, other than psychotherapeutic treatment, to his or her spouse or person in an equivalent domestic relationship.

(f) If a physician and surgeon, psychotherapist, or alcohol and drug abuse counselor in a professional partnership or similar group has sexual contact with a patient in violation of this section, another physician and surgeon, psychotherapist, or alcohol and drug abuse counselor in the partnership or group shall not be subject to action under this section solely because of the occurrence of that sexual contact.

731.Violations at work as unprofessional conduct
(a) Any person licensed, certified, registered, or otherwise subject to regulation pursuant to this division who engages in, or who aids or abets in, a violation of Section 266h, 266i, 315, 316, or 318 of, or subdivision (a) or

(b) of Section 647 of, the Penal Code occurring in the work premises of, or work area under the direct professional supervision or control of, that person, shall be guilty of unprofessional conduct. The license, certification, or registration of that person shall be subject to denial, suspension, or revocation by the appropriate regulatory entity under this division.
(b) In addition to any penalty provided under any other provision of law, a violation of subdivision (a) shall subject the person to a civil penalty in an amount not to exceed two thousand five hundred dollars ($2,500) for the first offense, and not to exceed five thousand dollars ($5,000) for each subsequent offense, which may be assessed and recovered in a civil action brought by any district attorney. If the action is brought by a district attorney, the penalty recovered shall be paid to the treasurer of the county in which the judgment was entered.

PCC Unprofessional Conduct, Enforcement, Penalties

Business and Professions Code
4999.80. Enforcement of Laws; Board Duties
In order to carry out the provisions of this chapter, the board shall do all of the following:
(a) Enforce laws designed to protect the public from incompetent, unethical, or unprofessional practitioners.
(b) Investigate complaints concerning the conduct of any licensed professional clinical counselor.
(c) Revoke, suspend, or fail to renew a license that it has authority to issue for just cause, as enumerated in rules and regulations of the board. The board may deny, suspend, or revoke any license granted under this chapter pursuant to Section 480, 481, 484, 496, 498, or 499.
(Added by Stats. 2009, Ch. 619, Sec. 3. Effective January 1, 2010.)

4999.82.Engaging in Practice; Unlawful Acts; Licensure Requirement
It shall be unlawful for any person to engage in any of the following acts:

(a) Engage in the practice of professional clinical counseling, as defined in Section 4999.20, without first having complied with the provisions of this chapter and without holding a valid license as required by this chapter.

(b) Represent himself or herself by the title "licensed professional clinical counselor," "LPCC," "licensed clinical counselor," or "professional clinical counselor" without being duly licensed according to the provisions of this chapter.

(c) Make any use of any title, words, letters, or abbreviations, that may reasonably be confused with a designation provided by this chapter to denote a standard of professional or occupational competence without being duly licensed.

(d) Materially refuse to furnish the board information or records required or requested pursuant to this chapter.

4999.84. Privileged Communication

It is the intent of the Legislature that any communication made by a person to a licensed professional clinical counselor in the course of professional services shall be deemed a privileged communication.

4999.86. Violation of Chapter Provisions; Misdemeanor

Any person who violates any of the provisions of this chapter is guilty of a misdemeanor punishable by imprisonment in a county jail not exceeding six months, or by a fine not exceeding two thousand five hundred dollars ($2,500), or by both that fine and imprisonment.

4999.88. Issuance of An Injunction To Restrain Conduct

In addition to other proceedings provided in this chapter, whenever any person has engaged, or is about to engage, in any acts or practices that constitute, or will constitute, an offense against this chapter, the superior court in and for the county wherein the acts or practices take place, or are about to take place, may issue an injunction, or other appropriate order, restraining that conduct on application of the board, the Attorney General, or the district attorney of the county.

The proceedings under this section shall be governed by Chapter 3 (commencing with Section 525) of Title 7 of Part 2 of the Code of Civil Procedure.

4999.90. Unprofessional Conduct

The board may refuse to issue any registration or license, or may suspend or revoke the registration or license of any associate or licensed professional clinical counselor, if the applicant, licensee, or registrant has been guilty of unprofessional conduct. Unprofessional conduct includes, but is not limited to, the following:

(a) The conviction of a crime substantially related to the qualifications, functions, or duties of a licensee or registrant under this chapter. The record of conviction shall be conclusive evidence only of the fact that the conviction occurred. The board may inquire into the circumstances surrounding the commission of the crime in order to fix the degree of discipline or to determine if the conviction is substantially related to the qualifications, functions, or duties of a licensee or registrant under this chapter. A plea or verdict of guilty or a conviction following a plea of nolo contendere made to a charge substantially related to the qualifications, functions, or duties of a licensee or registrant under this chapter shall be deemed to be a conviction within the meaning of this section. The board may order any license or registration suspended or revoked, or may decline to issue a license or registration when the time for appeal has elapsed, or the judgment of conviction has been affirmed on appeal, or, when an order granting probation is made suspending the imposition of sentence, irrespective of a subsequent order under Section 1203.4 of the Penal Code allowing the person to withdraw a plea of guilty and enter a plea of not guilty, or setting aside the verdict of guilty, or dismissing the accusation, information, or indictment.

(b) Securing a license or registration by fraud, deceit, or misrepresentation on any application for licensure or registration submitted to the board, whether engaged in by an applicant for a license or registration, or by a licensee in support of any application for licensure or registration.

(c) Administering to himself or herself any controlled substance or using any of the dangerous drugs specified in Section 4022, or any alcoholic beverage to the extent, or in a manner, as to be dangerous or injurious to the person applying for a registration or license or holding a registration or license under this chapter, or to any other person, or to the public, or, to the extent that the use impairs the ability of the person applying for or holding a registration or license to conduct with safety to the public the practice authorized by the registration or license. The board shall deny an application for a registration or license or revoke the license or registration of any person, other than one who is licensed as a physician and surgeon, who uses or offers to use drugs in the course of performing licensed professional clinical counseling services.

(d) Gross negligence or incompetence in the performance of licensed professional clinical counseling services.

(e) Violating, attempting to violate, or conspiring to violate any of the provisions of this chapter or any regulation adopted by the board.

(f) Misrepresentation as to the type or status of a license or registration held by the person, or otherwise misrepresenting or permitting misrepresentation of his or her education, professional qualifications, or professional affiliations to any person or entity.

(g) Impersonation of another by any licensee, registrant, or applicant for a license or registration, or, in the case of a licensee or registrant, allowing any other person to use his or her license or registration.

(h) Aiding or abetting, or employing, directly or indirectly, any unlicensed or unregistered person to engage in conduct for which a license or registration is required under this chapter.

(i) Intentionally or recklessly causing physical or emotional harm to any client.

(j) The commission of any dishonest, corrupt, or fraudulent act substantially related to the qualifications, functions, or duties of a licensee or registrant.

(k) Engaging in sexual relations with a client, or a former client within two years following termination of therapy, soliciting sexual relations with a client, or committing an act of sexual abuse, or sexual misconduct with a client, or committing an act punishable as a sexually related crime, if that act or solicitation is substantially related to the qualifications, functions, or duties of a licensed professional clinical counselor.

(l) Performing, or holding oneself out as being able to perform, or offering to perform, or permitting any trainee, applicant, or registrant under supervision to perform, any professional services beyond the scope of the license authorized by this chapter.

(m) Failure to maintain confidentiality, except as otherwise required or permitted by law, of all information that has been received from a client in confidence during the course of treatment and all information about the client which is obtained from tests or other means.

(n) Prior to the commencement of treatment, failing to disclose to the client or prospective client the fee to be charged for the professional services, or the basis upon which that fee will be computed.

(o) Paying, accepting, or soliciting any consideration, compensation, or remuneration, whether monetary or otherwise, for the referral of professional clients. All consideration, compensation, or remuneration shall be in relation to professional clinical counseling services actually provided by the licensee. Nothing in this subdivision shall prevent collaboration among two or more licensees in a case or cases. However, no fee shall be charged for that collaboration, except when disclosure of the fee has been made in compliance with subdivision (n).

(p) Advertising in a manner that is false, fraudulent, misleading, or deceptive, as defined in Section 651.

(q) Reproduction or description in public, or in any publication subject to general public distribution, of any psychological test or other assessment device, the value of which depends in whole or in part on the naivete of the subject, in ways that might invalidate the test or device.

(r) Any conduct in the supervision of any registered associate, trainee, or applicant for licensure by any licensee that violates this chapter or any rules or regulations adopted by the board.

(s) Performing or holding oneself out as being able to perform professional services beyond the scope of one's competence, as established by one's education, training, or experience. This subdivision shall not be construed to expand the scope of the license authorized by this chapter.

(t) Permitting a trainee, registered associate, or applicant for licensure under one's supervision or control to perform, or permitting the trainee, registered associate, or applicant for licensure to hold himself or herself out as competent to perform, mental health services beyond the trainee's, registered associate's, or applicant for licensure's level of education, training, or experience.

(u) The violation of any statute or regulation of the standards of the profession, and the nature of the services being rendered, governing the gaining and supervision of experience required by this chapter.

(v) Failure to keep records consistent with sound clinical judgment, the standards of the profession, and the nature of the services being rendered.

(w) Failure to comply with the child abuse reporting requirements of Section 11166 of the Penal Code.

(x) Failing to comply with the elder and dependent adult abuse reporting requirements of Section 15630 of the Welfare and Institutions Code.

(y) Repeated acts of negligence.

(z) (1) Engaging in an act described in Section 261, 286, 288a, or 289 of the Penal Code with a minor or an act described in Section 288 or 288.5 of the Penal Code regardless of whether the act occurred prior to or after the time the registration or license was issued by the board. An act described in this subdivision occurring prior to the effective date of this subdivision shall constitute unprofessional conduct and shall subject the licensee to refusal, suspension, or revocation of a license under this section.

(2) The Legislature hereby finds and declares that protection of the public,

and in particular minors, from sexual misconduct by a licensee is a compelling governmental interest, and that the ability to suspend or revoke a license for sexual conduct with a minor occurring prior to the effective date of this section is equally important to protecting the public as is the ability to refuse a license for sexual conduct with a minor occurring prior to the effective date of this section.

(aa) Engaging in any conduct that subverts or attempts to subvert any licensing examination or the administration of an examination as described in Section 123.

(ab) Revocation, suspension, or restriction by the board of a license, certificate, or registration to practice as a professional clinical counselor, clinical social worker, educational psychologist, or marriage and family therapist.

(ac) Failing to comply with the procedures set forth in Section 2290.5 when delivering health care via telehealth.

(ad) Willful violation of Chapter 1 (commencing with Section 123100) of Part 1 of Division 106 of the Health and Safety Code.

4999.91. Denial of Application or Suspension or Revocation of License or Registration; Grounds

The board may deny any application, or may suspend or revoke any license or registration issued under this chapter, for any of the following:

(a) Denial of licensure, revocation, suspension, restriction, or any other disciplinary action imposed by this state or another state or territory of the United States, or by any other governmental agency, on a license, certificate, or registration to practice professional clinical counseling or any other healing art shall constitute grounds for disciplinary action for unprofessional conduct. A certified copy of the disciplinary action decision or judgment shall be conclusive evidence of that action.

(b) Revocation, suspension, or restriction by the board of a license, certificate, or registration to practice clinical social work, professional clinical counseling, marriage and family therapy, or educational psychology shall also constitute grounds for disciplinary action for unprofessional conduct under this chapter.

(Added by Stats. 2011, Ch. 350, Sec. 40. Effective January 1, 2012.)

MFT Unprofessional Conduct, Enforcement, Penalties

4982. Unprofessional Conduct

The board may deny a license or registration or may suspend or revoke the license or registration of a licensee or registrant if he or she has been guilty of unprofessional conduct. Unprofessional conduct includes, but is not limited to, the following:

(a) The conviction of a crime substantially related to the qualifications, functions, or duties of a licensee or registrant under this chapter. The record of conviction shall be conclusive evidence only of the fact that the conviction occurred. The board may inquire into the circumstances surrounding the commission of the crime in order to fix the degree of discipline or to determine if the conviction is substantially related to the qualifications, functions, or duties of a licensee or registrant under this chapter. A plea or verdict of guilty or a conviction following a plea of nolo contendere made to a charge substantially related to the qualifications, functions, or duties of a licensee or registrant under this chapter shall be deemed to be a conviction within the meaning of this section. The board may order any license or registration suspended or revoked, or may decline to issue a license or registration when the time for appeal has elapsed, or the judgment of conviction has been affirmed on appeal, or, when an order granting probation is made suspending the imposition of sentence, irrespective of a subsequent order under Section 1203.4 of the Penal Code allowing the person to withdraw a plea of guilty and enter a plea of not guilty, or setting aside the verdict of guilty, or dismissing the accusation, information, or indictment.

(b) Securing a license or registration by fraud, deceit, or misrepresentation on any application for licensure or registration submitted to the board, whether engaged in by an applicant for a license or registration, or by a licensee in support of any application for licensure or registration.

(c) Administering to himself or herself any controlled substance or using of any of the dangerous drugs specified in Section 4022, or of any alcoholic beverage to the extent, or in a manner, as to be dangerous or injurious to the person applying for a registration or license or holding a registration or license under this chapter, or to any other person, or to the public, or, to the extent that the use impairs the ability of the person applying for or holding a registration or license to conduct with safety to the public the practice authorized by the registration or license. The board shall deny an application for a registration or license or revoke the license or registration of any person, other than one who is licensed as a physician and surgeon, who uses or offers to use drugs in the course of performing marriage and family therapy services.

(d) Gross negligence or incompetence in the performance of marriage and family therapy.

(e) Violating, attempting to violate, or conspiring to violate any of the provisions of this chapter or any regulation adopted by the board.

(f) Misrepresentation as to the type or status of a license or registration held by the person, or otherwise misrepresenting or permitting misrepresentation of his or her education, professional qualifications, or professional affiliations to any person or entity.

(g) Impersonation of another by any licensee, registrant, or applicant for a license or registration, or, in the case of a licensee, allowing any other person to use his or her license or registration.

(h) Aiding or abetting, or employing, directly or indirectly, any unlicensed or unregistered person to engage in conduct for which a license or registration is required under this chapter.

(i) Intentionally or recklessly causing physical or emotional harm to any client.

(j) The commission of any dishonest, corrupt, or fraudulent act substantially related to the qualifications, functions, or duties of a licensee or registrant.

(k) Engaging in sexual relations with a client, or a former client within two years following termination of therapy, soliciting sexual relations with a client, or committing an act of sexual abuse, or sexual misconduct with a client, or committing an act punishable as a sexually related crime, if that act or solicitation is substantially related to the qualifications, functions, or duties of a marriage and family therapist.

(l) Performing, or holding oneself out as being able to perform, or offering to perform, or permitting any trainee, registered associate, or applicant for licensure under supervision to perform, any professional services beyond the scope of the license authorized by this chapter.

(m) Failure to maintain confidentiality, except as otherwise required or permitted by law, of all information that has been received from a client in confidence during the course of treatment and all information about the client that is obtained from tests or other means.

(n) Prior to the commencement of treatment, failing to disclose to the client or prospective client the fee to be charged for the professional services, or the basis upon which that fee will be computed.

(o) Paying, accepting, or soliciting any consideration, compensation, or remuneration, whether monetary or otherwise, for the referral of professional clients. All consideration, compensation, or remuneration shall be in relation to professional counseling services actually provided by the licensee. Nothing in this subdivision shall prevent collaboration among two or more licensees in a case or cases. However, no fee shall be charged for that collaboration, except when disclosure of the fee has been made in compliance with subdivision (n).

(p) Advertising in a manner that is false, fraudulent, misleading, or deceptive, as defined in Section 651.

(q) Reproduction or description in public, or in any publication subject to general public distribution, of any psychological test or other assessment device, the value of which depends in whole or in part on the naivete of the subject, in ways that might invalidate the test or device.

(r) Any conduct in the supervision of any registered associate, trainee, or applicant for licensure by any licensee that violates this chapter or any rules or regulations adopted by the board.

(s) Performing or holding oneself out as being able to perform mental health services beyond the scope of one's competence, as established by one's education, training, or experience. This subdivision shall not be construed to expand the scope of the license authorized by this chapter.

(t) Permitting a trainee, registered associate, or applicant for licensure under one's supervision or control to perform, or permitting the trainee, registered associate, or applicant for licensure to hold himself or herself out as competent to perform, mental health services beyond the trainee's, registered associate's, or applicant for licensure's level of education, training, or experience.

(u) The violation of any statute or regulation governing the gaining and supervision of experience required by this chapter.

(v) Failure to keep records consistent with sound clinical judgment, the standards of the profession, and the nature of the services being rendered.
(w) Failure to comply with the child abuse reporting requirements of Section 11166 of the Penal Code.

(x) Failure to comply with the elder and dependent adult abuse reporting requirements of Section 15630 of the Welfare and Institutions Code.

(y) Willful violation of Chapter 1 (commencing with Section 123100) of Part 1 of Division 106 of the Health and Safety Code.

(z) Failure to comply with Section 2290.5.

(aa) (1) Engaging in an act described in Section 261, 286, 288a, or 289 of the Penal Code with a minor or an act described in Section 288 or 288.5 of the Penal Code regardless of whether the act occurred prior to or after the time the registration or license was issued by the board. An act described in this subdivision occurring prior to the effective date of this subdivision shall constitute unprofessional conduct and shall subject the licensee to refusal, suspension, or revocation of a license under this section.

(2) The Legislature hereby finds and declares that protection of the public, and in particular minors, from sexual misconduct by a licensee is a compelling governmental interest, and that the ability to suspend or revoke a license for sexual conduct with a minor occurring prior to the effective date of this section is equally important to protecting the public as is the ability to refuse a license for sexual conduct with a minor occurring prior to the effective date of this section.

(ab) Engaging in any conduct that subverts or attempts to subvert any licensing examination or the administration of an examination as described in Section 123.

4982.05. Enforcement Statute of Limitations

(a) Except as provided in subdivisions (b), (c), and (e), any accusation filed against a licensee pursuant to Section 11503 of the Government Code shall be filed within three years from the date the board discovers the alleged act or omission that is the basis for disciplinary action, or within seven years from the date the alleged act or omission that is the basis for disciplinary action occurred, whichever occurs first.

(b) An accusation filed against a licensee pursuant to Section 11503 of the Government Code alleging the procurement of a license by fraud or misrepresentation is not subject to the limitations set forth in subdivision (a).

(c) The limitation provided for by subdivision (a) shall be tolled for the length of time required to obtain compliance when a report required to be filed by the licensee or registrant with the board pursuant to Article 11 (commencing with Section 800) of Chapter 1 is not filed in a timely fashion.

(d) If an alleged act or omission involves a minor, the seven-year limitations period provided for by subdivision (a) and the 10-year limitations period provided for by subdivision (e) shall be tolled until the minor reaches the age of majority.

(e) An accusation filed against a licensee pursuant to Section 11503 of the Government Code alleging sexual misconduct shall be filed within three years after the board discovers the act or omission alleged as the grounds for disciplinary action, or within 10 years after the act or omission alleged as the grounds for disciplinary action occurs, whichever occurs first. This subdivision shall apply to a complaint alleging sexual misconduct received by the board on and after January 1, 2002.

(f) The limitations period provided by subdivision (a) shall be tolled during any period if material evidence necessary for prosecuting or determining whether a disciplinary action would be appropriate is unavailable to the board due to an ongoing criminal investigation.

(g) For purposes of this section, "discovers" means the later of the occurrence of any of the following with respect to each act or omission alleged as the basis for disciplinary action:

(1) The date the board received a complaint or report describing the act or omission.

(2) The date, subsequent to the original complaint or report, on which the board became aware of any additional acts or omissions alleged as the basis for disciplinary action against the same individual.

(3) The date the board receives from the complainant a written release of information pertaining to the complainant's diagnosis and treatment.

4982.1. Mental Illness or Chemical Dependency; Grounds for Refusal to License or Register

The board may refuse to issue any registration or license whenever it appears that an applicant may be unable to practice his or her profession safely due to mental illness or chemical dependency. The procedures set forth in Article 12.5 (commencing with Section 820) of Chapter 1 shall apply to any denial of a license or registration pursuant to this section.

4982.15. Placing a License or Registration on Probation; Circumstances

(a) The board may place a license or registration on probation under the following circumstances:

(1) In lieu of, or in addition to, any order of the board suspending or revoking the license or registration of any licensee or associate.

(2) Upon the issuance of a license to an individual who has been guilty of unprofessional conduct, but who had otherwise completed all education and training and experience required for licensure.

(3) As a condition upon the reissuance or reinstatement of any license that has been suspended or revoked by the board.

(b) The board may adopt regulations establishing a monitoring program to ensure compliance with any terms or conditions of probation imposed by the board pursuant to subdivision (a). The cost of probation or monitoring may be ordered to be paid by the licensee, registrant, or applicant.

(c) The board, in its discretion, may require any licensee or registrant who has been placed on probation, or whose license or registration has been suspended, to obtain additional professional training, and to pass an examination upon completion of that training, and to pay any necessary examination fee. The examination may be written, oral, or a practical or clinical examination.

4982.25. Denial of Application or Suspension or Revocation of License or Registration; Grounds

The board may deny an application, or may suspend or revoke a license or registration issued under this chapter, for any of the following:

(a) Denial of licensure, revocation, suspension, restriction, or any other disciplinary action imposed by another state or territory or possession of the

United States, or by any other governmental agency, on a license, certificate, or registration to practice marriage and family therapy, or any other healing art, shall constitute unprofessional conduct. A certified copy of the disciplinary action decision or judgment shall be conclusive evidence of that action.

(b) Revocation, suspension, or restriction by the board of a license, certificate, or registration to practice as a marriage and family therapist, clinical social worker, professional clinical counselor, or educational psychologist shall also constitute grounds for disciplinary action for unprofessional conduct against the licensee or registrant under this chapter.

4982.26. Decision Containing Finding That Licensee or Registrant Engaged in Sexual Contact with Patient or Formal Patient; Order of Revocation

The board shall revoke any license issued under this chapter upon a decision made in accordance with the procedures set forth in Chapter 5 (commencing with Section 11500) of Part 1 of Division 3 of Title 2 of the Government Code, that contains any finding of fact that the licensee or registrant engaged in any act of sexual contact, as defined in Section 729, when that act is with a patient, or with a former patient when the relationship was terminated primarily for the purpose of engaging in that act. The revocation shall not be stayed by the administrative law judge or the board.

4982.3. Conduct of Proceedings

The proceedings conducted under this article shall be held in accordance with Chapter 5 (commencing with Section 11500) of Part 1 of Division 3 of Title 2 of the Government Code.

4983. Violation; Misdemeanor; Punishment

Any person who violates any of the provisions of this chapter is guilty of a misdemeanor punishable by imprisonment in the county jail not exceeding six months, or by a fine not exceeding two thousand five hundred dollars ($2,500), or by both.

4983.1. Injunction

In addition to other proceedings provided for in this chapter, whenever any person has engaged, or is about to engage, in any acts or practices which constitute, or will constitute, an offense against this chapter, the superior court in and for the county wherein the acts or practices take place, or are about to take place, may issue an injunction, or other appropriate order, restraining such conduct on application of the board, the Attorney General, or the district attorney of the county.

The proceedings under this section shall be governed by Chapter 3 (commencing with Section 525) of Title 7 of Part 2 of the Code of Civil Procedure.

General Disciplinary Actions – MFT & PCC

Business and Professions Code
4990.28. Grounds for Refusal to Issue License or Registration; Mental Illness or Chemical Dependency
The board may refuse to issue a registration or license under the chapters it administers and enforces whenever it appears that the applicant may be unable to practice his or her profession safely due to mental illness or chemical dependency. The procedures set forth in Article 12.5 (commencing with Section 820) of Chapter 1 shall apply to denial of a license or registration pursuant to this section.

4990.30. Petition for Reinstatement or Modification of Penalty
(a) A licensed marriage and family therapist, marriage and family therapist intern, licensed clinical social worker, associate clinical social worker, licensed professional clinical counselor, professional clinical counselor intern, or licensed educational psychologist whose license or registration has been revoked, suspended, or placed on probation, may petition the board for reinstatement or modification of the penalty, including modification or termination of probation. The petition shall be on a form provided by the board and shall state any facts and information as may be required by the board including, but not limited to, proof of compliance with the terms and conditions of the underlying disciplinary order. The petition shall be verified by the petitioner who shall file an original and sufficient copies of the petition, together with any supporting documents, for the members of the board, the administrative law judge, and the Attorney General.

(b) The licensee or registrant may file the petition on or after the expiration of the following timeframes, each of which commences on the effective date of the decision ordering the disciplinary action or, if the order of the board, or any portion of it, is stayed by the board itself or by the superior court, from the date the disciplinary action is actually implemented in its entirety:

(1) Three years for reinstatement of a license or registration that was revoked for unprofessional conduct, except that the board may, in its sole discretion, specify in its revocation order that a petition for reinstatement may be filed after two years.

(2) Two years for early termination of any probation period of three years or more.

(3) One year for modification of a condition, reinstatement of a license or registration revoked for mental or physical illness, or termination of probation of less than three years.

(c) The petition may be heard by the board itself or the board may assign the petition to an administrative law judge pursuant to Section 11512 of the Government Code.

(d) The petitioner may request that the board schedule the hearing on the petition for a board meeting at a specific city where the board regularly meets.

(e) The petitioner and the Attorney General shall be given timely notice by letter of the time and place of the hearing on the petition and an opportunity to present both oral and documentary evidence and argument to the board or the administrative law judge.

(f) The petitioner shall at all times have the burden of production and proof to establish by clear and convincing evidence that he or she is entitled to the relief sought in the petition.

(g) The board, when it is hearing the petition itself, or an administrative law judge sitting for the board, may consider all activities of the petitioner since the disciplinary action was taken, the offense for which the petitioner was disciplined, the petitioner's activities during the time his or her license or registration was in good standing, and the petitioner's rehabilitative efforts, general reputation for truth, and professional ability.

(h) The hearing may be continued from time to time as the board or the administrative law judge deems appropriate but in no case may the hearing on the petition be delayed more than 180 days from its filing without the consent of the petitioner.

(i) The board itself, or the administrative law judge if one is designated by the board, shall hear the petition and shall prepare a written decision setting forth the reasons supporting the decision. In a decision granting a petition reinstating a license or modifying a penalty, the board itself, or the administrative law judge, may impose any terms and conditions that the agency deems reasonably appropriate, including those set forth in Sections 823 and 4990.40. If a petition is heard by an administrative law judge sitting alone, the administrative law judge shall prepare a proposed decision and submit it to the board. The board may take action with respect to the proposed decision and petition as it deems appropriate.

(j) The petitioner shall pay a fingerprinting fee and provide a current set of his or her fingerprints to the board. The petitioner shall execute a form authorizing release to the board or its designee, of all information concerning the petitioner's current physical and mental condition. Information provided to the board pursuant to the release shall be confidential and shall not be subject to discovery or subpoena in any other proceeding, and shall not be admissible in any action, other than before the board, to determine the petitioner's fitness to practice as required by Section 822.

(k) The board may delegate to its executive officer authority to order investigation of the contents of the petition.

(l) No petition shall be considered while the petitioner is under sentence for any criminal offense, including any period during which the petitioner is on court-imposed probation or parole or the petitioner is required to register pursuant to Section 290 of the Penal Code. No petition shall be considered while there is an accusation or petition to revoke probation pending against the petitioner.

(m) Except in those cases where the petitioner has been disciplined for violation of Section 822, the board may in its discretion deny without hearing or argument any petition that is filed pursuant to this section within a period of two years from the effective date of a prior decision following a hearing under this section.

4990.32. Enforcement Statute of Limitations
(a) Except as otherwise provided in this section, an accusation filed pursuant to Section 11503 of the Government Code against a licensee or registrant under the chapters the board administers and enforces shall be filed within three years from the date the board discovers the alleged act or omission that is the basis for disciplinary action or within seven years from the date the alleged act or omission that is the basis for disciplinary action occurred, whichever occurs first.

(b) An accusation filed against a licensee alleging the procurement of a license by fraud or misrepresentation is not subject to the limitations set forth in subdivision (a).

(c) The limitations period provided by subdivision (a) shall be tolled for the length of time required to obtain compliance when a report required to be filed by the licensee or registrant with the board pursuant to Article 11 (commencing with Section 800) of Chapter 1 is not filed in a timely fashion.

(d) An accusation alleging sexual misconduct shall be filed within three years after the board discovers the act or omission alleged as the grounds for disciplinary action or within 10 years after the act or omission alleged as the grounds for disciplinary action occurred, whichever occurs first. This subdivision shall apply to a complaint alleging sexual misconduct received by the board on and after January 1, 2002.

(e) If an alleged act or omission involves a minor, the seven-year limitations period provided for by subdivision (a) and the 10-year limitations period provided for by subdivision (d) shall be tolled until the minor reaches the age of majority. However, if the board discovers an alleged act of sexual contact with a minor under Section 261, 286, 288, 288.5, 288a, or 289 of the Penal Code after the limitations periods described in this subdivision have otherwise expired, and there is independent evidence that corroborates the allegation, an accusation shall be filed within three years from the date the board discovers that alleged act.

(f) The limitations period provided by subdivision (a) shall be tolled during any period if material evidence necessary for prosecuting or determining whether a disciplinary action would be appropriate is unavailable to the board due to an ongoing criminal investigation.

(g) For purposes of this section, "discovers" means the latest of the occurrence of any of the following with respect to each act or omission alleged as the basis for disciplinary action:

(1) The date the board received a complaint or report describing the act or omission.

(2) The date, subsequent to the original complaint or report, on which the board became aware of any additional acts or omissions alleged as the basis for disciplinary action against the same individual.

(3) The date the board receives from the complainant a written release of information pertaining to the complainant's diagnosis and treatment.

4990.34. Placing License or Registration on Probation; Monitoring Program
(a) The board may place a license or registration issued under the chapters it administers and enforces on probation under the following circumstances:

(1) In lieu of, or in addition to, any order of the board suspending or revoking the license or registration.

(2) Upon the issuance of a license or registration to an individual who has been guilty of unprofessional conduct but who otherwise completed all education, training, and experience required for licensure or registration.

(3) As a condition upon the reissuance or reinstatement of a license or

registration that has been suspended or revoked by the board.

(b) The board may adopt regulations establishing a monitoring program to ensure compliance with any terms or conditions of probation imposed by the board pursuant to subdivision (a). The cost of probation or monitoring may be ordered to be paid by the licensee or registrant.

4990.36. Training or Examination After Probation or Suspension
The board, in its discretion, may require a licensee or registrant whose license or registration has been placed on probation or whose license or registration has been suspended, to obtain additional professional training and to pass an examination upon completion of that training and to pay any necessary examination fee. The examination may be written, oral, or a practical or clinical examination.

4990.38. Disciplinary Action; Grounds for Denial, Suspension or Revocation
The board may deny an application or may suspend or revoke a license or registration issued under the chapters it administers and enforces for any disciplinary action imposed by this state or another state or territory or possession of the United States, or by a governmental agency on a license, certificate or registration to practice marriage and family therapy, clinical social work, educational psychology, professional clinical counseling, or any other healing art. The disciplinary action, which may include denial of licensure or revocation or suspension of the license or imposition of restrictions on it, constitutes unprofessional conduct. A certified copy of the disciplinary action decision or judgment shall be conclusive evidence of that action.

4990.40. Revocation of License or Registration Due to Sexual Contact with a Patient
The board shall revoke a license or registration issued under the chapters it administers and enforces upon a decision made in accordance with the procedures set forth in Chapter 5 (commencing with Section 11500) of Part 1 of Division 3 of Title 2 of the Government Code, that contains a finding of fact that the licensee or registrant engaged in an act of sexual contact, as defined in Section 729, when that act is with a patient or with a former patient when the relationship was terminated primarily for the purpose of engaging in that act. The revocation shall not be stayed by the administrative law judge or the board.

4990.42. Conduct of Proceedings
The proceedings under this article shall be conducted in accordance with Chapter 5 (commencing with Section 11500) of Part 1 of Division 3 of Title 2 of the Government Code.

CHAPTER 5
GENERAL TRAINING REQUIREMENTS

There are requirements specific to the profession of professional clinical counseling and marriage and family therapy, but there are also general requirements that all therapists must comply with in the State of California. This chapter is broken up into two sections; General Training Requirements for all Psychotherapists and General Unprofessional Conduct for Psychotherapists. You will note that in Chapter 3, unprofessional conduct was also reviewed and here there are overlaps, but you will also note that the statutory requirements listed in this chapter provides clinicians with a broad definition for unprofessional conduct for all psychotherapists, not just the PCC or MFT as described in chapter 3.

More Training?

Not exactly (referring specifically to more training). The training listed in this chapter has already been implemented and integrated into the content of most counseling and therapy related programs. However, continuing education becomes a continued source for information delivery and education maintenance. These trainings are fulfilled by successfully completing the continuing education (CE) courses by approved providers. The 5 specific areas are: (1) Human Sexuality (2) Child Abuse Assessment & Reporting (3) Dependent Adult and Elder Abuse Assessment & Reporting (4) Chemical Dependency & Alcoholism and (5) AIDS Training for Professionals. Proof of these trainings may be required to obtain license eligibility and to maintain the license.

Business & Professions Code
25. Training in Human Sexuality

Any person applying for a license, registration, or the first renewal of a license, after the effective date of this section, as a licensed marriage and family therapist, a licensed clinical social worker, a licensed psychologist, or a licensed professional clinical counselor shall, in addition to any other requirements, show by evidence satisfactory to the agency regulating the business or profession, that he or she has completed training in human sexuality as a condition of licensure. The training shall be creditable toward continuing education requirements as deemed appropriate by the agency regulating the business or profession, and the course shall not exceed more than 50 contact hours.

The Board of Psychology shall exempt from the requirements of this section any persons whose field of practice is such that they are not likely to have use for this training.

"Human sexuality" as used in this section means the study of a human being as a sexual being and how he or she functions with respect thereto.
The content and length of the training shall be determined by the administrative agency regulating the business or profession and the agency shall proceed immediately upon the effective date of this section to determine what training, and the quality of staff to provide the training, is available and shall report its determination to the Legislature on or before July 1, 1977.

If a licensing board or agency proposes to establish a training program in human sexuality, the board or agency shall first consult with other licensing boards or agencies that have established or propose to establish a training program in human sexuality to ensure that the programs are compatible in scope and content.

27. Information to be provided on Internet; Entities in Department of Consumer Affairs required to comply

(a) Each entity specified in subdivisions (c), (d), and (e) shall provide on the Internet information regarding the status of every license issued by that entity in accordance with the California Public Records Act (Chapter 3.5 (commencing with Section 6250) of Division 7 of Title 1 of the Government Code) and the Information Practices Act of 1977 (Chapter 1 (commencing with Section 1798) of Title 1.8 of Part 4 of Division 3 of the Civil Code). The public information to be provided on the Internet shall include information on suspensions and revocations of licenses issued by the entity and other related enforcement action, including accusations filed pursuant to the Administrative Procedure Act (Chapter 3.5 (commencing with Section 11340) of Part 1 of Division 3 of Title 2 of the Government Code) taken by the entity relative to persons, businesses, or facilities subject to licensure or regulation by the entity. The information may not include personal information, including home telephone number, date of birth, or social security number. Each entity shall disclose a licensee's address of record. However, each entity shall allow a licensee to provide a post office box number or other alternate address, instead of his or her home address, as the address of record. This section shall not preclude an entity from also requiring a licensee, who has provided a post office box number or other alternative mailing address as his or her address of record, to provide a physical business address or residence address only for the entity's internal administrative use and not for disclosure as the licensee's address of record or disclosure on the Internet.

(b) In providing information on the Internet, each entity specified in subdivisions (c) and (d) shall comply with the Department of Consumer Affairs' guidelines for access to public records.

(c) Each of the following entities within the Department of Consumer Affairs shall comply with the requirements of this section:

(1) The Board for Professional Engineers, Land Surveyors, and Geologists shall disclose information on its registrants and licensees.

(2) The Bureau of Automotive Repair shall disclose information on its licensees, including auto repair dealers, smog stations, lamp and brake stations, smog check technicians, and smog inspection certification stations.

(3) The Bureau of Electronic and Appliance Repair, Home Furnishings, and Thermal Insulation shall disclose information on its licensees and registrants, including major appliance repair dealers, combination dealers (electronic and appliance), electronic repair dealers, service contract sellers, and service contract administrators.

(4) The Cemetery and Funeral Bureau shall disclose information on its licensees, including cemetery brokers, cemetery salespersons, cemetery managers, crematory managers, cemetery authorities, crematories, cremated remains disposers, embalmers, funeral establishments, and funeral directors.

(5) The Professional Fiduciaries Bureau shall disclose information on its licensees.

(6) The Contractors' State License Board shall disclose information on its licensees and registrants in accordance with Chapter 9 (commencing with Section 7000) of Division 3. In addition to information related to licenses as specified in subdivision (a), the board shall also disclose information provided to the board by the Labor Commissioner pursuant to Section 98.9 of the Labor Code.

(7) The Bureau for Private Postsecondary Education shall disclose information on private postsecondary institutions under its jurisdiction, including disclosure of notices to comply issued pursuant to Section 94935 of the Education Code.

(8) The California Board of Accountancy shall disclose information on its licensees and registrants.

(9) The California Architects Board shall disclose information on its licensees, including architects and landscape architects.

(10) The State Athletic Commission shall disclose information on its licensees and registrants.

(11) The State Board of Barbering and Cosmetology shall disclose information on its licensees.

(12) The State Board of Guide Dogs for the Blind shall disclose information on its licensees and registrants.

(13) The Acupuncture Board shall disclose information on its licensees.

(14) The Board of Behavioral Sciences shall disclose information on its licensees, including licensed marriage and family therapists, licensed clinical social workers, licensed educational psychologists, and licensed professional clinical counselors.

(15) The Dental Board of California shall disclose information on its licensees.

(16) The State Board of Optometry shall disclose information regarding certificates of registration to practice optometry, statements of licensure, optometric corporation registrations, branch office licenses, and fictitious name permits of its licensees.

(17) The Board of Psychology shall disclose information on its licensees, including psychologists, psychological assistants, and registered psychologists.

(d) The State Board of Chiropractic Examiners shall disclose information on its licensees.

(e) The Structural Pest Control Board shall disclose information on its licensees, including applicators, field representatives, and operators in the areas of fumigation, general pest and wood destroying pests and organisms, and wood roof cleaning and treatment.

(f) "Internet" for the purposes of this section has the meaning set forth in paragraph (6) of subdivision (f) of Section 17538.
(Amended by Stats. 2014, Ch. 316, Sec. 1. Effective January 1, 2015.)

28. Child, elder, and dependent adult abuse assessment and reporting training

The Legislature finds that there is a need to ensure that professionals of the healing arts who have demonstrable contact with victims and potential victims of child, elder, and dependent adult abuse, and abusers and potential abusers of children, elders, and dependent adults are provided with adequate and appropriate training regarding the reporting of child, elder, and dependent adult abuse which reduce, and eliminate the trauma of abuse and neglect reporting of abuse in a timely manner to prevent additiona

The Board of Psychology and the Board of Behavioral   ..ı ıaıı establish required training in the area of child abuse assessment and reporting for all persons applying for initial licensure and renewal of a license as a psychologist, clinical social worker, professional clinical counselor, or marriage and family therapist. This training shall be required one time only for all persons applying for initial licensure or for licensure renewal.

All persons applying for initial licensure or renewal of a license as a psychologist, clinical social worker, professional clinical counselor, or marriage and family therapist shall, in addition to all other requirements for licensure or renewal, have completed coursework or training in child abuse assessment and reporting that meets the requirements of this section, including detailed knowledge of the Child Abuse and Neglect Reporting Act (Article 2.5 (commencing with Section 11164) of Chapter 2 of Title 1 of Part 4 of the Penal Code). The training shall meet all of the following requirements:

(a) Be obtained from one of the following sources:

(1) An accredited or approved educational institution, as defined in Sections 2902, 4980.36, 4980.37, 4996.18, and 4999.12, including extension courses offered by those institutions.

(2) A continuing education provider approved by the responsible board.

(3) A course sponsored or offered by a professional association or a local, county, or state department of health or mental health for continuing education and approved by the responsible board.

(b) Have a minimum of seven contact hours.

(c) Include the study of the assessment and method of reporting of sexual assault, neglect, severe neglect, general neglect, willful cruelty or unjustifiable punishment, corporal punishment or injury, and abuse in out-of-home care. The training shall also include physical and behavioral indicators of abuse, crisis counseling techniques, community resources, rights and responsibilities of reporting, consequences of failure to report, caring for a child's needs after a report is made, sensitivity to previously abused children and adults, and implications and methods of treatment for children and adults.

a) An applicant shall provide the appropriate board with documentation of completion of the required child abuse training.

The Board of Psychology and the Board of Behavioral Sciences shall exempt an applicant who applies for an exemption from the requirements of this section and who shows to the satisfaction of the board that there would be no need for the training in his or her practice because of the nature of that practice.

It is the intent of the Legislature that a person licensed as a psychologist, clinical social worker, professional clinical counselor, or marriage and family therapist have minimal but appropriate training in the areas of child, elder, and dependent adult abuse assessment and reporting. It is not intended that by solely complying with the requirements of this section, a practitioner is fully trained in the subject of treatment of child, elder, and dependent adult abuse victims and abusers.

The Board of Psychology and the Board of Behavioral Sciences are encouraged to include coursework regarding the assessment and reporting of elder and dependent adult abuse in the required training on aging and long-term care issues prior to licensure or license renewal.

29. Adoption of continuing education requirements regarding chemical dependency and alcoholism

(a) The Board of Psychology and the Board of Behavioral Sciences shall consider adoption of continuing education requirements including training in the area of recognizing chemical dependency and early intervention for all persons applying for renewal of a license as a psychologist, clinical social worker, marriage and family therapist, or professional clinical counselor.

(b) Prior to the adoption of any regulations imposing continuing education relating to alcohol and other chemical dependency, the boards are urged to consider coursework to include, but not necessarily be limited to, the following topics:

(1) Historical and contemporary perspectives on alcohol and other drug abuse.

(2) Extent of the alcohol and drug abuse epidemic and its effects on the individual, family, and community.

(3) Recognizing the symptoms of alcoholism and drug addiction.

(4) Making appropriate interpretations, interventions, and referrals.

(5) Recognizing and intervening with affected family members.

(6) Learning about current programs of recovery, such as 12 step programs, and how therapists can effectively utilize these programs.

32. Legislative findings; AIDS training for health care professionals

(a) The Legislature finds that there is a need to ensure that professionals of the healing arts who have or intend to have significant contact with patients who have, or are at risk to be exposed to, acquired immune deficiency syndrome (AIDS) are provided with training in the form of continuing education regarding the characteristics and methods of assessment and treatment of the condition.

(b) A board vested with the responsibility of regulating the following licensees shall consider including training regarding the characteristics and method of assessment and treatment of acquired immune deficiency syndrome (AIDS) in any continuing education or training requirements for those licensees: chiropractors, medical laboratory technicians, dentists, dental hygienists, dental assistants, physicians and surgeons, podiatrists, registered nurses, licensed vocational nurses, psychologists, physician assistants, respiratory therapists, acupuncturists, marriage and family therapists, licensed educational psychologists, clinical social workers, and professional clinical counselors.

CHAPTER 6
MANDATED REPORTING - MINORS

Child abuse is nothing to be taken lightly. Minors are vulnerable in society, whether they are infants or high school age, they must be protected against abuse and neglect. This is why the Child Abuse and Neglect Reporting Act was enacted, to ensure that professionals like you understand your role and responsibility when it comes to assessing for suspected child abuse and reporting those suspicions. As listed below directly from the California Penal Code, the types of suspected or alleged abuse that must be reported are: (1) child sexual abuse, sexual assault or sexual exploitation, (2) neglect, severe neglect or general neglect, (3) willful harm, injury of a child, or endangering of the person or health of a child, (4) unlawful corporal punishment or injury, and (5) child abuse or neglect in "out-of-home care". Notice however, emotional abuse (damage) is not listed as an abuse that is required to be reported. In fact, the law stated that mandated reports *may* report such abuse, but again, not required. However, note that unlike the other reportable abuse, this type requires "evidence" by way of observed behavioral changes (CPC 11166.05).

The list of professionals who make up the group "mandated reports" include marriage and family therapist and professional clinical counselors – trainees, interns and licensee's (PC 11165.7). We highly suggest that you become familiar with the language of the law. What is not acceptable in any situation is the "I didn't know I was supposed to report" statement. In the next section we will talk a bit more about the duties required under the law for mandated reporters. While the law does not require individuals not in a professional capacity to make reports (such as being off of work/off duty but becomes aware of abuse/neglect), it may be an ethical requirement of some professional organizations.

Reasonable Suspicion

When deciding what to report and went to report, the law has provided mandated reporters great latitude when it comes to reporting suspected or alleged child abuse. In fact suspected child abuse does not have to be directly observed, simply a suspicion of child abuse is enough to make a report. California Penal Code 11166(a)(1) states, "for the purpose of this article, "reasonable suspicion" means that it is objectively reasonable for a person to entertain a suspicion, based upon facts that could cause a reasonable person in a like position, drawing, when appropriate, on his or her training and experience, to suspect child abuse or neglect.

"Reasonable suspicion" does not require certainty that child abuse or neglect has occurred nor does it require a specific medical indication of child abuse or neglect; any reasonable suspicion" is sufficient.""

Reporting Timeframes

The law requires that the mandated reporter makes the initial report immediately upon observing abuse or being advised of suspected abuse, or as soon as possible by phone. A written report is then either mailed, faxed or submitted through an online system within 36 hours of receiving information on or observing suspected abuse. Note that the law is very specific about the time frames as there are no exceptions. These reports are submitted to an agency designated to receive child abuse reports in California. The form that is required is called the SS 8572 Suspected Child Abuse Report Form. Be aware that it is not the responsibility of mandated reporters to do any type of investigation. While it may be okay to ask some questions to clarify statements, completing an investigation would be unlawful and unprofessional.

The laws regarding mandated reporting also stipulate penalties for failing to make a report to an agency designated to receive such reports. These penalties include up to 6 months in jail, a fine of $1,000 or both. Further penalties could result if the mandated reporter attempts to conceal their failure to report, or their failure to report resulted in death or severe injury of the child. Therefore it should be clear that the law has been designed to allow for over reporting and gives no reason for therapist to come up with an excuse or an exception for not reporting. All suspected child abuse should be reported to the appropriate agency regardless if the child has moved, the alleged abuser no longer has access to the child, the death of a child, or the death of the alleged abuser.

Required Information in Reports

When making a report to an agency designated to accept child abuse reports, it is very important to ensure that your identifying information is provided on the report (PC 11167). This is not only required by law, but it also helps the agency by allowing them to contact you for further information (this may be the social worker assigned to the case or law enforcement). Information that should be reported on the telephone and on the report due within 36 hours is your name, the business or organization you work for, the address of the business organization you work for, your telephone number (whenever possible provide a direct number or an extension), your professional capacity/ title, and information necessary to support why the report was made. If the report was made not by observation but by statements from other individuals, those sources should be listed as well.

Information on the victim needs to be sufficient as well in order for the agency and/or law enforcement to follow up accordingly with an investigation. As listed in the law, the information regarding the child should include their name, their address, current location if they are not at home, school name, current grade and class, as well as any other pertinent information regarding the child. Information on the child's parents or guardians such as their names, addresses and telephone numbers need to be provided, as well as the information of others that might have been party to the abuse or neglect. However, even if this information is not known, the report should still be made and as much known information should be provided.

Mandated reporter information is considered confidential and is not released to the public or to the suspected abuser, however it may be shared among agencies that are involved in the investigation. Mandated reporters are not responsible for reports that are made and determined to be unfounded by the investigation agencies. This is however as long as it was not a false report to begin with. Should a therapist have a civil lawsuit against them as a result of making a report, with certain conditions, the therapist may be reimbursed up to $50,000 in attorney fees.

Minor Consensual Sexual Activity Reporting

When to report consensual sexual activity between minors largely depends on age and the type of sexual activity being engaged in (PC 261.5). There are several considerations that therapists must consider when determining to make a report or determining not to make a report. There are also a variety of resources that are available to therapist to assist in making these determinations such as the publication Understanding Confidentiality and Minor Consent in California: A Model of Adolescent Provider Toolkit published by the Adolescent Health Working Group-California Adolescent Health Collaborative or the published article, Reporting_Consensual Activity_Between_Minors: The Confusion Unraveled by the California Association of Marriage and Family Therapists. These can easily be found with an internet search.

What is paramount for a therapist to remember is that activities that include oral, anal or penetration with a foreign object is always reportable when the individual involved is a minor, regardless of the age the other individual involved. There are also times when a therapist has no duty to report sexual activity involving two consenting minors. Remember, that just because there may be no duty to report, this does not make the sexual contact legal. It just means that a therapist can use clinical judgment to not report such activities that are not mandated.

Because of the variety of resources and charts that are available to therapist today, we have not gone into depth regarding reporting consensual sexual activity involving minors but here are some quick tips:

1. If a minor is at least 14 years old and is engaging in sex with anyone between 14 years old and 20 years old and it is believed to be consensual, there is no duty to report.

2. If a minor is at least 16 years old and engaging in sex with anyone older than 14 years old, there is no duty to report.

Therapists need to consider factors such as coercion, bribery, intimidation, potentially exploitive relationships as well as the chronological and psychological ages of the individuals involved when determining to make a report or not make a report (if there is no mandate). Depending on the nature of the report and the ability to obtain additional information to assist in these assessments, it may be difficult to ascertain. As previously stated, the law has been made to allow for over reporting and safeguards therapists should they decide to make report in these situations.

Child Abuse and Neglect Reporting Act

California Penal Code
11164. Citation of article; Intent
(a) This article shall be known and may be cited as the Child Abuse and Neglect Reporting Act.

(b) The intent and purpose of this article is to protect children from abuse and neglect. In any investigation of suspected child abuse or neglect, all persons participating in the investigation of the case shall consider the needs of the child victim and shall do whatever is necessary to prevent psychological harm to the child victim.

Definitions

11165. "Child"
As used in this article "child" means a person under the age of 18 years.

11165.1. "Sexual abuse"; "Sexual assault"; "Sexual exploitation"
As used in this article, "sexual abuse" means sexual assault or sexual exploitation as defined by the following:
(a) "Sexual assault" means conduct in violation of one or more of the following sections: Section 261 (rape), subdivision (d) of Section 261.5 (statutory rape), 264.1 (rape in concert), 285 (incest), 286 (sodomy), subdivision (a) or (b), or paragraph (1) of subdivision (c) of Section 288 (lewd

or lascivious acts upon a child), 288a (oral copulation), 289 (sexual penetration), or 647.6 (child molestation).

(b) Conduct described as "sexual assault" includes, but is not limited to, all of the following:
(1) Penetration, however slight, of the vagina or anal opening of one person by the penis of another person, whether or not there is the emission of semen.
 (2) Sexual contact between the genitals or anal opening of one person and the mouth or tongue of another person.
(3) Intrusion by one person into the genitals or anal opening of another person, including the use of an object for this purpose, except that, it does not include acts performed for a valid medical purpose.
(4) The intentional touching of the genitals or intimate parts, including the breasts, genital area, groin, inner thighs, and buttocks, or the clothing covering them, of a child, or of the perpetrator by a child, for purposes of sexual arousal or gratification, except that it does not include acts which may reasonably be construed to be normal caretaker responsibilities; interactions with, or demonstrations of affection for, the child; or acts performed for a valid medical purpose.
(5) The intentional masturbation of the perpetrator's genitals in the presence of a child.

(c) "Sexual exploitation" refers to any of the following:
(1) Conduct involving matter depicting a minor engaged in obscene acts in violation of Section 311.2 (preparing, selling, or distributing obscene matter) or subdivision (a) of Section 311.4 (employment of minor to perform obscene acts).
(2) A person who knowingly promotes, aids, or assists, employs, uses, persuades, induces, or coerces a child, or a person responsible for a child's welfare, who knowingly permits or encourages a child to engage in, or assist others to engage in, prostitution or a live performance involving obscene sexual conduct, or to either pose or model alone or with others for purposes of preparing a film, photograph, negative, slide, drawing, painting, or other pictorial depiction, involving obscene sexual conduct. For the purpose of this section, "person responsible for a child's welfare" means a parent, guardian, foster parent, or a licensed administrator or employee of a public or private residential home, residential school, or other residential institution.
(3) A person who depicts a child in, or who knowingly develops, duplicates, prints, downloads, streams, accesses through any electronic or digital media, or exchanges, a film, photograph, videotape, video recording, negative, or slide in which a child is engaged in an act of obscene sexual conduct, except for those activities by law enforcement and prosecution agencies and other persons described in subdivisions (c) and (e) of Section 311.3.

11165.2. "Neglect"; "Severe neglect"; "General neglect"

As used in this article, "neglect" means the negligent treatment or the maltreatment of a child by a person responsible for the child's welfare under circumstances indicating harm or threatened harm to the child's health or welfare. The term includes both acts and omissions on the part of the responsible person.

(a) "Severe neglect" means the negligent failure of a person having the care or custody of a child to protect the child from severe malnutrition or medically diagnosed nonorganic failure to thrive. "Severe neglect" also means those situations of neglect where any person having the care or custody of a child willfully causes or permits the person or health of the child to be placed in a situation such that his or her person or health is endangered, as proscribed by Section 11165.3, including the intentional failure to provide adequate food, clothing, shelter, or medical care.

(b) "General neglect" means the negligent failure of a person having the care or custody of a child to provide adequate food, clothing, shelter, medical care, or supervision where no physical injury to the child has occurred.

For the purposes of this chapter, a child receiving treatment by spiritual means as provided in Section 16509.1 of the Welfare and Institutions Code or not receiving specified medical treatment for religious reasons, shall not for that reason alone be considered a neglected child. An informed and appropriate medical decision made by parent or guardian after consultation with a physician or physicians who have examined the minor does not constitute neglect.

11165.3. "Willful harming or injuring of a child or the endangering of the person or health of a child"

As used in this article, "the willful harming or injuring of a child or the endangering of the person or health of a child," means a situation in which any person willfully causes or permits any child to suffer, or inflicts thereon, unjustifiable physical pain or mental suffering, or having the care or custody of any child, willfully causes or permits the person or health of the child to be placed in a situation in which his or her person or health is endangered.

11165.4. "Unlawful corporal punishment or injury"

As used in this article, "unlawful corporal punishment or injury" means a situation where any person willfully inflicts upon any child any cruel or inhuman corporal punishment or injury resulting in a traumatic condition. It does not include an amount of force that is reasonable and necessary for a person employed by or engaged in a public school to quell a disturbance threatening physical injury to person or damage to property, for purposes of self-defense, or to obtain possession of weapons or other dangerous objects within the control of the pupil, as authorized by Section 49001 of the Education Code. It also does not include the exercise of the degree of physical control authorized by Section 44807 of the Education Code. It also does not include an injury caused by reasonable and necessary force used by a peace officer acting within the course and scope of his or her employment as a peace officer.

11165.5. "Abuse or neglect in out–of–home care"
As used in this article, the term "abuse or neglect in out-of-home care" includes physical injury or death inflicted upon a child by another person by other than accidental means, sexual abuse as defined in Section 11165.1, neglect as defined in Section 11165.2, unlawful corporal punishment or injury as defined in Section 11165.4, or the willful harming or injuring of a child or the endangering of the person or health of a child, as defined in Section 11165.3, where the person responsible for the child's welfare is a licensee, administrator, or employee of any facility licensed to care for children, or an administrator or employee of a public or private school or other institution or agency. "Abuse or neglect in out-of-home care" does not include an injury caused by reasonable and necessary force used by a peace officer acting within the course and scope of his or her employment as a peace officer.

11165.6. "Child abuse or neglect"
As used in this article, the term "child abuse or neglect" includes physical injury or death inflicted by other than accidental means upon a child by another person, sexual abuse as defined in Section 11165.1, neglect as defined in Section 11165.2, the willful harming or injuring of a child or the endangering of the person or health of a child, as defined in Section 11165.3, and unlawful corporal punishment or injury as defined in Section 11165.4. "Child abuse or neglect" does not include a mutual affray between minors. "Child abuse or neglect" does not include an injury caused by reasonable and necessary force used by a peace officer acting within the course and scope of his or her employment as a peace officer.

Mandated Reporters

11165.7. "Mandated reporter"; Training
(a) As used in this article, "mandated reporter" is defined as any of the following:
(1) A teacher.
(2) An instructional aide.
(3) A teacher's aide or teacher's assistant employed by a public or private school.
(4) A classified employee of a public school.
(5) An administrative officer or supervisor of child welfare and attendance,

or a certificated pupil personnel employee of a public or private school.

(6) An administrator of a public or private day camp.

(7) An administrator or employee of a public or private youth center, youth recreation program, or youth organization.

(8) An administrator or employee of a public or private organization whose duties require direct contact and supervision of children.

(9) An employee of a county office of education or the State Department of Education whose duties bring the employee into contact with children on a regular basis.

(10) A licensee, an administrator, or an employee of a licensed community care or child day care facility.

(11) A Head Start program teacher.

(12) A licensing worker or licensing evaluator employed by a licensing agency, as defined in Section 11165.11.

(13) A public assistance worker.

(14) An employee of a child care institution, including, but not limited to, foster parents, group home personnel, and personnel of residential care facilities.

(15) A social worker, probation officer, or parole officer.

(16) An employee of a school district police or security department.

(17) A person who is an administrator or presenter of, or a counselor in, a child abuse prevention program in a public or private school.

(18) A district attorney investigator, inspector, or local child support agency caseworker, unless the investigator, inspector, or caseworker is working with an attorney appointed pursuant to Section 317 of the Welfare and Institutions Code to represent a minor.

(19) A peace officer, as defined in Chapter 4.5 (commencing with Section 830) of Title 3 of Part 2, who is not otherwise described in this section.

(20) A firefighter, except for volunteer firefighters.

(21) A physician and surgeon, psychiatrist, psychologist, dentist, resident, intern, podiatrist, chiropractor, licensed nurse, dental hygienist, optometrist, marriage and family therapist, clinical social worker, professional clinical counselor, or any other person who is currently licensed under Division 2 (commencing with Section 500) of the Business and Professions Code.

(22) An emergency medical technician I or II, paramedic, or other person certified pursuant to Division 2.5 (commencing with Section 1797) of the Health and Safety Code.

(23) A psychological assistant registered pursuant to Section 2913 of the Business and Professions Code.

(24) A marriage and family therapist trainee, as defined in subdivision (c) of Section 4980.03 of the Business and Professions Code.

(25) An unlicensed marriage and family therapist intern registered under Section 4980.44 of the Business and Professions Code.

(26) A state or county public health employee who treats a minor for venereal disease or any other condition.

(27) A coroner.

(28) A medical examiner or other person who performs autopsies.

(29) A commercial film and photographic print or image processor as specified in subdivision (e) of Section 11166. As used in this article, "commercial film and photographic print or image processor" means a person who develops exposed photographic film into negatives, slides, or prints, or who makes prints from negatives or slides, or who prepares, publishes, produces, develops, duplicates, or prints any representation of information, data, or an image, including, but not limited to, any film, filmstrip, photograph, negative, slide, photocopy, videotape, video laser disc, computer hardware, computer software, computer floppy disk, data storage medium, CD-ROM, computer-generated equipment, or computer-generated image, for compensation. The term includes any employee of that person; it does not include a person who develops film or makes prints or images for a public agency.

(30) A child visitation monitor. As used in this article, "child visitation monitor" means a person who, for financial compensation, acts as a monitor of a visit between a child and another person when the monitoring of that visit has been ordered by a court of law.

(31) An animal control officer or humane society officer. For the purposes of this article, the following terms have the following meanings:

(A) "Animal control officer" means a person employed by a city, county, or city and county for the purpose of enforcing animal control laws or regulations.

(B) "Humane society officer" means a person appointed or employed by a public or private entity as a humane officer who is qualified pursuant to Section 14502 or 14503 of the Corporations Code.

(32) A clergy member, as specified in subdivision (d) of Section11166. As used in this article, "clergy member" means a priest, minister, rabbi, religious practitioner, or similar functionary of a church, temple, or recognized denomination or organization.

(33) Any custodian of records of a clergy member, as specified in this section and subdivision (d) of Section 11166.

(34) An employee of any police department, county sheriff's department, county probation department, or county welfare department.

(35) An employee or volunteer of a Court Appointed Special Advocate program, as defined in Rule 5.655 of the California Rules of Court.

(36) A custodial officer, as defined in Section 831.5.

(37) A person providing services to a minor child under Section 12300 or 12300.1 of the Welfare and Institutions Code.

(38) An alcohol and drug counselor. As used in this article, an "alcohol and drug counselor" is a person providing counseling, therapy, or other clinical services for a state licensed or certified drug, alcohol, or drug and alcohol treatment program. However, alcohol or drug abuse, or both alcohol and drug abuse, is not, in and of itself, a sufficient basis for reporting child abuse or neglect.

(39) A clinical counselor trainee, as defined in subdivision (g) of Section

4999.12 of the Business and Professions Code.

(40) A clinical counselor intern registered under Section 4999.42 of the Business and Professions Code.

(41) An employee or administrator of a public or private postsecondary educational institution, whose duties bring the administrator or employee into contact with children on a regular basis, or who supervises those whose duties bring the administrator or employee into contact with children on a regular basis, as to child abuse or neglect occurring on that institution's premises or at an official activity of, or program conducted by, the institution.

Nothing in this paragraph shall be construed as altering the lawyer-client privilege as set forth in Article 3 (commencing with Section 950) of Chapter 4 of Division 8 of the Evidence Code.

(42) An athletic coach, athletic administrator, or athletic director employed by any public or private school that provides any combination of instruction for kindergarten, or grades 1 to 12, inclusive.

(43) (A) A commercial computer technician as specified in subdivision (e) of Section 11166. As used in this article, "commercial computer technician" means a person who works for a

company that is in the business of repairing, installing, or otherwise servicing a computer or computer component, including, but not limited to, a computer part, device, memory storage or recording mechanism, auxiliary storage recording or memory capacity, or any other material relating to the operation and maintenance of a computer or computer network system, for a fee. An employer who provides an electronic communications service or a remote computing service to the public shall be deemed to comply with this article if that employer complies with Section 2258A of Title 18 of the United States Code.

(B) An employer of a commercial computer technician may implement internal procedures for facilitating reporting consistent with this article. These procedures may direct employees who are mandated reporters under this paragraph to report materials described in subdivision (e) of Section 11166 to an employee who is designated by the employer to receive the reports. An employee who is designated to receive reports under this subparagraph shall be a commercial computer technician for purposes of this article. A commercial computer technician who makes a report to the designated employee pursuant to this subparagraph shall be deemed to have complied with the requirements of this article and shall be subject to the protections afforded to mandated reporters, including, but not limited to, those protections afforded by Section 11172.

(44) Any athletic coach, including, but not limited to, an assistant coach or a graduate assistant involved in coaching, at public or private postsecondary educational institutions.

(b) Except as provided in paragraph (35) of subdivision (a), volunteers of public or private organizations whose duties require direct contact with and supervision of children are not mandated reporters but are encouraged to obtain training in the identification and reporting of child abuse and neglect and are further encouraged to report known or suspected instances of child abuse or neglect to an agency specified in Section 11165.9.

(c) Except as provided in subdivision (d), employers are strongly encouraged to provide their employees who are mandated reporters with training in the duties imposed by this article. This training shall include training in child abuse and neglect identification and training in child abuse and neglect reporting. Whether or not employers provide their employees with training in child abuse and neglect identification and reporting, the employers shall provide their employees who are mandated reporters with the statement required pursuant to subdivision (a) of Section 11166.5.

(d) Pursuant to Section 44691 of the Education Code, school districts, county offices of education, state special schools and diagnostic centers operated by the State Department of Education, and charter schools shall annually train their employees and persons working on their behalf specified in subdivision (a) in the duties of mandated reporters under the child abuse reporting laws. The training shall include, but not necessarily be limited to, training in child abuse and neglect identification and child abuse and neglect reporting.

(e) Unless otherwise specifically provided, the absence of training shall not excuse a mandated reporter from the duties imposed by this article.

(f) Public and private organizations are encouraged to provide their volunteers whose duties require direct contact with and supervision of children with training in the identification and reporting of child abuse and neglect.

11165.9. Reports to authorities
Reports of suspected child abuse or neglect shall be made by mandated reporters, or in the case of reports pursuant to Section 11166.05, may be made, to any police department or sheriff's department, not including a school district police or security department, county probation department, if designated by the county to receive mandated reports, or the county welfare department. Any of those agencies shall accept a report of suspected child abuse or neglect whether offered by a mandated reporter or another person, or referred by another agency, even if the agency to whom the report is being made lacks subject matter or geographical jurisdiction to investigate the reported case, unless the agency can immediately electronically transfer the call to an agency with proper jurisdiction. When an agency takes a report about a case of suspected child abuse or neglect in which that agency lacks jurisdiction, the agency shall immediately refer the case by telephone, fax, or electronic transmission to an agency with proper jurisdiction. Agencies that are required to receive reports of suspected child abuse or neglect may not refuse to accept a report of suspected child abuse or neglect from a mandated reporter or another person unless otherwise authorized pursuant

to this section, and shall maintain a record of all reports received.

11165.11. "Licensing Agency"

As used in this article, "licensing agency" means the State Department of Social Services office responsible for the licensing and enforcement of the California Community Care Facilities Act (Chapter 3 (commencing with Section 1500) of Division 2 of the Health and Safety Code), the California Child Day Care Act (Chapter 3.4 (commencing with Section 1596.70) of Division 2 of the Health and Safety Code), and Chapter 3.5 (commencing with Section 1596.90) of Division 2 of the Health and Safety Code), or the county licensing agency which has contracted with the state for performance of those duties.

11165.12. Definitions relating to reports

As used in this article, the following definitions shall control:

(a) "Unfounded report" means a report that is determined by the investigator who conducted the investigation to be false, to be inherently improbable, to involve an accidental injury, or not to constitute child abuse or neglect, as defined in Section 11165.6.

(b) "Substantiated report" means a report that is determined by the investigator who conducted the investigation to constitute child abuse or neglect, as defined in Section 11165.6, based upon evidence that makes it more likely than not that child abuse or neglect, as defined, occurred. A substantiated report shall not include a report where the investigator who conducted the investigation found the report to be false, inherently improbable, to involve an accidental injury, or to not constitute child abuse or neglect as defined in Section 11165.6. (c) "Inconclusive report" means a report that is determined by the investigator who conducted the investigation not to be unfounded, but the findings are inconclusive and there is insufficient evidence to determine whether child abuse or neglect, as defined in Section 11165.6, has occurred.

11165.13. Effect of positive toxicology screen at time of delivery of infant

For purposes of this article, a positive toxicology screen at the time of the delivery of an infant is not in and of itself a sufficient basis for reporting child abuse or neglect. However, any indication of maternal substance abuse shall lead to an assessment of the needs of the mother and child pursuant to Section 123605 of the Health and Safety Code. If other factors are present that indicate risk to a child, then a report shall be made. However, a report based on risk to a child which relates solely to the inability of the parent to provide the child with regular care due to the parent's substance abuse shall be made only to a county welfare or probation department, and not to a law enforcement agency.

11165.15. Basis for reporting abuse or neglect

For the purposes of this article, the fact that a child is homeless or is classified as an unaccompanied youth, as defined in Section 11434a of the federal McKinney-Vento Homeless Assistance Act (42 U.S.C. Sec. 11301 et seq.), is not, in and of itself, a sufficient basis for reporting child abuse or neglect. This section shall not limit a mandated reporter, as defined in Section 11165.7, from making a report pursuant to Section 11166 whenever the mandated reporter has knowledge of or observes an unaccompanied minor whom the mandated reporter knows or reasonably suspects to be the victim of abuse or neglect.

Duty to Report & Timeline

11166. Duty to report; Mandated reporters; Punishment for violation
(a) Except as provided in subdivision (d), and in Section 11166.05, a mandated reporter shall make a report to an agency specified in Section 11165.9 whenever the mandated reporter, in his or her professional capacity or within the scope of his or her employment, has knowledge of or observes a child whom the mandated reporter knows or reasonably suspects has been the victim of child abuse or neglect. The mandated reporter shall make an initial report by telephone to the agency immediately or as soon as is practicably possible, and shall prepare and send, fax, or electronically transmit a written followup report within 36 hours of receiving the information concerning the incident. The mandated reporter may include with the report any nonprivileged documentary evidence the mandated reporter possesses relating to the incident.
(1) For purposes of this article, "reasonable suspicion" means that it is objectively reasonable for a person to entertain a suspicion, based upon facts that could cause a reasonable person in a like position, drawing, when appropriate, on his or her training and experience, to suspect child abuse or neglect. "Reasonable suspicion" does not require certainty that child abuse or neglect has occurred nor does it require a specific medical indication of child abuse or neglect; any "reasonable suspicion" is sufficient. For purposes of this article, the pregnancy of a minor does not, in and of itself, constitute a basis for a reasonable suspicion of sexual abuse.
(2) The agency shall be notified and a report shall be prepared and sent, faxed, or electronically transmitted even if the child has expired, regardless of whether or not the possible abuse was a factor contributing to the death, and even if suspected child abuse was discovered during an autopsy.
(3) A report made by a mandated reporter pursuant to this section shall be known as a mandated report.

(b) If, after reasonable efforts, a mandated reporter is unable to submit an initial report by telephone, he or she shall immediately or as soon as is practicably possible, by fax or electronic transmission, make a one-time automated written report on the form prescribed by the Department of Justice, and shall also be available to respond to a telephone followup call by the agency with which he or she filed the report. A mandated reporter who files a one-time automated written report because he or she was unable to submit an initial report by telephone is not required to submit a written followup report.

(1) The one-time automated written report form prescribed by the Department of Justice shall be clearly identifiable so that it is not mistaken for a standard written followup report. In addition, the automated one-time report shall contain a section that allows the mandated reporter to state the reason the initial telephone call was not able to be completed. The reason for the submission of the one-time automated written report in lieu of the procedure prescribed in subdivision (a) shall be captured in the Child Welfare Services/Case Management System (CWS/CMS). The department shall work with stakeholders to modify reporting forms and the CWS/CMS as is necessary to accommodate the changes enacted by these provisions.

(2) This subdivision shall not become operative until the CWS/CMS is updated to capture the information prescribed in this subdivision.

(3) This subdivision shall become inoperative three years after this subdivision becomes operative or on January 1, 2009, whichever occurs first.

(4) On the inoperative date of these provisions, a report shall be submitted to the counties and the Legislature by the State Department of Social Services that reflects the data collected from automated one-time reports indicating the reasons stated as to why the automated one-time report was filed in lieu of the initial telephone report.

(5) Nothing in this section shall supersede the requirement that a mandated reporter first attempt to make a report via telephone, or that agencies specified in Section 11165.9 accept reports from mandated reporters and other persons as required.

(c) A mandated reporter who fails to report an incident of known or reasonably suspected child abuse or neglect as required by this section is guilty of a misdemeanor punishable by up to six months confinement in a county jail or by a fine of one thousand dollars ($1,000) or by both that imprisonment and fine. If a mandated reporter intentionally conceals his or her failure to report an incident known by the mandated reporter to be abuse or severe neglect under this section, the failure to report is a continuing offense until an agency specified in Section 11165.9 discovers the offense.

(d) (1) A clergy member who acquires knowledge or a reasonable suspicion of child abuse or neglect during a penitential communication is not subject to subdivision (a). For the purposes of this subdivision, "penitential communication" means a communication, intended to be in confidence, including, but not limited to, a sacramental confession, made to a clergy member who, in the course of the discipline or practice of his or her church, denomination, or organization, is authorized or accustomed to hear those communications, and under the discipline, tenets, customs, or practices of his or her church, denomination, or organization, has a duty to keep those communications secret.

(2) Nothing in this subdivision shall be construed to modify or limit a clergy member's duty to report known or suspected child abuse or neglect when the clergy member is acting in some other capacity that would otherwise make the clergy member a mandated reporter. (3) (A) On or before January 1, 2004, a clergy member or any custodian of records for the clergy member may report to an agency specified in Section 11165.9 that the clergy member or any custodian of records for the clergy member, prior to January 1, 1997, in his or her professional capacity or within the scope of his or her employment, other than during a penitential communication, acquired knowledge or had a reasonable suspicion that a child had been the victim of sexual abuse and that the clergy member or any custodian of records for the clergy member did not previously report the abuse to an agency specified in Section 11165.9. The provisions of Section 11172 shall apply to all reports made pursuant to this paragraph.

(B) This paragraph shall apply even if the victim of the known or suspected abuse has reached the age of majority by the time the required report is made. (C) The local law enforcement agency shall have jurisdiction to investigate any report of child abuse made pursuant to this paragraph even if the report is made after the victim has reached the age of majority.

(e)(1) A commercial film, photographic print, or image processor who has knowledge of or observes, within the scope of his or her professional capacity or employment, any film, photograph, videotape, negative, slide, or any representation of information, data, or an image, including, but not limited to, any film, filmstrip, photograph, negative, slide, photocopy, videotape, video laser disc, computer hardware, computer software, computer floppy disk, data storage medium, CD-ROM, computer-generated equipment, or computer-generated image depicting a child under 16 years of age engaged in an act of sexual conduct, shall, immediately or as soon as practicably possible, telephonically report the instance of suspected abuse to the law enforcement agency located in the county in which the images are seen. Within 36 hours of receiving the information concerning the incident, the reporter shall prepare and send, fax, or electronically transmit a written followup report of the incident with a copy of the image or material attached.

(2) A commercial computer technician who has knowledge of or observes, within the scope of his or her professional capacity or employment, any representation of information, data, or an image, including, but not limited to, any computer hardware, computer software, computer file, computer floppy disk, data storage medium, CD-ROM, computer-generated equipment, or computer-generated image that is retrievable in perceivable form and that is intentionally saved, transmitted, or organized on an electronic medium, depicting a child under 16 years of age

engaged in an act of sexual conduct, shall immediately, or as soon as practicably possible, telephonically report the instance of suspected abuse to the law enforcement agency located in the county in which the images or material are seen. As soon as practicably possible after receiving the information concerning the incident, the reporter shall prepare and send, fax, or electronically transmit a written followup report of the incident with a brief description of the images or materials.

(3) For purposes of this article, "commercial computer technician" includes an employee designated by an employer to receive reports pursuant to an established reporting process authorized by subparagraph (B) of paragraph (43) of subdivision (a) of Section 11165.7.
(4) As used in this subdivision, "electronic medium" includes, but is not limited to, a recording, CD-ROM, magnetic disk memory, magnetic tape memory, CD, DVD, thumbdrive, or any other computer hardware or media.

(5) As used in this subdivision, "sexual conduct" means any of the following:
(A) Sexual intercourse, including genital-genital, oral-genital, anal-genital, or oral-anal, whether between persons of the same or opposite sex or between humans and animals.   (B) Penetration of the vagina or rectum by any object.   (C) Masturbation for the purpose of sexual stimulation of the viewer.   (D) Sadomasochistic abuse for the purpose of sexual stimulation of the viewer.   (E) Exhibition of the genitals, pubic, or rectal areas of a person for the purpose of sexual stimulation of the viewer.   (f) Any mandated reporter who knows or reasonably suspects that the home or institution in which a child resides is unsuitable for the child because of abuse or neglect of the child shall bring the condition to the attention of the agency to which, and at the same time as, he or she makes a report of the abuse or neglect pursuant to subdivision (a).   (g) Any other person who has knowledge of or observes a child whom he or she knows or reasonably suspects has been a victim of child abuse or neglect may report the known or suspected instance of child abuse or neglect to an agency specified in Section 11165.9. For purposes of this section, "any other person" includes a mandated reporter who acts in his or her private capacity and not in his or her professional capacity or within the scope of his or her employment.   (h) When two or more persons, who are required to report, jointly have knowledge of a known or suspected instance of child abuse or neglect, and when there is agreement among them, the telephone report may be made by a member of the team selected by mutual agreement and a single report may be made and signed by the selected member of the reporting team. Any member who has knowledge that the member designated to report has failed to do so shall thereafter make the report.

(i) (1) The reporting duties under this section are individual, and no supervisor or administrator may impede or inhibit the reporting duties, and no person making a report shall be subject to any sanction for making the report. However, internal procedures to facilitate reporting and apprise supervisors and administrators of reports may be established provided that they are not inconsistent with this article.

(2) The internal procedures shall not require any employee required to make reports pursuant to this article to disclose his or her identity to the employer.   (3) Reporting the information regarding a case of possible child abuse or neglect to an employer, supervisor, school principal, school counselor, coworker, or other person shall not be a substitute for making a mandated report to an agency specified in Section 11165.9.

(j) A county probation or welfare department shall immediately, or as soon as practicably possible, report by telephone, fax, or electronic transmission to the law enforcement agency having jurisdiction over the case, to the agency given the responsibility for investigation of cases under Section 300 of the Welfare and Institutions Code, and to the district attorney's office every known or suspected instance of child abuse or neglect, as defined in Section 11165.6, except acts or omissions coming within subdivision (b) of Section 11165.2, or reports made pursuant to Section 11165.13 based on risk to a child which relates solely to the inability of the parent to provide the child with regular care due to the parent's substance abuse, which shall be reported only to the county welfare or probation department. A county probation or welfare department also shall send, fax, or electronically transmit a written report thereof within 36 hours of receiving the information concerning the incident to any agency to which it makes a telephone report under this subdivision.

(k) A law enforcement agency shall immediately, or as soon as practicably possible, report by telephone, fax, or electronic transmission to the agency given responsibility for investigation of cases under Section 300 of the Welfare and Institutions Code and to the district attorney's office every known or suspected instance of child abuse or neglect reported to it, except acts or omissions coming within subdivision (b) of Section 11165.2, which shall be reported only to the county welfare or probation department. A law enforcement agency shall report to the county welfare or probation department every known or suspected instance of child abuse or neglect reported to it which is alleged to have occurred as a result of the action of a person responsible for the child's welfare, or as the result of the failure of a person responsible for the child's welfare to adequately protect the minor from abuse when the person responsible for the child's welfare knew or reasonably should have known that the minor was in danger of abuse.

A law enforcement agency also shall send, fax, or electronically transmit a written report thereof within 36 hours of receiving the information concerning the incident to any agency to which it makes a telephone report under this subdivision.   11166.01.   (a) Except as provided in subdivision (b), any supervisor or administrator who violates paragraph (1) of subdivision (i) of Section 11166 shall be punished by not more than six months in a county jail, by a fine of not more than one thousand dollars ($1,000), or by both that fine and imprisonment.   (b) Notwithstanding Section 11162 or subdivision (c) of Section 11166, any mandated reporter who willfully fails to report abuse or neglect, or any person who impedes or inhibits a report of abuse or neglect, in violation of this article, where that abuse or neglect results in death or great bodily injury, shall be punished by not more than one year in a county jail, by a fine of not more than five thousand dollars ($5,000), or by both that fine and imprisonment.

11166.05. Reporting child suffering serious emotional damage
Any mandated reporter who has knowledge of or who reasonably suspects that a child is suffering serious emotional damage or is at a substantial risk of suffering serious emotional damage, evidenced by states of being or behavior, including, but not limited to, severe anxiety, depression, withdrawal, or untoward aggressive behavior toward self or others, may make a report to an agency specified in Section 11165.9.

11166.1. Duty of agency
(a) When an agency receives a report pursuant to Section 11166 that contains either of the following, it shall, within 24 hours, notify the licensing office with jurisdiction over the facility: (1) A report of abuse alleged to have occurred in facilities licensed to care for children by the State Department of Social Services.   (2) A report of the death of a child who was, at the time of death, living at, enrolled in, or regularly attending a facility licensed to care for children by the State Department of Social Services, unless the circumstances of the child's death are clearly unrelated to the child's care at the facility.   The agency shall send the licensing agency a copy of its investigation and any other pertinent materials.

(b) Any employee of an agency specified in Section 11165.9 who has knowledge of, or observes in his or her professional capacity or within the scope of his or her employment, a child in protective custody whom he or she knows or reasonably suspects has been the victim of child abuse or neglect shall, within 36 hours, send or have sent to the attorney who represents the child in dependency court, a copy of the report prepared in accordance with Section 11166. The agency shall maintain a copy of the written report. All information requested by the attorney for the child or the child's guardian ad litem shall be provided by the agency within 30 days of the request.

11166.2. Additional duty of agency
In addition to the reports required under Section 11166, any agency specified in Section 11165.9 shall immediately or as soon as practically possible report by telephone, fax, or electronic transmission to the

appropriate licensing agency every known or suspected instance of child abuse or neglect when the instance of abuse or neglect occurs while the child is being cared for in a child day care facility, involves a child day care licensed staff person, or occurs while the child is under the supervision of a community care facility or involves a community care facility licensee or staff person. The agency shall also send, fax, or electronically transmit a written report thereof within 36 hours of receiving the information concerning the incident to any agency to which it makes a telephone report under this subdivision. The agency shall send the licensing agency a copy of its investigation report and any other pertinent materials.

11166.3. Coordination of duties in connection with investigation of suspected child abuse or neglect cases

(a) The Legislature intends that in each county the law enforcement agencies and the county welfare or probation department shall develop and implement cooperative arrangements in order to coordinate existing duties in connection with the investigation of suspected child abuse or neglect cases. The local law enforcement agency having jurisdiction over a case reported under Section 11166 shall report to the county welfare or probation department that it is investigating the case within 36 hours after starting its investigation. The county welfare department or probation department shall, in cases where a minor is a victim of actions specified in Section 288 of this code and a petition has been filed pursuant to Section 300 of the Welfare and Institutions Code with regard to the minor, evaluate what action or actions would be in the best interest of the child victim. Notwithstanding any other provision of law, the county welfare department or probation department shall submit in writing its findings and the reasons therefor to the district attorney on or before the completion of the investigation. The written findings and the reasons therefor shall be delivered or made accessible to the defendant or his or her counsel in the manner specified in Section 859.

(b) The local law enforcement agency having jurisdiction over a case reported under Section 11166 shall report to the district office of the State Department of Social Services any case reported under this section if the case involves a facility specified in paragraph (5) or (6) of subdivision (a) of Section 1502, Section 1596.750 or 1596.76 of the Health and Safety Code, and the licensing of the facility has not been delegated to a county agency. The law enforcement agency shall send a copy of its investigation report and any other pertinent materials to the licensing agency upon the request of the licensing agency.

11166.5. Statement acknowledging awareness of reporting duties and promising compliance; Exemptions; Distribution in connection with licensure or certification

(a) (1) On and after January 1, 1985, any mandated reporter as specified in Section 11165.7, with the exception of child visitation monitors, prior to commencing his or her employment, and as a prerequisite to that employment, shall sign a statement on a form provided to him or her by his or her employer to the effect that he or she has knowledge of the provisions of Section 11166 and will comply with those provisions. The statement shall inform the employee that he or she is a mandated reporter and inform the employee of his or her reporting obligations under Section 11166 and of his or her confidentiality rights under subdivision (d) of Section 11167. The employer shall provide a copy of Sections 11165.7, 11166, and 11167 to the employee. On and after January 1, 1993, any person who acts as a child visitation monitor, as defined in paragraph (31) of subdivision (a) of Section 11165.7, prior to engaging in monitoring the first visit in a case, shall sign a statement on a form provided to him or her by the court which ordered the presence of that third person during the visit, to the effect that he or she has knowledge of the provisions of Section 11166 and will comply with those provisions.

(2) The signed statements shall be retained by the employer or the court, as the case may be. The cost of printing, distribution, and filing of these statements shall be borne by the employer or the court.

(3) This subdivision is not applicable to persons employed by public or private youth centers, youth recreation programs, and youth organizations as members of the support staff or maintenance staff and who do not work with, observe, or have knowledge of children as part of their official duties.
(b) On and after January 1, 1986, when a person is issued a state license or certificate to engage in a profession or occupation, the members of which are required to make a report pursuant to Section 11166, the state agency issuing the license or certificate shall send a statement substantially similar to the one contained in subdivision (a) to the person at the same time as it transmits the document indicating licensure or certification to the person. In addition to the requirements contained in subdivision (a), the statement also shall indicate that failure to comply with the requirements of Section 11166 is a misdemeanor, punishable by up to six months in a county jail, by a fine of one thousand dollars ($1,000), or by both that imprisonment and fine.
(c) As an alternative to the procedure required by subdivision (b), a state agency may cause the required statement to be printed on all application forms for a license or certificate printed on or after January 1, 1986.
(d) On and after January 1, 1993, any child visitation monitor, as defined in paragraph (31) of subdivision (a) of Section 11165.7, who desires to act in that capacity shall have received training in the duties imposed by this article, including training in child abuse identification and child abuse reporting. The person, prior to engaging in monitoring the first visit in a case, shall sign a statement on a form provided to him or her by the court which ordered the presence of that third person during the visit, to the effect that

he or she has received this training. This statement may be included in the statement required by subdivision (a) or it may be a separate statement.

This statement shall be filed, along with the statement required by subdivision (a), in the court file of the case for which the visitation monitoring is being provided.   (e) Any person providing services to a minor child, as described in paragraph (38) of subdivision (a) of Section 11165.7, shall not be required to make a report pursuant to Section 11166 unless that person has received training, or instructional materials in the appropriate language, on the duties imposed by this article, including identifying and reporting child abuse and neglect.

11167. Required information; Confidentiality of reporter's identity; Advising individual of complaint or allegations

(a) Reports of suspected child abuse or neglect pursuant to Section 11166 or Section 11166.05 shall include the name, business address, and telephone number of the mandated reporter; the capacity that makes the person a mandated reporter; and the information that gave rise to the reasonable suspicion of child abuse or neglect and the source or sources of that information. If a report is made, the following information, if known, shall also be included in the report: the child's name, the child's address, present location, and, if applicable, school, grade, and class; the names, addresses, and telephone numbers of the child's parents or guardians; and the name, address, telephone number, and other relevant personal information about the person or persons who might have abused or neglected the child. The mandated reporter shall make a report even if some of this information is not known or is uncertain to him or her.

(b) Information relevant to the incident of child abuse or neglect and information relevant to a report made pursuant to Section 11166.05 may be given to an investigator from an agency that is investigating the known or suspected case of child abuse or neglect.

(c) Information relevant to the incident of child abuse or neglect, including the investigation report and other pertinent materials, and information relevant to a report made pursuant to Section 11166.05 may be given to the licensing agency when it is investigating a known or suspected case of child abuse or neglect.

(d) (1) The identity of all persons who report under this article shall be confidential and disclosed only among agencies receiving or investigating mandated reports, to the prosecutor in a criminal prosecution or in an action initiated under Section 602 of the Welfare and Institutions Code arising from alleged child abuse, or to counsel appointed pursuant to subdivision (c) of Section 317 of the Welfare and Institutions Code, or to the county counsel or prosecutor in a proceeding under Part 4 (commencing with Section 7800) of Division 12 of the Family Code or Section 300 of the Welfare and Institutions Code, or to a licensing agency when abuse or neglect in out-of-home care is reasonably suspected, or when those persons waive confidentiality, or by court order.

(2) No agency or person listed in this subdivision shall disclose the identity of any person who reports under this article to that person's employer, except with the employee's consent or by court order. (e) Notwithstanding the confidentiality requirements of this section, a representative of a child protective services agency performing an investigation that results from a report of suspected child abuse or neglect made pursuant to Section 11166 or Section 11166.05, at the time of the initial contact with the individual who is subject to the investigation, shall advise the individual of the complaints or allegations against him or her, in a manner that is consistent with laws protecting the identity of the reporter under this article. (f) Persons who may report pursuant to subdivision (g) of Section 11166 are not required to include their names.

11167.5. Confidentiality and disclosure of reports

(a) The reports required by Sections 11166 and 11166.2, or authorized by Section 11166.05, and child abuse or neglect investigative reports that result in a summary report being filed with the Department of Justice pursuant to subdivision (a) of Section 11169 shall be confidential and may be disclosed only as provided in subdivision (b). Any violation of the confidentiality provided by this article is a misdemeanor punishable by imprisonment in a county jail not to exceed six months, by a fine of five hundred dollars ($500), or by both that imprisonment and fine. (b) Reports of suspected child abuse or neglect and information contained therein may be disclosed only to the following:

(1) Persons or agencies to whom disclosure of the identity of the reporting party is permitted under Section 11167.

(2) Persons or agencies to whom disclosure of information is permitted under subdivision (b) of Section 11170 or subdivision (a) of Section 11170.5.

(3) Persons or agencies with whom investigations of child abuse or neglect are coordinated under the regulations promulgated under Section 11174.

(4) Multidisciplinary personnel teams as defined in subdivision (d) of Section 18951 of the Welfare and Institutions Code.

(5) Persons or agencies responsible for the licensing of facilities which care for children, as specified in Section 11165.7.

(6) The State Department of Social Services or any county licensing agency which has contracted with the state, as specified in paragraph (4) of subdivision (b) of Section 11170, when an individual has applied for a community care license or child day care license, or for employment in an out-of-home care facility, or when a complaint alleges child abuse or neglect by an operator or employee of an out-of-home care facility.

(7) Hospital scan teams. As used in this paragraph, "hospital scan team"

means a team of three or more persons established by a hospital, or two or more hospitals in the same county, consisting of health care professionals and representatives of law enforcement and child protective services, the members of which are engaged in the identification of child abuse or neglect. The disclosure authorized by this section includes disclosure among all hospital scan teams.

(8) Coroners and medical examiners when conducting a post mortem examination of a child.

(9) The Board of Parole Hearings, which may subpoena an employee of a county welfare department who can provide relevant evidence and reports that both (A) are not unfounded, pursuant to Section 11165.12, and (B) concern only the current incidents upon which parole revocation proceedings are pending against a parolee charged with child abuse or neglect. The reports and information shall be confidential pursuant to subdivision (d) of Section 11167. (10) Personnel from an agency responsible for making a placement of a child pursuant to Section 361.3 of, and Article 7 (commencing with Section 305) of Chapter 2 of Part 1 of Division 2 of, the Welfare and Institutions Code.

(11) Persons who have been identified by the Department of Justice as listed in the Child Abuse Central Index pursuant to paragraph (7) of subdivision (b) of Section 11170 or subdivision (c) of Section 11170, or persons who have verified with the Department of Justice that they are listed in the Child Abuse Central Index as provided in subdivision (f) of Section 11170. Disclosure under this paragraph is required notwithstanding the California Public Records Act, Chapter 3.5 (commencing with Section 6250) of Division 7 of Title 1 of the Government Code. Nothing in this paragraph shall preclude a submitting agency prior to disclosure from redacting any information necessary to maintain confidentiality as required by law.

(12) Out-of-state law enforcement agencies conducting an investigation of child abuse or neglect only when an agency makes the request for reports of suspected child abuse or neglect in writing and on official letterhead, or as designated by the Department of Justice, identifying the suspected abuser or victim by name and date of birth or approximate age. The request shall be signed by the department supervisor of the requesting law enforcement agency. The written request shall cite the out-of-state statute or interstate compact provision that requires that the information contained within these reports is to be disclosed only to law enforcement, prosecutorial entities, or multidisciplinary investigative teams, and shall cite the safeguards in place to prevent unlawful disclosure provided by the requesting state or the applicable interstate compact provision.

(13) Out-of-state agencies responsible for approving prospective foster or adoptive parents for placement of a child only when the agency makes the request in compliance with the Adam Walsh Child Protection and Safety Act of 2006 (Public Law 109-248). The request shall also cite the safeguards in place to prevent unlawful disclosure provided by the

requesting state or the applicable interstate compact provision and indicate that the requesting state shall maintain continual compliance with the requirement in paragraph (20) of subdivision (a) of Section 671 of Title 42 of the United States Code that requires the state have in place safeguards to prevent the unauthorized disclosure of information in any child abuse and neglect registry maintained by the state and prevent the information from being used for a purpose other than the conducting of background checks in foster or adoptive placement cases.

(14) Each chairperson of a county child death review team, or his or her designee, to whom disclosure of information is permitted under this article, relating to the death of one or more children and any prior child abuse or neglect investigation reports maintained involving the same victim, siblings, or suspects. Local child death review teams may share any relevant information regarding case reviews involving child death with other child death review teams.   (c) Authorized persons within county health departments shall be permitted to receive copies of any reports made by health practitioners, as defined in paragraphs (21) to (28), inclusive, of subdivision (a) of Section 11165.7, and pursuant to Section 11165.13, and copies of assessments completed pursuant to Sections 123600 and 123605 of the Health and Safety Code, to the extent permitted by federal law. Any information received pursuant to this subdivision is protected by subdivision (e). (d) Nothing in this section requires the Department of Justice to disclose information contained in records maintained under Section 11170 or under the regulations promulgated pursuant to Section 11174, except as otherwise provided in this article.   (e) This section shall not be interpreted to allow disclosure of any reports or records relevant to the reports of child abuse or neglect if the disclosure would be prohibited by any other provisions of state or federal law applicable to the reports or records relevant to the reports of child abuse or neglect.

11168. Form of Written Report

The written reports required by Section 11166 shall be submitted on forms adopted by the Department of Justice after consultation with representatives of the various professional medical associations and hospital associations and county probation or welfare departments. Those forms shall be distributed by the agencies specified in Section 11165.9.

11169. Forwarding of reports to Department of Justice

(a) An agency specified in Section 11165.9 shall forward to the Department of Justice a report in writing of every case it investigates of known or suspected child abuse or severe neglect that is determined to be substantiated, other than cases coming within subdivision (b) of Section 11165.2. An agency shall not forward a report to the Department of Justice unless it has conducted an active investigation and determined that the report is substantiated, as defined in Section 11165.12. If a report has previously been filed which subsequently proves to be not substantiated, the Department of Justice shall be notified in writing of that fact and shall not retain the report. The reports required by this section shall be in a form approved by the Department of Justice and may be sent by fax or electronic transmission. An agency specified in Section 11165.9 receiving a written report from another agency specified in Section 11165.9 shall not send that report to the Department of Justice.

(b) On and after January 1, 2012, a police department or sheriff's department specified in Section 11165.9 shall no longer forward to the Department of Justice a report in writing of any case it investigates of known or suspected child abuse or severe neglect.

(c) At the time an agency specified in Section 11165.9 forwards a report in writing to the Department of Justice pursuant to subdivision (a), the agency shall also notify in writing the known or suspected child abuser that he or she has been reported to the Child Abuse Central Index (CACI).The notice required by this section shall be in a form approved by the Department of Justice. The requirements of this subdivision shall apply with respect to reports forwarded to the department on or after the date on which this subdivision becomes operative.

(d) Subject to subdivision (e), any person who is listed on the CACI has the right to a hearing before the agency that requested his or her inclusion in the CACI to challenge his or her listing on the CACI. The hearing shall satisfy due process requirements. It is the intent of the Legislature that the hearing provided for by this subdivision shall not be construed to be inconsistent with hearing proceedings available to persons who have been listed on the CACI prior to the enactment of the act that added this subdivision.

(e) A hearing requested pursuant to subdivision (d) shall be denied when a court of competent jurisdiction has determined that suspected child abuse or neglect has occurred, or when the allegation of child abuse or neglect resulting in the referral to the CACI is pending before the court. A person who is listed on the CACI and has been denied a hearing pursuant to this subdivision has a right to a hearing pursuant to subdivision (d) only if the court's jurisdiction has terminated, the court has not made a finding concerning whether the suspected child abuse or neglect was substantiated, and a hearing has not previously been provided to the listed person pursuant to subdivision (d).

(f) Any person listed in the CACI who has reached 100 years of age shall have his or her listing removed from the CACI.

(g) Any person listed in the CACI as of January 1, 2013, who was listed prior to reaching 18 years of age, and who is listed once in CACI with no subsequent listings, shall be removed from the CACI 10 years from the date of the incident resulting in the CACI listing.

(h) If, after a hearing pursuant to subdivision (d) or a court proceeding described in subdivision (e), it is determined the person' s CACI listing was based on a report that was not substantiated, the agency shall notify the Department of Justice of that result and the department shall remove that person's name from the CACI.

(i) Agencies, including police departments and sheriff's departments, shall retain child abuse or neglect investigative reports that result or resulted in a report filed with the Department of Justice pursuant to subdivision (a) for the same period of time that the information is required to be maintained on the CACI pursuant to this section and subdivision (a) of Section 11170. Nothing in this section precludes an agency from retaining the reports for a longer period of time if required by law.

(j) The immunity provisions of Section 11172 shall not apply to the submission of a report by an agency pursuant to this section. However, nothing in this section shall be construed to alter or diminish any other immunity provisions of state or federal law.

11170.5. Disclosure of Report Index to Adoption Agencies
(a) Notwithstanding paragraph (4) of subdivision (b) of Section 11170, the Department of Justice shall make available to a licensed adoption agency, as defined in Section 8530 of the Family Code, information regarding a known or suspected child abuser maintained in the Child Abuse Central Index, pursuant to subdivision (a) of Section 11170, concerning any person who has submitted to the agency an application for adoption.   (b) A licensed adoption agency, to which disclosure of any information pursuant to subdivision (a) is authorized, is responsible for obtaining the original investigative report from the reporting agency, and for drawing independent conclusions regarding the quality of the evidence disclosed and the sufficiency of the evidence for making decisions when evaluating an application for adoption.   (c) Whenever information contained in the Department of Justice files is furnished as the result of an application for adoption pursuant to subdivision (a), the Department of Justice may charge the agency making the request a fee. The fee shall not exceed the reasonable costs to the department of providing the information. The only increase shall be at a rate not to exceed the legislatively approved cost-of-living adjustment for the department. In no case shall the fee exceed fifteen dollars ($15).   All moneys received by the department pursuant to this subdivision shall be deposited in the Department of Justice Sexual Habitual Offender Fund pursuant to subparagraph (C) of paragraph (9) of subdivision (b) of Section 11170.

11171.5. Peace officer's application for order directing X-rays of
suspected child abuse or neglect victim (a) If a peace officer, in the course

of an investigation of child abuse or neglect, has reasonable cause to believe that the child has been the victim of physical abuse, the officer may apply to a magistrate for an order directing that the victim be X-rayed without parental consent. Any X-ray taken pursuant to this subdivision shall be administered by a physician and surgeon or dentist or their agents. (b) With respect to the cost of an X-ray taken by the county coroner or at the request of the county coroner in suspected child abuse or neglect cases, the county may charge the parent or legal guardian of the child-victim the costs incurred by the county for the X-ray. (c) No person who administers an X-ray pursuant to this section shall be entitled to reimbursement from the county for any administrative cost that exceeds 5 percent of the cost of the X-ray.

11172. Liability of person making report; Reimbursement by state of attorney fees incurred in defending action

(a) No mandated reporter shall be civilly or criminally liable for any report required or authorized by this article, and this immunity shall apply even if the mandated reporter acquired the knowledge or reasonable suspicion of child abuse or neglect outside of his or her professional capacity or outside the scope of his or her employment. Any other person reporting a known or suspected instance of child abuse or neglect shall not incur civil or criminal liability as a result of any report authorized by this article unless it can be proven that a false report was made and the person knew that the report was false or was made with reckless disregard of the truth or falsity of the report, and any person who makes a report of child abuse or neglect known to be false or with reckless disregard of the truth or falsity of the report is liable for any damages caused. No person required to make a report pursuant to this article, nor any person taking photographs at his or her direction, shall incur any civil or criminal liability for taking photographs of a suspected victim of child abuse or neglect, or causing photographs to be taken of a suspected victim of child abuse or neglect, without parental consent, or for disseminating the photographs, images, or material with the reports required by this article. However, this section shall not be construed to grant immunity from this liability with respect to any other use of the photographs.

(b) Any person, who, pursuant to a request from a government agency investigating a report of suspected child abuse or neglect, provides the requesting agency with access to the victim of a known or suspected instance of child abuse or neglect shall not incur civil or criminal liability as a result of providing that access.

(c) Any commercial computer technician, and any employer of any commercial computer technician, who, pursuant to a warrant from a law enforcement agency investigating a report of suspected child abuse or neglect, provides the law enforcement agency with a computer or computer component which contains possible evidence of a known or suspected instance of child abuse or neglect, shall not incur civil or criminal liability as a result of providing that computer or computer component to the law enforcement agency.

(d) (1) The Legislature finds that even though it has provided immunity from liability to persons required or authorized to make reports pursuant to this article, that immunity does not eliminate the possibility that actions may be brought against those persons based upon required or authorized reports. In order to further limit the financial hardship that those persons may incur as a result of fulfilling their legal responsibilities, it is necessary that they not be unfairly burdened by legal fees incurred in defending those actions. Therefore, a mandated reporter may present a claim to the California Victim Compensation and Government Claims Board for reasonable attorney's fees and costs incurred in any action against that person on the basis of making a report required or authorized by this article if the court has dismissed the action upon a demurrer or motion for summary judgment made by that person, or if he or she prevails in the action. The California Victim Compensation and Government Claims Board shall allow that claim if the requirements of this subdivision are met, and the claim shall be paid from an appropriation to be made for that purpose. Attorney's fees awarded pursuant to this section shall not exceed an hourly rate greater than the rate charged by the Attorney General of the State of California at the time the award is made and shall not exceed an aggregate amount of fifty thousand dollars ($50,000).

(2) This subdivision shall not apply if a public entity has provided for the defense of the action pursuant to Section 995 of the Government Code.

(e) A court may award attorney's fees and costs to a commercial film and photographic print processor when a suit is brought against the processor because of a disclosure mandated by this article and the court finds this suit to be frivolous

Minor Sexual Activity in Law

California Penal Code
261.5.

(a) Unlawful sexual intercourse is an act of sexual intercourse accomplished with a person who is not the spouse of the perpetrator, if the person is a minor. For the purposes of this section, a "minor" is a person under the age of 18 years and an "adult" is a person who is at least 18 years of age.

(b) Any person who engages in an act of unlawful sexual intercourse with a minor who is not more than three years older or three years younger than the perpetrator, is guilty of a misdemeanor.

(c) Any person who engages in an act of unlawful sexual intercourse with a minor who is more than three years younger than the perpetrator is guilty of either a misdemeanor or a felony, and shall be punished by imprisonment in a county jail not exceeding one year, or by imprisonment pursuant to subdivision (h) of Section 1170.

(d) Any person 21 years of age or older who engages in an act of unlawful sexual intercourse with a minor who is under 16 years of age is guilty of either a misdemeanor or a felony, and shall be punished by imprisonment in a county jail not exceeding one year, or by imprisonment pursuant to subdivision (h) of Section 1170 for two, three, or four years.

(e) (1) Notwithstanding any other provision of this section, an adult who engages in an act of sexual intercourse with a minor in violation of this section may be liable for civil penalties in the following amounts:

(A) An adult who engages in an act of unlawful sexual intercourse with a minor less than two years younger than the adult is liable for a civil penalty not to exceed two thousand dollars ($2,000).

(B) An adult who engages in an act of unlawful sexual intercourse with a minor at least two years younger than the adult is liable for a civil penalty not to exceed five thousand dollars ($5,000).

(C) An adult who engages in an act of unlawful sexual intercourse with a minor at least three years younger than the adult is liable for a civil penalty not to exceed ten thousand dollars ($10,000).

(D) An adult over the age of 21 years who engages in an act of unlawful sexual intercourse with a minor under 16 years of age is liable for a civil penalty not to exceed twenty-five thousand dollars ($25,000).

(2) The district attorney may bring actions to recover civil penalties pursuant to this subdivision. From the amounts collected for each case, an amount equal to the costs of pursuing the action shall be deposited with the treasurer of the county in which the judgment was entered, and the remainder shall be deposited in the Underage Pregnancy Prevention Fund, which is hereby created in the State Treasury. Amounts deposited in the Underage Pregnancy Prevention Fund may be used only for the purpose of preventing underage pregnancy upon appropriation by the Legislature.

(3) In addition to any punishment imposed under this section, the judge may assess a fine not to exceed seventy dollars ($70) against any person who violates this section with the proceeds of this fine to be used in accordance with Section 1463.23. The court shall, however, take into consideration the defendant's ability to pay, and no defendant shall be denied probation because of his or her inability to pay the fine permitted under this subdivision.

CHAPTER 7
MANDATED REPORTING - ADULTS

Because some adults are vulnerable to abuse, neglect and undue influence, laws and regulations have been put in place to protect this groups of individuals. In this chapter you will become familiar with age requirements for making reports on adults, considerations of disabilities or diagnosis as well as the process of making reports to agencies designated to receive reports for elder and dependent adult abuse.

To acquaint yourself with specific terms, this chapter includes the definitions for abandonment, abduction, abuse of an elder or dependent adult, Adult Protective Services, care custodian, clergy member, clients rights advocate, dependent adult, developmentally disabled person, elder, financial abuse, imminent danger, isolation, mental suffering, neglect, physical abuse and reasonable suspicion.

Reasonable Suspicion

So let's start off with reasonable suspicion. Welfare and Institutions Code 15610.65 cites "Reasonable Suspicion" as "an objectively reasonable suspicion that a person would entertain, based upon facts that could cause a reasonable person in a like position, drawing when appropriate upon his or her training and experience, to suspected abuse". This means regardless if you are a trainee or a licensed individual, if you suspect or have been informed of abuse, and the individual meets the criteria of an elder or dependent adult, a report needs to be made.

Dependent adult for this reason is someone who is between the ages of 18 and 64 years old and has a physical or mental limitation that restricts their ability to carry out normal activities i.e., activities of daily living (ADLs) or instrumental activities of daily living (IADLs). While a diagnosis alone does not make someone dependent, it should be taken into consideration with other factors. An elder is anyone that is 65 years or older and lives in California. The Elder does not have to have any physical or mental limitations.

Reporting Timeframes

When abuse or neglect is suspected, mandated reporters are required to make a report to the appropriate agency designed to accept reports for elder abuse (typically the local law enforcement and Adult Protective

Services Agency) as soon as possible by phone. A written report needs to be submitted within 2 working days. The form that needs to be submitted in writing either by mail or by fax is the SOC 341 'Report of Suspected Dependent Adult /Elder Abuse' form. Because of internet capabilities, if the report was originally made through the internet (as some agencies have converted the form to digital format) then no follow up written report needs to be mailed or faxed. This is the typical process for suspected or alleged abuse that takes place outside of a long-term care facility. Additional requirements are found within this chapter for those that are victims of abuse that took place inside a long-term care facility.

Required Information

Consistent with the information required on reporting forms for suspected child abuse as discussed in the prior chapter, information pertaining to both the victim and the suspect abuser should be reported in as much detail as possible on the reporting forms. Additionally mandated reporter information should be provided as appropriate so that law enforcement and Adult Protective Services investigators can follow up appropriately.

Reporters of suspected abuse or neglect should know that their names and information will be kept confidential throughout the process and it's only shared amongst other investigative agencies as necessary. Failure to make a report of suspected abuse can result in a misdemeanor conviction, a fine of $1,000 or both.

There are exceptions to making a report even when the individual meets age and dependency requirements. Welfare and Institutions Code Section 15630(b)(3)(A) essentially states that psychotherapists are not required to make a report of suspected abuse when the following exists:

> (1) The mandated reporter has been told by an elder or a dependent adult that he or she has experienced behavior constituting
> physical abuse (including sexual abuse), abandonment, isolation, financial abuse, abduction, or neglect (including self-neglect).
> (2) The mandated reporter is not aware of any independent evidence that corroborates the statement that the abuse has occurred.
> (3) The elder or the dependent adult has been diagnosed with a mental illness or dementia, or is the subject of a court-ordered conservatorship because of a mental illness or dementia.
> (4) In the exercise of clinical judgment, the physician and surgeon, the registered nurse, or the psychotherapist, as defined in
> Section 1010 of the Evidence Code, reasonably believes that the abuse did not occur.

Elder Abuse and Dependent Adult Civil Protection Act

Welfare & Institutions Code
15630. Legislative Findings

(a) The Legislature recognizes that elders and dependent adults may be subjected to abuse, neglect, or abandonment and that this state has a responsibility to protect these persons.

(b) The Legislature further recognizes that a significant number of these persons are elderly. The Legislature desires to direct special attention to the needs and problems of elderly persons, recognizing that these persons constitute a significant and identifiable segment of the population and that they are more subject to risks of abuse, neglect, and abandonment.

(c) The Legislature further recognizes that a significant number of these persons have developmental disabilities and that mental and verbal limitations often leave them vulnerable to abuse and incapable of asking for help and protection.

(d) The Legislature recognizes that most elders and dependent adults who are at the greatest risk of abuse, neglect, or abandonment by their families or caretakers suffer physical impairments and other poor health that place them in a dependent and vulnerable position.

(e) The Legislature further recognizes that factors which contribute to abuse, neglect, or abandonment of elders and dependent adults are economic instability of the family, resentment of caretaker responsibilities, stress on the caretaker, and abuse by the caretaker of drugs or alcohol.

(f) The Legislature declares that this state shall foster and promote community services for the economic, social, and personal well-being of its citizens in order to protect those persons described in this section.

(g) The Legislature further declares that uniform state guidelines, which specify when county adult protective service agencies are to investigate allegations of abuse of elders and dependent adults and the appropriate role of local law enforcement is necessary in order to ensure that a minimum level of protection is provided to elders and dependent adults in each county.

(h) The Legislature further finds and declares that infirm elderly persons and dependent adults are a disadvantaged class, that cases of abuse of these persons are seldom prosecuted as criminal matters, and few civil cases are brought in connection with this abuse due to problems of proof, court delays, and the lack of incentives to prosecute these suits.

(i) Therefore, it is the intent of the Legislature in enacting this chapter to provide that adult protective services agencies, local long-term care ombudsman programs, and local law enforcement agencies shall receive referrals or complaints from public or private agencies, from any mandated reporter submitting reports pursuant to Section 15630, or from any other source having reasonable cause to know that the welfare of an elder or dependent adult is endangered, and shall take any actions considered necessary to protect the elder or dependent adult and correct the situation and ensure the individual's safety.

(j) It is the further intent of the Legislature in adding Article 8.5 (commencing with Section 15657) to this chapter to enable interested persons to engage attorneys to take up the cause of abused elderly persons and dependent adults.

15601. Purpose of Act
The purposes of this act are to: (a) Require health practitioners, care custodians, clergy members, and employees of county adult protective services agencies and local law enforcement agencies to report known or suspected cases of abuse of elders and dependent adults and to encourage community members in general to do so.   (b) Collect information on the numbers of abuse victims, circumstances surrounding the act of abuse, and other data which will aid the state in establishing adequate services to aid all victims of abuse in a timely, compassionate manner.   (c) Provide for protection under the law for all those persons who report suspected cases of abuse, provided that the report is not made with malicious intent.

Definitions

Welfare & Institutions Code
15610. Abandonment
"Abandonment" means the desertion or willful forsaking of an elder or a dependent adult by anyone having care or custody of that person under circumstances in which a reasonable person would continue to provide care and custody.

15610.06. Abduction
"Abduction" means the removal from this state and the restraint from returning to this state, or the restraint from returning to this state, of any elder or dependent adult who does not have the capacity to consent to the removal from this state and the restraint from returning to this state, or the restraint from returning to this state, as well as the removal from this state or the restraint from returning to this state, of any conservatee without the consent of the conservator or the court.

15610.07. "Abuse of an elder or a dependent adult"

"Abuse of an elder or a dependent adult" means either of the following:
(a) Physical abuse, neglect, financial abuse, abandonment, isolation, abduction, or other treatment with resulting physical harm or pain or mental suffering.   (b) The deprivation by a care custodian of goods or services that are necessary to avoid physical harm or mental suffering.

15610.10. "Adult protective services"

Adult protective services" means those preventive and remedial activities performed on behalf of elders and dependent adults who are unable to protect their own interests, harmed or threatened with harm, caused physical or mental injury due to the action or inaction of another person or their own action as a result of ignorance, illiteracy, incompetence, mental limitation, substance abuse, or poor health, lacking in adequate food, shelter, or clothing, exploited of their income and resources, or deprived of entitlement due them.

15610.17. Care custodian

"Care custodian" means an administrator or an employee of any of the following public or private facilities or agencies, or persons providing care or services for elders or dependent adults, including members of the support staff and maintenance staff:
(a) Twenty-four-hour health facilities, as defined in Sections 1250, 1250.2, and 1250.3 of the Health and Safety Code.
(b) Clinics.
(c) Home health agencies.
(d) Agencies providing publicly funded in-home supportive services, nutrition services, or other home and community-based support services.
(e) Adult day health care centers and adult day care.
(f) Secondary schools that serve 18- to 22-year-old dependent adults and postsecondary educational institutions that serve dependent adults or elders.
(g) Independent living centers.
(h) Camps.
(i) Alzheimer's Disease day care resource centers.
(j) Community care facilities, as defined in Section 1502 of the Health and Safety Code, and residential care facilities for the elderly, as defined in Section 1569.2 of the Health and Safety Code.
(k) Respite care facilities.
(l) Foster homes.
(m) Vocational rehabilitation facilities and work activity centers.
(n) Designated area agencies on aging.
(o) Regional centers for persons with developmental disabilities.
(p) State Department of Social Services and State Department of Health Services licensing divisions.
(q) County welfare departments.

(r) Offices of patients' rights advocates and clients' rights advocates, including attorneys.   (s) The office of the long-term care ombudsman.

(t) Offices of public conservators, public guardians, and court investigators.

(u) Any protection or advocacy agency or entity that is designated by the Governor to fulfill the requirements and assurances of the following: (1) The federal Developmental Disabilities Assistance and Bill of Rights Act of 2000, contained in Chapter 144 (commencing with Section 15001) of Title 42 of the United States Code, for protection and advocacy of the rights of persons with developmental disabilities.   (2) The Protection and Advocacy for the Mentally Ill Individuals Act of 1986, as amended, contained in Chapter 114 (commencing with Section 10801) of Title 42 of the United States Code, for the protection and advocacy of the rights of persons with mental illness.

(v) Humane societies and animal control agencies.

(w) Fire departments.

(x) Offices of environmental health and building code enforcement.

(y) Any other protective, public, sectarian, mental health, or private assistance or advocacy agency or person providing health services or social services to elders or dependent adults.

15610.19. Clergy Member
"Clergy member" means a priest, minister, rabbi, religious practitioner, or similar functionary of a church, synagogue, temple, mosque, or recognized religious denomination or organization. "Clergy member" does not include unpaid volunteers whose principal occupation or vocation does not involve active or ordained ministry in a church, synagogue, temple, mosque, or recognized religious denomination or organization, and who periodically visit elder or dependent adults on behalf of that church, synagogue, temple, mosque, or recognized religious denomination or organization.

15610.20. Clients rights advocate
"Clients' rights advocate" means the individual or individuals assigned by a regional center or state hospital developmental center to be responsible for clients' rights assurance for persons with developmental disabilities.

15610.23. Dependent adult
(a) "Dependent adult" means any person between the ages of 18 and 64 years who resides in this state and who has physical or mental limitations that restrict his or her ability to carry out normal activities or to protect his or her rights, including, but not limited to, persons who have physical or developmental disabilities, or whose physical or mental abilities have diminished because of age.   (b) "Dependent adult" includes any person between the ages of 18 and 64 years who is admitted as an inpatient to a 24-hour health facility, as defined in Sections 1250, 1250.2, and 1250.3 of the Health and Safety Code.

15610.25. Developmentally disabled person
"Developmentally disabled person" means a person with a developmental disability specified by or as described in subdivision (a) of Section 4512.

15610.27. Elder
"Elder" means any person residing in this state, 65 years of age or older.

15610.30. Financial Abuse
(a) "Financial abuse" of an elder or dependent adult occurs when a person or entity does any of the following: (1) Takes, secretes, appropriates, obtains, or retains real or personal property of an elder or dependent adult for a wrongful use or with intent to defraud, or both.   (2) Assists in taking, secreting, appropriating, obtaining, or retaining real or personal property of an elder or dependent adult for a wrongful use or with intent to defraud, or both.   (3) Takes, secretes, appropriates, obtains, or retains, or assists in taking, secreting, appropriating, obtaining, or retaining, real or personal property of an elder or dependent adult by undue influence, as defined in Section 15610.70.

(b) A person or entity shall be deemed to have taken, secreted, appropriated, obtained, or retained property for a wrongful use if, among other things, the person or entity takes, secretes, appropriates, obtains, or retains the property and the person or entity knew or should have known that this conduct is likely to be harmful to the elder or dependent adult.

(c) For purposes of this section, a person or entity takes, secretes, appropriates, obtains, or retains real or personal property when an elder or dependent adult is deprived of any property right, including by means of an agreement, donative transfer, or testamentary bequest, regardless of whether the property is held directly or by a representative of an elder or dependent adult.

(d) For purposes of this section, "representative" means a person or entity that is either of the following: (1) A conservator, trustee, or other representative of the estate of an elder or dependent adult.   (2) An attorney-in-fact of an elder or dependent adult who acts within the authority of the power of attorney.

15610.35. Goods and services
"Goods and services necessary to avoid physical harm or mental suffering" include, but are not limited to, all of the following: (a) The provision of medical care for physical and mental health needs.   (b) Assistance in personal hygiene.   (c) Adequate clothing.   (d) Adequately heated and ventilated shelter.   (e) Protection from health and safety hazards.   (f) Protection from malnutrition, under those circumstances where the results

include, but are not limited to, malnutrition and deprivation of necessities or physical punishment.   (g) Transportation and assistance necessary to secure any of the needs set forth in subdivisions (a) to (f), inclusive.

15610.37. Health Practitioner
"Health practitioner" means a physician and surgeon, psychiatrist, psychologist, dentist, resident, intern, podiatrist, chiropractor, registered nurse, dental hygienist, licensed clinical social worker or associate clinical social worker, marriage and family therapist, licensed professional clinical counselor, or any other person who is currently licensed under Division 2 (commencing with Section 500) of the Business and Professions Code, any emergency medical technician I or II, paramedic, or person certified pursuant to Division 2.5 (commencing with Section 1797) of the Health and Safety Code, a psychological assistant registered pursuant to Section 2913 of the Business and Professions Code, a marriage and family therapist trainee, as defined in subdivision (c) of Section 4980.03 of the Business and Professions Code, an unlicensed marriage and family therapist intern registered under Section 4980.44 of the Business and Professions Code, a clinical counselor trainee, as defined in subdivision (g) of Section 4999.12 of the Business and Professions Code, a clinical counselor intern registered under Section 4999.42 of the Business and Professions Code, a state or county public health or social service employee who treats an elder or a dependent adult for any condition, or a coroner.

15610.39. Imminent Danger
"Imminent danger" means a substantial probability that an elder or dependent adult is in imminent or immediate risk of death or serious physical harm, through either his or her own action or inaction, or as a result of the action or inaction of another person.

15610.40. Investigation
"Investigation" means that activity undertaken to determine the validity of a report of elder or dependent adult abuse.

15610.43. Isolation
(a) "Isolation" means any of the following:
(1) Acts intentionally committed for the purpose of preventing, and that do serve to prevent, an elder or dependent adult from receiving his or her mail or telephone calls.
(2) Telling a caller or prospective visitor that an elder or dependent adult is not present, or does not wish to talk with the caller, or does not wish to meet with the visitor where the statement is false, is contrary to the express wishes of the elder or the dependent adult, whether he or she is competent or not, and is made for the purpose of preventing the elder or dependent adult from having contact with family, friends, or concerned persons.
(3) False imprisonment, as defined in Section 236 of the Penal Code.

(4) Physical restraint of an elder or dependent adult, for the purpose of preventing the elder or dependent adult from meeting with visitors.

(b) The acts set forth in subdivision (a) shall be subject to a rebuttable presumption that they do not constitute isolation if they are performed pursuant to the instructions of a physician and surgeon licensed to practice medicine in the state, who is caring for the elder or dependent adult at the time the instructions are given, and who gives the instructions as part of his or her medical care.

(c) The acts set forth in subdivision (a) shall not constitute isolation if they are performed in response to a reasonably perceived threat of danger to property or physical safety.

15610.53. Mental Suffering
"Mental suffering" means fear, agitation, confusion, severe depression, or other forms of serious emotional distress that is brought about by forms of intimidating behavior, threats, harassment, or by deceptive acts performed or false or misleading statements made with malicious intent to agitate, confuse, frighten, or cause severe depression or serious emotional distress of the elder or dependent adult.

15610.57. Neglect
(a) "Neglect" means either of the following: (1) The negligent failure of any person having the care or custody of an elder or a dependent adult to exercise that degree of care that a reasonable person in a like position would exercise.   (2) The negligent failure of an elder or dependent adult to exercise that degree of self care that a reasonable person in a like position would exercise.

(b) Neglect includes, but is not limited to, all of the following: (1) Failure to assist in personal hygiene, or in the provision of food, clothing, or shelter.   (2) Failure to provide medical care for physical and mental health needs. No person shall be deemed neglected or abused for the sole reason that he or she voluntarily relies on treatment by spiritual means through prayer alone in lieu of medical treatment.   (3) Failure to protect from health and safety hazards.   (4) Failure to prevent malnutrition or dehydration.   (5) Failure of an elder or dependent adult to satisfy the needs specified in paragraphs (1) to (4), inclusive, for himself or herself as a result of poor cognitive functioning, mental limitation, substance abuse, or chronic poor health.

15610.63. Physical Abuse
"Physical abuse" means any of the following:
(a) Assault, as defined in Section 240 of the Penal Code.
(b) Battery, as defined in Section 242 of the Penal Code.

(c) Assault with a deadly weapon or force likely to produce great bodily injury, as defined in Section 245 of the Penal Code.

(d) Unreasonable physical constraint, or prolonged or continual deprivation of food or water.

(e) Sexual assault, that means any of the following: (1) Sexual battery, as defined in Section 243.4 of the Penal Code. (2) Rape, as defined in Section 261 of the Penal Code. (3) Rape in concert, as described in Section 264.1 of the Penal Code. (4) Spousal rape, as defined in Section 262 of the Penal Code. (5) Incest, as defined in Section 285 of the Penal Code. (6) Sodomy, as defined in Section 286 of the Penal Code. (7) Oral copulation, as defined in Section 288a of the Penal Code. (8) Sexual penetration, as defined in Section 289 of the Penal Code. (9) Lewd or lascivious acts as defined in paragraph (2) of subdivision (b) of Section 288 of the Penal Code.

(f) Use of a physical or chemical restraint or psychotropic medication under any of the following conditions: (1) For punishment. (2) For a period beyond that for which the medication was ordered pursuant to the instructions of a physician and surgeon licensed in the State of California, who is providing medical care to the elder or dependent adult at the time the instructions are given. (3) For any purpose not authorized by the physician and surgeon.

15610.65. Reasonable suspicion

"Reasonable suspicion" means an objectively reasonable suspicion that a person would entertain, based upon facts that could cause a reasonable person in a like position, drawing when appropriate upon his or her training and experience, to suspect abuse.

Duty to Report & Timeline

Welfare & Institutions Code
15630. Mandated Reporter

(a) Any person who has assumed full or intermittent responsibility for the care or custody of an elder or dependent adult, whether or not he or she receives compensation, including administrators, supervisors, and any licensed staff of a public or private facility that provides care or services for elder or dependent adults, or any elder or dependent adult care custodian, health practitioner, clergy member, or employee of a county adult protective services agency or a local law enforcement agency, is a mandated reporter.

(b) (1) Any mandated reporter who, in his or her professional capacity, or within the scope of his or her employment, has observed or has knowledge of an incident that reasonably appears to be physical abuse, as defined in Section 15610.63, abandonment, abduction, isolation, financial abuse, or neglect, or is told by an elder or dependent adult that he or she has experienced behavior, including an act or omission, constituting physical abuse, as defined in Section 15610.63, abandonment, abduction, isolation, financial abuse, or neglect, or reasonably suspects that abuse, shall report the known or suspected instance of abuse by telephone or through a confidential Internet reporting tool, as authorized by Section 15658, immediately or as soon as practicably possible. If reported by telephone, a written report shall be sent, or an Internet report shall be made through the confidential Internet reporting tool established in Section 15658, within two working days, as follows:

(A) If the abuse has occurred in a long-term care facility, except a state mental health hospital or a state developmental center, the report shall be made to the local ombudsperson or the local law enforcement agency. The local ombudsperson and the local law enforcement agency shall, as soon as practicable, except in the case of an emergency or pursuant to a report required to be made pursuant to clause (v), in which case these actions shall be taken immediately, do all of the following:
(i) Report to the State Department of Public Health any case of known or suspected abuse occurring in a long-term health care facility, as defined in subdivision (a) of Section 1418 of the Health and Safety Code.
(ii) Report to the State Department of Social Services any case of known or suspected abuse occurring in a residential care facility for the elderly, as defined in Section 1569.2 of the Health and Safety Code, or in an adult day care facility, as defined in paragraph (2) of subdivision (a) of Section 1502.
(iii) Report to the State Department of Public Health and the California Department of Aging any case of known or suspected abuse occurring in an adult day health care center, as defined in subdivision (b) of Section 1570.7 of the Health and Safety Code.
(iv) Report to the Bureau of Medi-Cal Fraud and Elder Abuse any case of known or suspected criminal activity.
(v) Report all cases of known or suspected physical abuse and financial abuse to the local district attorney's office in the county where the abuse occurred.

(B) If the suspected or alleged abuse occurred in a state mental hospital or a state developmental center, the report shall be made to designated investigators of the State Department of State Hospitals or the State Department of Developmental Services, or to the local law enforcement agency. Except in an emergency, the local law enforcement agency shall, as soon as practicable, report any case of known or suspected criminal activity to the Bureau of Medi-Cal Fraud and Elder Abuse.

(C) If the abuse has occurred any place other than one described in subparagraph (A), the report shall be made to the adult protective services agency or the local law enforcement agency.

(2) (A) A mandated reporter who is a clergy member who acquires knowledge or reasonable suspicion of elder or dependent adult abuse during a penitential communication is not subject to paragraph (1). For purposes of this subdivision, "penitential communication" means a communication that is intended to be in confidence, including, but not limited to, a sacramental confession made to a clergy member who, in the course of the discipline or practice of his or her church, denomination, or organization is authorized or accustomed to hear those communications and under the discipline tenets, customs, or practices of his or her church, denomination, or organization, has a duty to keep those communications secret.

(B) Nothing in this subdivision shall be construed to modify or limit a clergy member's duty to report known or suspected elder and dependent adult abuse when he or she is acting in the capacity of a care custodian, health practitioner, or employee of an adult protective services agency.

(C) Notwithstanding any other provision in this section, a clergy member who is not regularly employed on either a full-time or part-time basis in a long-term care facility or does not have care or custody of an elder or dependent adult shall not be responsible for reporting abuse or neglect that is not reasonably observable or discernible to a reasonably prudent person having no specialized training or experience in elder or dependent care.

(3) (A) A mandated reporter who is a physician and surgeon, a registered nurse, or a psychotherapist, as defined in Section 1010 of the Evidence Code, shall not be required to report, pursuant to paragraph (1), an incident where all of the following conditions exist:

(i) The mandated reporter has been told by an elder or dependent adult that he or she has experienced behavior constituting physical abuse, as defined in Section 15610.63, abandonment, abduction, isolation, financial abuse, or neglect.

(ii) The mandated reporter is not aware of any independent evidence that corroborates the statement that the abuse has occurred.

(iii) The elder or dependent adult has been diagnosed with a mental illness or dementia, or is the subject of a court-ordered conservatorship because of a mental illness or dementia.

(iv) In the exercise of clinical judgment, the physician and surgeon, the registered nurse, or the psychotherapist, as defined in Section 1010 of the Evidence Code, reasonably believes that the abuse did not occur.

(B) This paragraph shall not be construed to impose upon mandated reporters a duty to investigate a known or suspected incident of abuse and shall not be construed to lessen or restrict any existing duty of mandated reporters.

(4) (A) In a long-term care facility, a mandated reporter shall not be required to report as a suspected incident of abuse, as defined in Section

15610.07, an incident where all of the following conditions exist:

(i) The mandated reporter is aware that there is a proper plan of care.

(ii) The mandated reporter is aware that the plan of care was properly provided or executed.

(iii) A physical, mental, or medical injury occurred as a result of care provided pursuant to clause (i) or (ii).

(iv) The mandated reporter reasonably believes that the injury was not the result of abuse.

(B) This paragraph shall not be construed to require a mandated reporter to seek, nor to preclude a mandated reporter from seeking, information regarding a known or suspected incident of abuse prior to reporting. This paragraph shall apply only to those categories of mandated reporters that the State Department of Public Health determines, upon approval by the Bureau of Medi-Cal Fraud and Elder Abuse and the state long-term care ombudsperson, have access to plans of care and have the training and experience necessary to determine whether the conditions specified in this section have been met.

(c) (1) Any mandated reporter who has knowledge, or reasonably suspects, that types of elder or dependent adult abuse for which reports are not mandated have been inflicted upon an elder or dependent adult, or that his or her emotional well-being is endangered in any other way, may report the known or suspected instance of abuse.

(2) If the suspected or alleged abuse occurred in a long-term care facility other than a state mental health hospital or a state developmental center, the report may be made to the long-term care ombudsperson program. Except in an emergency, the local ombudsperson shall report any case of known or suspected abuse to the State Department of Public Health and any case of known or suspected criminal activity to the Bureau of Medi-Cal Fraud and Elder Abuse, as soon as is practicable.

(3) If the suspected or alleged abuse occurred in a state mental health hospital or a state developmental center, the report may be made to the designated investigator of the State Department of State Hospitals or the State Department of Developmental Services or to a local law enforcement agency or to the local ombudsperson. Except in an emergency, the local ombudsperson and the local law enforcement agency shall report any case of known or suspected criminal activity to the Bureau of Medi-Cal Fraud and Elder Abuse, as soon as is practicable.

(4) If the suspected or alleged abuse occurred in a place other than a place described in paragraph (2) or (3), the report may be made to the county adult protective services agency.

(5) If the conduct involves criminal activity not covered in subdivision (b), it may be immediately reported to the appropriate law enforcement agency.

(d) When two or more mandated reporters are present and jointly have knowledge or reasonably suspect that types of abuse of an elder or a dependent adult for which a report is or is not mandated have occurred, and when there is agreement among them, the telephone report or Internet report, as authorized by Section 15658, may be made by a member of the team selected by mutual agreement, and a single report may be made and signed by the selected member of the reporting team. Any member who has knowledge that the member designated to report has failed to do so shall thereafter make the report.

(e) A telephone report or Internet report, as authorized by Section 15658, of a known or suspected instance of elder or dependent adult abuse shall include, if known, the name of the person making the report, the name and age of the elder or dependent adult, the present location of the elder or dependent adult, the names and addresses of family members or any other adult responsible for the elder's or dependent adult's care, the nature and extent of the elder' s or dependent adult's condition, the date of the incident, and any other information, including information that led that person to suspect elder or dependent adult abuse, as requested by the agency receiving the report.

(f) The reporting duties under this section are individual, and no supervisor or administrator shall impede or inhibit the reporting duties, and no person making the report shall be subject to any sanction for making the report. However, internal procedures to facilitate reporting, ensure confidentiality, and apprise supervisors and administrators of reports may be established, provided they are not inconsistent with this chapter.

(g) (1) Whenever this section requires a county adult protective services agency to report to a law enforcement agency, the law enforcement agency shall, immediately upon request, provide a copy of its investigative report concerning the reported matter to that county adult protective services agency.
(2) Whenever this section requires a law enforcement agency to report to a county adult protective services agency, the county adult protective services agency shall, immediately upon request, provide to that law enforcement agency a copy of its investigative report concerning the reported matter.
(3) The requirement to disclose investigative reports pursuant to this subdivision shall not include the disclosure of social services records or case files that are confidential, nor shall this subdivision be construed to allow disclosure of any reports or records if the disclosure would be prohibited by any other provision of state or federal law.

(h) Failure to report, or impeding or inhibiting a report of, physical abuse, as defined in Section 15610.63, abandonment, abduction, isolation, financial abuse, or neglect of an elder or dependent adult, in violation of this section, is a misdemeanor, punishable by not more than six months in the county jail, by a fine of not more than one thousand dollars ($1,000), or by both that fine and imprisonment. Any mandated reporter who willfully fails to report, or impedes or inhibits a report of, physical abuse, as defined in Section 15610.63, abandonment, abduction, isolation, financial abuse, or neglect of an elder or dependent adult, in violation of this section, where that abuse results in death or great bodily injury, shall be punished by not more than one year in a county jail, by a fine of not more than five thousand dollars ($5,000), or by both that fine and imprisonment. If a mandated reporter intentionally conceals his or her failure to report an incident known by the mandated reporter to be abuse or severe neglect under this section, the failure to report is a continuing offense until a law enforcement agency specified in paragraph (1) of subdivision (b) of Section 15630 discovers the offense.

(i) For purposes of this section, "dependent adult" shall have the same meaning as in Section 15610.23.

15630.1. Mandated Reporter of Suspected Financial Abuse

(a) As used in this section, "mandated reporter of suspected financial abuse of an elder or dependent adult" means all officers and employees of financial institutions.

(b) As used in this section, the term "financial institution" means any of the following:
(1) A depository institution, as defined in Section 3(c) of the Federal Deposit Insurance Act (12 U.S.C. Sec. 1813(c)).
(2) An institution-affiliated party, as defined in Section 3(u) of the Federal Deposit Insurance Act (12 U.S.C. Sec. 1813(u)).
(3) A federal credit union or state credit union, as defined in Section 101 of the Federal Credit Union Act (12 U.S.C. Sec. 1752), including, but not limited to, an institution-affiliated party of a credit union, as defined in Section 206(r) of the Federal Credit Union Act (12 U.S.C. Sec. 1786(r)).

(c) As used in this section, "financial abuse" has the same meaning as in Section 15610.30.

(d) (1) Any mandated reporter of suspected financial abuse of an elder or dependent adult who has direct contact with the elder or dependent adult or who reviews or approves the elder or dependent adult's financial documents, records, or transactions, in connection with providing financial services with respect to an elder or dependent adult, and who, within the scope of his or her employment or professional practice, has observed or has knowledge of an incident, that is directly related to the transaction or matter that is within that scope of employment or professional practice, that reasonably appears to be financial abuse, or who reasonably suspects that abuse, based solely on the information before him or her at the time of reviewing or approving the document, record, or transaction in the case of mandated reporters who do not have direct contact with the elder or dependent adult, shall report the known or suspected instance of financial abuse by telephone or through a confidential Internet reporting tool, as authorized pursuant to Section 15658, immediately, or as soon as practicably possible. If reported by telephone, a written report shall be sent, or an Internet report shall be made through the confidential Internet reporting tool established in Section 15658, within two working days to the local adult protective services agency or the local law enforcement agency.

(2) When two or more mandated reporters jointly have knowledge or reasonably suspect that financial abuse of an elder or a dependent adult for which the report is mandated has occurred, and when there is an agreement among them, the telephone report or Internet report, as authorized by Section 15658, may be made by a member of the reporting team who is selected by mutual agreement. A single report may be made and signed by the selected member of the reporting team. Any member of the team who has knowledge that the member designated to report has failed to do so shall thereafter make that report.

(3) If the mandated reporter knows that the elder or dependent adult resides in a long-term care facility, as defined in Section 15610.47, the report shall be made to the local ombudsman or local law enforcement agency.

(e) An allegation by the elder or dependent adult, or any other person, that financial abuse has occurred is not sufficient to trigger the reporting requirement under this section if both of the following conditions are met:

(1) The mandated reporter of suspected financial abuse of an elder or dependent adult is aware of no other corroborating or independent evidence of the alleged financial abuse of an elder or dependent adult. The mandated reporter of suspected financial abuse of an elder or dependent adult is not required to investigate any accusations.

(2) In the exercise of his or her professional judgment, the mandated reporter of suspected financial abuse of an elder or dependent adult reasonably believes that financial abuse of an elder or dependent adult did not occur.

(f) Failure to report financial abuse under this section shall be subject to a civil penalty not exceeding one thousand dollars ($1,000) or if the failure to report is willful, a civil penalty not exceeding five thousand dollars ($5,000), which shall be paid by the financial institution that is the employer of the mandated reporter to the party bringing the action. Subdivision (h) of Section 15630 shall not apply to violations of this section.

(g) (1) The civil penalty provided for in subdivision (f) shall be recovered only in a civil action brought against the financial institution by the Attorney General, district attorney, or county counsel. No action shall be brought under this section by any person other than the Attorney General, district attorney, or county counsel. Multiple actions for the civil penalty may not be brought for the same violation.

(2) Nothing in the Financial Elder Abuse Reporting Act of 2005 shall be construed to limit, expand, or otherwise modify any civil liability or remedy that may exist under this or any other law.

(h) As used in this section, "suspected financial abuse of an elder or dependent adult" occurs when a person who is required to report under subdivision (a) observes or has knowledge of behavior or unusual circumstances or transactions, or a pattern of behavior or unusual circumstances or transactions, that would lead an individual with like training or experience, based on the same facts, to form a reasonable belief that an elder or dependent adult is the victim of financial abuse as defined in Section 15610.30.

(i) Reports of suspected financial abuse of an elder or dependent adult made by an employee or officer of a financial institution pursuant to this section are covered under subdivision (b) of Section 47 of the Civil Code.

15631. Permissive Reporting

(a) Any person who is not a mandated reporter under Section 15630, who knows, or reasonably suspects, that an elder or a dependent adult has been the victim of abuse may report that abuse to a long-term care ombudsman program or local law enforcement agency when the abuse is alleged to have occurred in a long-term care facility.

(b) Any person who is not a mandated reporter under Section 15630, who knows, or reasonably suspects, that an elder or a dependent adult has been the victim of abuse in any place other than a long-term care facility may report the abuse to the county adult protective services agency or local law enforcement agency.

15632. Waiver of Privilege

(a) In any court proceeding or administrative hearing, neither the physician-patient privilege nor the psychotherapist-patient privilege applies to the specific information reported pursuant to this chapter.

(b) Nothing in this chapter shall be interpreted as requiring an attorney to violate his or her oath and duties pursuant to Section 6067 or subdivision (e) of Section 6068 of the Business and Professions Code, and Article 3 (commencing with Section 950) of Chapter 4 of Division 8 of the Evidence Code.

Confidentiality of Reports

15633. Confidentiality of Reports

(a) The reports made pursuant to Sections 15630, 15630.1, and 15631 shall be confidential and may be disclosed only as provided in subdivision (b).

Any violation of the confidentiality required by this chapter is a misdemeanor punishable by not more than six months in the county jail, by a fine of five hundred dollars ($500), or by both that fine and imprisonment.
(b) Reports of suspected abuse of an elder or dependent adult and information contained therein may be disclosed only to the following:
(1) Persons or agencies to whom disclosure of information or the identity of the reporting party is permitted under Section 15633.5.
(2) (A) Persons who are trained and qualified to serve on multidisciplinary personnel teams may disclose to one another information and records that are relevant to the prevention, identification, or treatment of abuse of elderly or dependent persons.
(B) Except as provided in subparagraph (A), any personnel of the multidisciplinary team or agency that receives information pursuant to this chapter, shall be under the same obligations and subject to the same confidentiality penalties as the person disclosing or providing that information. The information obtained shall be maintained in a manner that ensures the maximum protection of privacy and confidentiality rights.
(c) This section shall not be construed to allow disclosure of any reports or records relevant to the reports of abuse of an elder or dependent adult if the disclosure would be prohibited by any other provisions of state or federal law applicable to the reports or records relevant to the reports of the abuse, nor shall it be construed to prohibit the disclosure by a financial institution of any reports or records relevant to the reports of abuse of an elder or dependent adult if the disclosure would be required of a financial institution by otherwise applicable state or federal law or court order.

15633.5. Means of Discharging Duty to Report
(a) Information relevant to the incident of elder or dependent adult abuse may be given to an investigator from an adult protective services agency, a local law enforcement agency, the office of the district attorney, the office of the public guardian, the probate court, the bureau, or an investigator of the Department of Consumer Affairs, Division of Investigation who is investigating a known or suspected case of elder or dependent adult abuse.
(b) The identity of any person who reports under this chapter shall be confidential and disclosed only among the following agencies or persons representing an agency:
(1) An adult protective services agency.
(2) A long-term care ombudsperson program.
(3) A licensing agency.
(4) A local law enforcement agency.
(5) The office of the district attorney.
(6) The office of the public guardian.
(7) The probate court.
(8) The bureau.
(9) The Department of Consumer Affairs, Division of Investigation.

(10) Counsel representing an adult protective services agency.

(c) The identity of a person who reports under this chapter may also be disclosed under the following circumstances:

(1) To the district attorney in a criminal prosecution.

(2) When a person reporting waives confidentiality.

(3) By court order.

(d) Notwithstanding subdivisions (a), (b), and (c), any person reporting pursuant to Section 15631 shall not be required to include his or her name in the report.

15634. Immunity for Making Mandated or Authorized Report

(a) No care custodian, clergy member, health practitioner, mandated reporter of suspected financial abuse of an elder or dependent adult, or employee of an adult protective services agency or a local law enforcement agency who reports a known or suspected instance of abuse of an elder or dependent adult shall be civilly or criminally liable for any report required or authorized by this article. Any other person reporting a known or suspected instance of abuse of an elder or dependent adult shall not incur civil or criminal liability as a result of any report authorized by this article, unless it can be proven that a false report was made and the person knew that the report was false. No person required to make a report pursuant to this article, or any person taking photographs at his or her discretion, shall incur any civil or criminal liability for taking photographs of a suspected victim of abuse of an elder or dependent adult or causing photographs to be taken of such a suspected victim or for disseminating the photographs with the reports required by this article. However, this section shall not be construed to grant immunity from this liability with respect to any other use of the photographs.

(b) No care custodian, clergy member, health practitioner, mandated reporter of suspected financial abuse of an elder or dependent adult, or employee of an adult protective services agency or a local law enforcement agency who, pursuant to a request from an adult protective services agency or a local law enforcement agency investigating a report of known or suspected abuse of an elder or dependent adult, provides the requesting agency with access to the victim of a known or suspected instance of abuse of an elder or dependent adult, shall incur civil or criminal liability as a result of providing that access.

(c) The Legislature finds that, even though it has provided immunity from liability to persons required to report abuse of an elder or dependent adult, immunity does not eliminate the possibility that actions may be brought against those persons based upon required reports of abuse. In order to further limit the financial hardship that those persons may incur as a result of fulfilling their legal responsibilities, it is necessary that they not be unfairly burdened by legal fees incurred in defending those actions. Therefore, a care custodian, clergy member, health practitioner, or an employee of an adult protective services agency or a local law enforcement agency may present to the California Victim Compensation and Government Claims Board a claim for reasonable attorneys' fees incurred in any action against that person on the basis of making a report required or authorized by this article if the court has dismissed the action upon a demurrer or motion for summary judgment made by that person, or if he or she prevails in the action. The California Victim Compensation and Government Claims Board shall allow that claim if the requirements of this subdivision are met, and the claim shall be paid from an appropriation to be made for that purpose. Attorneys' fees awarded pursuant to this section shall not exceed an hourly rate greater than the rate charged by the Attorney General at the time the award is made and shall not exceed an aggregate amount of fifty thousand dollars ($50,000). This subdivision shall not apply if a public entity has provided for the defense of the action pursuant to Section 995 of the Government Code.

15636. Consent of Victim Required for Other Than Criminal Allegation
(a) Any victim of elder or dependent adult abuse may refuse or withdraw consent at any time to an investigation or the provision of protective services by an adult protective services agency or long-term care ombudsman program. The adult protective services agency shall act only with the consent of the victim unless a violation of the Penal Code has been alleged. A local long-term care ombudsman shall act only with the consent of the victim and shall disclose confidential information only after consent to disclose is given by the victim or pursuant to court order.

(b) If the elder or dependent adult abuse victim is so incapacitated that he or she cannot legally give or deny consent to protective services, a petition for temporary conservatorship or guardianship may be initiated in accordance with Section 2250 of the Probate Code.

15637. Waiver of Privilege
In any court proceeding or administrative hearing, neither the physician-patient privilege nor the psychotherapist-patient privilege applies to the specific information required to be reported pursuant to this chapter. Nothing in this chapter shall be interpreted as requiring an attorney to violate his or her oath and duties pursuant to Section 6067 or subdivision (e) of Section 6068 of the Business and Professions Code, and Article 3 (commencing with Section 950) of Chapter 4 of Division 8 of the Evidence Code.

Local Agency Cross-Reporting

15640. Duty of Adult Protective Services, Ombudsman and Law Enforcement To Investigate and Report
(a) (1) An adult protective services agency shall immediately, or as soon as

practically possible, report by telephone to the law enforcement agency having jurisdiction over the case any known or suspected instance of criminal activity, and to any public agency given responsibility for investigation in that jurisdiction of cases of elder and dependent adult abuse, every known or suspected instance of abuse pursuant to Section 15630 or 15630.1 of an elder or dependent adult. A county adult protective services agency shall also send a written report thereof within two working days of receiving the information concerning the incident to each agency to which it is required to make a telephone report under this subdivision. Prior to making any cross-report of allegations of financial abuse to law enforcement agencies, an adult protective services agency shall first determine whether there is reasonable suspicion of any criminal activity.

(2) If an adult protective services agency receives a report of abuse alleged to have occurred in a long-term care facility, that adult protective services agency shall immediately inform the person making the report that he or she is required to make the report to the long-term care ombudsman program or to a local law enforcement agency. The adult protective services agency shall not accept the report by telephone but shall forward any written report received to the long-term care ombudsman.

(b) If an adult protective services agency or local law enforcement agency or ombudsman program receiving a report of known or suspected elder or dependent adult abuse determines, pursuant to its investigation, that the abuse is being committed by a health practitioner licensed under Division 2 (commencing with Section 500) of the Business and Professions Code, or any related initiative act, or by a person purporting to be a licensee, the adult protective services agency or local law enforcement agency or ombudsman program shall immediately, or as soon as practically possible, report this information to the appropriate licensing agency. The licensing agency shall investigate the report in light of the potential for physical harm. The transmittal of information to the appropriate licensing agency shall not relieve the adult protective services agency or local law enforcement agency or ombudsman program of the responsibility to continue its own investigation as required under applicable provisions of law. The information reported pursuant to this paragraph shall remain confidential and shall not be disclosed.

(c) A local law enforcement agency shall immediately, or as soon as practically possible, report by telephone to the long-term care ombudsman program when the abuse is alleged to have occurred in a long-term care facility or to the county adult protective services agency when it is alleged to have occurred anywhere else, and to the agency given responsibility for the investigation of cases of elder and dependent adult abuse every known or suspected instance of abuse of an elder or dependent adult. A local law enforcement agency shall also send a written report thereof within two working days of receiving the information concerning the incident to any agency to which it is required to make a telephone report under this subdivision.

(d) A long-term care ombudsman coordinator may report the instance of abuse to the county adult protective services agency or to the local law enforcement agency for assistance in the investigation of the abuse if the victim gives his or her consent. A long-term care ombudsman program and the Licensing and Certification Division of the State Department of Public Health shall immediately report by telephone and in writing within two working days to the bureau any instance of neglect occurring in a health care facility, that has seriously harmed any patient or reasonably appears to present a serious threat to the health or physical well-being of a patient in that facility. If a victim or potential victim of the neglect withholds consent to being identified in that report, the report shall contain circumstantial information about the neglect but shall not identify that victim or potential victim and the bureau and the reporting agency shall maintain the confidentiality of the report until the report becomes a matter of public record.

(e) When a county adult protective services agency, a long-term care ombudsman program, or a local law enforcement agency receives a report of abuse, neglect, or abandonment of an elder or dependent adult alleged to have occurred in a long-term care facility, that county adult protective services agency, long-term care ombudsman coordinator, or local law enforcement agency shall report the incident to the licensing agency by telephone as soon as possible.

(f) County adult protective services agencies, long-term care ombudsman programs, and local law enforcement agencies shall report the results of their investigations of referrals or reports of abuse to the respective referring or reporting agencies.

Prosecution of Elder and Dependent Adult Abuse Cases

15656. Elder or Dependent Adult Abuse Criminal Penalties
(a) Any person who knows or reasonably should know that a person is an elder or dependent adult and who, under circumstances or conditions likely to produce great bodily harm or death, willfully causes or permits any elder or dependent adult to suffer, or inflicts unjustifiable physical pain or mental suffering upon him or her, or having the care or custody of any elder or dependent adult, willfully causes or permits the person or health of the elder or dependent adult to be injured, or willfully causes or permits the elder or dependent adult to be placed in a situation such that his or her person or health is endangered, is punishable by imprisonment in the

county jail not exceeding one year, or in the state prison for two, three, or four years.

(b) Any person who knows or reasonably should know that a person is an elder or dependent adult and who, under circumstances or conditions other than those likely to produce great bodily harm or death, willfully causes or permits any elder or dependent adult to suffer, or inflicts unjustifiable physical pain or mental suffering on him or her, or having the care or custody of any elder or dependent adult, willfully causes or permits the person or health of the elder or dependent adult to be injured or willfully causes or permits the elder or dependent adult to be placed in a situation such that his or her person or health may be endangered, is guilty of a misdemeanor.

(c) Any caretaker of an elder or a dependent adult who violates any provision of law prescribing theft or embezzlement, with respect to the property of that elder or dependent adult, is punishable by imprisonment in the county jail not exceeding one year, or in the state prison for two, three, or four years when the money, labor, or real or personal property taken is of a value exceeding nine hundred fifty dollars ($950), and by a fine not exceeding one thousand dollars ($1,000), or by imprisonment in the county jail not exceeding one year, or by both that imprisonment and fine, when the money, labor, or real or personal property taken is of a value not exceeding nine hundred fifty dollars ($950).

(d) As used in this section, "caretaker" means any person who has the care, custody, or control of or who stands in a position of trust with, an elder or a dependent adult.

(e) Conduct covered in subdivision (b) of Section 15610.57 shall not be subject to this section.

15657. Adult Abuse Enhanced Civil Penalties

Where it is proven by clear and convincing evidence that a defendant is liable for physical abuse as defined in Section 15610.63, or neglect as defined in Section 15610.57, and that the defendant has been guilty of recklessness, oppression, fraud, or malice in the commission of this abuse, the following shall apply, in addition to all other remedies otherwise provided by law:

(a) The court shall award to the plaintiff reasonable attorney's fees and costs. The term "costs" includes, but is not limited to, reasonable fees for the services of a conservator, if any, devoted to the litigation of a claim brought under this article.

(b) The limitations imposed by Section 377.34 of the Code of Civil Procedure on the damages recoverable shall not apply. However, the damages recovered shall not exceed the damages permitted to be recovered pursuant to subdivision (b) of Section 3333.2 of the Civil Code.

(c) The standards set forth in subdivision (b) of Section 3294 of the Civil Code regarding the imposition of punitive damages on an employer based upon the acts of an employee shall be satisfied before any damages or attorney's fees permitted under this section may be imposed against an employer.

15657.05. Abduction Enhanced Civil Penalties

Where it is proven by clear and convincing evidence that an individual is liable for abduction, as defined in Section 15610.06, in addition to all other remedies otherwise provided by law:

(a) (1) The court shall award to the plaintiff reasonable attorney's fees and costs. The term "costs" shall include, but is not limited to, costs of representing the abductee and his or her family in this state and any other state in any action related to the abduction and returning of the abductee to this state, as well as travel expenses for returning the abductee to this state and reasonable fees for the services of a conservator, if any, devoted to the litigation of a claim brought under this article.

(2) The award of attorney's fees shall be governed by the principles set forth in Section 15657.1.

(b) The limitations imposed by Section 377.34 of the Code of Civil Procedure on the damages recoverable shall not apply. However, the damages recovered shall not exceed the damages permitted to be recovered pursuant to subdivision (b) of Section 3333.2 of the Civil Code.

(c) The standards set forth in subdivision (b) of Section 3294 of the Civil Code regarding the imposition of punitive damages on an employer based upon the acts of an employee shall be satisfied before any damages or attorney's fees permitted under this section may be imposed against an employer.

15657.5. Financial Abuse Enhanced Civil Penalties

(a) Where it is proven by a preponderance of the evidence that a defendant is liable for financial abuse, as defined in Section 15610.30, in addition to compensatory damages and all other remedies otherwise provided by law, the court shall award to the plaintiff reasonable attorney's fees and costs. The term "costs" includes, but is not limited to, reasonable fees for the services of a conservator, if any, devoted to the litigation of a claim brought under this article.

(b) Where it is proven by a preponderance of the evidence that a defendant is liable for financial abuse, as defined in Section 15610.30, and where it is proven by clear and convincing evidence that the defendant has been guilty of recklessness, oppression, fraud, or malice in the commission of the abuse, in addition to reasonable attorney's fees and costs set forth in subdivision (a), compensatory damages, and all other remedies otherwise provided by law, the limitations imposed by Section 377.34 of the Code of Civil Procedure on the damages recoverable shall not apply.

(c) The standards set forth in subdivision (b) of Section 3294 of the Civil Code regarding the imposition of punitive damages on an employer based upon the acts of an employee shall be satisfied before any punitive damages may be imposed against an employer found liable for financial abuse as defined in Section 15610.30. This subdivision shall not apply to the recovery of compensatory damages or attorney' s fees and costs.

(d) Nothing in this section affects the award of punitive damages under Section 3294 of the Civil Code.

(e) Any money judgment in an action under this section shall include a statement that the damages are awarded based on a claim for financial abuse of an elder or dependent adult, as defined in Section 15610.30. If only part of the judgment is based on that claim, the judgment shall specify what amount was awarded on that basis.

Reporting Forms

15658. Manner of Reporting

(1) On a form adopted by the State Department of Social Services after consultation with representatives of the various law enforcement agencies, the California Department of Aging, the State Department of Developmental Services, the State Department of Mental Health, the bureau, professional medical and nursing agencies, hospital associations, and county welfare departments. These reporting forms shall be distributed by the county adult protective services agencies and the long-term care ombudsman programs. This reporting form may also be used for documenting the telephone report of a known or suspected instance of abuse of an elder or dependent adult by the county adult protective services agency, local ombudsman program, and local law enforcement agencies.

(2) Through a confidential Internet reporting tool, if the county or long-term care ombudsman program chooses to implement such a system. This Internet reporting tool shall be developed and implemented in a manner that ensures the confidentiality and security of all information contained in the reports, pursuant to the confidentiality standards set forth in Sections 10850, 15633, and 15633.5.

(A) A county or long-term care ombudsman program that chooses to implement this system shall report to the Assembly Committee on Aging and Long-Term Care, the Assembly Committee on Human Services, the Senate Committee on Human Services, the Assembly Committee on Public Safety, and the Senate Committee on Public Safety one year after full implementation. The report shall include changes in the number of mandated reporters reporting through the confidential Internet reporting tool, changes in the number of abandoned calls, and any other quantitative or qualitative data that indicates the success, or lack thereof, in employing a confidential Internet reporting tool to better protect the safety and financial security of elder and dependent adults.

(B) Information sent and received through the confidential Internet reporting tool shall be used only for its intended purpose and shall be subject to the same confidentiality and privacy requirements that govern nonelectronic transmission of the same information, and that are set forth in Sections 10850, 15633, and 15633.5.

(b) The form required by this section and the confidential Internet reporting tool, if implemented, shall contain the following items:
(1) The name, address, telephone number, and occupation of the person reporting.
(2) The name and address of the victim.
(3) The date, time, and place of the incident.
(4) Other details, including the reporter's observations and beliefs concerning the incident.
(5) Any statement relating to the incident made by the victim.
(6) The name of any individuals believed to have knowledge of the incident.
(7) The name of the individuals believed to be responsible for the incident and their connection to the victim.

(c) (1) Each county adult protective services agency shall report to the State Department of Social Services monthly on the reports received pursuant to this chapter. The reports shall be made on forms adopted by the department. The information reported shall include, but shall not be limited to, the number of incidents of abuse, the number of persons abused, the type of abuse sustained, and the actions taken on the reports. For purposes of these reports, sexual abuse shall be reported separately from physical abuse.
(2) The county's report to the department shall not include reports it receives from the long-term care ombudsman program pursuant to subdivision (d).
(3) The department shall refer to the bureau monthly data summaries of the reports of elder and dependent adult abuse, neglect, abandonment, isolation, financial abuse, and other abuse it receives from county adult protective services agencies.

(d) Each long-term care ombudsman program shall report to the Office of the State Long-Term Care Ombudsman of the California Department of Aging monthly on the reports it receives pursuant to this chapter and shall send a copy to the county adult protective services agency. The Office of the State Long-Term Care Ombudsman shall submit a summarized quarterly report to the department based on the monthly reports submitted by local long-term care ombudsman programs. The reports shall be on forms adopted by the department and the Office of the State Long-Term Care Ombudsman. The information reported shall include, but shall not be limited to, the number of incidents of abuse, the numbers of persons abused, the type of abuse, and the actions taken on the reports. For purposes of these reports, sexual abuse shall be reported separately from physical abuse.

Employee Statement

15659. Employee Statement – Acknowledgement of Mandated Reporter Status

(a) Any person who enters into employment on or after January 1, 1995, as a care custodian, clergy member, health practitioner, or with an adult protective services agency or a local law enforcement agency, prior to commencing his or her employment and as a prerequisite to that employment, shall sign a statement on a form that shall be provided by the prospective employer, to the effect that he or she has knowledge of Section 15630 and will comply with its provisions. The employer shall provide a copy of Section 15630 to the employee. The statement shall inform the employee that he or she is a mandated reporter and inform the employee of his or her reporting obligations under Section 15630. The signed statement shall be retained by the employer.

(b) Agencies or facilities that employ persons who were employed prior to January 1, 1995, and who are required to make reports pursuant to Section 15630, shall inform those persons of their responsibility to make reports by delivering to them a copy of the statement specified in subdivision (a).

(c) The cost of printing, distribution, and filing of these statements shall be borne by the employer.

(d) On and after January 1, 1995, when a person is issued a state license or certificate to
engage in a profession or occupation the members of which are required to make a report pursuant to Section 15630, the state agency issuing the license or certificate shall send to the person a statement substantially similar to the one contained in subdivision (a) at the same time that it transmits to the person the document indicating licensure or certification.

(e) As an alternative to the procedure required by subdivision (d), a state agency may cause the required statement to be printed on all application forms for a license or certificate printed on or after January 1, 1995.

(f) The retention of statements required by subdivision (a), and the delivery of statements required by subdivision (b), shall be the full extent of the employer's duty pursuant to this section. The failure of any employee or other person associated with the employer to report abuse of elders or dependent adults pursuant to Section 15630 or otherwise meet the requirements of this chapter shall be the sole responsibility of that person. The employer or facility shall incur no civil or other liability for the failure of these persons to comply with the requirements of this chapter.

CHAPTER 8
CONFIDENTIALITY, PRIVILEGE
& EXCEPTIONS

Confidentiality is central to the work that we do as therapists. Our clients need to know that the information they share with us in therapy is kept confidential and private and that we will not haphazardly disclose and share that information. All therapists must recognize and uphold confidentiality and protect client's information. This is both a legal requirement and an ethical obligation.

There are some exceptions to confidentiality that we will discuss in a bit, but the rule of thumb is to remember that all information shared by clients in therapy is private and confidential information. If you believe that there is an exception to this information, review the law. You may also seek consultation for additional information and clarification, but it is your duty to ensure you either report as provided by the exception or you keep the information private and confidential as required by the law.

Confidentiality, Privilege, and Exceptions to both these are tied together in this chapter because they share similar information and responsibilities. Confidentiality is information that is shared during our clinical therapeutic process with the client this is information that is about the client either told to us directly from the client or information about the client that was shared to us by another party that also has a duty to maintain confidentiality as well. When we discuss privilege, generally it is that same confidential information that we obtained previously about our client, but it is now used in a legal setting. Again, confidentiality information regarding clients in sessions that becomes part of a legal process (a criminal case or other court proceedings) that then is called privileged information. There are exceptions to when we can share confidential information and exceptions when privileged information can and must be shared. Both ethical standards and legal requirements govern confidentiality and privilege and the rights to confidentiality and privileged information for clients as well as the responsibilities for therapists in practice.

There are many legal precedents that exist, and several court cases have established why having confidentiality as the foundation and the bedrock of counseling and psychotherapy is important. In Ewing v. Northridge in 2004, it identified that confidentiality and confidential information is important to help clients avoid the stigma that is part of mental health. This is so they know that the information that they share is going to be private and that they do not have to worry about that information being disclosed to other individuals. In re Lifschultz 1970 Supreme Court Case, it was determined that information that is divulged by clients should not be disclosed. It supported the notion that clients need to be protected from feeling guilty about things that they are disclosing to their therapist. In People v. Stritzinger in 1983, again it indicated that clients should be able to freely disclose information and be uninhibited about the information that they share with therapists because that information is going to be held confidential. Ewing v Northridge in 2004 we see again that this case resulted in the identification of confidentiality again being a place in which trust is established between the client and the therapist and again that information is not going to be released to the general public.

When you are going to disclose information, typically in most situations the information needs to be approved and agreed to by your client. Therefore, you have them sign a release of information also known (ROI) as an authorization to release information or authorization to receive information if you are going to receive information from other individuals. We want to as much as possible get our clients permission to disclose that information. That may just be routine information to share with another provider, another health care practitioner, or another colleague in order to help and support our client. Again, have them sign that ROI to disclose that information. If we are going to obtain confidential information from other providers, then we want to have a signed authorization to obtain and receive information on file as well. There are times when we must disclose confidential information and it may be without our client's explicit consent. These times might be considered exceptions to confidentiality and we will look at these further.

When our client has died and is no longer with us physically, confidentiality continues... it survives, it just does not end. It means that we cannot just go around disclosing their information just because they've passed, and in fact, the law indicates that if a client dies and perhaps their spouse comes to us and says "hey I would like to obtain the clinical records from my spouse...I want to know what they were talking about. I'm concerned maybe it was me...maybe it was someone else," well, unfortunately, we cannot disclose that information. We cannot provide the records unless that individual is identified as the clients authorized representative. So, it is important as a therapist, as an associate professional clinical counselor, as a trainee to know how to manage confidentiality. The law is very clear that confidentiality survives death and if we are asked to disclose that information it must be to their authorized representative and it may not be the spouse.

When you are clinically treating a family unit or couples you need to obtain a document of confidentiality indicating that each one of these individuals understands that the information that is disclosed or may be disclosed based upon each one of them signing a document agreeing to that confidential information being disclosed. If you are treating a family unit, you cannot disclose any information about the individuals in that family unit unless each person signs a release of information. The same thing goes for couples as well. We want to ensure that we are very clear about that, so if one person is unwilling to sign, then we have a problem, you are not going to be able to disclose that information. A therapist might find it prudent to have general releases signed early on and in the event, that information needs to be disclosed.

Since you are treating the family unit your notes and your files (the records) are going to have different family unit names in it, therefore you have a requirement to protect each one of the individuals in the unit. When you are treating individuals, who are in group therapy, you have a responsibility to maintain confidentiality.

Let's talk a little bit about when there are breaches to confidentiality. These are times when we have maybe not have been on top of our game, monitoring what we are doing, monitoring what is happening in our office and then there is a breach. It may be times in which we discuss one of our client's issues with another client, that would be completely inappropriate, that would be a breach. There may be times when we allow another client to overhear our voice messages or allow the client to see our computer screen where a client message or client file visible, these would be breaches of confidentiality. We also want to be careful about when we have appointment books (if we have a physical appointment log that a client signs-in on), we want to make sure that this is something that only one person can sign in on at a time or that it has a tear-off where we can remove their name the moment that we call them. We want to make sure that we protect our clients as much as possible in those particular situations. Note that it would be a breach of confidentiality if we were to share information with a client's partner or their family member without a release of information. Yes, there are some exceptions to this, but in general, it would be a breach.

You cannot discuss client information in consultation unless you have had a document signed by the client authorizing this. You may, however, disclose the situation and the concerns that you have and try to get up some assistance in general and disguise any personally identifiable information, but unless you have that release information you cannot just go around disclosing the clients personally-identifying information.

Exceptions to Confidentiality

(1) When a minor has expressed, or the therapist has knowledge that

there is child abuse or neglect. The therapist is required to report that information. The Child Abuse and Neglect Reporting Act provide guidance regarding suspected or known child abuse, we must report that information to the appropriate authorities and appropriate agencies.

(2) If there is suspicion or knowledge of elder and/or dependent adult abuse we must disclose that information to the appropriate authorities and the appropriate agencies that are responsible for investigating and following up on those particular reports. These are two very common exceptions to confidentiality. There are some other provisions that allow a therapist to disclose information, and are expected and mandated to disclose that information. Therapists might find it helpful to discuss some of these exceptions with the client at the beginning of therapy.

Danger: Let's look at when individuals are a danger to themselves. This is found both in California Evidence Code 1024, but really was supported by the case Bellah v. Greenson and this was decided in 1978 and in summary, a client had committed overdose by consuming pills and the parents of that client decided to sue the psychiatrist because she had engaged in and discussed suicidal ideation and intention. So here we have a requirement by law to protect clients and to support clients in these situations. You might have already heard of the Tarasoff v. California Board of Regents ruling in your law and ethics class, this is something that should have been discussed but we'll go over it just briefly here. In summary, a student studying at the University of California Berkeley campus named Tatiana Tarasoff and she met an individual that was also studying there named Poddar. Poddar eventually became obsessed with her and wanted to pursue a romantic relationship. This didn't go the way he wanted.

When Poddar was seeing his therapist, a psychologist on campus, he disclosed his dreams and fantasies and urges to violently hurt her and essentially expressed that he was going to hurt her, it was determined the psychologists did not do enough to warn and protect her according to the parents. Her parents sued the campus and the psychologist, and the ruling came from this case was that it would be important for therapists to intervene in these situations. What we need to do is not only attempt to warn the intended victim, but we also must contact law enforcement. These are the requirements that we do, but we also need to take any other steps and measures to protect the client. You might have heard of something called duty to warn and duty to protect. The goal here is to protect! Warning them would be great, but we have to also take steps to protect. Protect might mean warning the intended victim, but it may mean contacting other individuals that know the intended victim such as family or friends. Again, we need to contact law enforcement and then take any other reasonable steps.

There is something identified as the Tarasoff immunity and this is found within section 43.92 of the California Civil Code which states that as long as we follow this requirement we are immune from any civil lawsuit that may come as a result in the harm of the intended victim. If we have done all that we could to protect the victim or intended victim, we have met the immunity requirement. Our role is not to get out in front and to take the bullet for the victim or to do any of those particular things but to do whatever we can to protect them as much as possible by making those phone calls and making sure that we do whatever we can to protect.

When you have done your duty and you have attempted and taken the best actions possible to warn the intended victim as well as contacted and notified the law enforcement agency you have done what you are required to do under this particular requirement. When you act in this particular way you are given something called immunity right and this is immunity from lawsuits that might arise from subsequent harm that may come from the threatened violence. Specifically, the law says "(a) There shall be no monetary liability on the part of, and no cause of action shall arise against, any person who is a psychotherapist as defined in Section 1010 of the Evidence Code in failing to protect from a patient's threatened violent behavior or failing to predict and protect from a patient's violent behavior except if the patient has communicated to the psychotherapist a serious threat of physical violence against a reasonably identifiable victim or victims.

(b) There shall be no monetary liability on the part of, and no cause of action shall arise against, a psychotherapist who, under the limited circumstances specified in subdivision (a), discharges his or her duty to protect by making reasonable efforts to communicate the threat to the victim or victims and to a law enforcement agency.

This clarifies that these are the two actions you must do in order to be protected from liability when you are informed that your client is going to be a danger to other individuals (1)warn the intended victim and make every reasonable effort to do so and then make sure that you (2) call law enforcement. In these particular situations, documentation of your actions is key. What is meant by that? You attempt to contact the intended victim, but perhaps you do not have their phone number and only have the phone number of the spouse or the parent or of the child, well you contact that individual(s) in order obtain the contact information for the intended victim or perhaps you are relay information through those particular individuals to the intended victim. You want to document that information. You want to make every reasonable possible effort to get in contact with the intended victim based upon the information that you have.

When you contact law enforcement, it might be helpful that it is the law enforcement agency that is closest to the intended victim and perhaps your client as well and notify both agencies if they are in different cities or different counties or even if in different states. You want to get the badge number and the name of the person that you spoke to or the person that is taking the report. If you speak to the dispatch, you want to get their information to document. You may also want to perhaps send a certified letter to the law enforcement agency as well as perhaps to the intended victim if you have that information expressing what the concerns are. Remember that calling is the quickest way and the letter should be a follow-up. One thing to know is that there is no reporting form that exists for making these types of reports. There is a reporting form for Adult Protective Services and there is a reporting form for Child Protective Services, but not necessarily a form for this particular situation.

Make sure that you are documenting this information in several places so that if there are any concerns about why you did not act, or why you did act in a specific way, you have information to substantiate those particular reasons. All of the information that you disclose here (again because we are talking about confidentiality, and here specifically the exceptions to it) but even in these particular situations you want to be as discreet as possible. You want to disclose only the information that is necessary to protect the intended victim. You do not want to just give the entire record over to everyone you are speaking to, but just enough information as necessary to protect that particular individual. This substantiated by the Menendez versus Superior Court ruling.

As a therapist your job is not to predict that there is going to be violence, you do not have the ability to do that and you cannot foresee the future, but you have to exercise a reasonable degree of skills knowledge and care in these particular situations, so you want to really be mindful about how you go about assessing the risk and assessing the harm and what information that you gathered or utilized to make the decision either act or not to act. These may be statements that the client has made as identified in Tarasoff 1974 and then the later 1976 ruling. It might be the clients behavior and how they are speaking (how they are talking) that is identified in the Ewing v. Goldstein 2004 decision, or might be by the clients physical behavior and the way they position their body, the nonverbal communication that you are receiving that you might be deriving your information from, and that would be from the Calderon v. Glick 2005 ruling. You do not have to be perfect...you do not have to foresee in the future, but you have to take all this information into account as part of your clinical training.

In California Civil Code 56.10 there are a variety of exceptions when it comes to confidentiality, and common exception is when a therapist receives a court order. We have not yet gone over court orders or subpoenas as this information is in a later chapter, but court orders times when a judge orders you to provide information, either verbally in testimony or in writing and you must disclose that information. There is no right to confidentiality for the client in this situation. When the therapist is part of an investigation by State Board or Commission or Administrative Agency (an example of that would be the Board of Behavioral Sciences) then that information must be disclosed. When the Boards does an investigation on a specific client regarding an allegation, they would require the client to sign a release of information.

When the therapist receives a search warrant, the therapist cannot block or stop the investigation agency, they have right to access that information based upon the warrant when the therapist is named on the warrant. When a corner requests information in the course of their investigation, then that information can be disclosed. There are a variety of other exceptions found under California Civil Code 56.10 which includes disclosing of medical information and treatment with other healthcare providers and health care plans for the purposes of treatment as well as disclosure of medical information and treatment with other healthcare providers and healthcare plans for the purposes of payment. Additionally, a disclosure made to probate court investigation offices and other investigators for the purposes of guardianship or conservatorship that is allowed as part of the disclosure. We can look further in California Civil Code under Section 56 and we see that there are a variety of other situations in which information can be disclosed and is required to be disclosed based upon the situation at hand. We encourage counselors to review this information.

Let's go back and look at California Evidence Code 1024 that we indicated previously, it reads: "There is no privilege under this article if the psychotherapist has reasonable cause to believe that the patient is in such mental or emotional condition as to be dangerous to himself or to the person or property of another and that disclosure of the communication is necessary to prevent the threatened danger."

So, there is no privilege (right to confidentiality) if a client is a danger to themselves, to other individuals or to property. A question you might ask then is, should I disclose and give confidential information that is pertinent about the protection of someone is property? This is one of those professional judgment situations that may require consultation with an attorney and/or professional association. If the client is going to their neighbor and kick their car and put a dent in it, is that something that you think you should disclose? Or if the clients going to go to the neighbor's house and perhaps kick in the front door, does that change whether you believe you should make that report? Does the property being damaged put people at risk to be hurt? Let's say one your clients were going to put a hole someone's care tire causing a slow leak. If the intended individual was driving on the freeway, they may get hurt. What if they were to damage the mechanical parts (cut the brake lines) of a car, would that be the reason to disclose?

California Evidence Code 1020 has to do with communication and privilege under this particular section, it says, "There is no privilege under this article as to a communication relevant to an issue of breach, by the psychotherapist or by the patient, of a duty arising out of the psychotherapist-patient relationship." What does this mean? Well perhaps the client is accusing the therapist of breaking some form of duty, and therefore the therapist may need to disclose just enough information to provide a defense to say "no, that is not true...this is what happened." This often happens in situations where a client makes a threatening statement to the therapist or engages in threating behavior towards the therapist, and they may need to contact law enforcement during a session and explain to the law enforcement officer what the situation is regarding the client.

Here the client makes a breach in the client (patient) expected behavior as part of the informed consent process, it may be appropriate for that therapist to disclose certain information due to that breach. Perhaps the breach is about non-payment? Therapists may need to send a bill or decided whether to go through a collection agency because payments were not received. Non-payment may be a breach of the relationship and that therapist would need to provide enough information to the collection agency to collecting the fees. They may provide things such as the client name, address, dates, times and the location of the services, but maybe not necessarily what the diagnosis is, that would probably be too much information.

Privilege

Privilege is commonly confused by new therapists with the term confidentiality, while they are similar and shared the same assumption of privacy, they have different guidelines and expectations. Privilege is a term used specifically in a legal proceeding. Privileged information is essentially the same confidential information communicated between a client and the therapist that may be requested or subjected to disclosure in legal proceedings. The term privilege essentially protects and supports the clients right to not have this confidential information revealed, specifically in open proceedings and in almost all circumstances, therapists have a legal obligation to assert privilege on behalf of a client.

Exceptions to Privilege

There are however a few circumstances in which there are exceptions. In most circumstances, clients are the holders of their own privilege, this means that they can determine what information they would like to have revealed during legal proceedings. This is supported by California Evidence Code 1013 which provides the definition of the holders of privilege. Much like we talked about confidentiality applies to interns and trainees, associates and those that are licensed so does privilege, and privilege exists between both a therapist and the client, but also a professional corporation from which a client is receiving services from. We have an obligation to assert privilege and to maintain that privilege on behalf of our client unless the client or the court directs us to do otherwise. Therapists are never the holders of privilege although we assert privilege.

So who actually is the holder of privilege? The patient is the holder of privilege. Privilege is confidential information in a legal proceeding. It does not matter what the age of the patient is they, hold privilege and the only way that they do not hold privilege is if they are a minor and there has been a guardian ad litem that has been assigned by the court or if there is a conservator assigned by the court, if they are an adult and have mental or cognitive impairments where they cannot consent and make those particular decisions. In essentially all other circumstances it is the patient regardless of age. The second individual that is identified as who can hold privilege is the client's personal representative. If a client has died, their personal representative (the person they previously identified) would hold privilege. These are the individuals that hold privilege and who can assert privilege. The client has the right to have us as therapists assert privilege on their behalf when they direct us to or if we are unable to reach them to find out what they want us to do in those particular situations. We would assert privilege on behalf of a client should they ask us, or again, if we are unable to reach them to get information on otherwise what they would like us to do. Additionally, there are other individuals under California Evidence Code that are required to assert privilege on a client's behalf when there is confidential information that is being sought in a legal proceeding.

Who can waive privilege? Waiving privilege means that the individual can say in a legal proceeding, "I do not care if this confidential information is kept quiet or private, I am okay with it being disclosed, I'm okay with it being out there in the public." There are only certain individuals that can exercise that right, that obviously would be the (1) client themselves but other individuals can waive. That could be either the (2) designated conservator as mentioned earlier or the (3) guardian ad litem. The latter two have been appointed by the court on behalf of the client and can exercise that right. Additionally, a judge can waive privilege as well as the client's personal representative.

It should be known that if a client decides to waive privilege, the judge may determine that it would be inappropriate for that information to be disclosed and may actually deny or block that waiving of privilege if the judge believes that that information would not be in the best interest of the client during the legal proceeding. Note here that therapists do not have the right to waive privilege. Again, therapists are not holders of privilege and can only assert privilege on behalf of our clients.

Summary of Exceptions to Privilege

A few of some interesting exceptions are listed below, however these are just a few and the rest are found within this chapter.

1. When a client introduces his or her mental or emotional condition during legal proceedings.
2. When a client sues the therapist for malpractice.
3. If the therapist has been appointed by the court to examine the client.
4. If the client sought therapy in order to plan or commit a crime or to escape punishment of a crime.
5. If the therapist has reason to believe that a patient under the age of 16 has been the victim of a crime and that by disclosing the information it would be in the best interest of the child.
6. If the client is a danger to self or others.

Confidentiality of Medical Information Act

California Civil Code
Section 56.05 Definitions
(a) "Authorization" means permission granted in accordance with Section 56.11 or 56.21 for the disclosure of medical information.

(b) "Authorized recipient" means any person who is authorized to receive medical information pursuant to Section 56.10 or 56.20.

(c) "Contractor" means any person or entity that is a medical group, independent practice association, pharmaceutical benefits manager, or a medical service organization and is not a health care service plan or provider of health care. "Contractor" does not include insurance institutions as defined in subdivision (k) of Section 791.02 of the Insurance Code or pharmaceutical benefits managers licensed pursuant to the Knox-Keene Health Care Service Plan Act of 1975 (Chapter 2.2 (commencing with Section 1340) of Division 2 of the Health and Safety Code).

(d) "Health care service plan" means any entity regulated pursuant to the Knox-Keene Health Care Service Plan Act of 1975 (Chapter 2.2 (commencing with Section 1340) of Division 2 of the Health and Safety Code).

(e) "Licensed health care professional" means any person licensed or certified pursuant to Division 2 (commencing with Section 500) of the Business and Professions Code, the Osteopathic Initiative Act or the Chiropractic Initiative Act, or Division 2.5 (commencing with Section 1797) of the Health and Safety Code.

(f) "Marketing" means to make a communication about a product or service that encourages recipients of the communication to purchase or use the product or service. "Marketing" does not include any of the following:

(1) Communications made orally or in writing for which the communicator does not receive direct or indirect remuneration, including, but not limited to, gifts, fees, payments, subsidies, or other economic benefits, from a third party for making the communication.

(2) Communications made to current enrollees solely for the purpose of describing a provider's participation in an existing health care provider network or health plan network of a Knox-Keene licensed health plan to which the enrollees already subscribe; communications made to current enrollees solely for the purpose of describing if, and the extent to which, a product or service, or payment for a product or service, is provided by a provider, contractor, or plan or included in a plan of benefits of a Knox-Keene licensed health plan to which the enrollees already subscribe; or communications made to plan enrollees describing the availability of more cost-effective pharmaceuticals.

(3) Communications that are tailored to the circumstances of a particular individual to educate or advise the individual about treatment options, and otherwise maintain the individual's adherence to a prescribed course of medical treatment, as provided in Section 1399.901 of the Health and Safety Code, for a chronic and seriously debilitating or life-threatening condition as defined in subdivisions (d) and (e) of Section 1367.21 of the Health and Safety Code, if the health care provider, contractor, or health plan receives direct or indirect remuneration, including, but not limited to, gifts, fees, payments, subsidies, or other economic benefits, from a third party for making the communication, if all of the following apply:

(A) The individual receiving the communication is notified in the communication in typeface no smaller than 14-point type of the fact that the provider, contractor, or health plan has been remunerated and the source of the remuneration.

(B) The individual is provided the opportunity to opt out of receiving future remunerated communications.

(C) The communication contains instructions in typeface no smaller than 14-point type describing how the individual can opt out of receiving further communications by calling a toll-free number of the health care provider, contractor, or health plan making the remunerated communications. No further communication may be made to an individual who has opted out after 30 calendar days from the date the individual makes the opt out request.

(g) "Medical information" means any individually identifiable information, in electronic or physical form, in possession of or derived from a provider of health care, health care service plan, pharmaceutical company, or contractor regarding a patient's medical history, mental or physical condition, or treatment. "Individually identifiable" means that the medical information includes or contains any element of personal identifying information sufficient to allow identification of the individual, such as the patient's name, address, electronic mail address, telephone number, or social security number, or other information that, alone or in combination with other publicly available information, reveals the individual's identity.

(h) "Patient" means any natural person, whether or not still living, who received health care services from a provider of health care and to whom medical information pertains.

(i) "Pharmaceutical company" means any company or business, or an agent or representative thereof, that manufactures, sells, or distributes pharmaceuticals, medications, or prescription drugs. "Pharmaceutical company" does not include a pharmaceutical benefits manager, as included in subdivision (c), or a provider of health care.

(j) "Provider of health care" means any person licensed or certified pursuant to Division 2 (commencing with Section 500) of the Business and Professions Code; any person licensed pursuant to the Osteopathic Initiative Act or the Chiropractic Initiative Act; any person certified pursuant to Division 2.5 (commencing with Section 1797) of the Health and Safety Code; any clinic, health dispensary, or health facility licensed pursuant to Division 2 (commencing with Section 1200) of the Health and Safety Code. "Provider of health care" does not include insurance institutions as defined in subdivision (k) of Section 791.02 of the Insurance Code.

Disclosure of Medical Information by Providers

California Civil Code
Section 56.10 Patient Information
(a) A provider of health care, health care service plan, or contractor shall

not disclose medical information regarding a patient of the provider of health care or an enrollee or subscriber of a health care service plan without first obtaining an authorization, except as provided in subdivision (b) or (c).

(b) A provider of health care, a health care service plan, or a contractor shall disclose medical information if the disclosure is compelled by any of the following:

(1) By a court pursuant to an order of that court.

(2) By a board, commission, or administrative agency for purposes of adjudication pursuant to its lawful authority.

(3) By a party to a proceeding before a court or administrative agency pursuant to a subpoena, subpoena duces tecum, notice to appear served pursuant to Section 1987 of the Code of Civil Procedure, or any provision authorizing discovery in a proceeding before a court or administrative agency.

(4) By a board, commission, or administrative agency pursuant to an investigative subpoena issued under Article 2 (commencing with Section 11180) of Chapter 2 of Part 1 of Division 3 of Title 2 of the Government Code.

(5) By an arbitrator or arbitration panel, when arbitration is lawfully requested by either party, pursuant to a subpoena duces tecum issued under Section 1282.6 of the Code of Civil Procedure, or another provision authorizing discovery in a proceeding before an arbitrator or arbitration panel.

(6) By a search warrant lawfully issued to a governmental law enforcement agency.

(7) By the patient or the patient's representative pursuant to Chapter 1 (commencing with Section 123100) of Part 1 of Division 106 of the Health and Safety Code.

(8) By a coroner, when requested in the course of an investigation by the coroner's office for the purpose of identifying the decedent or locating next of kin, or when investigating deaths that may involve public health concerns, organ or tissue donation, child abuse, elder abuse, suicides, poisonings, accidents, sudden infant deaths, suspicious deaths, unknown deaths, or criminal deaths, or when otherwise authorized by the decedent's representative. Medical information requested by the coroner under this paragraph shall be limited to information regarding the patient who is the decedent and who is the subject of the investigation and shall be disclosed

to the coroner without delay upon request.

(9) When otherwise specifically required by law.

(c) A provider of health care or a health care service plan may disclose medical information as follows:

(1) The information may be disclosed to providers of health care, health care service plans, contractors, or other health care professionals or facilities for purposes of diagnosis or treatment of the patient. This includes, in an emergency situation, the communication of patient information by radio transmission or other means between emergency medical personnel at the scene of an emergency, or in an emergency medical transport vehicle, and emergency medical personnel at a health facility licensed pursuant to Chapter 2 (commencing with Section 1250) of Division 2 of the Health and Safety Code.

(2) The information may be disclosed to an insurer, employer, health care service plan, hospital service plan, employee benefit plan, governmental authority, contractor, or any other person or entity responsible for paying for health care services rendered to the patient, to the extent necessary to allow responsibility for payment to be determined and payment to be made.

If (A) the patient is, by reason of a comatose or other disabling medical condition, unable to consent to the disclosure of medical information and (B) no other arrangements have been made to pay for the health care services being rendered to the patient, the information may be disclosed to a governmental authority to the extent necessary to determine the patient's eligibility for, and to obtain, payment under a governmental program for health care services provided to the patient. The information may also be disclosed to another provider of health care or health care service plan as necessary to assist the other provider or health care service plan in obtaining payment for health care services rendered by that provider of health care or health care service plan to the patient.

(3) The information may be disclosed to a person or entity that provides billing, claims management, medical data processing, or other administrative services for providers of health care or health care service plans or for any of the persons or entities specified in paragraph (2). However, information so disclosed shall not be further disclosed by the recipient in a way that would violate this part.

(4) The information may be disclosed to organized committees and agents of professional societies or of medical staffs of licensed hospitals, licensed health care service plans, professional standards review organizations,

independent medical review organizations and their selected reviewers, utilization and quality control peer review organizations as established by Congress in Public Law 97-248 in 1982, contractors, or persons or organizations insuring, responsible for, or defending professional liability that a provider may incur, if the committees, agents, health care service plans, organizations, reviewers, contractors, or persons are engaged in reviewing the competence or qualifications of health care professionals or in reviewing health care services with respect to medical necessity, level of care, quality of care, or justification of charges.

(5) The information in the possession of a provider of health care or health care service plan may be reviewed by a private or public body responsible for licensing or accrediting the provider of health care or health care service plan. However, no patient-identifying medical information may be removed from the premises except as expressly permitted or required elsewhere by law, nor shall that information be further disclosed by the recipient in a way that would violate this part.

(6) The information may be disclosed to the county coroner in the course of an investigation by the coroner's office when requested for all purposes not included in paragraph (8) of subdivision (b).

(7) The information may be disclosed to public agencies, clinical investigators, including investigators conducting epidemiologic studies, health care research organizations, and accredited public or private nonprofit educational or health care institutions for bona fide research purposes. However, no information so disclosed shall be further disclosed by the recipient in a way that would disclose the identity of a patient or violate this part.

(8) A provider of health care or health care service plan that has created medical information as a result of employment-related health care services to an employee conducted at the specific prior written request and expense of the employer may disclose to the employee's employer that part of the information that:

(A) Is relevant in a lawsuit, arbitration, grievance, or other claim or challenge to which the employer and the employee are parties and in which the patient has placed in issue his or her medical history, mental or physical condition, or treatment, provided that information may only be used or disclosed in connection with that proceeding.

(B) Describes functional limitations of the patient that may entitle the patient to leave from work for medical reasons or limit the patient's fitness to perform his or her present employment, provided that no statement of medical cause is included in the information disclosed.

(9) Unless the provider of health care or a health care service plan is notified in writing of an agreement by the sponsor, insurer, or administrator to the contrary, the information may be disclosed to a sponsor, insurer, or administrator of a group or individual insured or uninsured plan or policy that the patient seeks coverage by or benefits from, if the information was created by the provider of health care or health care service plan as the result of services conducted at the specific prior written request and expense of the sponsor, insurer, or administrator for the purpose of evaluating the application for coverage or benefits.

(10) The information may be disclosed to a health care service plan by providers of health care that contract with the health care service plan and may be transferred among providers of health care that contract with the health care service plan, for the purpose of administering the health care service plan. Medical information shall not otherwise be disclosed by a health care service plan except in accordance with this part.

(11) This part does not prevent the disclosure by a provider of health care or a health care service plan to an insurance institution, agent, or support organization, subject to Article 6.6 (commencing with Section 791) of Chapter 1 of Part 2 of Division 1 of the Insurance Code, of medical information if the insurance institution, agent, or support organization has complied with all of the requirements for obtaining the information pursuant to Article 6.6 (commencing with Section 791) of Chapter 1 of Part 2 of Division 1 of the Insurance Code.

(12) The information relevant to the patient's condition, care, and treatment provided may be disclosed to a probate court investigator in the course of an investigation required or authorized in a conservatorship proceeding under the Guardianship-Conservatorship Law as defined in Section 1400 of the Probate Code, or to a probate court investigator, probation officer, or domestic relations investigator engaged in determining the need for an initial guardianship or continuation of an existing guardianship.

(13) The information may be disclosed to an organ procurement organization or a tissue bank processing the tissue of a decedent for transplantation into the body of another person, but only with respect to the donating decedent, for the purpose of aiding the transplant. For the purpose of this paragraph, "tissue bank" and "tissue" have the same meanings as defined in Section 1635 of the Health and Safety Code.

(14) The information may be disclosed when the disclosure is otherwise specifically authorized by law, including, but not limited to, the voluntary reporting, either directly or indirectly, to the federal Food and Drug

Administration of adverse events related to drug products or medical device problems, or to disclosures made pursuant to subdivisions (b) and (c) of Section 11167 of the Penal Code by a person making a report pursuant to Sections 11165.9 and 11166 of the Penal Code, provided that those disclosures concern a report made by that person.

(15) Basic information, including the patient's name, city of residence, age, sex, and general condition, may be disclosed to a state-recognized or federally recognized disaster relief organization for the purpose of responding to disaster welfare inquiries.

(16) The information may be disclosed to a third party for purposes of encoding, encrypting, or otherwise anonymizing data. However, no information so disclosed shall be further disclosed by the recipient in a way that would violate this part, including the unauthorized manipulation of coded or encrypted medical information that reveals individually identifiable medical information.

(17) For purposes of disease management programs and services as defined in Section 1399.901 of the Health and Safety Code, information may be disclosed as follows:

(A) to an entity contracting with a health care service plan or the health care service plan's contractors to monitor or administer care of enrollees for a covered benefit, if the disease management services and care are authorized by a treating physician, or

B) to a disease management organization, as defined in Section 1399.900 of the Health and Safety Code, that complies fully with the physician authorization requirements of Section 1399.902 of the Health and Safety Code, if the health care service plan or its contractor provides or has provided a description of the disease management services to a treating physician or to the health care service plan's or contractor's network of physicians. This paragraph does not require physician authorization for the care or treatment of the adherents of a well-recognized church or religious denomination who depend solely upon prayer or spiritual means for healing in the practice of the religion of that church or denomination.

(18) The information may be disclosed, as permitted by state and federal law or regulation, to a local health department for the purpose of preventing or controlling disease, injury, or disability, including, but not limited to, the reporting of disease, injury, vital events, including, but not limited to, birth or death, and the conduct of public health surveillance, public health investigations, and public health interventions, as authorized or required by state or federal law or regulation.

(19) The information may be disclosed, consistent with applicable law and standards of ethical conduct, by a psychotherapist, as defined in Section 1010 of the Evidence Code, if the psychotherapist, in good faith, believes the disclosure is necessary to prevent or lessen a serious and imminent threat to the health or safety of a reasonably foreseeable victim or victims, and the disclosure is made to a person or persons reasonably able to prevent or lessen the threat, including the target of the threat.

(20) The information may be disclosed as described in Section 56.103.

(21) (A) The information may be disclosed to an employee welfare benefit plan, as defined under Section 3(1) of the Employee Retirement Income Security Act of 1974 (29 U.S.C. Sec. 1002(1)), which is formed under Section 302(c)(5) of the Taft-Hartley Act (29 U.S.C. Sec. 186(c)(5)), to the extent that the employee welfare benefit plan provides medical care, and may also be disclosed to an entity contracting with the employee welfare benefit plan for billing, claims management, medical data processing, or other administrative services related to the provision of medical care to persons enrolled in the employee welfare benefit plan for health care coverage, if all of the following conditions are met:

(i) The disclosure is for the purpose of determining eligibility, coordinating benefits, or allowing the employee welfare benefit plan, or the contracting entity, to advocate on the behalf of a patient or enrollee with a provider, a health care service plan, or a state or federal regulatory agency.

(ii) The request for the information is accompanied by a written authorization for the release of the information submitted in a manner consistent with subdivision (a) and Section 56.11.

(iii) The disclosure is authorized by and made in a manner consistent with the Health Insurance Portability and Accountability Act of 1996 (Public Law 104-191).

(iv) Any information disclosed is not further used or disclosed by the recipient in any way that would directly or indirectly violate this part or the restrictions imposed by Part 164 of Title 45 of the Code of Federal Regulations, including the manipulation of the information in any way that might reveal individually identifiable medical information.

(B) For purposes of this paragraph, Section 1374.8 of the Health and Safety Code shall not apply.

(22) Information may be disclosed pursuant to subdivision (a) of Section 15633.5 of the Welfare and Institutions Code by a person required to make

a report pursuant to Section 15630 of the Welfare and Institutions Code, provided that the disclosure under subdivision (a) of Section 15633.5 concerns a report made by that person. Covered entities, as they are defined in Section 160.103 of Title 45 of the Code of Federal Regulations, shall comply with the requirements of the Health Insurance Portability and Accountability Act (HIPAA) privacy rule pursuant to subsection (c) of Section 164.512 of Title 45 of the Code of Federal Regulations if the disclosure is not for the purpose of public health surveillance, investigation, intervention, or reporting an injury or death.

(d) Except to the extent expressly authorized by a patient or enrollee or subscriber or as provided by subdivisions (b) and (c), a provider of health care, health care service plan, contractor, or corporation and its subsidiaries and affiliates shall not intentionally share, sell, use for marketing, or otherwise use medical information for a purpose not necessary to provide health care services to the patient.

(e) Except to the extent expressly authorized by a patient or enrollee or subscriber or as provided by subdivisions (b) and (c), a contractor or corporation and its subsidiaries and affiliates shall not further disclose medical information regarding a patient of the provider of health care or an enrollee or subscriber of a health care service plan or insurer or self-insured employer received under this section to a person or entity that is not engaged in providing direct health care services to the patient or his or her provider of health care or health care service plan or insurer or self-insured employer.

Limited Disclosure to Family, Relative, Domestic Partner

Section 56.1007.
(a) A provider of health care, health care service plan, or contractor may, in accordance with subdivision (c) or (d), disclose to a family member, other relative, domestic partner, or a close personal friend of the patient, or any other person identified by the patient, the medical information directly relevant to that person's involvement with the patient's care or payment related to the patient's health care.

(b) A provider of health care, health care service plan, or contractor may use or disclose medical information to notify, or assist in the notification of, including identifying or locating, a family member, a personal representative of the patient, a domestic partner, or another person responsible for the care of the patient of the patient's location, general condition, or death. Any use or disclosure of medical information for those notification purposes shall be in accordance with the provisions of subdivision (c), (d), or (e), as applicable.

(c) (1) Except as provided in paragraph (2), if the patient is present for, or otherwise available prior to, a use or disclosure permitted by subdivision (a) or (b) and has the capacity to make health care decisions, the provider of health care, health care service plan, or contractor may use or disclose the medical information if it does any of the following:

(A) Obtains the patient's agreement.

(B) Provides the patient with the opportunity to object to the disclosure, and the patient does not express an objection.

(C) Reasonably infers from the circumstances, based on the exercise of professional judgment, that the patient does not object to the disclosure.

(2) A provider of health care who is a psychotherapist, as defined in Section 1010 of the Evidence Code, may use or disclose medical information pursuant to this subdivision only if the psychotherapist complies with subparagraph (A) or (B) of paragraph (1).

(d) If the patient is not present, or the opportunity to agree or object to the use or disclosure cannot practicably be provided because of the patient's incapacity or an emergency circumstance, the provider of health care, health care service plan, or contractor may, in the exercise of professional judgment, determine whether the disclosure is in the best interests of the patient and, if so, disclose only the medical information that is directly relevant to the person's involvement with the patient's health care. A provider of health care, health care service plan, or contractor may use professional judgment and its experience with common practice to make reasonable inferences of the patient's best interest in allowing a person to act on behalf of the patient to pick up filled prescriptions, medical supplies, X-rays, or other similar forms of medical information.

(e) A provider of health care, health care service plan, or contractor may use or disclose medical information to a public or private entity authorized by law or by its charter to assist in disaster relief efforts, for the purpose of coordinating with those entities the uses or disclosures permitted by subdivision (b). The requirements in subdivisions (c) and (d) apply to those uses and disclosures to the extent that the provider of health care, health care service plan, or contractor, in the exercise of professional judgment, determines that the requirements do not interfere with the ability to respond to the emergency circumstances.

(f) Nothing in this section shall be construed to interfere with or limit the access authority of Protection and Advocacy, Inc., the Office of Patients'

Rights, or any county patients' rights advocates to access medical information pursuant to any state or federal law.

Storage & Destruction of Information

Section 56.101.

(a) Every provider of health care, health care service plan, pharmaceutical company, or contractor who creates, maintains, preserves, stores, abandons, destroys, or disposes of medical information shall do so in a manner that preserves the confidentiality of the information contained therein. Any provider of health care, health care service plan, pharmaceutical company, or contractor who negligently creates, maintains, preserves, stores, abandons, destroys, or disposes of medical information shall be subject to the remedies and penalties provided under subdivisions (b) and (c) of Section 56.36.

(b) (1) An electronic health record system or electronic medical record system shall do the following:

(A) Protect and preserve the integrity of electronic medical information.

(B) Automatically record and preserve any change or deletion of any electronically stored medical information. The record of any change or deletion shall include the identity of the person who accessed and changed the medical information, the date and time the medical information was accessed, and the change that was made to the medical information.

(2) A patient's right to access or receive a copy of his or her electronic medical records upon request shall be consistent with applicable state and federal laws governing patient access to, and the use and disclosures of, medical information.

(c) This section shall apply to an "electronic medical record" or "electronic health record" that meets the definition of "electronic health record," as that term is defined in Section 17921(5) of Title 42 of the United States Code.

Section 56.102.

(a) A pharmaceutical company may not require a patient, as a condition of receiving pharmaceuticals, medications, or prescription drugs, to sign an authorization, release, consent, or waiver that would permit the disclosure of medical information that otherwise may not be disclosed under Section 56.10 or any other provision of law, unless the disclosure is for one of the following purposes:

(1) Enrollment of the patient in a patient assistance program or prescription drug discount program.

(2) Enrollment of the patient in a clinical research project.

(3) Prioritization of distribution to the patient of a prescription medicine in limited supply in the United States.
(4) Response to an inquiry from the patient communicated in writing, by telephone, or by electronic mail.

(b) Except as provided in subdivision (a) or Section 56.10, a pharmaceutical company may not disclose medical information provided to it without first obtaining a valid authorization from the patient.

Section 56.103.
(a) A provider of health care may disclose medical information to a county social worker, a probation officer, or any other person who is legally authorized to have custody or care of a minor for the purpose of coordinating health care services and medical treatment provided to the minor.

(b) For purposes of this section, health care services and medical treatment includes one or more providers of health care providing, coordinating, or managing health care and related services, including, but not limited to, a provider of health care coordinating health care with a third party, consultation between providers of health care and medical treatment relating to a minor, or a provider of health care referring a minor for health care services to another provider of health care.

(c) For purposes of this section, a county social worker, a probation officer, or any other person who is legally authorized to have custody or care of a minor shall be considered a third party who may receive any of the following:

(1) Medical information described in Sections 56.05 and 56.10.

(2) Protected health information described in Section 160.103 of Title 45 of the Code of Federal Regulations.

(d) Medical information disclosed to a county social worker, probation officer, or any other person who is legally authorized to have custody or care of a minor shall not be further disclosed by the recipient unless the disclosure is for the purpose of coordinating health care services and medical treatment of the minor and the disclosure is authorized by law. Medical information disclosed pursuant to this section may not be admitted into evidence in any criminal or delinquency proceeding against the minor.

Nothing in this subdivision shall prohibit identical evidence from being admissible in a criminal proceeding if that evidence is derived solely from lawful means other than this section and is permitted by law.

(e) (1) Notwithstanding Section 56.104, if a provider of health care determines that the disclosure of medical information concerning the diagnosis and treatment of a mental health condition of a minor is reasonably necessary for the purpose of assisting in coordinating the treatment and care of the minor, that information may be disclosed to a county social worker, probation officer, or any other person who is legally authorized to have custody or care of the minor. The information shall not be further disclosed by the recipient unless the disclosure is for the purpose of coordinating mental health services and treatment of the minor and the disclosure is authorized by law.

(2) As used in this subdivision, "medical information" does not include psychotherapy notes as defined in Section 164.501 of Title 45 of the Code of Federal Regulations.

(f) The disclosure of information pursuant to this section is not intended to limit the disclosure of information when that disclosure is otherwise required by law.

(g) For purposes of this section, "minor" means a minor taken into temporary custody or as to who a petition has been filed with the court, or who has been adjudged to be a dependent child or ward of the juvenile court pursuant to Section 300 or 601 of the Welfare and Institutions Code.

(h) (1) Except as described in paragraph (1) of subdivision (e), nothing in this section shall be construed to limit or otherwise affect existing privacy protections provided for in state or federal law.

(2) Nothing in this section shall be construed to expand the authority of a social worker, probation officer, or custodial caregiver beyond the authority provided under existing law to a parent or a patient representative regarding access to medical information.

Release of Information & Authorization

Section 56.104.
(a) Notwithstanding subdivision (c) of Section 56.10, except as provided in subdivision (e), no provider of health care, health care service plan, or contractor may release medical information to persons or entities who have requested that information and who are authorized by law to receive that information pursuant to subdivision (c) of Section 56.10, if the requested information specifically relates to the patient's participation in outpatient

treatment with a psychotherapist, unless the person or entity requesting that information submits to the patient pursuant to subdivision (b) and to the provider of health care, health care service plan, or contractor a written request, signed by the person requesting the information or an authorized agent of the entity requesting the information, that includes all of the following:

(1) The specific information relating to a patient's participation in outpatient treatment with a psychotherapist being requested and its specific intended use or uses.

(2) The length of time during which the information will be kept before being destroyed or disposed of. A person or entity may extend that timeframe, provided that the person or entity notifies the provider, plan, or contractor of the extension. Any notification of an extension shall include the specific reason for the extension, the intended use or uses of the information during the extended time, and the expected date of the destruction of the information.

(3) A statement that the information will not be used for any purpose other than its intended use.

(4) A statement that the person or entity requesting the information will destroy the information and all copies in the person' s or entity's possession or control, will cause it to be destroyed, or will return the information and all copies of it before or immediately after the length of time specified in paragraph (2) has expired.

(b) The person or entity requesting the information shall submit a copy of the written request required by this section to the patient within 30 days of receipt of the information requested, unless the patient has signed a written waiver in the form of a letter signed and submitted by the patient to the provider of health care or health care service plan waiving notification.

(c) For purposes of this section, "psychotherapist" means a person who is both a "psychotherapist" as defined in Section 1010 of the Evidence Code and a "provider of health care" as defined in subdivision (i) of Section 56.05.

(d) This section does not apply to the disclosure or use of medical information by a law enforcement agency or a regulatory agency when required for an investigation of unlawful activity or for licensing, certification, or regulatory purposes, unless the disclosure is otherwise prohibited by law.
(e) This section shall not apply to any of the following:

(1) Information authorized to be disclosed pursuant to paragraph (1) of

subdivision (c) of Section 56.10.

(2) Information requested from a psychotherapist by law enforcement or by the target of the threat subsequent to a disclosure by that psychotherapist authorized by paragraph (19) of subdivision (c) of Section 56.10, in which the additional information is clearly necessary to prevent the serious and imminent threat disclosed under that paragraph.

(3) Information disclosed by a psychotherapist pursuant to paragraphs (14) and (22) of subdivision (c) of Section 56.10 and requested by an agency investigating the abuse reported pursuant to those paragraphs.

(f) Nothing in this section shall be construed to grant any additional authority to a provider of health care, health care service plan, or contractor to disclose information to a person or entity without the patient's consent.

Section 56.105.

Whenever, prior to the service of a complaint upon a defendant in any action arising out of the professional negligence of a person holding a valid physician's and surgeon's certificate issued pursuant to Chapter 5 (commencing with Section 2000) of Division 2 of the Business and Professions Code, a demand for settlement or offer to compromise is made on a patient's behalf, the demand or offer shall be accompanied by an authorization to disclose medical information to persons or organizations insuring, responsible for, or defending professional liability that the certificate holder may incur. The authorization shall be in accordance with Section 56.11 and shall authorize disclosure of that information that is necessary to investigate issues of liability and extent of potential damages in evaluating the merits of the demand for settlement or offer to compromise.

Notice of any request for medical information made pursuant to an authorization as provided by this section shall be given to the patient or the patient's legal representative. The notice shall describe the inclusive subject matter and dates of the materials requested and shall also authorize the patient or the patient's legal representative to receive, upon request, copies of the information at his or her expense.

Nothing in this section shall be construed to waive or limit any applicable privileges set forth in the Evidence Code except for the disclosure of medical information subject to the patient's authorization. Nothing in this section shall be construed as authorizing a representative of any person from whom settlement has been demanded to communicate in violation of the physician-patient privilege with a treating physician except for the medical information request. The requirements of this section are independent of the requirements of Section 364 of the Code of Civil Procedure.

Section 56.11.
Any person or entity that wishes to obtain medical information pursuant to subdivision (a) of Section 56.10, other than a person or entity authorized to receive medical information pursuant to subdivision (b) or (c) of Section 56.10, except as provided in paragraph (21) of subdivision (c) of Section 56.10, shall obtain a valid authorization for the release of this information. An authorization for the release of medical information by a provider of health care, health care service plan, pharmaceutical company, or contractor shall be valid if it:

(a) Is handwritten by the person who signs it or is in a typeface no smaller than 14-point type.

(b) Is clearly separate from any other language present on the same page and is executed by a signature which serves no other purpose than to execute the authorization.

(c) Is signed and dated by one of the following:

(1) The patient. A patient who is a minor may only sign an authorization for the release of medical information obtained by a provider of health care, health care service plan, pharmaceutical company, or contractor in the course of furnishing services to which the minor could lawfully have consented under Part 1 (commencing with Section 25) or Part 2.7 (commencing with Section 60).

(2) The legal representative of the patient, if the patient is a minor or an incompetent. However, authorization may not be given under this subdivision for the disclosure of medical information obtained by the provider of health care, health care service plan, pharmaceutical company, or contractor in the course of furnishing services to which a minor patient could lawfully have consented under Part 1 (commencing with Section 25) or Part 2.7 (commencing with Section 60).

(3) The spouse of the patient or the person financially responsible for the patient, where the medical information is being sought for the sole purpose of processing an application for health insurance or for enrollment in a nonprofit hospital plan, a health care service plan, or an employee benefit plan, and where the patient is to be an enrolled spouse or dependent under the policy or plan.

(4) The beneficiary or personal representative of a deceased patient.

(d) States the specific uses and limitations on the types of medical information to be disclosed.

(e) States the name or functions of the provider of health care, health care service plan, pharmaceutical company, or contractor that may disclose the medical information.

(f) States the name or functions of the persons or entities authorized to receive the medical information.

(g) States the specific uses and limitations on the use of the medical information by the persons or entities authorized to receive the medical information.

(h) States a specific date after which the provider of health care, health care service plan, pharmaceutical company, or contractor is no longer authorized to disclose the medical information.

(i) Advises the person signing the authorization of the right to receive a copy of the authorization.

Section 56.12.
Upon demand by the patient or the person who signed an authorization, a provider of health care, health care service plan, pharmaceutical company, or contractor possessing the authorization shall furnish a true copy thereof.

Section 56.13.
A recipient of medical information pursuant to an authorization as provided by this chapter or pursuant to the provisions of subdivision (c) of Section 56.10 may not further disclose that medical information except in accordance with a new authorization that meets the requirements of Section 56.11, or as specifically required or permitted by other provisions of this chapter or by law.

Section 56.14.
A provider of health care, health care service plan, or contractor that discloses medical information pursuant to the authorizations required by this chapter shall communicate to the person or entity to which it discloses the medical information any limitations in the authorization regarding the use of the medical information. No provider of health care, health care service plan, or contractor that has attempted in good faith to comply with this provision shall be liable for any unauthorized use of the medical information by the person or entity to which the provider, plan, or contractor disclosed the medical information.

Section 56.15.
Nothing in this part shall be construed to prevent a person who could sign

the authorization pursuant to subdivision (c) of Section 56.11 from cancelling or modifying an authorization. However, the cancellation or modification shall be effective only after the provider of health care actually receives written notice of the cancellation or modification.

Section 56.16.
For disclosures not addressed by Section 56.1007, unless there is a specific written request by the patient to the contrary, nothing in this part shall be construed to prevent a general acute care hospital, as defined in subdivision (a) of Section 1250 of the Health and Safety Code, upon an inquiry concerning a specific patient, from releasing at its discretion any of the following information: the patient's name, address, age, and sex; a general description of the reason for treatment (whether an injury, a burn, poisoning, or some unrelated condition); the general nature of the injury, burn, poisoning, or other condition; the general condition of the patient; and any information that is not medical information as defined in subdivision (c) of Section 56.05.

Breach & Violations of Confidentiality

California Civil Code
Section 56.35
In addition to any other remedies available at law, a patient whose medical information has been used or disclosed in violation of Section 56.10 or 56.104 or 56.20 or subdivision (a) of Section 56.26 and who has sustained economic loss or personal injury therefrom may recover compensatory damages, punitive damages not to exceed three thousand dollars ($3,000), attorneys' fees not to exceed one thousand dollars ($1,000), and the costs of litigation.

Section 56.36.
(a) Any violation of the provisions of this part that results in economic loss or personal injury to a patient is punishable as a misdemeanor.
(b) In addition to any other remedies available at law, any individual may bring an action against any person or entity who has negligently released confidential information or records concerning him or her in violation of this part, for either or both of the following:

(1) Nominal damages of one thousand dollars ($1,000). In order to recover under this paragraph, it shall not be necessary that the plaintiff suffered or was threatened with actual damages.

(2) The amount of actual damages, if any, sustained by the patient.

(c) (1) In addition, any person or entity that negligently discloses medical information in violation of the provisions of this part shall also be liable, irrespective of the amount of damages suffered by the patient as a result of that violation, for an administrative fine or civil penalty not to exceed two thousand five hundred dollars ($2,500) per violation.

(2) (A) Any person or entity, other than a licensed health care professional, who knowingly and willfully obtains, discloses, or uses medical information in violation of this part shall be liable for an administrative fine or civil penalty not to exceed twenty-five thousand dollars ($25,000) per violation.

(B) Any licensed health care professional, who knowingly and willfully obtains, discloses, or uses medical information in violation of this part shall be liable on a first violation, for an administrative fine or civil penalty not to exceed two thousand five hundred dollars ($2,500) per violation, or on a second violation for an administrative fine or civil penalty not to exceed ten thousand dollars ($10,000) per violation, or on a third and subsequent violation for an administrative fine or civil penalty not to exceed twenty-five thousand dollars ($25,000) per violation. Nothing in this subdivision shall be construed to limit the liability of a health care service plan, a contractor, or a provider of health care that is not a licensed health care professional for any violation of this part.

(3) (A) Any person or entity, other than a licensed health care professional, who knowingly or willfully obtains or uses medical information in violation of this part for the purpose of financial gain shall be liable for an administrative fine or civil penalty not to exceed two hundred fifty thousand dollars ($250,000) per violation and shall also be subject to disgorgement of any proceeds or other consideration obtained as a result of the violation.

(B) Any licensed health care professional, who knowingly and willfully obtains, discloses, or uses medical information in violation of this part for financial gain shall be liable on a first violation, for an administrative fine or civil penalty not to exceed five thousand dollars ($5,000) per violation, or on a second violation for an administrative fine or civil penalty not to exceed twenty-five thousand dollars ($25,000) per violation, or on a third and subsequent violation for an administrative fine or civil penalty not to exceed two hundred fifty thousand dollars ($250,000) per violation and shall also be subject to disgorgement of any proceeds or other consideration obtained as a result of the violation. Nothing in this subdivision shall be construed to limit the liability of a health care service plan, a contractor, or a provider of health care that is not a licensed health care professional for any violation of this part.

(4) Nothing in this subdivision shall be construed as authorizing an administrative fine or civil penalty under both paragraphs (2) and (3) for the same violation.

(5) Any person or entity who is not permitted to receive medical information pursuant to this part and who knowingly and willfully obtains, discloses, or uses medical information without written authorization from the patient shall be liable for a civil penalty not to exceed two hundred fifty thousand dollars ($250,000) per violation.

(d) In assessing the amount of an administrative fine or civil penalty pursuant to subdivision (c), the Office of Health Information Integrity, licensing agency, or certifying board or court shall consider any one or more of the relevant circumstances presented by any of the parties to the case including, but not limited to, the following:

(1) Whether the defendant has made a reasonable, good faith attempt to comply with this part.

(2) The nature and seriousness of the misconduct.

(3) The harm to the patient, enrollee, or subscriber.

(4) The number of violations.

(5) The persistence of the misconduct.

(6) The length of time over which the misconduct occurred.

(7) The willfulness of the defendant's misconduct.

(8) The defendant's assets, liabilities, and net worth.

(e) (1) The civil penalty pursuant to subdivision (c) shall be assessed and recovered in a civil action brought in the name of the people of the State of California in any court of competent jurisdiction by any of the following:

(A) The Attorney General.

(B) Any district attorney.

(C) Any county counsel authorized by agreement with the district attorney in actions involving violation of a county ordinance.

(D) Any city attorney of a city.

(E) Any city attorney of a city and county having a population in excess of 750,000, with the consent of the district attorney.

(F) A city prosecutor in any city having a full-time city prosecutor or, with the consent of the district attorney, by a city attorney in any city and county.

(G) The Director of the Office of Health Information Integrity may recommend that any person described in subparagraphs (A) to (F), inclusive, bring a civil action under this section.

(2) If the action is brought by the Attorney General, one-half of the penalty collected shall be paid to the treasurer of the county in which the judgment was entered, and one-half to the General Fund. If the action is brought by a district attorney or county counsel, the penalty collected shall be paid to the treasurer of the county in which the judgment was entered. Except as provided in paragraph (3), if the action is brought by a city attorney or city prosecutor, one-half of the penalty collected shall be paid to the treasurer of the city in which the judgment was entered and one-half to the treasurer of the county in which the judgment was entered.

(3) If the action is brought by a city attorney of a city and county, the entire amount of the penalty collected shall be paid to the treasurer of the city and county in which the judgment was entered.

(4) Nothing in this section shall be construed as authorizing both an administrative fine and civil penalty for the same violation.

(5) Imposition of a fine or penalty provided for in this section shall not preclude imposition of any other sanctions or remedies authorized by law.

(6) Administrative fines or penalties issued pursuant to Section 1280.15 of the Health and Safety Code shall offset any other administrative fine or civil penalty imposed under this section for the same violation.

(f) For purposes of this section, "knowing" and "willful" shall have the same meanings as in Section 7 of the Penal Code.

(g) No person who discloses protected medical information in accordance with the provisions of this part shall be subject to the penalty provisions of this part.

(h) Paragraph (6) of subdivision (e) shall only become operative if Senate Bill 541 of the 2007-08 Regular Session is enacted and becomes effective on or before January 1, 2009.

Section 56.37.
(a) No provider of health care, health care service plan, or contractor may require a patient, as a condition of receiving health care services, to sign

an authorization, release, consent, or waiver that would permit the disclosure of medical information that otherwise may not be disclosed under Section 56.10 or any other provision of law. However, a health care service plan or disability insurer may require relevant enrollee or subscriber medical information as a condition of the medical underwriting process, provided that Sections 1374.7 and 1389.1 of the Health and Safety Code are strictly observed.

(b) Any waiver by a patient of the provisions of this part, except as authorized by Section 56.11 or 56.21 or subdivision (b) of Section 56.26, shall be deemed contrary to public policy and shall be unenforceable.

California Civil Code
Section 43.92
(a) There shall be no monetary liability on the part of, and no cause of action shall arise against, any person who is a psychotherapist as defined in Section 1010 of the Evidence Code in failing to warn of and protect from a patient's threatened violent behavior or failing to predict and warn of and protect from a patient' s violent behavior except where the patient has communicated to the psychotherapist a serious threat of physical violence against a reasonably identifiable victim or victims.

(b) There shall be no monetary liability on the part of, and no cause of action shall arise against, a psychotherapist who, under the limited circumstances specified above, discharges his or her duty to warn and protect by making reasonable efforts to communicate the threat to the victim or victims and to a law enforcement agency.

Psychotherapist-Patient Privilege

California Evidence Code
Section 912
(a) Except as otherwise provided in this section, the right of any person to claim a privilege provided by Section 954 (lawyer-client privilege), 980 (privilege for confidential marital communications), 994 (physician-patient privilege), 1014 (psychotherapist-patient privilege), 1033 (privilege of penitent), 1034 (privilege of clergyman), 1035.8 (sexual assault counselor-victim privilege), or 1037.5 (domestic violence counselor-victim privilege) is waived with respect to a communication protected by the privilege if any holder of the privilege, without coercion, has disclosed a significant part of the communication or has consented to disclosure made by anyone. Consent to disclosure is manifested by any statement or other conduct of the holder of the privilege indicating consent to the disclosure, including failure to claim the privilege in any proceeding in which the holder has the legal standing and opportunity to claim the privilege.

(b) Where two or more persons are joint holders of a privilege provided by Section 954 (lawyer-client privilege), 994 (physician-patient privilege), 1014 (psychotherapist-patient privilege), 1035.8 (sexual assault counselor-victim privilege), or 1037.5 (domestic violence counselor-victim privilege), a waiver of the right of a particular joint holder of the privilege to claim the privilege does not affect the right of another joint holder to claim the privilege. In the case of the privilege provided by Section 980 (privilege for confidential marital communications), a waiver of the right of one spouse to claim the privilege does not affect the right of the other spouse to claim the privilege.

(c) A disclosure that is itself privileged is not a waiver of any privilege.

(d) A disclosure in confidence of a communication that is protected by a privilege provided by Section 954 (lawyer-client privilege), 994 (physician-patient privilege), 1014 (psychotherapist-patient privilege), 1035.8 (sexual assault counselor-victim privilege), or 1037.5 (domestic violence counselor-victim privilege), when disclosure is reasonably necessary for the accomplishment of the purpose for which the lawyer, physician, psychotherapist, sexual assault counselor, or domestic violence counselor was consulted, is not a waiver of the privilege.

California Evidence Code
Section 1010.
As used in this article, "psychotherapist" means a person who is, or is reasonably believed by the patient to be:

(a) A person authorized to practice medicine in any state or nation who devotes, or is reasonably believed by the patient to devote, a substantial portion of his or her time to the practice of psychiatry.

(b) A person licensed as a psychologist under Chapter 6.6 (commencing with Section 2900) of Division 2 of the Business and Professions Code.

(c) A person licensed as a clinical social worker under Article 4 (commencing with Section 4996) of Chapter 14 of Division 2 of the Business and Professions Code, when he or she is engaged in applied psychotherapy of a nonmedical nature.

(d) A person who is serving as a school psychologist and holds a credential authorizing that service issued by the state.

(e) A person licensed as a marriage and family therapist under Chapter 13 (commencing with Section 4980) of Division 2 of the Business and Professions Code.
(f) A person registered as a psychological assistant who is under the

supervision of a licensed psychologist or board certified psychiatrist as required by Section 2913 of the Business and Professions Code, or a person registered as a marriage and family therapist intern who is under the supervision of a licensed marriage and family therapist, a licensed clinical social worker, a licensed psychologist, or a licensed physician and surgeon certified in psychiatry, as specified in Section 4980.44 of the Business and Professions Code.

(g) A person registered as an associate clinical social worker who is under supervision as specified in Section 4996.23 of the Business and Professions Code.

(h) A person exempt from the Psychology Licensing Law pursuant to subdivision (d) of Section 2909 of the Business and Professions Code who is under the supervision of a licensed psychologist or board certified psychiatrist.

(i) A psychological intern as defined in Section 2911 of the Business and Professions Code who is under the supervision of a licensed psychologist or board certified psychiatrist.

(j) A trainee, as defined in subdivision (c) of Section 4980.03 of the Business and Professions Code, who is fulfilling his or her supervised practicum required by subparagraph (B) of paragraph (1) of subdivision (d) of Section 4980.36 of, or subdivision (c) of Section 4980.37 of, the Business and Professions Code and is supervised by a licensed psychologist, a board certified psychiatrist, a licensed clinical social worker, a licensed marriage and family therapist, or a licensed professional clinical counselor.

(k) A person licensed as a registered nurse pursuant to Chapter 6 (commencing with Section 2700) of Division 2 of the Business and Professions Code, who possesses a master's degree in psychiatric-mental health nursing and is listed as a psychiatric-mental health nurse by the Board of Registered Nursing.

(l) An advanced practice registered nurse who is certified as a clinical nurse specialist pursuant to Article 9 (commencing with Section 2838) of Chapter 6 of Division 2 of the Business and Professions Code and who participates in expert clinical practice in the specialty of psychiatric-mental health nursing.

(m) A person rendering mental health treatment or counseling services as authorized pursuant to Section 6924 of the Family Code.

(n) A person licensed as a professional clinical counselor under Chapter 16 (commencing with Section 4999.10) of Division 2 of the Business and Professions Code.

(o) A person registered as a clinical counselor intern who is under the supervision of a licensed professional clinical counselor, a licensed marriage and family therapist, a licensed clinical social worker, a licensed psychologist, or a licensed physician and surgeon certified in psychiatry, as specified in Sections 4999.42 to 4999.46, inclusive, of the Business and Professions Code.

(p) A clinical counselor trainee, as defined in subdivision (g) of Section 4999.12 of the Business and Professions Code, who is fulfilling his or her supervised practicum required by paragraph (3) of subdivision (c) of Section 4999.32 of, or paragraph (3) of subdivision (c) of Section 4999.33 of, the Business and Professions Code, and is supervised by a licensed psychologist, a board-certified psychiatrist, a licensed clinical social worker, a licensed marriage and family therapist, or a licensed professional clinical counselor.

Section 1010.5.
A communication between a patient and an educational psychologist, licensed under Article 5 (commencing with Section 4986) of Chapter 13 of Division 2 of the Business and Professions Code, shall be privileged to the same extent, and subject to the same limitations, as a communication between a patient and a psychotherapist described in subdivisions (c), (d), and (e) of Section 1010.

Section 1011.
As used in this article, "patient" means a person who consults a psychotherapist or submits to an examination by a psychotherapist for the purpose of securing a diagnosis or preventive, palliative, or curative treatment of his mental or emotional condition or who submits to an examination of his mental or emotional condition for the purpose of scientific research on mental or emotional problems.

Section 1012.
As used in this article, "confidential communication between patient and psychotherapist" means information, including information obtained by an examination of the patient, transmitted between a patient and his psychotherapist in the course of that relationship and in confidence by a means which, so far as the patient is aware, discloses the information to no third persons other than those who are present to further the interest of the patient in the consultation, or those to whom disclosure is reasonably necessary for the transmission of the information or the accomplishment of the purpose for which the psychotherapist is consulted, and includes a diagnosis made and the advice given by the psychotherapist in the course of that relationship.

Section 1013.
As used in this article, "holder of the privilege" means:
(a) The patient when he has no guardian or conservator.
(b) A guardian or conservator of the patient when the patient has a guardian or conservator.
(c) The personal representative of the patient if the patient is dead.

Section 1014.
Subject to Section 912 and except as otherwise provided in this article, the patient, whether or not a party, has a privilege to refuse to disclose, and to prevent another from disclosing, a confidential communication between patient and psychotherapist if the privilege is claimed by:

(a) The holder of the privilege.

(b) A person who is authorized to claim the privilege by the holder of the privilege.

(c) The person who was the psychotherapist at the time of the confidential communication, but the person may not claim the privilege if there is no holder of the privilege in existence or if he or she is otherwise instructed by a person authorized to permit disclosure. The relationship of a psychotherapist and patient shall exist between a psychological corporation as defined in Article 9 (commencing with Section 2995) of Chapter 6.6 of Division 2 of the Business and Professions Code, a marriage and family therapist corporation as defined in Article 6 (commencing with Section 4987.5) of Chapter 13 of Division 2 of the Business and Professions Code, a licensed clinical social workers corporation as defined in Article 5 (commencing with Section 4998) of Chapter 14 of Division 2 of the Business and Professions Code, or a professional clinical counselor corporation as defined in Article 7 (commencing with Section 4999.123) of Chapter 16 of Division 2 of the Business and Professions Code, and the patient to whom it renders professional services, as well as between those patients and psychotherapists employed by those corporations to render services to those patients. The word "persons" as used in this subdivision includes partnerships, corporations, limited liability companies, associations, and other groups and entities.

Section 1015.
The psychotherapist who received or made a communication subject to the privilege under this article shall claim the privilege whenever he is present when the communication is sought to be disclosed and is authorized to claim the privilege under subdivision (c) of Section 1014.

Section 1016.
There is no privilege under this article as to a communication relevant to an

issue concerning the mental or emotional condition of the patient if such issue has been tendered by:

(a) The patient;

(b) Any party claiming through or under the patient;

(c) Any party claiming as a beneficiary of the patient through a contract to which the patient is or was a party; or

(d) The plaintiff in an action brought under Section 376 or 377 of the Code of Civil Procedure for damages for the injury or death of the patient.

Section 1017.
(a) There is no privilege under this article if the psychotherapist is appointed by order of a court to examine the patient, but this exception does not apply where the psychotherapist is appointed by order of the court upon the request of the lawyer for the defendant in a criminal proceeding in order to provide the lawyer with information needed so that he or she may advise the defendant whether to enter or withdraw a plea based on insanity or to present a defense based on his or her mental or emotional condition.

(b) There is no privilege under this article if the psychotherapist is appointed by the Board of Prison Terms to examine a patient pursuant to the provisions of Article 4 (commencing with Section 2960) of Chapter 7 of Title 1 of Part 3 of the Penal Code.

Section 1018.
There is no privilege under this article if the services of the psychotherapist were sought or obtained to enable or aid anyone to commit or plan to commit a crime or a tort or to escape detection or apprehension after the commission of a crime or a tort.

Section 1019.
There is no privilege under this article as to a communication relevant to an issue between parties all of whom claim through a deceased patient, regardless of whether the claims are by testate or intestate succession or by inter vivos transaction.

Section 1020.
There is no privilege under this article as to a communication relevant to an issue of breach, by the psychotherapist or by the patient, of a duty arising out of the psychotherapist-patient relationship.

Section 1021.
There is no privilege under this article as to a communication relevant to an issue concerning the intention of a patient, now deceased, with respect to a deed of conveyance, will, or other writing, executed by the patient, purporting to affect an interest in property.

Section 1022.
There is no privilege under this article as to a communication relevant to an issue concerning the validity of a deed of conveyance, will, or other writing, executed by a patient, now deceased, purporting to affect an interest in property.

Section 1023.
There is no privilege under this article in a proceeding under Chapter 6 (commencing with Section 1367) of Title 10 of Part 2 of the Penal Code initiated at the request of the defendant in a criminal action to determine his sanity.

Section 1024.
There is no privilege under this article if the psychotherapist has reasonable cause to believe that the patient is in such mental or emotional condition as to be dangerous to himself or to the person or property of another and that disclosure of the communication is necessary to prevent the threatened danger.

Section 1025.
There is no privilege under this article in a proceeding brought by or on behalf of the patient to establish his competence.

Section 1026.
There is no privilege under this article as to information that the psychotherapist or the patient is required to report to a public employee or as to information required to be recorded in a public office, if such report or record is open to public inspection.

Section 1027.
There is no privilege under this article if all of the following circumstances exist:
(a) The patient is a child under the age of 16.
(b) The psychotherapist has reasonable cause to believe that the patient has been the victim of a crime and that disclosure of the communication is in the best interest of the child.

Sexual Assault Counselor-Victim Privilege

California Evidence Code
Section 1035.
As used in this article, "victim" means a person who consults a sexual assault counselor for the purpose of securing advice or assistance concerning a mental, physical, or emotional condition caused by a sexual assault.

Section 1035.2.
As used in this article, "sexual assault counselor" means any of the following:

(a) A person who is engaged in any office, hospital, institution, or center commonly known as a rape crisis center, whose primary purpose is the rendering of advice or assistance to victims of sexual assault and who has received a certificate evidencing completion of a training program in the counseling of sexual assault victims issued by a counseling center that meets the criteria for the award of a grant established pursuant to Section 13837 of the Penal Code and who meets one of the following requirements:

(1) Is a psychotherapist as defined in Section 1010; has a master's degree in counseling or a related field; or has one year of counseling experience, at least six months of which is in rape crisis counseling.

(2) Has 40 hours of training as described below and is supervised by an individual who qualifies as a counselor under paragraph (1). The training, supervised by a person qualified under paragraph (1), shall include, but not be limited to, the following areas:

(A) Law.
(B) Medicine.
(C) Societal attitudes.
(D) Crisis intervention and counseling techniques.
(E) Role playing.
(F) Referral services.
(G) Sexuality.

(b) A person who is employed by any organization providing the programs specified in Section 13835.2 of the Penal Code, whether financially compensated or not, for the purpose of counseling and assisting sexual assault victims, and who meets one of the following requirements:
(1) Is a psychotherapist as defined in Section 1010; has a master's degree in counseling or a related field; or has one year of counseling experience, at least six months of which is in rape assault counseling.

(2) Has the minimum training for sexual assault counseling required by guidelines established by the employing agency pursuant to subdivision (c)

of Section 13835.10 of the Penal Code, and is supervised by an individual who qualifies as a counselor under paragraph (1). The training, supervised by a person qualified under paragraph (1), shall include, but not be limited to, the following areas:

(A) Law.
(B) Victimology.
(C) Counseling.
(D) Client and system advocacy.
(E) Referral services.

Section 1035.4.

As used in this article, "confidential communication between the sexual assault counselor and the victim" means information transmitted between the victim and the sexual assault counselor in the course of their relationship and in confidence by a means which, so far as the victim is aware, discloses the information to no third persons other than those who are present to further the interests of the victim in the consultation or those to whom disclosures are reasonably necessary for the transmission of the information or an accomplishment of the purposes for which the sexual assault counselor is consulted. The term includes all information regarding the facts and circumstances involving the alleged sexual assault and also includes all information regarding the victim's prior or subsequent sexual conduct, and opinions regarding the victim' s sexual conduct or reputation in sexual matters. The court may compel disclosure of information received by the sexual assault counselor which constitutes relevant evidence of the facts and circumstances involving an alleged sexual assault about which the victim is complaining and which is the subject of a criminal proceeding if the court determines that the probative value outweighs the effect on the victim, the treatment relationship, and the treatment services if disclosure is compelled. The court may also compel disclosure in proceedings related to child abuse if the court determines the probative value outweighs the effect on the victim, the treatment relationship, and the treatment services if disclosure is compelled. When a court is ruling on a claim of privilege under this article, the court may require the person from whom disclosure is sought or the person authorized to claim the privilege, or both, to disclose the information in chambers out of the presence and hearing of all persons except the person authorized to claim the privilege and such other persons as the person authorized to claim the privilege is willing to have present. If the judge determines that the information is privileged and must not be disclosed, neither he or she nor any other person may ever disclose, without the consent of a person authorized to permit disclosure, what was disclosed in the course of the proceedings in chambers. If the court determines certain information shall be disclosed, the court shall so order and inform the defendant. If the court finds there is a reasonable likelihood that particular information is subject to disclosure pursuant to the balancing test provided in this section, the following procedure shall be followed:

(1) The court shall inform the defendant of the nature of the information which may be subject to disclosure.

(2) The court shall order a hearing out of the presence of the jury, if any, and at the hearing allow the questioning of the sexual assault counselor regarding the information which the court has determined may be subject to disclosure.

(3) At the conclusion of the hearing, the court shall rule which items of information, if any, shall be disclosed. The court may make an order stating what evidence may be introduced by the defendant and the nature of questions to be permitted. The defendant may then offer evidence pursuant to the order of the court. Admission of evidence concerning the sexual conduct of the complaining witness is subject to Sections 352, 782, and 1103.

Section 1035.6.
As used in this article, "holder of the privilege" means:
(a) The victim when such person has no guardian or conservator.
(b) A guardian or conservator of the victim when the victim has a guardian or conservator.
(c) The personal representative of the victim if the victim is dead.

Section 1035.8.
A victim of a sexual assault, whether or not a party, has a privilege to refuse to disclose, and to prevent another from disclosing, a confidential communication between the victim and a sexual assault counselor if the privilege is claimed by any of the following :

(a) The holder of the privilege;

(b) A person who is authorized to claim the privilege by the holder of the privilege; or

(c) The person who was the sexual assault counselor at the time of the confidential communication, but that person may not claim the privilege if there is no holder of the privilege in existence or if he or she is otherwise instructed by a person authorized to permit disclosure.

Section 1036.
The sexual assault counselor who received or made a communication subject to the privilege under this article shall claim the privilege if he or she is present when the communication is sought to be disclosed and is authorized to claim the privilege under subdivision (c) of Section 1035.8.

Section 1036.2.
As used in this article, "sexual assault" includes all of the following:

(a) Rape, as defined in Section 261 of the Penal Code.
(b) Unlawful sexual intercourse, as defined in Section 261.5 of the Penal Code.
(c) Rape in concert with force and violence, as defined in Section 264.1 of the Penal Code.
(d) Rape of a spouse, as defined in Section 262 of the Penal Code.
(e) Sodomy, as defined in Section 286 of the Penal Code, except a violation of subdivision (e) of that section.
(f) A violation of Section 288 of the Penal Code.
(g) Oral copulation, as defined in Section 288a of the Penal Code, except a violation of subdivision (e) of that section.
(h) Sexual penetration, as defined in Section 289 of the Penal Code.
(i) Annoying or molesting a child under 18, as defined in Section 647a of the Penal Code.
(j) Any attempt to commit any of the above acts.

Domestic Violence Counselor-Victim Privilege

Section 1037.
As used in this article, "victim" means any person who suffers domestic violence, as defined in Section 1037.7.

Section 1037.1.
(a) (1) As used in this article, "domestic violence counselor" means a person who is employed by a domestic violence victim service organization, as defined in this article, whether financially compensated or not, for the purpose of rendering advice or assistance to victims of domestic violence and who has at least 40 hours of training as specified in paragraph (2).

(2) The 40 hours of training shall be supervised by an individual who qualifies as a counselor under paragraph (1), and who has at least one year of experience counseling domestic violence victims for the domestic violence victim service organization. The training shall include, but need not be limited to, the following areas: history of domestic violence, civil and criminal law as it relates to domestic violence, the domestic violence victim-counselor privilege and other laws that protect the confidentiality of victim records and information, societal attitudes towards domestic violence, peer counseling techniques, housing, public assistance and other financial resources available to meet the financial needs of domestic violence victims, and referral services available to domestic violence victims.

(3) A domestic violence counselor who has been employed by the domestic violence victim service organization for a period of less than six months shall be supervised by a domestic violence counselor who has at least one year of experience counseling domestic violence victims for the domestic violence victim service organization.

(b) As used in this article, "domestic violence victim service organization" means a nongovernmental organization or entity that provides shelter, programs, or services to victims of domestic violence and their children, including, but not limited to, either of the following:

(1) Domestic violence shelter-based programs, as described in Section 18294 of the Welfare and Institutions Code.

(2) Other programs with the primary mission to provide services to victims of domestic violence whether or not that program exists in an agency that provides additional services.

Section 1037.2.
(a) As used in this article, "confidential communication" means any information, including, but not limited to, written or oral communication, transmitted between the victim and the counselor in the course of their relationship and in confidence by a means which, so far as the victim is aware, discloses the information to no third persons other than those who are present to further the interests of the victim in the consultation or those to whom disclosures are reasonably necessary for the transmission of the information or an accomplishment of the purposes for which the domestic violence counselor is consulted. The term includes all information regarding the facts and circumstances involving all incidences of domestic violence, as well as all information about the children of the victim or abuser and the relationship of the victim with the abuser.

(b) The court may compel disclosure of information received by a domestic violence counselor which constitutes relevant evidence of the facts and circumstances involving a crime allegedly perpetrated against the victim or another household member and which is the subject of a criminal proceeding, if the court determines that the probative value of the information outweighs the effect of disclosure of the information on the victim, the counseling relationship, and the counseling services. The court may compel disclosure if the victim is either dead or not the complaining witness in a criminal action against the perpetrator. The court may also compel disclosure in proceedings related to child abuse if the court determines that the probative value of the evidence outweighs the effect of the disclosure on the victim, the counseling relationship, and the counseling services.

(c) When a court rules on a claim of privilege under this article, it may require the person from whom disclosure is sought or the person authorized to claim the privilege, or both, to disclose the information in chambers out of the presence and hearing of all persons except the person authorized to claim the privilege and such other persons as the person authorized to claim the privilege consents to have present. If the judge determines that the information is privileged and shall not be disclosed, neither he nor she nor any other person may disclose, without the consent of a person authorized to permit disclosure, any information disclosed in the course of the proceedings in chambers.

(d) If the court determines that information shall be disclosed, the court shall so order and inform the defendant in the criminal action. If the court finds there is a reasonable likelihood that any information is subject to disclosure pursuant to the balancing test provided in this section, the procedure specified in subdivisions (1), (2), and (3) of Section 1035.4 shall be followed.

Section 1037.3.
Nothing in this article shall be construed to limit any obligation to report instances of child abuse as required by Section 11166 of the Penal Code.

Section 1037.4.
As used in this article, "holder of the privilege" means:

(a) The victim when he or she has no guardian or conservator.
(b) A guardian or conservator of the victim when the victim has a guardian or conservator, unless the guardian or conservator is accused of perpetrating domestic violence against the victim.

Section 1037.5.
A victim of domestic violence, whether or not a party to the action, has a privilege to refuse to disclose, and to prevent another from disclosing, a confidential communication between the victim and a domestic violence counselor in any proceeding specified in Section 901 if the privilege is claimed by any of the following persons:

(a) The holder of the privilege.
(b) A person who is authorized to claim the privilege by the holder of the privilege.
(c) The person who was the domestic violence counselor at the time of the confidential communication. However, that person may not claim the privilege if there is no holder of the privilege in existence or if he or she is otherwise instructed by a person authorized to permit disclosure.

Section 1037.6.
The domestic violence counselor who received or made a communication

subject to the privilege granted by this article shall claim the privilege whenever he or she is present when the communication is sought to be disclosed and he or she is authorized to claim the privilege under subdivision (c) of Section 1037.5.

Section 1037.7.
As used in this article, "domestic violence" means "domestic violence" as defined in Section 6211 of the Family Code.

Section 1037.8.
A domestic violence counselor shall inform a domestic violence victim of any applicable limitations on confidentiality of communications between the victim and the domestic violence counselor. This information may be given orally.

Human Trafficking Caseworker-Victim Privilege

Section 1038.
(a) A trafficking victim, whether or not a party to the action, has a privilege to refuse to disclose, and to prevent another from disclosing, a confidential communication between the victim and a human trafficking caseworker if the privilege is claimed by any of the following persons:

(1) The holder of the privilege.

(2) A person who is authorized to claim the privilege by the holder of the privilege.

(3) The person who was the human trafficking caseworker at the time of the confidential communication. However, that person may not claim the privilege if there is no holder of the privilege in existence or if he or she is otherwise instructed by a person authorized to permit disclosure. The human trafficking caseworker who received or made a communication subject to the privilege granted by this article shall claim the privilege whenever he or she is present when the communication is sought to be disclosed and he or she is authorized to claim the privilege under this section.

(b) A human trafficking caseworker shall inform a trafficking victim of any applicable limitations on confidentiality of communications between the victim and the caseworker. This information may be given orally.

Section 1038.1.
(a) The court may compel disclosure of information received by a human trafficking caseworker that constitutes relevant evidence of the facts and circumstances involving a crime allegedly perpetrated against the victim

and that is the subject of a criminal proceeding, if the court determines that the probative value of the information outweighs the effect of disclosure of the information on the victim, the counseling relationship, and the counseling services. The court may compel disclosure if the victim is either dead or not the complaining witness in a criminal action against the perpetrator.

(b) When a court rules on a claim of privilege under this article, it may require the person from whom disclosure is sought or the person authorized to claim the privilege, or both, to disclose the information in chambers out of the presence and hearing of all persons except the person authorized to claim the privilege and those other persons that the person authorized to claim the privilege consents to have present.

(c) If the judge determines that the information is privileged and shall not be disclosed, neither he nor she nor any other person may disclose, without the consent of a person authorized to permit disclosure, any information disclosed in the course of the proceedings in chambers. If the court determines that information shall be disclosed, the court shall so order and inform the defendant in the criminal action. If the court finds there is a reasonable likelihood that any information is subject to disclosure pursuant to the balancing test provided in this section, the procedure specified in paragraphs (1), (2), and (3) of Section 1035.4 shall be followed.

Section 1038.2.
(a) As used in this article, "victim" means any person who is a "trafficking victim" as defined in Section 236.1.

(b) As used in this article, "human trafficking caseworker" means any of the following:
(1) A person who is employed by any organization providing the programs specified in Section 18294 of the Welfare and Institutions Code, whether financially compensated or not, for the purpose of rendering advice or assistance to victims of human trafficking, who has received specialized training in the counseling of human trafficking victims, and who meets one of the following requirements:

(A) Has a master's degree in counseling or a related field; or has one year of counseling experience, at least six months of which is in the counseling of human trafficking victims.

(B) Has at least 40 hours of training as specified in this paragraph and is supervised by an individual who qualifies as a counselor under subparagraph (A), or is a psychotherapist, as defined in Section 1010. The training, supervised by a person qualified under subparagraph (A), shall include, but need not be limited to, the following areas: history of human trafficking, civil and criminal law as it relates to human trafficking, societal attitudes towards human trafficking, peer counseling techniques, housing, public assistance and other financial resources available to meet the financial needs of human trafficking victims, and referral services available to human trafficking victims. A portion of this training must include an explanation of privileged communication.

(2) A person who is employed by any organization providing the programs specified in Section 13835.2 of the Penal Code, whether financially compensated or not, for the purpose of counseling and assisting human trafficking victims, and who meets one of the following requirements:

(A) Is a psychotherapist as defined in Section 1010, has a master' s degree in counseling or a related field, or has one year of counseling experience, at least six months of which is in rape assault counseling.

(B) Has the minimum training for human trafficking counseling required by guidelines established by the employing agency pursuant to subdivision (c) of Section 13835.10 of the Penal Code, and is supervised by an individual who qualifies as a counselor under subparagraph (A). The training, supervised by a person qualified under subparagraph (A), shall include, but not be limited to, law, victimology, counseling techniques, client and system advocacy, and referral services. A portion of this training must include an explanation of privileged communication.

(c) As used in this article, "confidential communication" means information transmitted between the victim and the caseworker in the course of their relationship and in confidence by a means which, so far as the victim is aware, discloses the information to no third persons other than those who are present to further the interests of the victim in the consultation or those to whom disclosures are reasonably necessary for the transmission of the information or an accomplishment of the purposes for which the human trafficking counselor is consulted. It includes all information regarding the facts and circumstances involving all incidences of human trafficking.

(d) As used in this article, "holder of the privilege" means the victim when he or she has no guardian or conservator, or a guardian or conservator of the victim when the victim has a guardian or conservator.

CHAPTER 9
Record Keeping

According to the Business and Professions Code 4999.75 and 4980.49 therapists are required to retain clients or patient's healthcare records for a minimum of seven years from the date therapy is terminated. If the client or patient is a minor, healthcare service record shall be retained for a minimum of seven years from the date the client or the patient reaches 18 years of age. The healthcare records may be retained in either written or electronic format. In this section, 'patient' is used synonymously with 'client.' Therapists can keep the records longer than that required duration; there is no limit on that; however, they must meet the minimum timeframes.

When we look at what needs to be contained in clinical records, you won't find any singular place in the law that gives you specific guidance. California Health and Safety Code 123130 gives some information about what the law is requiring or expecting to be part of records. This section discusses situations when a client asks for a copy of their records, and we provide them a summary of those records. Here, the law gives us some information about what should be included in this summary. There are eight specific items:

(1) chief complaint or complaints including pertinent history

(2) findings from consultations and referrals to other health care providers

(3) diagnosis, where determined

(4) treatment plan and regimen including medications prescribed

(5) progress of the treatment

6) prognosis including significant continuing problems or conditions pertinent

(7) pertinent reports of diagnostic procedures and tests and all discharge summaries

(8) objective findings from the most relevant physical exam, such as blood pressure, weight, and actual values from routine laboratory tests.

While some of the information required much more pertinent to those in the medical field than versus mental health, these are the requirements that both groups must follow. It may be necessary for therapists to refer to their professional organizations to determine what additional information might be required or would be recommended to be kept in clinical records and how those records should be formatted.

California Health and Safety Code 123105 provides some important definitions as it relates to who is responsible for clinical records and what they may contain. It discusses that patient records includes only records pertaining to the patient requesting the records or whose representative requests the records and that it does not include information given in confidence to a healthcare provider by a person other than another healthcare provider that material may be removed from any records prior to inspection or copying, per the patients right to do so under sections 123110 and 123115.

When patients request access to their records, there are essentially three ways in which a therapist can respond to a patient request to either (1) inspect their records or to (2) receive a copy. The therapist can either accept and allow the client to receive a copy of their records or to inspect the records (reviewing the records there in the office) or if the client asked to receive a copy of the record, the therapist could decide instead of having the client have access to the entire record they provide a summary. The therapists can also decide to decline the patient's request to either inspect or either receive a copy of the record.

Access and Restrictions Summary
of
California Health and Safety Code 123110 & 123115

1.   A patient can ask to inspect the records (that would be there in the office), or for a copy of the records. When they ask for a copy of the records or to inspect the records, the request must be in writing.

2.   If the patient requests an inspection of their record in writing, the therapist must make that record available during normal business hours and within five working days of the request being made.

3.   If the patient is asking for a copy of their records in writing, the

therapist must provide the copy of those records (either the entire records or the specific part they are requesting) within 15 days after receiving the request.

4.   The law does allow the healthcare providers to charge for copying of the records and that charge is no more than 25 cents per page as well as any additional costs that are reasonable for locating and making the record available. Note there are some exceptions.

5.   This section prohibits a healthcare provider from withholding patient records or summaries of patient records because of an unpaid bill for healthcare services.

6.   A healthcare practitioner is allowed to provide the client with a summary of the treatment record instead of providing the complete and entire record. If the therapist decides that they are going to give a summary of the record, they must provide that document or set of documents within 10 working days after the date of the request.

7.   If the record is a large data set and the therapist cannot make the required timeframe, the therapist has up to 30 days (from the original date of request) to produce them as long as they have notified the client.

8.   California Health and Safety Code 123115 informs that the representative of a minor are not entitled to inspect or obtain copies of the records (a) if the minor consented to their own treatment or (b) the health care provider determines that access to the patient's records requested by the representative would have a detrimental effect on the providers professional relationship with the minor patient or the minors physical safety or psychological well-being.

9.   If an adult patient submits a request for their records in writing, the request may be denied if the health care provider determines that there is a substantial risk of significant adverse or detrimental consequences to the patient if they obtained their records or inspected them. The therapist must include a note in the file explaining the reason for the denial, the date of the request and description of the specific adverse or detrimental consequences to the patient that the provider anticipates would occur if permitted.

10.   Copies or the inspection of records can be provided to another healthcare provider at the patients request if they were denied. Note: If the receiving or inspecting provider is a BBS Registered Associate, the supervisor has to sign a receipt for the records. The receiving provider cannot then allow the client to review or have a copy of the records; they were already denied.

11.   Patients have the right to attach an addendum 250 words per item or statement in their record that they believe is incorrect or incomplete.   The provider would document and disclose this addendum was completed by the patient, even if the provider believes the patient's addendum is not correct.

12.   Note that HIPAA Covered Entities are required to follow HIPAA rules and regulations; the restriction or denial reasons are a bit different.   Under 45 Code of Federal Regulations 164.524 "individuals' access to protected health information that is contained in records that are subject to Privacy Act 5 USC 552a may be denied if the denial of access under the Privacy Act would meet the requirements of that law.

a.   A licensed healthcare professional may determine, in the exercise of professional judgment that the access requested is reasonably likely to endanger the life or physical safety of the individual or another person.

California Health and Safety Code
123105
As used in this chapter:
(a) "Health care provider" means any of the following:

(1) A health facility licensed pursuant to Chapter 2 (commencing with Section 1250) of Division 2.

(2) A clinic licensed pursuant to Chapter 1 (commencing with Section 1200) of Division 2.

(3) A home health agency licensed pursuant to Chapter 8 (commencing with Section 1725) of Division 2.

(4) A physician and surgeon licensed pursuant to Chapter 5 (commencing with Section 2000) of Division 2 of the Business and Professions Code or pursuant to the Osteopathic Act.

(5) A podiatrist licensed pursuant to Article 22 (commencing with Section

2460) of Chapter 5 of Division 2 of the Business and Professions Code.

(6) A dentist licensed pursuant to Chapter 4 (commencing with Section 1600) of Division 2 of the Business and Professions Code.

(7) A psychologist licensed pursuant to Chapter 6.6 (commencing with Section 2900) of Division 2 of the Business and Professions Code.

(8) An optometrist licensed pursuant to Chapter 7 (commencing with Section 3000) of Division 2 of the Business and Professions Code.

(9) A chiropractor licensed pursuant to the Chiropractic Initiative Act.

(10) A marriage and family therapist licensed pursuant to Chapter 13 (commencing with Section 4980) of Division 2 of the Business and Professions Code.

(11) A clinical social worker licensed pursuant to Chapter 14 (commencing with Section 4990) of Division 2 of the Business and Professions Code.

(12) A physical therapist licensed pursuant to Chapter 5.7 (commencing with Section 2600) of Division 2 of the Business and Professions Code.

(13) An occupational therapist licensed pursuant to Chapter 5.6 (commencing with Section 2570).

(14) A professional clinical counselor licensed pursuant to Chapter 16 (commencing with Section 4999.10) of Division 2 of the Business and Professions Code.

(b) "Mental health records" means patient records, or discrete portions thereof, specifically relating to evaluation or treatment of a mental disorder. "Mental health records" includes, but is not limited to, all alcohol and drug abuse records.

(c) "Patient" means a patient or former patient of a health care provider.

(d) "Patient records" means records in any form or medium maintained by, or in the custody or control of, a health care provider relating to the health history, diagnosis, or condition of a patient, or relating to treatment provided or proposed to be provided to the patient. "Patient records" includes only records pertaining to the patient requesting the records or whose representative requests the records. "Patient records" does not include information given in confidence to a health care provider by a person other than another health care provider or the patient, and that material may be removed from any records prior to inspection or copying under Section 123110 or 123115. "Patient records" does not include information contained in aggregate form, such as indices, registers, or logs.

(e) "Patient's representative," "patient's personal representative," or "representative" means any of the following:

(1) A parent or guardian of a minor who is a patient.

(2) The guardian or conservator of the person of an adult patient.

(3) An agent as defined in Section 4607 of the Probate Code, to the extent necessary for the agent to fulfill his or her duties as set forth in Division 4.7 (commencing with Section 4600) of the Probate Code.

(4) The beneficiary as defined in Section 24 of the Probate Code or personal representative as defined in Section 58 of the Probate Code, of a deceased patient.

(f) "Alcohol and drug abuse records" means patient records, or discrete portions thereof, specifically relating to evaluation and treatment of alcoholism or drug abuse.

123110
(a) Notwithstanding Section 5328 of the Welfare and Institutions Code, and except as provided in Sections 123115 and 123120, any adult patient of a health care provider, any minor patient authorized by law to consent to medical treatment, and any patient's personal representative shall be entitled to inspect patient records upon presenting to the health care provider a request for those records and upon payment of reasonable costs, as specified in subdivision (k). However, a patient who is a minor shall be entitled to inspect patient records pertaining only to health care of a type for which the minor is lawfully authorized to consent. A health care provider shall permit this inspection during business hours within five working days after receipt of the request. The inspection shall be conducted by the patient or patient's personal representative requesting the inspection, who may be accompanied by one other person of his or her choosing.

(b) (1) Additionally, any patient or patient's personal representative shall be entitled to a paper or electronic copy of all or any portion of the patient records that he or she has a right to inspect, upon presenting a request to the health care provider specifying the records to be copied, together with a fee to defray the costs of producing the copy or summary, as specified in subdivision (k). The health care provider shall ensure that the copies are transmitted within 15 days after receiving the request.

(2) The health care provider shall provide the patient or patient's personal

representative with a copy of the record in the form and format requested if it is readily producible in the requested form and format, or, if not, in a readable paper copy form or other form and format as agreed to by the health care provider and the patient or patient's personal representative. If the requested patient records are maintained electronically and if the patient or patient's personal representative requests an electronic copy of those records, the health care provider shall provide them in the electronic form and format requested if they are readily producible in that form and format, or, if not, in a readable electronic form and format as agreed to by the health care provider and the patient or patient's personal representative.

(c) Copies of X-rays or tracings derived from electrocardiography, electroencephalography, or electromyography need not be provided to the patient or patient's personal representative under this section, if the original X-rays or tracings are transmitted to another health care provider upon written request of the patient or patient's personal representative and within 15 days after receipt of the request. The request shall specify the name and address of the health care provider to whom the records are to be delivered. All reasonable costs, not exceeding actual costs, incurred by a health care provider in providing copies pursuant to this subdivision may be charged to the patient or representative requesting the copies.

(d) (1) Notwithstanding any provision of this section, and except as provided in Sections 123115 and 123120, a patient, former patient, or the personal representative of a patient or former patient, is entitled to a copy, at no charge, of the relevant portion of the patient's records, upon presenting to the provider a written request, and proof that the records or supporting forms are needed to support a claim or appeal regarding eligibility for a public benefit program. These programs shall be the Medi-Cal program, the In-Home Supportive Services Program, the California Work Opportunity and Responsibility to Kids (CalWORKs) program, social security disability insurance benefits, Supplemental Security Income/State Supplementary Program for the Aged, Blind and Disabled (SSI/SSP) benefits, federal veterans service-connected compensation and nonservice connected pension disability benefits, and CalFresh.

(2) Although a patient shall not be limited to a single request, the patient or patient's personal representative shall be entitled to no more than one copy of any relevant portion of his or her record free of charge.

(3) This subdivision shall not apply to any patient who is represented by a private attorney who is paying for the costs related to the patient's claim or appeal, pending the outcome of that claim or appeal. For purposes of this subdivision, "private attorney" means any attorney not employed by a nonprofit legal services entity.

(e) If the patient's appeal regarding eligibility for a public benefit program specified in subdivision (d) is successful, the hospital or other health care provider may bill the patient, at the rates specified in subdivisions (b) and (c), for the copies of the medical records previously provided free of charge.

(f) If a patient or his or her personal representative requests a record pursuant to subdivision (d), the health care provider shall ensure that the copies are transmitted within 30 days after receiving the written request.

(g) This section shall not be construed to preclude a health care provider from requiring reasonable verification of identity prior to permitting inspection or copying of patient records, provided this requirement is not used oppressively or discriminatorily to frustrate or delay compliance with this section. Nothing in this chapter shall be deemed to supersede any rights that a patient or personal representative might otherwise have or exercise under Section 1158 of the Evidence Code or any other provision of law. Nothing in this chapter shall require a health care provider to retain records longer than required by applicable statutes or administrative regulations.

(h) This chapter shall not be construed to render a health care provider liable for the quality of his or her records or the copies provided in excess of existing law and regulations with respect to the quality of medical records. A health care provider shall not be liable to the patient or any other person for any consequences that result from disclosure of patient records as required by this chapter. A health care provider shall not discriminate against classes or categories of providers in the transmittal of X-rays or other patient records, or copies of these X-rays or records, to other providers as authorized by this section.

Every health care provider shall adopt policies and establish procedures for the uniform transmittal of X-rays and other patient records that effectively prevent the discrimination described in this subdivision. A health care provider may establish reasonable conditions, including a reasonable deposit fee, to ensure the return of original X-rays transmitted to another health care provider, provided the conditions do not discriminate on the basis of, or in a manner related to, the license of the provider to which the X-rays are transmitted.

(i) Any health care provider described in paragraphs (4) to (10), inclusive, of subdivision (a) of Section 123105 who willfully violates this chapter is guilty of unprofessional conduct. Any health care provider described in paragraphs (1) to (3), inclusive, of subdivision (a) of Section 123105 that willfully violates this chapter is guilty of an infraction punishable by a fine of not more than one hundred dollars ($100). The state agency, board, or commission that issued the health care provider's professional or institutional license shall consider a violation as grounds for disciplinary action with respect to the licensure, including suspension or revocation of the license or certificate.

(j) This section prohibits a health care provider from withholding patient records or summaries of patient records because of an unpaid bill for health care services. Any health care provider who willfully withholds patient records or summaries of patient records because of an unpaid bill for health care services is subject to the sanctions specified in subdivision (i).

(k) (1) Except as provided in subdivision (d), a health care provider may impose a reasonable, cost-based fee for providing a paper or electronic copy or summary of patient records, provided the fee includes only the cost of the following:

(A) Labor for copying the patient records requested by the patient or patient's personal representative, whether in paper or electronic form.

(B) Supplies for creating the paper copy or electronic media if the patient or patient's personal representative requests that the electronic copy be provided on portable media.

(C) Postage, if the patient or patient's personal representative has requested the copy, or the summary or explanation, be mailed.

(D) Preparing an explanation or summary of the patient record, if agreed to by the patient or patient's personal representative.

(2) The fee from a health care provider shall not exceed twenty-five cents ($0.25) per page for paper copies or fifty cents ($0.50) per page for records that are copied from microfilm.

123111
(a) A patient who inspects his or her patient records pursuant to Section 123110 has the right to provide to the health care provider a written addendum with respect to any item or statement in his or her records that the patient believes to be incomplete or incorrect. The addendum shall be limited to 250 words per alleged incomplete or incorrect item in the patient's record and shall clearly indicate in writing that the patient requests the addendum to be made a part of his or her record.

(b) The health care provider shall attach the addendum to the patient's records and shall include that addendum if the health care provider makes a disclosure of the allegedly incomplete or incorrect portion of the patient's records to any third party.

(c) The receipt of information in a patient's addendum which contains defamatory or otherwise unlawful language, and the inclusion of this information in the patient's records, in accordance with subdivision (b), shall not, in and of itself, subject the health care provider to liability in any civil, criminal, administrative, or other proceeding.

(d) Subdivision (i) of Section 123110 and Section 123120 are applicable with respect to any violation of this section by a health care provider.

123115
(a) The representative of a minor shall not be entitled to inspect or obtain copies of the minor's patient records in either of the following circumstances:

(1) With respect to which the minor has a right of inspection under Section 123110.

(2) Where the health care provider determines that access to the patient records requested by the representative would have a detrimental effect on the provider's professional relationship with the minor patient or the minor's physical safety or psychological well-being. The decision of the health care provider as to whether or not a minor's records are available for inspection or copying under this section shall not attach any liability to the provider, unless the decision is found to be in bad faith.

(b) When a health care provider determines there is a substantial risk of significant adverse or detrimental consequences to a patient in seeing or receiving a copy of mental health records requested by the patient, the provider may decline to permit inspection or provide copies of the records to the patient, subject to the following conditions:

(1) The health care provider shall make a written record, to be included with the mental health records requested, noting the date of the request and explaining the health care provider's reason for refusing to permit inspection or provide copies of the records, including a description of the specific adverse or detrimental consequences to the patient that the provider anticipates would occur if inspection or copying were permitted.

(2) (A) The health care provider shall permit inspection by, or provide copies of the mental health records to, a licensed physician and surgeon, licensed psychologist, licensed marriage and family therapist, licensed clinical social worker, or licensed professional clinical counselor, designated by request of the patient.

(B) Any person registered as a marriage and family therapist intern, as defined in Chapter 13 (commencing with Section 4980) of Division 2 of the Business and Professions Code, may not inspect the patient's mental health records or obtain copies thereof, except pursuant to the direction or supervision of a licensed professional specified in subdivision (g) of Section 4980.03 of the Business and Professions Code. Prior to providing copies of mental health records to a registered marriage and family therapist intern, a receipt for those records shall be signed by the supervising licensed professional.

(C) Any person registered as a clinical counselor intern, as defined in Chapter 16 (commencing with Section 4999.10) of Division 2 of the Business and Professions Code, may not inspect the patient's mental health records or obtain copies thereof, except pursuant to the direction or supervision of a licensed professional specified in subdivision (h) of Section 4999.12 of the Business and Professions Code. Prior to providing copies of mental health records to a person registered as a clinical counselor intern, a receipt for those records shall be signed by the supervising licensed professional.

(D) A licensed physician and surgeon, licensed psychologist, licensed marriage and family therapist, licensed clinical social worker, licensed professional clinical counselor, registered marriage and family therapist intern, or person registered as a clinical counselor intern to whom the records are provided for inspection or copying shall not permit inspection or copying by the patient.

(3) The health care provider shall inform the patient of the provider's refusal to permit him or her to inspect or obtain copies of the requested records, and inform the patient of the right to require the provider to permit inspection by, or provide copies to, a licensed physician and surgeon, licensed psychologist, licensed marriage and family therapist, licensed clinical social worker, or licensed professional clinical counselor designated by written authorization of the patient.

(4) The health care provider shall indicate in the mental health records of the patient whether the request was made under paragraph (2).

123130
(a) A health care provider may prepare a summary of the record, according to the requirements of this section, for inspection and copying by a patient. If the health care provider chooses to prepare a summary of the record rather than allowing access to the entire record, he or she shall make the summary of the record available to the patient within 10 working days from the date of the patient's request. However, if more time is needed because the record is of extraordinary length or because the patient was discharged from a licensed health facility within the last 10 days, the health care provider shall notify the patient of this fact and the

date that the summary will be completed, but in no case shall more than 30 days elapse between the request by the patient and the delivery of the summary. In preparing the summary of the record the health care provider shall not be obligated to include information that is not contained in the original record.

(b) A health care provider may confer with the patient in an attempt to clarify the patient's purpose and goal in obtaining his or her record. If as a consequence the patient requests information about only certain injuries, illnesses, or episodes, this subdivision shall not require the provider to prepare the summary required by this subdivision for other than the injuries, illnesses, or episodes so requested by the patient. The summary shall contain for each injury, illness, or episode any information included in the record relative to the following:

> (1) Chief complaint or complaints including pertinent history.
>
> (2) Findings from consultations and referrals to other health care providers.
>
> (3) Diagnosis, where determined.
>
> (4) Treatment plan and regimen including medications prescribed.
>
> (5) Progress of the treatment.
>
> (6) Prognosis including significant continuing problems or conditions.
>
> (7) Pertinent reports of diagnostic procedures and tests and all discharge summaries.
>
> (8) Objective findings from the most recent physical examination, such as blood pressure, weight, and actual values from routine laboratory tests.

(c) This section shall not be construed to require any medical records to be written or maintained in any manner not otherwise required by law.

(d) The summary shall contain a list of all current medications prescribed, including dosage, and any sensitivities or allergies to medications recorded by the provider.

(e) Subdivision (c) of Section 123110 shall be applicable whether or not the health care provider elects to prepare a summary of the record.

(f) The health care provider may charge no more than a reasonable fee based on actual time and cost for the preparation of the summary. The cost shall be based on a computation of the actual time spent preparing the summary for availability to the patient or the patient's representative. It is the intent of the Legislature that summaries of the records be made available at the lowest possible cost to the patient.

CHAPTER 10
HEALTH INSURANCE PORTABILITY
AND ACCOUNTABILITY ACT (HIPAA)

There is a lot of responsibility that comes with the protection of the health information of our clients. HIPAA is the umbrella notation that mandates you attend to and constantly monitor the privacy of our clients in whatever setting you may be providing services. In short review of the history, HIPAA was created to protect the consumer of health services. It not only encompasses direct service providers and the patient, but the health care organization as a whole. There are strict regulations on how information is distributed amongst people within the organization, as well as outside of the organization. If any negligence occurs, you and your organization are both held liable for releasing this protected information of your clients.

Many find HIPAA regulations to be a daunting reminder of how important it is to protect the identity of your clients. Each organization that you will work for not only follows these federal guidelines, but often times have supplementary policies that you will be trained in, at the very least on an annual basis. Further, adherence to HIPAA regulations and organization wide practices are going to be a daily task for you and your co-workers. The best way YOU can follow the letters of the law is to stay informed and knowledgeable of the latest regulations.

Remember when your supervisors or professors told you about protecting your documents? HIPAA has strict outlines about who can access, release, review and disclose information about consumers of your services. The "minimum necessary" rule applies here too. This means that you have a legal responsibility to release the minimum necessary information about your clients when discussing them with a third party. For example, licensed professionals in private practice often speak directly with insurance companies to render payment for therapy sessions provided.

As a reminder, HIPAA applies to health providers who (1) engage in certain covered transactions on behalf of the client with other third parties and (2) engage in those transactions through electronic means. Whether the transaction was initiated by the therapist or by another third-party, if it is a covered transaction then the therapist must comply with HIPAA and is forever a covered entity.

Common covered transactions are submitting claims for reimbursement to health care plan, submitting a referral authorization to health care plans, receiving responses for inquiries or claims about eligibility or potential services. These are but a few, but essentially any communication that is transmitted electronically for referrals or billing as well as other communication fall under "covered transactions".

Code of Federal Regulations
164.501

As used in this subpart, the following terms have the following meanings:

Correctional institution means any penal or correctional facility, jail, reformatory, detention center, work farm, halfway house, or residential community program center operated by, or under contract to, the United States, a State, a territory, a political subdivision of a State or territory, or an Indian tribe, for the confinement or rehabilitation of persons charged with or convicted of a criminal offense or other persons held in lawful custody. Other persons held in lawful custody includes juvenile offenders adjudicated delinquent, aliens detained awaiting deportation, persons committed to mental institutions through the criminal justice system, witnesses, or others awaiting charges or trial.

Data aggregation means, with respect to protected health information created or received by a business associate in its capacity as the business associate of a covered entity, the combining of such protected health information by the business associate with the protected health information received by the business associate in its capacity as a business associate of another covered entity, to permit data analyses that relate to the health care operations of the respective covered entities.

Designated record set means:

(1) A group of records maintained by or for a covered entity that is:

(i) The medical records and billing records about individuals maintained by or for a covered health care provider;

(ii) The enrollment, payment, claims adjudication, and case or medical management record systems maintained by or for a health plan; or

(iii) Used, in whole or in part, by or for the covered entity to make decisions about individuals.

(2) For purposes of this paragraph, the term record means any item, collection, or grouping of information that includes protected health information and is maintained, collected, used, or disseminated by or for a covered entity.

Direct treatment relationship means a treatment relationship between an individual and a health care provider that is not an indirect treatment relationship.

Health care operations means any of the following activities of the covered entity to the extent that the activities are related to covered functions:

(1) Conducting quality assessment and improvement activities, including

outcomes evaluation and development of clinical guidelines, provided that the obtaining of generalizable knowledge is not the primary purpose of any studies resulting from such activities; patient safety activities (as defined in42 CFR 3.20); population-based activities relating to improving health or reducing health care costs, protocol development, case management and care coordination, contacting of health care providers and patients with information about treatment alternatives; and related functions that do not include treatment;

(2) Reviewing the competence or qualifications of health care professionals, evaluating practitioner and provider performance, health plan performance, conducting training programs in which students, trainees, or practitioners in areas of health care learn under supervision to practice or improve their skills as health care providers, training of non-health care professionals, accreditation, certification, licensing, or credentialing activities;

(3) Except as prohibited under§ 164.502(a)(5)(i), underwriting, enrollment, premium rating, and other activities related to the creation, renewal, or replacement of a contract of health insurance or health benefits, and ceding, securing, or placing a contract for reinsurance of risk relating to claims for health care (including stop-loss insurance and excess of loss insurance), provided that the requirements of § 164.514(g) are met, if applicable;

(4) Conducting or arranging for medical review, legal services, and auditing functions, including fraud and abuse detection and compliance programs;

(5) Business planning and development, such as conducting cost-management and planning-related analyses related to managing and operating the entity, including formulary development and administration, development or improvement of methods of payment or coverage policies; and

(6) Business management and general administrative activities of the entity, including, but not limited to:

(i) Management activities relating to implementation of and compliance with the requirements of this subchapter;

(ii) Customer service, including the provision of data analyses for policy holders, plan sponsors, or other customers, provided that protected health information is not disclosed to such policy holder, plan sponsor, or customer.

(iii) Resolution of internal grievances;

(iv) The sale, transfer, merger, or consolidation of all or part of the covered entity with another covered entity, or an entity that following such activity will become a covered entity and due diligence related to such activity; and

(v) Consistent with the applicable requirements of§ 164.514, creating de-identified health information or a limited data set, and fundraising for the benefit of the covered entity.

Health oversight agency means an agency or authority of the United

States, a State, a territory, a political subdivision of a State or territory, or an Indian tribe, or a person or entity acting under a grant of authority from or contract with such public agency, including the employees or agents of such public agency or its contractors or persons or entities to whom it has granted authority, that is authorized by law to oversee the health care system (whether public or private) or government programs in which health information is necessary to determine eligibility or compliance, or to enforce civil rights laws for which health information is relevant.

Indirect treatment relationship means a relationship between an individual and a health care provider in which:

(1) The health care provider delivers health care to the individual based on the orders of another health care provider; and

(2) The health care provider typically provides services or products, or reports the diagnosis or results associated with the health care, directly to another health care provider, who provides the services or products or reports to the individual.

Inmate means a person incarcerated in or otherwise confined to a correctional institution.

Marketing:

(1) Except as provided in paragraph (2) of this definition, marketing means to make a communication about a product or service that encourages recipients of the communication to purchase or use the product or service.

(2) Marketing does not include a communication made:

(i) To provide refill reminders or otherwise communicate about a drug or biologic that is currently being prescribed for the individual, only if any financial remuneration received by the covered entity in exchange for making the communication is reasonably related to the covered entity's cost of making the communication.

(ii) For the following treatment and health care operations purposes, except where the covered entity receives financial remuneration in exchange for making the communication:

(A) For treatment of an individual by a health care provider, including case management or care coordination for the individual, or to direct or recommend alternative treatments, therapies, health care providers, or settings of care to the individual;

(B) To describe a health-related product or service (or payment for such product or service) that is provided by, or included in a plan of benefits of, the covered entity making the communication, including communications about: the entities participating in a health care provider network or health plan network; replacement of, or enhancements to, a health plan; and health-related products or services available only to a health plan enrollee that add value to, but are not part of, a plan of benefits; or

(C) For case management or care coordination, contacting of individuals with information about treatment alternatives, and related functions to the extent these activities do not fall within the definition of treatment.

(3) Financial remuneration means direct or indirect payment from or on behalf of a third party whose product or service is being described. Direct or indirect payment does not include any payment for treatment of an individual.

Payment means:

(1) The activities undertaken by:

(i) Except as prohibited under§ 164.502(a)(5)(i), a health plan to obtain premiums or to determine or fulfill its responsibility for coverage and provision of benefits under the health plan; or

(ii) A health care provider or health plan to obtain or provide reimbursement for the provision of health care; and

(2) The activities in paragraph (1) of this definition relate to the individual to whom health care is provided and include, but are not limited to:

(i) Determinations of eligibility or coverage (including coordination of benefits or the determination of cost sharing amounts), and adjudication or subrogation of health benefit claims;

(ii) Risk adjusting amounts due based on enrollee health status and demographic characteristics;

(iii) Billing, claims management, collection activities, obtaining payment under a contract for reinsurance (including stop-loss insurance and excess of loss insurance), and related health care data processing;

(iv) Review of health care services with respect to medical necessity, coverage under a health plan, appropriateness of care, or justification of charges;

(v) Utilization review activities, including precertification and preauthorization of services, concurrent and retrospective review of services; and

(vi) Disclosure to consumer reporting agencies of any of the following protected health information relating to collection of premiums or reimbursement:

(A) Name and address;

(B) Date of birth;

(C) Social security number;

(D) Payment history;

(E) Account number; and

(F) Name and address of the health care provider and/or health plan.

Psychotherapy notes means notes recorded (in any medium) by a health care provider who is a mental health professional documenting or analyzing the contents of conversation during a private counseling session or a group, joint, or family counseling session and that are separated from the rest of the individual's medical record. Psychotherapy notes excludes medication prescription and monitoring, counseling session start and stop times, the modalities and frequencies of treatment furnished, results of clinical tests, and any summary of the following items: Diagnosis, functional status, the treatment plan, symptoms, prognosis, and progress to date.

Public health authority means an agency or authority of the United States, a State, a territory, a political subdivision of a State or territory, or an Indian tribe, or a person or entity acting under a grant of authority from or contract with such public agency, including the employees or agents of such public agency or its contractors or persons or entities to whom it has granted authority, that is responsible for public health matters as part of its official mandate.

Research means a systematic investigation, including research development, testing, and evaluation, designed to develop or contribute to generalizable knowledge.

Treatment means the provision, coordination, or management of health care and related services by one or more health care providers, including the coordination or management of health care by a health care provider with a third party; consultation between health care providers relating to a patient; or the referral of a patient for health care from one health care provider to another.

164.502 Uses and disclosures of protected health information: General rules.

(a) Standard. A covered entity or business associate may not use or disclose protected health information, except as permitted or required by this subpart or by subpart C of part 160 of this subchapter.

(1) Covered entities: Permitted uses and disclosures. A covered entity is permitted to use or disclose protected health information as follows:

(i) To the individual;

(ii) For treatment, payment, or health care operations, as permitted by and in compliance with§ 164.506;

(iii) Incident to a use or disclosure otherwise permitted or required by this subpart, provided that the covered entity has complied with the applicable requirements of§§ 164.502(b), 164.514(d), and 164.530(c) with respect to such otherwise permitted or required use or disclosure;

(iv) Except for uses and disclosures prohibited under§ 164.502(a)(5)(i), pursuant to and in compliance with a valid authorization under § 164.508;

(v) Pursuant to an agreement under, or as otherwise permitted by,§ 164.510; and

(vi) As permitted by and in compliance with this section,§ 164.512, § 164.514(e), (f), or (g).

(2) Covered entities: Required disclosures. A covered entity is required to disclose protected health information:

(i) To an individual, when requested under, and required by§ 164.524 or § 164.528; and

(ii) When required by the Secretary under subpart C ofpart 160 of this subchapter to investigate or determine the covered entity's compliance with this subchapter.

(3) Business associates: Permitted uses and disclosures. A business associate may use or disclose protected health information only as permitted or required by its business associate contract or other

arrangement pursuant to § 164.504(e) or as required by law. The business associate may not use or disclose protected health information in a manner that would violate the requirements of this subpart, if done by the covered entity, except for the purposes specified under § 164.504(e)(2)(i)(A) or (B) if such uses or disclosures are permitted by its contract or other arrangement.

(4) Business associates: Required uses and disclosures. A business associate is required to disclose protected health information:

(i) When required by the Secretary under subpart C of part 160 of this subchapter to investigate or determine the business associate's compliance with this subchapter.

(ii) To the covered entity, individual, or individual's designee, as necessary to satisfy a covered entity's obligations under§ 164.524(c)(2)(ii) and (3)(ii) with respect to an individual's request for an electronic copy of protected health information.

(5) Prohibited uses and disclosures.

(i) Use and disclosure of genetic information for underwriting purposes: Notwithstanding any other provision of this subpart, a health plan, excluding an issuer of a long-term care policy falling within paragraph (1)(viii) of the definition of health plan, shall not use or disclose protected health information that is genetic information for underwriting purposes. For purposes of paragraph (a)(5)(i) of this section, underwriting purposes means, with respect to a health plan:

(A) Except as provided in paragraph (a)(5)(i)(B) of this section:

(1) Rules for, or determination of, eligibility (including enrollment and continued eligibility) for, or determination of, benefits under the plan, coverage, or policy (including changes in deductibles or other cost-sharing mechanisms in return for activities such as completing a health risk assessment or participating in a wellness program);

(2) The computation of premium or contribution amounts under the plan, coverage, or policy (including discounts, rebates, payments in kind, or other premium differential mechanisms in return for activities such as completing a health risk assessment or participating in a wellness program);

(3) The application of any pre-existing condition exclusion under the plan, coverage, or policy; and

(4) Other activities related to the creation, renewal, or replacement of a contract of health insurance or health benefits.

(B) Underwriting purposes does not include determinations of medical appropriateness where an individual seeks a benefit under the plan, coverage, or policy.

(ii) Sale of protected health information:

(A) Except pursuant to and in compliance with§ 164.508(a)(4), a covered entity or business associate may not sell protected health information.

(B) For purposes of this paragraph, sale of protected health information means:

(1) Except as provided in paragraph (a)(5)(ii)(B)(2) of this section, a

disclosure of protected health information by a covered entity or business associate, if applicable, where the covered entity or business associate directly or indirectly receives remuneration from or on behalf of the recipient of the protected health information in exchange for the protected health information.

(2) Sale of protected health information does not include a disclosure of protected health information:

(i) For public health purposes pursuant to§ 164.512(b) or § 164.514(e);

(ii) For research purposes pursuant to§ 164.512(i) or § 164.514(e), where the only remuneration received by the covered entity or business associate is a reasonable cost-based fee to cover the cost to prepare and transmit the protected health information for such purposes;

(iii) For treatment and payment purposes pursuant to§ 164.506(a);

(iv) For the sale, transfer, merger, or consolidation of all or part of the covered entity and for related due diligence as described in paragraph (6)(iv) of the definition of health care operations and pursuant to§ 164.506(a);

(v) To or by a business associate for activities that the business associate undertakes on behalf of a covered entity, or on behalf of a business associate in the case of a subcontractor, pursuant to§§ 164.502(e) and 164.504(e), and the only remuneration provided is by the covered entity to the business associate, or by the business associate to the subcontractor, if applicable, for the performance of such activities;

(vi) To an individual, when requested under§ 164.524 or § 164.528;

(vii) Required by law as permitted under§ 164.512(a); and

(viii) For any other purpose permitted by and in accordance with the applicable requirements of this subpart, where the only remuneration received by the covered entity or business associate is a reasonable, cost-based fee to cover the cost to prepare and transmit the protected health information for such purpose or a fee otherwise expressly permitted by other law.

(b) Standard: Minimum necessary — Minimum necessary applies. When using or disclosing protected health information or when requesting protected health information from another covered entity or business associate, a covered entity or business associate must make reasonable efforts to limit protected health information to the minimum necessary to accomplish the intended purpose of the use, disclosure, or request.

(2) Minimum necessary does not apply. This requirement does not apply to:

(i) Disclosures to or requests by a health care provider for treatment;

(ii) Uses or disclosures made to the individual, as permitted under paragraph (a)(1)(i) of this section or as required by paragraph (a)(2)(i) of this section;

(iii) Uses or disclosures made pursuant to an authorization under§ 164.508;

(iv) Disclosures made to the Secretary in accordance with subpart C ofpart 160 of this subchapter;

(v) Uses or disclosures that are required by law, as described by§ 164.512(a); and

(vi) Uses or disclosures that are required for compliance with applicable requirements of this subchapter.

(c) Standard: Uses and disclosures of protected health information subject to an agreed upon restriction. A covered entity that has agreed to a restriction pursuant to § 164.522(a)(1) may not use or disclose the protected health information covered by the restriction in violation of such restriction, except as otherwise provided in § 164.522(a).

(d) Standard: Uses and disclosures of de-identified protected health information.

(1) Uses and disclosures to create de-identified information. A covered entity may use protected health information to create information that is not individually identifiable health information or disclose protected health information only to a business associate for such purpose, whether or not the de-identified information is to be used by the covered entity.

(2) Uses and disclosures of de-identified information. Health information that meets the standard and implementation specifications for de-identification under § 164.514(a) and (b) is considered not to be individually identifiable health information, i.e., de-identified. The requirements of this subpart do not apply to information that has been de-identified in accordance with the applicable requirements of § 164.514, provided that:

(i) Disclosure of a code or other means of record identification designed to enable coded or otherwise de-identified information to be re-identified constitutes disclosure of protected health information; and

(ii) If de-identified information is re-identified, a covered entity may use or disclose such re-identified information only as permitted or required by this subpart.

(e)

(1) Standard: Disclosures to business associates.

(i) A covered entity may disclose protected health information to a business associate and may allow a business associate to create, receive, maintain, or transmit protected health information on its behalf, if the covered entity obtains satisfactory assurance that the business associate will appropriately safeguard the information. A covered entity is not required to obtain such satisfactory assurances from a business associate that is a subcontractor.

(ii) A business associate may disclose protected health information to a business associate that is a subcontractor and may allow the subcontractor to create, receive, maintain, or transmit protected health information on its behalf, if the business associate obtains satisfactory assurances, in accordance with§ 164.504(e)(1)(i), that the subcontractor will appropriately safeguard the information.

(2) Implementation specification: Documentation. The satisfactory assurances required by paragraph (e)(1) of this section must be documented through a written contract or other written agreement or

arrangement with the business associate that meets the applicable requirements of § 164.504(e).

(f) Standard: Deceased individuals. A covered entity must comply with the requirements of this subpart with respect to the protected health information of a deceased individual for a period of 50 years following the death of the individual.

(g)

(1) Standard: Personal representatives. As specified in this paragraph, a covered entity must, except as provided in paragraphs (g)(3) and (g)(5) of this section, treat a personal representative as the individual for purposes of this subchapter.

(2) Implementation specification: Adults and emancipated minors. If under applicable law a person has authority to act on behalf of an individual who is an adult or an emancipated minor in making decisions related to health care, a covered entity must treat such person as a personal representative under this subchapter, with respect to protected health information relevant to such personal representation.

(3)

(i) Implementation specification: Unemancipated minors. If under applicable law a parent, guardian, or other person acting in loco parentis has authority to act on behalf of an individual who is an unemancipated minor in making decisions related to health care, a covered entity must treat such person as a personal representative under this subchapter, with respect to protected health information relevant to such personal representation, except that such person may not be a personal representative of an unemancipated minor, and the minor has the authority to act as an individual, with respect to protected health information pertaining to a health care service, if:

(A) The minor consents to such health care service; no other consent to such health care service is required by law, regardless of whether the consent of another person has also been obtained; and the minor has not requested that such person be treated as the personal representative;

(B) The minor may lawfully obtain such health care service without the consent of a parent, guardian, or other person actingin loco parentis, and the minor, a court, or another person authorized by law consents to such health care service; or

(C) A parent, guardian, or other person actingin loco parentis assents to an agreement of confidentiality between a covered health care provider and the minor with respect to such health care service.

(ii) Notwithstanding the provisions of paragraph (g)(3)(i) of this section:

(A) If, and to the extent, permitted or required by an applicable provision of State or other law, including applicable case law, a covered entity may disclose, or provide access in accordance with§ 164.524 to, protected health information about an unemancipated minor to a parent, guardian, or other person acting in loco parentis;

(B) If, and to the extent, prohibited by an applicable provision of State or other law, including applicable case law, a covered entity may not disclose, or provide access in accordance with§ 164.524 to, protected health information about an unemancipated minor to a parent, guardian, or other person acting in loco parentis; and

(C) Where the parent, guardian, or other person actingin loco parentis, is not the personal representative under paragraphs (g)(3)(i)(A), (B), or (C) of this section and where there is no applicable access provision under State or other law, including case law, a covered entity may provide or deny access under § 164.524 to a parent, guardian, or other person acting in loco parentis, if such action is consistent with State or other applicable law, provided that such decision must be made by a licensed health care professional, in the exercise of professional judgment.

(4) Implementation specification: Deceased individuals. If under applicable law an executor, administrator, or other person has authority to act on behalf of a deceased individual or of the individual's estate, a covered entity must treat such person as a personal representative under this subchapter, with respect to protected health information relevant to such personal representation.

(5) Implementation specification: Abuse, neglect, endangerment situations. Notwithstanding a State law or any requirement of this paragraph to the contrary, a covered entity may elect not to treat a person as the personal representative of an individual if:

(i) The covered entity has a reasonable belief that:

(A) The individual has been or may be subjected to domestic violence, abuse, or neglect by such person; or

(B) Treating such person as the personal representative could endanger the individual; and

(ii) The covered entity, in the exercise of professional judgment, decides that it is not in the best interest of the individual to treat the person as the individual's personal representative.

(h) Standard: Confidential communications. A covered health care provider or health plan must comply with the applicable requirements of § 164.522(b) in communicating protected health information.

(i) Standard: Uses and disclosures consistent with notice. A covered entity that is required by § 164.520 to have a notice may not use or disclose protected health information in a manner inconsistent with such notice. A covered entity that is required by § 164.520(b)(1)(iii) to include a specific statement in its notice if it intends to engage in an activity listed in § 164.520(b)(1)(iii)(A)-(C), may not use or disclose protected health information for such activities, unless the required statement is included in the notice.

(j) Standard: Disclosures by whistleblowers and workforce member crime victims

(1) Disclosures by whistleblowers. A covered entity is not considered to have violated the requirements of this subpart if a member of its workforce or a business associate discloses protected health information, provided

that:

(i) The workforce member or business associate believes in good faith that the covered entity has engaged in conduct that is unlawful or otherwise violates professional or clinical standards, or that the care, services, or conditions provided by the covered entity potentially endangers one or more patients, workers, or the public; and

(ii) The disclosure is to:

(A) A health oversight agency or public health authority authorized by law to investigate or otherwise oversee the relevant conduct or conditions of the covered entity or to an appropriate health care accreditation organization for the purpose of reporting the allegation of failure to meet professional standards or misconduct by the covered entity; or

(B) An attorney retained by or on behalf of the workforce member or business associate for the purpose of determining the legal options of the workforce member or business associate with regard to the conduct described in paragraph (j)(1)(i) of this section.

(2) Disclosures by workforce members who are victims of a crime. A covered entity is not considered to have violated the requirements of this subpart if a member of its workforce who is the victim of a criminal act discloses protected health information to a law enforcement official, provided that:

(i) The protected health information disclosed is about the suspected perpetrator of the criminal act; and

(ii) The protected health information disclosed is limited to the information listed in§ 164.512(f)(2)(i).

[65 FR 82802, Dec. 28, 2000, as amended at 67 FR 53267, Aug. 14, 2002; 78 FR 5696, Jan. 25, 2013]

164.504 Uses and disclosures: Organizational requirements.

(a) Definitions. As used in this section:

Plan administration functions means administration functions performed by the plan sponsor of a group health plan on behalf of the group health plan and excludes functions performed by the plan sponsor in connection with any other benefit or benefit plan of the plan sponsor.

Summary health information means information, that may be individually identifiable health information, and:

(1) That summarizes the claims history, claims expenses, or type of claims experienced by individuals for whom a plan sponsor has provided health benefits under a group health plan; and

(2) From which the information described at§ 164.514(b)(2)(i) has been deleted, except that the geographic information described in § 164.514(b)(2)(i)(B) need only be aggregated to the level of a five digit zip code.

(b)

(d) [Reserved]

(e)

(1) Standard: Business associate contracts.

(i) The contract or other arrangement required by§ 164.502(e)(2) must meet the requirements of paragraph (e)(2), (e)(3), or (e)(5) of this section, as applicable.

(ii) A covered entity is not in compliance with the standards in§ 164.502(e) and this paragraph, if the covered entity knew of a pattern of activity or practice of the business associate that constituted a material breach or violation of the business associate's obligation under the contract or other arrangement, unless the covered entity took reasonable steps to cure the breach or end the violation, as applicable, and, if such steps were unsuccessful, terminated the contract or arrangement, if feasible.

(iii) A business associate is not in compliance with the standards in§ 164.502(e) and this paragraph, if the business associate knew of a pattern of activity or practice of a subcontractor that constituted a material breach or violation of the subcontractor's obligation under the contract or other arrangement, unless the business associate took reasonable steps to cure the breach or end the violation, as applicable, and, if such steps were unsuccessful, terminated the contract or arrangement, if feasible.

(2) Implementation specifications: Business associate contracts. A contract between the covered entity and a business associate must:

(i) Establish the permitted and required uses and disclosures of protected health information by the business associate. The contract may not authorize the business associate to use or further disclose the information in a manner that would violate the requirements of this subpart, if done by the covered entity, except that:

(A) The contract may permit the business associate to use and disclose protected health information for the proper management and administration of the business associate, as provided in paragraph (e)(4) of this section; and

(B) The contract may permit the business associate to provide data aggregation services relating to the health care operations of the covered entity.

(ii) Provide that the business associate will:

(A) Not use or further disclose the information other than as permitted or required by the contract or as required by law;

(B) Use appropriate safeguards and comply, where applicable, with subpart C of this part with respect to electronic protected health information, to prevent use or disclosure of the information other than as provided for by its contract;

(C) Report to the covered entity any use or disclosure of the information not provided for by its contract of which it becomes aware, including breaches of unsecured protected health information as required by§ 164.410;

(D) In accordance with§ 164.502(e)(1)(ii), ensure that any subcontractors that create, receive, maintain, or transmit protected health information on behalf of the business associate agree to the same restrictions and conditions that apply to the business associate with respect to such information;

(E) Make available protected health information in accordance with§ 164.524;

(F) Make available protected health information for amendment and incorporate any amendments to protected health information in accordance with§ 164.526;

(G) Make available the information required to provide an accounting of disclosures in accordance with§ 164.528;

(H) To the extent the business associate is to carry out a covered entity's obligation under this subpart, comply with the requirements of this subpart that apply to the covered entity in the performance of such obligation.

(I) Make its internal practices, books, and records relating to the use and disclosure of protected health information received from, or created or received by the business associate on behalf of, the covered entity available to the Secretary for purposes of determining the covered entity's compliance with this subpart; and

(J) At termination of the contract, if feasible, return or destroy all protected health information received from, or created or received by the business associate on behalf of, the covered entity that the business associate still maintains in any form and retain no copies of such information or, if such return or destruction is not feasible, extend the protections of the contract to the information and limit further uses and disclosures to those purposes that make the return or destruction of the information infeasible.

(iii) Authorize termination of the contract by the covered entity, if the covered entity determines that the business associate has violated a material term of the contract.

(3) Implementation specifications: Other arrangements.

(i) If a covered entity and its business associate are both governmental entities:

(A) The covered entity may comply with this paragraph and§ 164.314(a)(1), if applicable, by entering into a memorandum of understanding with the business associate that contains terms that accomplish the objectives of paragraph (e)(2) of this section and § 164.314(a)(2), if applicable.

(B) The covered entity may comply with this paragraph and§ 164.314(a)(1), if applicable, if other law (including regulations adopted by the covered entity or its business associate) contains requirements applicable to the business associate that accomplish the objectives of paragraph (e)(2) of this section and § 164.314(a)(2), if applicable.

(ii) If a business associate is required by law to perform a function or activity on behalf of a covered entity or to provide a service described in the definition of business associate in§ 160.103 of this subchapter to a covered entity, such covered entity may disclose protected health information to the business associate to the extent necessary to comply with the legal mandate without meeting the requirements of this paragraph and § 164.314(a)(1), if applicable, provided that the covered entity attempts in good faith to obtain satisfactory assurances as required by paragraph (e)(2) of this section and § 164.314(a)(1), if applicable, and, if such attempt fails, documents the attempt and the reasons that such assurances cannot be obtained.

(iii) The covered entity may omit from its other arrangements the termination authorization required by paragraph (e)(2)(iii) of this section, if such authorization is inconsistent with the statutory obligations of the covered entity or its business associate.

(iv) A covered entity may comply with this paragraph and§ 164.314(a)(1) if the covered entity discloses only a limited data set to a business associate for the business associate to carry out a health care operations function and the covered entity has a data use agreement with the business associate that complies with § 164.514(e)(4) and § 164.314(a)(1), if applicable.

(4) Implementation specifications: Other requirements for contracts and other arrangements.

(i) The contract or other arrangement between the covered entity and the business associate may permit the business associate to use the protected health information received by the business associate in its capacity as a business associate to the covered entity, if necessary:

(A) For the proper management and administration of the business associate; or

(B) To carry out the legal responsibilities of the business associate.

(ii) The contract or other arrangement between the covered entity and the business associate may permit thebusiness associate to disclose the protected health information received by the business associate in its capacity as a business associate for the purposes described in paragraph (e)(4)(i) of this section, if:

(A) The disclosure is required by law; or

(B)

(1) The business associate obtains reasonable assurances from the person to whom the information is disclosed that it will be held confidentially and used or further disclosed only as required by law or for the purposes for which it was disclosed to the person; and

(2) The person notifies the business associate of any instances of which it is aware in which the confidentiality of the information has been breached.

(5) Implementation specifications: Business associate contracts with subcontractors. The requirements of § 164.504(e)(2) through (e)(4) apply to the contract or other arrangement required by § 164.502(e)(1)(ii) between a business associate and a business associate that is a subcontractor in the same manner as such requirements apply to contracts or other arrangements between a covered entity and business associate.

(f)

(1) Standard: Requirements for group health plans.

(i) Except as provided under paragraph (f)(1)(ii) or (iii) of this section or as otherwise authorized under§ 164.508, a group health plan, in order to disclose protected health information to the plan sponsor or to provide for or permit the disclosure of protected health information to the plan sponsor by a health insurance issuer or HMO with respect to the group health plan, must ensure that the plan documents restrict uses and disclosures of such information by the plan sponsor consistent with the requirements of this subpart.

(ii) Except as prohibited by§ 164.502(a)(5)(i), the group health plan, or a health insurance issuer or HMO with respect to the group health plan, may disclose summary health information to the plan sponsor, if the plan sponsor requests the summary health information for purposes of:

(A) Obtaining premium bids from health plans for providing health insurance coverage under the group health plan; or

(B) Modifying, amending, or terminating the group health plan.

(iii) The group health plan, or a health insurance issuer or HMO with respect to the group health plan, may disclose to the plan sponsor information on whether the individual is participating in the group health plan, or is enrolled in or has disenrolled from a health insurance issuer or HMO offered by the plan.

(2) Implementation specifications: Requirements for plan documents. The plan documents of the group health plan must be amended to incorporate provisions to:

(i) Establish the permitted and required uses and disclosures of such information by the plan sponsor, provided that such permitted and required uses and disclosures may not be inconsistent with this subpart.

(ii) Provide that the group health plan will disclose protected health information to the plan sponsor only upon receipt of a certification by the plan sponsor that the plan documents have been amended to incorporate the following provisions and that the plan sponsor agrees to:

(A) Not use or further disclose the information other than as permitted or required by the plan documents or as required by law;

(B) Ensure that any agents to whom it provides protected health information received from the group health plan agree to the same restrictions and conditions that apply to the plan sponsor with respect to such information;

(C) Not use or disclose the information for employment-related actions and decisions or in connection with any other benefit or employee benefit plan of the plan sponsor;

(D) Report to the group health plan any use or disclosure of the information that is inconsistent with the uses or disclosures provided for of which it becomes aware;

(E) Make available protected health information in accordance with§ 164.524;

(F) Make available protected health information for amendment and incorporate any amendments to protected health information in accordance with§ 164.526;

(G) Make available the information required to provide an accounting of disclosures in accordance with§ 164.528;

(H) Make its internal practices, books, and records relating to the use and disclosure of protected health information received from the group health plan available to the Secretary for purposes of determining compliance by the group health plan with this subpart;

(I) If feasible, return or destroy all protected health information received from the group health plan that the sponsor still maintains in any form and retain no copies of such information when no longer needed for the purpose for which disclosure was made, except that, if such return or destruction is not feasible, limit further uses and disclosures to those purposes that make the return or destruction of the information infeasible; and

(J) Ensure that the adequate separation required in paragraph (f)(2)(iii) of this section is established.

(iii) Provide for adequate separation between the group health plan and the plan sponsor. The plan documents must:

(A) Describe those employees or classes of employees or other persons under the control of the plan sponsor to be given access to the protected health information to be disclosed, provided that any employee or person who receives protected health information relating to payment under, health care operations of, or other matters pertaining to the group health plan in the ordinary course of business must be included in such description;

(B) Restrict the access to and use by such employees and other persons described in paragraph (f)(2)(iii)(A) of this section to the plan administration functions that the plan sponsor performs for the group health plan; and

(C) Provide an effective mechanism for resolving any issues of noncompliance by persons described in paragraph (f)(2)(iii)(A) of this section with the plan document provisions required by this paragraph.

(3) Implementation specifications: Uses and disclosures. A group health plan may:

(i) Disclose protected health information to a plan sponsor to carry out plan administration functions that the plan sponsor performs only consistent with the provisions of paragraph (f)(2) of this section;

(ii) Not permit a health insurance issuer or HMO with respect to the group health plan to disclose protected health information to the plan sponsor except as permitted by this paragraph;

(iii) Not disclose and may not permit a health insurance issuer or HMO to disclose protected health information to a plan sponsor as otherwise permitted by this paragraph unless a statement required by§ 164.520(b)(1)(iii)(C) is included in the appropriate notice; and (iv) Not disclose protected health information to the plan sponsor for the purpose of employment-related actions or decisions or in connection with any other benefit or employee benefit plan of the plan sponsor.

(g) Standard: Requirements for a covered entity with multiple covered functions.

(1) A covered entity that performs multiple covered functions that would make the entity any combination of a health plan, a covered health care provider, and a health care clearinghouse, must comply with the standards, requirements, and implementation specifications of this subpart, as applicable to the health plan, health care provider, or health care clearinghouse covered functions performed.

(2) A covered entity that performs multiple covered functions may use or disclose the protected health information of individuals who receive the covered entity's health plan or health care provider services, but not both, only for purposes related to the appropriate function being performed.

164.506 Uses and disclosures to carry out treatment, payment, or health care operations.

(a) Standard: Permitted uses and disclosures. Except with respect to uses or disclosures that require an authorization under § 164.508(a)(2) through (4) or that are prohibited under § 164.502(a)(5)(i), a covered entity may use or disclose protected health information for treatment, payment, or health care operations as set forth in paragraph (c) of this section, provided that such use or disclosure is consistent with other applicable requirements of this subpart.

(b) Standard: Consent for uses and disclosures permitted.

(1) A covered entity may obtain consent of the individual to use or disclose protected health information to carry out treatment, payment, or health care operations.

(2) Consent, under paragraph (b) of this section, shall not be effective to permit a use or disclosure of protected health information when an authorization, under§ 164.508, is required or when another condition must be met for such use or disclosure to be permissible under this subpart.

(c) Implementation specifications: Treatment, payment, or health care operations.

(1) A covered entity may use or disclose protected health information for its own treatment, payment, or health care operations.

(2) A covered entity may disclose protected health information for treatment activities of a health care provider.

(3) A covered entity may disclose protected health information to another covered entity or a health care provider for the payment activities of the entity that receives the information.

(4) A covered entity may disclose protected health information to another covered entity for health care operations activities of the entity that receives the information, if each entity either has or had a relationship with the individual who is the subject of the protected health information being requested, the protected health information pertains to such relationship, and the disclosure is:

(i) For a purpose listed in paragraph (1) or (2) of the definition of health care operations; or

(ii) For the purpose of health care fraud and abuse detection or compliance.

(5) A covered entity that participates in an organized health care arrangement may disclose protected health information about an individual to other participants in the organized health care arrangement for any health care operations activities of the organized health care arrangement.

164.508 Uses and disclosures for which an authorization is required.

(a) Standard: Authorizations for uses and disclosures

(1) Authorization required: General rule. Except as otherwise permitted or required by this subchapter, a covered entity may not use or disclose protected health information without an authorization that is valid under this section. When a covered entity obtains or receives a valid authorization for its use or disclosure of protected health information, such use or disclosure must be consistent with such authorization.

(2) Authorization required: Psychotherapy notes. Notwithstanding any provision of this subpart, other than the transition provisions in § 164.532, a covered entity must obtain an authorization for any use or disclosure of psychotherapy notes, except:

(i) To carry out the following treatment, payment, or health care operations:

(A) Use by the originator of the psychotherapy notes for treatment;

(B) Use or disclosure by the covered entity for its own training programs in which students, trainees, or practitioners in mental health learn under supervision to practice or improve their skills in group, joint, family, or individual counseling; or

(C) Use or disclosure by the covered entity to defend itself in a legal action or other proceeding brought by the individual; and

(ii) A use or disclosure that is required by§ 164.502(a)(2)(ii) or permitted by § 164.512(a); § 164.512(d) with respect to the oversight of the originator of the psychotherapy notes; § 164.512(g)(1); or § 164.512(j)(1)(i).

(3) Authorization required: Marketing.

(i) Notwithstanding any provision of this subpart, other than the transition provisions in§ 164.532, a covered entity must obtain an authorization for any use or disclosure of protected health information for marketing, except if the communication is in the form of:

(A) A face-to-face communication made by a covered entity to an individual; or

(B) A promotional gift of nominal value provided by the covered entity.

(ii) If the marketing involves financial remuneration, as defined in paragraph (3) of the definition of marketing at§ 164.501, to the covered entity from a third party, the authorization must state that such remuneration is involved.

(4) Authorization required: Sale of protected health information.

(i) Notwithstanding any provision of this subpart, other than the transition provisions in§ 164.532, a covered entity must obtain an authorization for any disclosure of protected health information which is a sale of protected health information, as defined in § 164.501 of this subpart. (ii) Such authorization must state that the disclosure will result in remuneration to the covered entity.

(b) Implementation specifications: General requirements

(1) Valid authorizations.

(i) A valid authorization is a document that meets the requirements in paragraphs (a)(3)(ii), (a)(4)(ii), (c)(1), and (c)(2) of this section, as applicable.

(ii) A valid authorization may contain elements or information in addition to the elements required by this section, provided that such additional elements or information are not inconsistent with the elements required by this section.

(2) Defective authorizations. An authorization is not valid, if the document submitted has any of the following defects:

(i) The expiration date has passed or the expiration event is known by the covered entity to have occurred;

(ii) The authorization has not been filled out completely, with respect to an element described by paragraph (c) of this section, if applicable;

(iii) The authorization is known by the covered entity to have been revoked;

(iv) The authorization violates paragraph (b)(3) or (4) of this section, if applicable;

(v) Any material information in the authorization is known by the covered entity to be false.

(3) Compound authorizations. An authorization for use or disclosure of protected health information may not be combined with any other document to create a compound authorization, except as follows:

(i) An authorization for the use or disclosure of protected health information for a research study may be combined with any other type of written permission for the same or another research study. This exception includes combining an authorization for the use or disclosure of protected health information for a research study with another authorization for the same research study, with an authorization for the creation or maintenance of a research database or repository, or with a consent to participate in research. Where a covered health care provider has conditioned the provision of research-related treatment on the provision of one of the authorizations, as permitted under paragraph (b)(4)(i) of this section, any compound authorization created under this paragraph must clearly differentiate between the conditioned and unconditioned components and provide the individual with an opportunity to opt in to the research activities described in the unconditioned authorization.

(ii) An authorization for a use or disclosure of psychotherapy notes may only be combined with another authorization for a use or disclosure of psychotherapy notes.

(iii) An authorization under this section, other than an authorization for a use or disclosure of psychotherapy notes, may be combined with any other such authorization under this section, except when a covered entity has conditioned the provision of treatment, payment, enrollment in the health plan, or eligibility for benefits under paragraph (b)(4) of this section on the provision of one of the authorizations. The prohibition in this paragraph on combining authorizations where one authorization conditions the provision of treatment, payment, enrollment in a health plan, or eligibility for benefits under paragraph (b)(4) of this section does not apply to a compound authorization created in accordance with paragraph (b)(3)(i) of this section.

(4) Prohibition on conditioning of authorizations. A covered entity may not condition the provision to an individual of treatment, payment, enrollment in the health plan, or eligibility for benefits on the provision of an authorization, except:

(i) A covered health care provider may condition the provision of research-related treatment on provision of an authorization for the use or disclosure of protected health information for such research under this section;

(ii) A health plan may condition enrollment in the health plan or eligibility for benefits on provision of an authorization requested by the health plan prior to an individual's enrollment in the health plan, if:

(A) The authorization sought is for the health plan's eligibility or enrollment determinations relating to the individual or for its underwriting or risk rating determinations; and

(B) The authorization is not for a use or disclosure of psychotherapy notes under paragraph (a)(2) of this section; and

(iii) A covered entity may condition the provision of health care that is solely for the purpose of creating protected health information for disclosure to a third party on provision of an authorization for the disclosure of the protected health information to such third party.

(5) Revocation of authorizations. An individual may revoke an authorization provided under this section at any time, provided that the revocation is in writing, except to the extent that:

(i) The covered entity has taken action in reliance thereon; or

(ii) If the authorization was obtained as a condition of obtaining insurance coverage, other law provides the insurer with the right to contest a claim under the policy or the policy itself.

(6) Documentation. A covered entity must document and retain any signed authorization under this section as required by § 164.530(j).

(c) Implementation specifications: Core elements and requirements

(1) Core elements. A valid authorization under this section must contain at least the following elements:

(i) A description of the information to be used or disclosed that identifies the information in a specific and meaningful fashion.

(ii) The name or other specific identification of the person(s), or class of persons, authorized to make the requested use or disclosure.

(iii) The name or other specific identification of the person(s), or class of persons, to whom the covered entity may make the requested use or disclosure.

(iv) A description of each purpose of the requested use or disclosure. The statement "at the request of the individual" is a sufficient description of the purpose when an individual initiates the authorization and does not, or elects not to, provide a statement of the purpose.

(v) An expiration date or an expiration event that relates to the individual or the purpose of the use or disclosure. The statement "end of the research study," "none," or similar language is sufficient if the authorization is for a use or disclosure of protected health information for research, including for the creation and maintenance of a research database or research repository.

(vi) Signature of the individual and date. If the authorization is signed by a personal representative of the individual, a description of such representative's authority to act for the individual must also be provided.

(2) Required statements. In addition to the core elements, the authorization must contain statements adequate to place the individual on notice of all of the following:

(i) The individual's right to revoke the authorization in writing, and either:

(A) The exceptions to the right to revoke and a description of how the individual may revoke the authorization; or

(B) To the extent that the information in paragraph (c)(2)(i)(A) of this section is included in the notice required by§ 164.520, a reference to the covered entity's notice.

(ii) The ability or inability to condition treatment, payment, enrollment or eligibility for benefits on the authorization, by stating either:

(A) The covered entity may not condition treatment, payment, enrollmentor eligibility for benefits on whether the individual signs the authorization when the prohibition on conditioning of authorizations in paragraph (b)(4) of this section applies; or

(B) The consequences to the individual of a refusal to sign the authorization when, in accordance with paragraph (b)(4) of this section, the covered entity can condition treatment, enrollment in the health plan, or eligibility for benefits on failure to obtain such authorization.

(iii) The potential for information disclosed pursuant to the authorization to be subject to redisclosure by the recipient and no longer be protected by this subpart.

(3) Plain language requirement. The authorization must be written in plain language.

(4) Copy to the individual. If a covered entity seeks an authorization from an individual for a use or disclosure of protected health information, the covered entity must provide the individual with a copy of the signed authorization.

164.510 Uses and disclosures requiring an opportunity for the individual to agree or to object.

A covered entity may use or disclose protected health information, provided that the individual is informed in advance of the use or disclosure and has the opportunity to agree to or prohibit or restrict the use or disclosure, in accordance with the applicable requirements of this section. The covered entity may orally inform the individual of and obtain the individual's oral agreement or objection to a use or disclosure permitted by this section.

(a) Standard: Use and disclosure for facility directories

(1) Permitted uses and disclosure. Except when an objection is expressed in accordance with paragraphs (a)(2) or (3) of this section, a covered health care provider may:

(i) Use the following protected health information to maintain a directory of individuals in its facility:

(A) The individual's name;

(B) The individual's location in the covered health care provider's facility;

(C) The individual's condition described in general terms that does not communicate specific medical information about the individual; and

(D) The individual's religious affiliation; and

(ii) Use or disclose for directory purposes such information:

(A) To members of the clergy; or

(B) Except for religious affiliation, to other persons who ask for the individual by name.

(2) Opportunity to object. A covered health care provider must inform an individual of the protected health information that it may include in a directory and the persons to whom it may disclose such information (including disclosures to clergy of information regarding religious affiliation) and provide the individual with the opportunity to restrict or prohibit some or all of the uses or disclosures permitted by paragraph (a)(1) of this section.

(3) Emergency circumstances.

(i) If the opportunity to object to uses or disclosures required by paragraph (a)(2) of this section cannot practicably be provided because of the individual's incapacity or an emergency treatment circumstance, a covered health care provider may use or disclose some or all of the protected health information permitted by paragraph (a)(1) of this section for the facility's directory, if such disclosure is:

(A) Consistent with a prior expressed preference of the individual, if any, that is known to the covered health care provider; and

(B) In the individual's best interest as determined by the covered health care provider, in the exercise of professional judgment.

(ii) The covered health care provider must inform the individual and provide an opportunity to object to uses or disclosures for directory purposes as required by paragraph (a)(2) of this section when it becomes practicable to do so.

(b) Standard: Uses and disclosures for involvement in the individual's care and notification purposes

(1) Permitted uses and disclosures.

(i) A covered entity may, in accordance with paragraphs (b)(2), (b)(3), or (b)(5) of this section, disclose to a family member, other relative, or a close personal friend of the individual, or any other person identified by the individual, the protected health information directly relevant to such person's involvement with the individual's health care or payment related to the individual's health care.

(ii) A covered entity may use or disclose protected health information to notify, or assist in the notification of (including identifying or locating), a family member, a personal representative of the individual, or another person responsible for the care of the individual of the individual's location, general condition, or death. Any such use or disclosure of protected health information for such notification purposes must be in accordance with paragraphs (b)(2), (b)(3), (b)(4), or (b)(5) of this section, as applicable.

(2) Uses and disclosures with the individual present. If the individual is present for, or otherwise available prior to, a use or disclosure permitted by paragraph (b)(1) of this section and has the capacity to make health care decisions, the covered entity may use or disclose the protected health information if it:

(i) Obtains the individual's agreement;

(ii) Provides the individual with the opportunity to object to the disclosure, and the individual does not express an objection; or

(iii) Reasonably infers from the circumstances, based on the exercise of professional judgment, that the individual does not object to the disclosure.

(3) Limited uses and disclosures when the individual is not present. If the individual is not present, or the opportunity to agree or object to the use or disclosure cannot practicably be provided because of the individual's incapacity or an emergency circumstance, the covered entity may, in the exercise of professional judgment, determine whether the disclosure is in the best interests of the individual and, if so, disclose only the protected health information that is directly relevant to the person's involvement with the individual's care or payment related to the individual's health care or needed for notification purposes. A covered entity may use professional judgment and its experience with common practice to make reasonable inferences of the individual's best interest in allowing a person to act on behalf of the individual to pick up filled prescriptions, medical supplies, X-rays, or other similar forms of protected health information.

(4) Uses and disclosures for disaster relief purposes. A covered entity may use or disclose protected health information to a public or private entity authorized by law or by its charter to assist in disaster relief efforts, for the purpose of coordinating with such entities the uses or disclosures permitted by paragraph (b)(1)(ii) of this section. The requirements in paragraphs (b)(2), (b)(3), or (b)(5) of this section apply to such uses and disclosures to the extent that the covered entity, in the exercise of professional judgment, determines that the requirements do not interfere with the ability to respond

to the emergency circumstances.

(5) Uses and disclosures when the individual is deceased. If the individual is deceased, a covered entity may disclose to a family member, or other persons identified in paragraph (b)(1) of this section who were involved in the individual's care or payment for health care prior to the individual's death, protected health information of the individual that is relevant to such person's involvement, unless doing so is inconsistent with any prior expressed preference of the individual that is known to the covered entity.

164.512 Uses and disclosures for which an authorization or opportunity to agree or object is not required.

A covered entity may use or disclose protected health information without the written authorization of the individual, as described in § 164.508, or the opportunity for the individual to agree or object as described in § 164.510, in the situations covered by this section, subject to the applicable requirements of this section. When the covered entity is required by this section to inform the individual of, or when the individual may agree to, a use or disclosure permitted by this section, the covered entity's information and the individual's agreement may be given orally.

(a) Standard: Uses and disclosures required by law.

(1) A covered entity may use or disclose protected health information to the extent that such use or disclosure is required by law and the use or disclosure complies with and is limited to the relevant requirements of such law.

(2) A covered entity must meet the requirements described in paragraph (c), (e), or (f) of this section for uses or disclosures required by law.

(b) Standard: Uses and disclosures for public health activities.

(1) Permitted uses and disclosures. A covered entity may use or disclose protected health information for the public health activities and purposes described in this paragraph to:

(i) A public health authority that is authorized by law to collect or receive such information for the purpose of preventing or controlling disease, injury, or disability, including, but not limited to, the reporting of disease, injury, vital events such as birth or death, and the conduct of public health surveillance, public health investigations, and public health interventions; or, at the direction of a public health authority, to an official of a foreign government agency that is acting in collaboration with a public health authority;

(ii) A public health authority or other appropriate government authority authorized by law to receive reports of child abuse or neglect;

(iii) A person subject to the jurisdiction of the Food and Drug Administration (FDA) with respect to an FDA-regulated product or activity for which that person has responsibility, for the purpose of activities related to the quality, safety or effectiveness of such FDA-regulated product or activity. Such purposes include:

(A) To collect or report adverse events (or similar activities with respect to food or dietary supplements), product defects or problems (including problems with the use or labeling of a product), or biological product deviations;

(B) To track FDA-regulated products;

(C) To enable product recalls, repairs, or replacement, or lookback (including locating and notifying individuals who have received products that have been recalled, withdrawn, or are the subject of lookback); or

(D) To conduct post marketing surveillance;

(iv) A person who may have been exposed to a communicable disease or may otherwise be at risk of contracting or spreading a disease or condition, if the covered entity or public health authority is authorized by law to notify such person as necessary in the conduct of a public health intervention or investigation; or

(v) An employer, about an individual who is a member of the workforce of the employer, if:

(A) The covered entity is a covered health care provider who provides health care to the individual at the request of the employer:

(1) To conduct an evaluation relating to medical surveillance of the workplace; or

(2) To evaluate whether the individual has a work-related illness or injury;

(B) The protected health information that is disclosed consists of findings concerning a work-related illness or injury or a workplace-related medical surveillance;

(C) The employer needs such findings in order to comply with its obligations, under29 CFR parts 1904 through 1928, 30 CFR parts 50 through 90, or under state law having a similar purpose, to record such illness or injury or to carry out responsibilities for workplace medical surveillance; and

(D) The covered health care provider provides written notice to the individual that protected health information relating to the medical surveillance of the workplace and work-related illnesses and injuries is disclosed to the employer:

(1) By giving a copy of the notice to the individual at the time the health care is provided; or

(2) If the health care is provided on the work site of the employer, by posting the notice in a prominent place at the location where the health care is provided.

(vi) A school, about an individual who is a student or prospective student of the school, if:

(A) The protected health information that is disclosed is limited to proof of immunization;

(B) The school is required by State or other law to have such proof of immunization prior to admitting the individual; and

(C) The covered entity obtains and documents the agreement to the disclosure from either:

(1) A parent, guardian, or other person acting in loco parentis of the individual, if the individual is an unemancipated minor; or

(2) The individual, if the individual is an adult or emancipated minor.

(2) Permitted uses. If the covered entity also is a public health authority, the covered entity is permitted to use protected health information in all cases in which it is permitted to disclose such information for public health activities under paragraph (b)(1) of this section.

(c) Standard: Disclosures about victims of abuse, neglect or domestic violence

(1) Permitted disclosures. Except for reports of child abuse or neglect permitted by paragraph (b)(1)(ii) of this section, a covered entity may disclose protected health information about an individual whom the covered entity reasonably believes to be a victim of abuse, neglect, or domestic violence to a government authority, including a social service or protective services agency, authorized by law to receive reports of such abuse, neglect, or domestic violence:

(i) To the extent the disclosure is required by law and the disclosure complies with and is limited to the relevant requirements of such law;

(ii) If the individual agrees to the disclosure; or

(iii) To the extent the disclosure is expressly authorized by statute or regulation and:

(A) The covered entity, in the exercise of professional judgment, believes the disclosure is necessary to prevent serious harm to the individual or other potential victims; or

(B) If the individual is unable to agree because of incapacity, a law enforcement or other public official authorized to receive the report represents that the protected health information for which disclosure is sought is not intended to be used against the individual and that an immediate enforcement activity that depends upon the disclosure would be materially and adversely affected by waiting until the individual is able to agree to the disclosure.

(2) Informing the individual. A covered entity that makes a disclosure permitted by paragraph (c)(1) of this section must promptly inform the individual that such a report has been or will be made, except if:

(i) The covered entity, in the exercise of professional judgment, believes informing the individual would place the individual at risk of serious harm; or

(ii) The covered entity would be informing a personal representative, and the covered entity reasonably believes the personal representative is responsible for the abuse, neglect, or other injury, and that informing such person would not be in the best interests of the individual as determined by the covered entity, in the exercise of professional judgment.

(d) Standard: Uses and disclosures for health oversight activities

(1) Permitted disclosures. A covered entity may disclose protected health information to a health oversight agency for oversight activities authorized by law, including audits; civil, administrative, or criminal investigations; inspections; licensure or disciplinary actions; civil, administrative, or criminal proceedings or actions; or other activities necessary for appropriate oversight of:

(i) The health care system;

(ii) Government benefit programs for which health information is relevant to beneficiary eligibility;

(iii) Entities subject to government regulatory programs for which health information is necessary for determining compliance with program standards; or

(iv) Entities subject to civil rights laws for which health information is necessary for determining compliance.

(2) Exception to health oversight activities. For the purpose of the disclosures permitted by paragraph (d)(1) of this section, a health oversight activity does not include an investigation or other activity in which the individual is the subject of the investigation or activity and such investigation or other activity does not arise out of and is not directly related to:

(i) The receipt of health care;

(ii) A claim for public benefits related to health; or

(iii) Qualification for, or receipt of, public benefits or services when a patient's health is integral to the claim for public benefits or services.

(3) Joint activities or investigations. Nothwithstanding paragraph (d)(2) of this section, if a health oversight activity or investigation is conducted in conjunction with an oversight activity or investigation relating to a claim for public benefits not related to health, the joint activity or investigation is considered a health oversight activity for purposes of paragraph (d) of this section.

(4) Permitted uses. If a covered entity also is a health oversight agency, the covered entity may use protected health information for health oversight activities as permitted by paragraph (d) of this section.

(e) Standard: Disclosures for judicial and administrative proceedings

(1) Permitted disclosures. A covered entity may disclose protected health information in the course of any judicial or administrative proceeding:

(i) In response to an order of a court or administrative tribunal, provided that the covered entity discloses only the protected health information expressly authorized by such order; or

(ii) In response to a subpoena, discovery request, or other lawful process, that is not accompanied by an order of a court or administrative tribunal, if:

(A) The covered entity receives satisfactory assurance, as described in paragraph (e)(1)(iii) of this section, from the party seeking the information that reasonable efforts have been made by such party to ensure that the individual who is the subject of the protected health information that has been requested has been given notice of the request; or

(B) The covered entity receives satisfactory assurance, as described in paragraph (e)(1)(iv) of this section, from the party seeking the information that reasonable efforts have been made by such party to secure a qualified protective order that meets the requirements of paragraph (e)(1)(v) of this section.

(iii) For the purposes of paragraph (e)(1)(ii)(A) of this section, a covered entity receives satisfactory assurances from a party seeking protected health information if the covered entity receives from such party a written statement and accompanying documentation demonstrating that:

(A) The party requesting such information has made a good faith attempt to provide written notice to the individual (or, if the individual's location is unknown, to mail a notice to the individual's last known address);

(B) The notice included sufficient information about the litigation or proceeding in which the protected health information is requested to permit the individual to raise an objection to the court or administrative tribunal; and

(C) The time for the individual to raise objections to the court or administrative tribunal has elapsed, and:

(1) No objections were filed; or

(2) All objections filed by the individual have been resolved by the court or the administrative tribunal and the disclosures being sought are consistent with such resolution.

(iv) For the purposes of paragraph (e)(1)(ii)(B) of this section, a covered entity receives satisfactory assurances from a party seeking protected health information, if the covered entity receives from such party a written statement and accompanying documentation demonstrating that:

(A) The parties to the dispute giving rise to the request for information have agreed to a qualified protective order and have presented it to the court or administrative tribunal with jurisdiction over the dispute; or

(B) The party seeking the protected health information has requested a qualified protective order from such court or administrative tribunal.

(v) For purposes of paragraph (e)(1) of this section, a qualified protective order means, with respect to protected health information requested under paragraph (e)(1)(ii) of this section, an order of a court or of an administrative tribunal or a stipulation by the parties to the litigation or administrative proceeding that:

(A) Prohibits the parties from using or disclosing the protected health information for any purpose other than the litigation or proceeding for which such information was requested; and

(B) Requires the return to the covered entity or destruction of the protected health information (including all copies made) at the end of the litigation or proceeding.

(vi) Notwithstanding paragraph (e)(1)(ii) of this section, a covered entity may disclose protected health information in response to lawful process described in paragraph (e)(1)(ii) of this section without receiving satisfactory assurance under paragraph (e)(1)(ii)(A) or (B) of this section, if the covered entity makes reasonable efforts to provide notice to the individual sufficient to meet the requirements of paragraph (e)(1)(iii) of this section or to seek a qualified protective order sufficient to meet the requirements of paragraph (e)(1)(v) of this section.

(2) Other uses and disclosures under this section. The provisions of this paragraph do not supersede other provisions of this section that otherwise permit or restrict uses or disclosures of protected health information.

(f) Standard: Disclosures for law enforcement purposes. A covered entity may disclose protected health information for a law enforcement purpose to a law enforcement official if the conditions in paragraphs (f)(1) through (f)(6) of this section are met, as applicable.

(1) Permitted disclosures: Pursuant to process and as otherwise required by law. A covered entity may disclose protected health information:

(i) As required by law including laws that require the reporting of certain types of wounds or other physical injuries, except for laws subject to paragraph (b)(1)(ii) or (c)(1)(i) of this section; or

(ii) In compliance with and as limited by the relevant requirements of:

(A) A court order or court-ordered warrant, or a subpoena or summons issued by a judicial officer;

(B) A grand jury subpoena; or

(C) An administrative request, including an administrative subpoena or summons, a civil or an authorized investigative demand, or similar process authorized under law, provided that:

(1) The information sought is relevant and material to a legitimate law enforcement inquiry;

(2) The request is specific and limited in scope to the extent reasonably practicable in light of the purpose for which the information is sought; and

(3) De-identified information could not reasonably be used.

(2) Permitted disclosures: Limited information for identification and

location purposes. Except for disclosures required by law as permitted by paragraph (f)(1) of this section, a covered entity may disclose protected health information in response to a law enforcement official's request for such information for the purpose of identifying or locating a suspect, fugitive, material witness, or missing person, provided that:

(i) The covered entity may disclose only the following information:

(A) Name and address;

(B) Date and place of birth;

(C) Social security number;

(D) ABO blood type and rh factor;

(E) Type of injury;

(F) Date and time of treatment;

(G) Date and time of death, if applicable; and

(H) A description of distinguishing physical characteristics, including height, weight, gender, race, hair and eye color, presence or absence of facial hair (beard or moustache), scars, and tattoos.

(ii) Except as permitted by paragraph (f)(2)(i) of this section, the covered entity may not disclose for the purposes of identification or location under paragraph (f)(2) of this section any protected health information related to the individual's DNA or DNA analysis, dental records, or typing, samples or analysis of body fluids or tissue.

(3) Permitted disclosure: Victims of a crime. Except for disclosures required by law as permitted by paragraph (f)(1) of this section, a covered entity may disclose protected health information in response to a law enforcement official's request for such information about an individual who is or is suspected to be a victim of a crime, other than disclosures that are subject to paragraph (b) or (c) of this section, if:

(i) The individual agrees to the disclosure; or

(ii) The covered entity is unable to obtain the individual's agreement because of incapacity or other emergency circumstance, provided that:

(A) The law enforcement official represents that such information is needed to determine whether a violation of law by a person other than the victim has occurred, and such information is not intended to be used against the victim;

(B) The law enforcement official represents that immediate law enforcement activity that depends upon the disclosure would be materially and adversely affected by waiting until the individual is able to agree to the disclosure; and

(C) The disclosure is in the best interests of the individual as determined by the covered entity, in the exercise of professional judgment.

(4) Permitted disclosure: Decedents. A covered entity may disclose protected health information about an individual who has died to a law enforcement official for the purpose of alerting law enforcement of the death of the individual if the covered entity has a suspicion that such death

may have resulted from criminal conduct.

(5) Permitted disclosure: Crime on premises. A covered entity may disclose to a law enforcement official protected health information that the covered entity believes in good faith constitutes evidence of criminal conduct that occurred on the premises of the covered entity.

(6) Permitted disclosure: Reporting crime in emergencies.
(i) A covered health care provider providing emergency health care in response to a medical emergency, other than such emergency on the premises of the covered health care provider, may disclose protected health information to a law enforcement official if such disclosure appears necessary to alert law enforcement to:
(A) The commission and nature of a crime;
(B) The location of such crime or of the victim(s) of such crime; and
(C) The identity, description, and location of the perpetrator of such crime.
(ii) If a covered health care provider believes that the medical emergency described in paragraph (f)(6)(i) of this section is the result of abuse, neglect, or domestic violence of the individual in need of emergency health care, paragraph (f)(6)(i) of this section does not apply and any disclosure to a law enforcement official for law enforcement purposes is subject to paragraph (c) of this section.
(g) Standard: Uses and disclosures about decedents

(1) Coroners and medical examiners. A covered entity may disclose protected health information to a coroner or medical examiner for the purpose of identifying a deceased person, determining a cause of death, or other duties as authorized by law. A covered entity that also performs the duties of a coroner or medical examiner may use protected health information for the purposes described in this paragraph.

(2) Funeral directors. A covered entity may disclose protected health information to funeral directors, consistent with applicable law, as necessary to carry out their duties with respect to the decedent. If necessary for funeral directors to carry out their duties, the covered entity may disclose the protected health information prior to, and in reasonable anticipation of, the individual's death.
(h) Standard: Uses and disclosures for cadaveric organ, eye or tissue donation purposes. A covered entity may use or disclose protected health information to organ procurement organizations or other entities engaged in the procurement, banking, or transplantation of cadaveric organs, eyes, or tissue for the purpose of facilitating organ, eye or tissue donation and transplantation.
(i) Standard: Uses and disclosures for research purposes
(1) Permitted uses and disclosures. A covered entity may use or disclose

protected health information for research, regardless of the source of funding of the research, provided that:

(i) Board approval of a waiver of authorization. The covered entity obtains documentation that an alteration to or waiver, in whole or in part, of the individual authorization required by § 164.508 for use or disclosure of protected health information has been approved by either:

(A) An Institutional Review Board (IRB), established in accordance with 7 CFR lc.107,10 CFR 745.107, CFR 1230.107, 15 CFR 27.107, CFR 1028.107, 21 CFR 56.107, CFR 225.107, 24 CFR 60.107, CFR 46.107, 32 CFR 219.107, CFR 97.107, 38 CFR 16.107, CFR 26.107, 45 CFR 46.107, CFR 690.107, or 49 CFR 11.107; or

(B) A privacy board that:

(1) Has members with varying backgrounds and appropriate professional competency as necessary to review the effect of the research protocol on the individual's privacy rights and related interests;

(2) Includes at least one member who is not affiliated with the covered entity, not affiliated with any entity conducting or sponsoring the research, and not related to any person who is affiliated with any of such entities; and

(3) Does not have any member participating in a review of any project in which the member has a conflict of interest.

(ii) Reviews preparatory to research. The covered entity obtains from the researcher representations that:

(A) Use or disclosure is sought solely to review protected health information as necessary to prepare a research protocol or for similar purposes preparatory to research;

(B) No protected health information is to be removed from the covered entity by the researcher in the course of the review; and

(C) The protected health information for which use or access is sought is necessary for the research purposes.

(iii) Research on decedent's information. The covered entity obtains from the researcher:

(A) Representation that the use or disclosure sought is solely for research on the protected health information of decedents;

(B) Documentation, at the request of the covered entity, of the death of such individuals; and

(C) Representation that the protected health information for which use or disclosure is sought is necessary for the research purposes.

(2) Documentation of waiver approval. For a use or disclosure to be permitted based on documentation of approval of an alteration or waiver, under paragraph (i)(1)(i) of this section, the documentation must include all of the following:

(i) Identification and date of action. A statement identifying the IRB or privacy board and the date on which the alteration or waiver of authorization was approved;

(ii) Waiver criteria. A statement that the IRB or privacy board has determined that the alteration or waiver, in whole or in part, of authorization satisfies the following criteria:

(A) The use or disclosure of protected health information involves no more than a minimal risk to the privacy of individuals, based on, at least, the presence of the following elements;

(1) An adequate plan to protect the identifiers from improper use and disclosure;

(2) An adequate plan to destroy the identifiers at the earliest opportunity consistent with conduct of the research, unless there is a health or research justification for retaining the identifiers or such retention is otherwise required by law; and

(3) Adequate written assurances that the protected health information will not be reused or disclosed to any other person or entity, except as required by law, for authorized oversight of the research study, or for other research for which the use or disclosure of protected health information would be permitted by this subpart;

(B) The research could not practicably be conducted without the waiver or alteration; and

(C) The research could not practicably be conducted without access to and use of the protected health information.

(iii) Protected health information needed. A brief description of the protected health information for which use or access has been determined to be necessary by the institutional review board or privacy board, pursuant to paragraph (i)(2)(ii)(C) of this section;

(iv) Review and approval procedures. A statement that the alteration or waiver of authorization has been reviewed and approved under either normal or expedited review procedures, as follows:

(A) An IRB must follow the requirements of the Common Rule, including the normal review procedures (7 CFR 1c.108(b), CFR 745.108(b), 14 CFR 1230.108(b), CFR 27.108(b), 16 CFR 1028.108(b), 21 CFR 56.108(b), CFR 225.108(b), 24 CFR 60.108(b), CFR 46.108(b), 32 CFR 219.108(b), CFR 97.108(b), 38 CFR 16.108(b), CFR 26.108(b), 45 CFR 46.108(b), CFR 690.108(b), or 49 CFR 11.108(b)) or the expedited review procedures (7 CFR 1c.110, CFR 745.110, 14 CFR 1230.110, CFR 27.110, 16 CFR 1028.110, CFR 56.110, 22 CFR 225.110, CFR 60.110, 28 CFR 46.110, CFR 219.110, 34 CFR 97.110, CFR 16.110, 40 CFR 26.110, CFR 46.110, 45 CFR 690.110, or 49 CFR 11.110);

(B) A privacy board must review the proposed research at convened meetings at which a majority of the privacy board members are present, including at least one member who satisfies the criterion stated in paragraph (i)(1)(i)(B)(2) of this section, and the alteration or waiver of authorization must be approved by the majority of the privacy board members present at the meeting, unless the privacy board elects to use an expedited review procedure in accordance with paragraph (i)(2)(iv)(C) of this section;

(C) A privacy board may use an expedited review procedure if the research involves no more than minimal risk to the privacy of the individuals who are the subject of the protected health information for which use or disclosure is being sought. If the privacy board elects to use an expedited review procedure, the review and approval of the alteration or waiver of authorization may be carried out by the chair of the privacy board, or by one or more members of the privacy board as designated by the chair; and

(v) Required signature. The documentation of the alteration or waiver of authorization must be signed by the chair or other member, as designated by the chair, of the IRB or the privacy board, as applicable.

(j) Standard: Uses and disclosures to avert a serious threat to health or safety

(1) Permitted disclosures. A covered entity may, consistent with applicable law and standards of ethical conduct, use or disclose protected health information, if the covered entity, in good faith, believes the use or disclosure:

(i)

(A) Is necessary to prevent or lessen a serious and imminent threat to the health or safety of a person or the public; and

(B) Is to a person or persons reasonably able to prevent or lessen the threat, including the target of the threat; or

(ii) Is necessary for law enforcement authorities to identify or apprehend an individual:

(A) Because of a statement by an individual admitting participation in a violent crime that the covered entity reasonably believes may have caused serious physical harm to the victim; or

(B) Where it appears from all the circumstances that the individual has escaped from a correctional institution or from lawful custody, as those terms are defined in§ 164.501.

(2) Use or disclosure not permitted. A use or disclosure pursuant to paragraph (j)(1)(ii)(A) of this section may not be made if the information described in paragraph (j)(1)(ii)(A) of this section is learned by the covered entity:

(i) In the course of treatment to affect the propensity to commit the criminal conduct that is the basis for the disclosure under paragraph (j)(1)(ii)(A) of this section, or counseling or therapy; or

(ii) Through a request by the individual to initiate or to be referred for the treatment, counseling, or therapy described in paragraph (j)(2)(i) of this section.

(3) Limit on information that may be disclosed. A disclosure made pursuant to paragraph (j)(1)(ii)(A) of this section shall contain only the statement described in paragraph (j)(1)(ii)(A) of this section and the protected health information described in paragraph (f)(2)(i) of this section.

(4) Presumption of good faith belief. A covered entity that uses or discloses protected health information pursuant to paragraph (j)(1) of this section is presumed to have acted in good faith with regard to a belief described in paragraph (j)(1)(i) or (ii) of this section, if the belief is based upon the covered entity's actual knowledge or in reliance on a credible representation by a person with apparent knowledge or authority.

(k) Standard: Uses and disclosures for specialized government functions

(1) Military and veterans activities—(i) Armed Forces personnel. A covered entity may use and disclose the protected health information of individuals who are Armed Forces personnel for activities deemed necessary by appropriate military command authorities to assure the proper execution of the military mission, if the appropriate military authority has published by notice in the Federal Register the following information:

(A) Appropriate military command authorities; and

(B) The purposes for which the protected health information may be used or disclosed.

(ii) Separation or discharge from military service. A covered entity that is a component of the Departments of Defense or Homeland Security may disclose to the Department of Veterans Affairs (DVA) the protected health information of an individual who is a member of the Armed Forces upon the separation or discharge of the individual from military service for the purpose of a determination by DVA of the individual's eligibility for or entitlement to benefits under laws administered by the Secretary of Veterans Affairs.

(iii) Veterans. A covered entity that is a component of the Department of Veterans Affairs may use and disclose protected health information to components of the Department that determine eligibility for or entitlement to, or that provide, benefits under the laws administered by the Secretary of Veterans Affairs.

(iv) Foreign military personnel. A covered entity may use and disclose the protected health information of individuals who are foreign military personnel to their appropriate foreign military authority for the same purposes for which uses and disclosures are permitted for Armed Forces personnel under the notice published in the Federal Register pursuant to paragraph (k)(1)(i) of this section.

(2) National security and intelligence activities. A covered entity may disclose protected health information to authorized federal officials for the conduct of lawful intelligence, counter-intelligence, and other national security activities authorized by the National Security Act (50 U.S.C. 401, et seq.) and implementing authority (e.g., Executive Order 12333).

(3) Protective services for the President and others. A covered entity may disclose protected health information to authorized Federal officials for the provision of protective services to the President or other persons authorized by 18 U.S.C. 3056 or to foreign heads of state or other persons authorized by 22 U.S.C. 2709(a)(3), or for the conduct of investigations authorized by 18 U.S.C. 871 and 879.

(4) Medical suitability determinations. A covered entity that is a component of the Department of State may use protected health information to make medical suitability determinations and may disclose whether or not the individual was determined to be medically suitable to the officials in the Department of State who need access to such information for the following purposes:

(i) For the purpose of a required security clearance conducted pursuant to Executive Orders 10450 and 12968;

(ii) As necessary to determine worldwide availability or availability for mandatory service abroad undersections 101(a)(4) and 504 of the Foreign Service Act; or

(iii) For a family to accompany a Foreign Service member abroad, consistent withsection 101(b)(5) and 904 of the Foreign Service Act.

(5) Correctional institutions and other law enforcement custodial situations.

(i) Permitted disclosures. A covered entity may disclose to a correctional institution or a law enforcement official having lawful custody of an inmate or other individual protected health information about such inmate or individual, if the correctional institution or such law enforcement official represents that such protected health information is necessary for:

(A) The provision of health care to such individuals;

(B) The health and safety of such individual or other inmates;

(C) The health and safety of the officers or employees of or others at the correctional institution;

(D) The health and safety of such individuals and officers or other personsresponsible for the transporting of inmates or their transfer from one institution, facility, or setting to another;

(E) Law enforcement on the premises of the correctional institution; or

(F) The administration and maintenance of the safety, security, and good order of the correctional institution.

(ii) Permitted uses. A covered entity that is a correctional institution may use protected health information of individuals who are inmates for any purpose for which such protected health information may be disclosed.

(iii) No application after release. For the purposes of this provision, an individual is no longer an inmate when released on parole, probation, supervised release, or otherwise is no longer in lawful custody.

(6) Covered entities that are government programs providing public benefits.

(i) A health plan that is a government program providing public benefits may disclose protected health information relating to eligibility for or enrollment in the health plan to another agency administering a government program providing public benefits if the sharing of eligibility or enrollment information among such government agencies or the maintenance of such information in a single or combined data system accessible to all such government agencies is required or expressly authorized by statute or regulation.

(ii) A covered entity that is a government agency administering a government program providing public benefits may disclose protected health information relating to the program to another covered entity that is a government agency administering a government program providing public benefits if the programs serve the same or similar populations and the disclosure of protected health information is necessary to coordinate the covered functions of such programs or to improve administration and management relating to the covered functions of such programs.

(l) Standard: Disclosures for workers' compensation. A covered entity may disclose protected health information as authorized by and to the extent necessary to comply with laws relating to workers' compensation or other similar programs, established by law, that provide benefits for work-related injuries or illness without regard to fault.

164.514 Other requirements relating to uses and disclosures of protected health information.

(a) Standard: De-identification of protected health information. Health information that does not identify an individual and with respect to which there is no reasonable basis to believe that the information can be used to identify an individual is not individually identifiable health information.

(b) Implementation specifications: Requirements for de-identification of protected health information. A covered entity may determine that health information is not individually identifiable health information only if:

(1) A person with appropriate knowledge of and experience with generally accepted statistical and scientific principles and methods for rendering information not individually identifiable:

(i) Applying such principles and methods, determines that the risk is very small that the information could be used, alone or in combination with other reasonably available information, by an anticipated recipient to identify an individual who is a subject of the information; and

(ii) Documents the methods and results of the analysis that justify such determination; or

(2)

(i) The following identifiers of the individual or of relatives, employers, or household members of the individual, are removed:

(A) Names;

(B) All geographic subdivisions smaller than a State, including street address, city, county, precinct, zip code, and their equivalent geocodes, except for the initial three digits of a zip code if, according to the current publicly available data from the Bureau of the Census:

(1) The geographic unit formed by combining all zip codes with the same three initial digits contains more than 20,000 people; and

(2) The initial three digits of a zip code for all such geographic units containing 20,000 or fewer people is changed to 000.

(C) All elements of dates (except year) for dates directly related to an individual, including birth date, admission date, discharge date, date of death; and all ages over 89 and all elements of dates (including year) indicative of such age, except that such ages and elements may be aggregated into a single category of age 90 or older;

(D) Telephone numbers;

(E) Fax numbers;

(F) Electronic mail addresses;

(G) Social security numbers;

(H) Medical record numbers;

(I) Health plan beneficiary numbers;

(J) Account numbers;

(K) Certificate/license numbers;

(L) Vehicle identifiers and serial numbers, including license plate numbers;

(M) Device identifiers and serial numbers;

(N) Web Universal Resource Locators (URLs);

(O) Internet Protocol (IP) address numbers;

(P) Biometric identifiers, including finger and voice prints;

(Q) Full face photographic images and any comparable images; and

(R) Any other unique identifying number, characteristic, or code, except as permitted by paragraph (c) of this section; and

(ii) The covered entity does not have actual knowledge that the information could be used alone or in combination with other information to identify an individual who is a subject of the information.

(c) Implementation specifications: Re-identification. A covered entity may assign a code or other means of record identification to allow information de-identified under this section to be re-identified by the covered entity, provided that:

(1) Derivation. The code or other means of record identification is not derived from or related to information about the individual and is not otherwise capable of being translated so as to identify the individual; and

(2) Security. The covered entity does not use or disclose the code or other means of record identification for any other purpose, and does not disclose the mechanism for re-identification.

(d)

(1) Standard: minimum necessary requirements. In order to comply with § 164.502(b) and this section, a covered entity must meet the requirements of paragraphs (d)(2) through (d)(5) of this section with respect to a request for, or the use and disclosure of, protected health information.

(2) Implementation specifications: Minimum necessary uses of protected health information.

(i) A covered entity must identify:

(A) Those persons or classes of persons, as appropriate, in its workforce who need access to protected health information to carry out their duties; and

(B) For each such person or class of persons, the category or categories of protected health information to which access is needed and any conditions appropriate to such access.

(ii) A covered entity must make reasonable efforts to limit the access of such persons or classes identified in paragraph (d)(2)(i)(A) of this section to protected health information consistent with paragraph (d)(2)(i)(B) of this section.

(3) Implementation specification: Minimum necessary disclosures of protected health information.

(i) For any type of disclosure that it makes on a routine and recurring basis, a covered entity must implement policies and procedures (which may be standard protocols) that limit the protected health information disclosed to the amount reasonably necessary to achieve the purpose of the disclosure.

(ii) For all other disclosures, a covered entity must:

(A) Develop criteria designed to limit the protected health information disclosed to the information reasonably necessary to accomplish the purpose for which disclosure is sought; and

(B) Review requests for disclosure on an individual basis in accordance with such criteria.

(iii) A covered entity may rely, if such reliance is reasonable under the circumstances, on a requested disclosure as the minimum necessary for the stated purpose when:

(A) Making disclosures to public officials that are permitted under§ 164.512, if the public official represents that the information requested is the minimum necessary for the stated purpose(s);

(B) The information is requested by another covered entity;

(C) The information is requested by a professional who is a member of its workforce or is a business associate of the covered entity for the purpose of providing professional services to the covered entity, if the professional represents that the information requested is the minimum necessary for the stated purpose(s); or

(D) Documentation or representations that comply with the applicable requirements of§ 164.512(i) have been provided by a person requesting the information for research purposes.

(4) Implementation specifications: Minimum necessary requests for protected health information.

(i) A covered entity must limit any request for protected health information to that which is reasonably necessary to accomplish the purpose for which the request is made, when requesting such information from other covered entities.

(ii) For a request that is made on a routine and recurring basis, a covered entity must implement policies and procedures (which may be standard protocols) that limit the protected health information requested to the amount reasonably necessary to accomplish the purpose for which the request is made.

(iii) For all other requests, a covered entity must:

(A) Develop criteria designed to limit the request for protected health information to the information reasonably necessary to accomplish the purpose for which the request is made; and

(B) Review requests for disclosure on an individual basis in accordance with such criteria.

(5) Implementation specification: Other content requirement. For all uses, disclosures, or requests to which the requirements in paragraph (d) of this section apply, a covered entity may not use, disclose or request an entire medical record, except when the entire medical record is specifically justified as the amount that is reasonably necessary to accomplish the purpose of the use, disclosure, or request.

(e)

(1) Standard: Limited data set. A covered entity may use or disclose a limited data set that meets the requirements of paragraphs (e)(2) and (e)(3) of this section, if the covered entity enters into a data use agreement with the limited data set recipient, in accordance with paragraph (e)(4) of this section.

(2) Implementation specification: Limited data set: A limited data set is protected health information that excludes the following direct identifiers of the individual or of relatives, employers, or household members of the individual:

(i) Names;

(ii) Postal address information, other than town or city, State, and zip code;

(iii) Telephone numbers;

(iv) Fax numbers;

(v) Electronic mail addresses;

(vi) Social security numbers;

(vii) Medical record numbers;

(viii) Health plan beneficiary numbers;

(ix) Account numbers;

(x) Certificate/license numbers;

(xi) Vehicle identifiers and serial numbers, including license plate numbers;

(xii) Device identifiers and serial numbers;

(xiii) Web Universal Resource Locators (URLs);

(xiv) Internet Protocol (IP) address numbers;

(xv) Biometric identifiers, including finger and voice prints; and

(xvi) Full face photographic images and any comparable images.

(3) Implementation specification: Permitted purposes for uses and disclosures.

(i) A covered entity may use or disclose a limited data set under paragraph (e)(1) of this section only for the purposes of research, public health, or health care operations.

(ii) A covered entity may use protected health information to create a limited data set that meets the requirements of paragraph (e)(2) of this section, or disclose protected health information only to a business associate for such purpose, whether or not the limited data set is to be used by the covered entity.

(4) Implementation specifications: Data use agreement

(i) Agreement required. A covered entity may use or disclose a limited data set under paragraph (e)(1) of this section only if the covered entity obtains satisfactory assurance, in the form of a data use agreement that meets the requirements of this section, that the limited data set recipient will only use or disclose the protected health information for limited purposes.

(ii) Contents. A data use agreement between the covered entity and the limited data set recipient must:

(A) Establish the permitted uses and disclosures of such information by the limited data set recipient, consistent with paragraph (e)(3) of this section. The data use agreement may not authorize the limited data set recipient to use or further disclose the information in a manner that would violate the requirements of this subpart, if done by the covered entity;
(B) Establish who is permitted to use or receive the limited data set; and
(C) Provide that the limited data set recipient will:

(1) Not use or further disclose the information other than as permitted by the data use agreement or as otherwise required by law;
(2) Use appropriate safeguards to prevent use or disclosure of the information other than as provided for by the data use agreement;
(3) Report to the covered entity any use or disclosure of the information not provided for by its data use agreement of which it becomes aware;
(4) Ensure that any agents to whom it provides the limited data set agree to the same restrictions and conditions that apply to the limited data set recipient with respect to such information; and
(5) Not identify the information or contact the individuals.

(iii) Compliance.
(A) A covered entity is not in compliance with the standards in paragraph (e) of this section if the covered entity knew of a pattern of activity or practice of the limited data set recipient that constituted a material breach or violation of the data use agreement, unless the covered entity took reasonable steps to cure the breach or end the violation, as applicable, and, if such steps were unsuccessful:
(1) Discontinued disclosure of protected health information to the recipient; and
(2) Reported the problem to the Secretary.
(B) A covered entity that is a limited data set recipient and violates a

data use agreement will be in noncompliance with the standards, implementation specifications, and requirements of paragraph (e) of this section.

(f) Fundraising communications.

(1) Standard: Uses and disclosures for fundraising. Subject to the conditions of paragraph (f)(2) of this section, a covered entity may use, or disclose to a business associate or to an institutionally related foundation, the following protected health information for the purpose of raising funds for its own benefit, without an authorization meeting the requirements of § 164.508:

(i) Demographic information relating to an individual, including name, address, other contact information, age, gender, and date of birth;

(ii) Dates of health care provided to an individual;

(iii) Department of service information;

(iv) Treating physician;

(v) Outcome information; and

(vi) Health insurance status.

(2) Implementation specifications: Fundraising requirements.

(i) A covered entity may not use or disclose protected health information for fundraising purposes as otherwise permitted by paragraph (f)(1) of this section unless a statement required by§ 164.520(b)(1)(iii)(A) is included in the covered entity's notice of privacy practices.

(ii) With each fundraising communication made to an individual under this paragraph, a covered entity must provide the individual with a clear and conspicuous opportunity to elect not to receive any further fundraising communications. The method for an individual to elect not to receive further fundraising communications may not cause the individual to incur an undue burden or more than a nominal cost.

(iii) A covered entity may not condition treatment or payment on the individual's choice with respect to the receipt of fundraising communications.

(iv) A covered entity may not make fundraising communications to an individual under this paragraph where the individual has elected not to receive such communications under paragraph (f)(2)(ii) of this section.

(v) A covered entity may provide an individual who has elected not to receive further fundraising communications with a method to opt back in to receive such communications.

(g) Standard: Uses and disclosures for underwriting and related purposes. If a health plan receives protected health information for the purpose of underwriting, premium rating, or other activities relating to the creation, renewal, or replacement of a contract of health insurance or health benefits, and if such health insurance or health benefits are not placed with the health plan, such health plan may only use or disclose such protected health information for such purpose or as may be required by law, subject to the prohibition at § 164.502(a)(5)(i) with respect to genetic information included in the protected health information.

(h)

(1) Standard: Verification requirements. Prior to any disclosure permitted by this subpart, a covered entity must:

(i) Except with respect to disclosures under§ 164.510, verify the identity of a person requesting protected health information and the authority of any such person to have access to protected health information under this subpart, if the identity or any such authority of such person is not known to the covered entity; and

(ii) Obtain any documentation, statements, or representations, whether oral or written, from the person requesting the protected health information when such documentation, statement, or representation is a condition of the disclosure under this subpart.

(2) Implementation specifications: Verification.

(i) Conditions on disclosures. If a disclosure is conditioned by this subpart on particular documentation, statements, or representations from the person requesting the protected health information, a covered entity may rely, if such reliance is reasonable under the circumstances, on documentation, statements, or representations that, on their face, meet the applicable requirements.

(A) The conditions in§ 164.512(f)(1)(ii)(C) may be satisfied by the administrative subpoena or similar process or by a separate written statement that, on its face, demonstrates that the applicable requirements have been met.

(B) The documentation required by§ 164.512(i)(2) may be satisfied by one or more written statements, provided that each is appropriately dated and signed in accordance with § 164.512(i)(2)(i) and (v).

(ii) Identity of public officials. A covered entity may rely, if such reliance is reasonable under the circumstances, on any of the following to verify identity when the disclosure of protected health information is to a public official or a person acting on behalf of the public official:

(A) If the request is made in person, presentation of an agency identification badge, other official credentials, or other proof of government status;

(B) If the request is in writing, the request is on the appropriate government letterhead; or

(C) If the disclosure is to a person acting on behalf of a public official, a written statement on appropriate government letterhead that the person is acting under the government's authority or other evidence or documentation of agency, such as a contract for services, memorandum of understanding, or purchase order, that establishes that the person is acting on behalf of the public official.

(iii) Authority of public officials. A covered entity may rely, if such reliance is reasonable under the circumstances, on any of the following to verify authority when the disclosure of protected health information is to a public official or a person acting on behalf of the public official:

(A) A written statement of the legal authority under which the information is requested, or, if a written statement would be impracticable, an oral statement of such legal authority;

(B) If a request is made pursuant to legal process, warrant, subpoena, order, or other legal process issued by a grand jury or a judicial or administrative tribunal is presumed to constitute legal authority.

(iv) Exercise of professional judgment. The verification requirements of this paragraph are met if the covered entity relies on the exercise of professional judgment in making a use or disclosure in accordance with § 164.510 or acts on a good faith belief in making a disclosure in accordance with § 164.512(j).

CHAPTER 11
Mental Health Psychiatric Holds

Involuntary hospitalizations may be initiated by therapist when a client poses a danger to self, a danger to others, or is gravely disabled and unable or unwilling to accept appropriate care. While a therapist may initiate the process for involuntary hospitalization, it is a physician, peace officer or authorized professional who makes the final determination. There are essentially 5 types of involuntarily hospitalizations, 4 of them are addressed here.

The term gravely disabled is defined in Welfare and Institutions Code 5008 as an individual who (a) cannot provide for their basic needs such as food, clothing or shelter, as a result of a mental disorder or, (b) has been found mentally incompetent under Penal Code 1370 and all of the following exist: We did go into all the facts that exist here because these are items that would be more determined by either law enforcement or by a court, so the first portion of the definition would be most appropriate for mental health professionals, however, therapist are encouraged to review the entirety of the section.

1. 5150 - this is the hold that can be initiated by the therapist, and if invoked and determined appropriate by the physician, peace officer or authorized professional, the client will be held 72 hours for treatment and evaluation. Only the psychiatrist responsible for the care of the client may release the individual.

2. 5250 - if the client does not respond positively to the treatment, requires additional testing is necessary or is a danger to self, they may be held up to 14 days. The individual is eligible and required to have a certification hearing within the first four days of the 14-day hold.

3. 5260 - If they behave in a manner that continues to place themselves or others in danger or is gravely disabled either because of a mental health disorder or impairment by chronic alcoholism, they be held an additional 14 days.

4. 5270 - If after the 14-day treatment from the 5250 the individual is still found to be gravely disabled due to a mental disorder or impairment by chronic alcoholism and is unwilling or is unable to accept treatment voluntarily, they may be certified for an additional 30 days.

Definitions & Gravely Disabled

Welfare and Institutions Code
5008

Unless the context otherwise requires, the following definitions shall govern the construction of this part:

(a) "Evaluation" consists of multidisciplinary professional analyses of a person's medical, psychological, educational, social, financial, and legal conditions as may appear to constitute a problem. Persons providing evaluation services shall be properly qualified professionals and may be full-time employees of an agency providing face-to-face, which includes telehealth, evaluation services or may be part-time employees or may be employed on a contractual basis.

(b) "Court-ordered evaluation" means an evaluation ordered by a superior court pursuant to Article 2 (commencing with Section 5200) or by a superior court pursuant to Article 3 (commencing with Section 5225) of Chapter 2.

(c) "Intensive treatment" consists of such hospital and other services as may be indicated. Intensive treatment shall be provided by properly qualified professionals and carried out in facilities qualifying for reimbursement under the California Medical Assistance Program (Medi-Cal) set forth in Chapter 7 (commencing with Section 14000) of Part 3 of Division 9, or under Title XVIII of the federal Social Security Act and regulations thereunder. Intensive treatment may be provided in hospitals of the United States government by properly qualified professionals. This part does not prohibit an intensive treatment facility from also providing 72-hour evaluation and treatment.

(d) "Referral" is referral of persons by each agency or facility providing assessment, evaluation, crisis intervention, or treatment services to other agencies or individuals. The purpose of referral shall be to provide for continuity of care, and may include, but need not be limited to, informing the person of available services, making appointments on the person's behalf, discussing the person's problem with the agency or individual to which the person has been referred, appraising the outcome of referrals, and arranging for personal escort and transportation when necessary. Referral shall be considered complete when the agency or individual to whom the person has been referred accepts responsibility for providing the necessary services. All persons shall be advised of available precare services that prevent initial recourse to hospital treatment or aftercare services that support adjustment to community living following hospital treatment. These services may be provided through county or city mental health departments, state hospitals under the jurisdiction of the State Department of State Hospitals, regional centers under contract with the

State Department of Developmental Services, or other public or private entities.

Each agency or facility providing evaluation services shall maintain a current and comprehensive file of all community services, both public and private. These files shall contain current agreements with agencies or individuals accepting referrals, as well as appraisals of the results of past referrals.

(e) "Crisis intervention" consists of an interview or series of interviews within a brief period of time, conducted by qualified professionals, and designed to alleviate personal or family situations which present a serious and imminent threat to the health or stability of the person or the family. The interview or interviews may be conducted in the home of the person or family, or on an inpatient or outpatient basis with such therapy, or other services, as may be appropriate. The interview or interviews may include family members, significant support persons, providers, or other entities or individuals, as appropriate and as authorized by law. Crisis intervention may, as appropriate, include suicide prevention, psychiatric, welfare, psychological, legal, or other social services.

(f) "Prepetition screening" is a screening of all petitions for court-ordered evaluation as provided in Article 2 (commencing with Section 5200) of Chapter 2, consisting of a professional review of all petitions; an interview with the petitioner and, whenever possible, the person alleged, as a result of a mental health disorder, to be a danger to others, or to himself or herself, or to be gravely disabled, to assess the problem and explain the petition; when indicated, efforts to persuade the person to receive, on a voluntary basis, comprehensive evaluation, crisis intervention, referral, and other services specified in this part.

(g) "Conservatorship investigation" means investigation by an agency appointed or designated by the governing body of cases in which conservatorship is recommended pursuant to Chapter 3 (commencing with Section 5350).

(h) (1) For purposes of Article 1 (commencing with Section 5150), Article 2 (commencing with Section 5200), and Article 4 (commencing with Section 5250) of Chapter 2, and for the purposes of Chapter 3 (commencing with Section 5350), "gravely disabled" means either of the following:

(A) A condition in which a person, as a result of a mental health disorder, is unable to provide for his or her basic personal needs for food, clothing, or shelter.

(B) A condition in which a person, has been found mentally incompetent under Section 1370 of the Penal Code and all of the following facts exist:

(i) The complaint, indictment, or information pending against the person at the time of commitment charges a felony involving death, great bodily harm, or a serious threat to the physical well-being of another person.

(ii) There has been a finding of probable cause on a complaint pursuant to paragraph (2) of subdivision (a) of Section 1368.1 of the Penal Code, a preliminary examination pursuant to Section 859b of the Penal Code, or a grand jury indictment, and the complaint, indictment, or information has not been dismissed.

(iii) As a result of a mental health disorder, the person is unable to understand the nature and purpose of the proceedings taken against him or her and to assist counsel in the conduct of his or her defense in a rational manner.

(iv) The person represents a substantial danger of physical harm to others by reason of a mental disease, defect, or disorder.

(2) For purposes of Article 3 (commencing with Section 5225) and Article 4 (commencing with Section 5250), of Chapter 2, and for the purposes of Chapter 3 (commencing with Section 5350), "gravely disabled" means a condition in which a person, as a result of impairment by chronic alcoholism, is unable to provide for his or her basic personal needs for food, clothing, or shelter.

(3) The term "gravely disabled" does not include persons with intellectual disabilities by reason of that disability alone.

(i) "Peace officer" means a duly sworn peace officer as that term is defined in Chapter 4.5 (commencing with Section 830) of Title 3 of Part 2 of the Penal Code who has completed the basic training course established by the Commission on Peace Officer Standards and Training, or any parole officer or probation officer specified in Section 830.5 of the Penal Code when acting in relation to cases for which he or she has a legally mandated responsibility.

(j) "Postcertification treatment" means an additional period of treatment pursuant to Article 6 (commencing with Section 5300) of Chapter 2.

(k) "Court," unless otherwise specified, means a court of record.

(l) "Antipsychotic medication" means any medication customarily prescribed for the treatment of symptoms of psychoses and other severe mental and emotional disorders.

(m) "Emergency" means a situation in which action to impose treatment over the person's objection is immediately necessary for the preservation of life or the prevention of serious bodily harm to the patient or others, and it is impracticable to first gain consent. It is not necessary for harm to take place or become unavoidable prior to treatment.

(n) "Designated facility" or "facility designated by the county for evaluation and treatment" means a facility that is licensed or certified as a mental health treatment facility or a hospital, as defined in subdivision (a) or (b) of Section 1250 of the Health and Safety Code, by the State Department of Public Health, and may include, but is not limited to, a licensed psychiatric hospital, a licensed psychiatric health facility, and a certified crisis stabilization unit.

5150 – 72 hours

5150

(a) When a person, as a result of a mental health disorder, is a danger to others, or to himself or herself, or gravely disabled, a peace officer, professional person in charge of a facility designated by the county for evaluation and treatment, member of the attending staff, as defined by regulation, of a facility designated by the county for evaluation and treatment, designated members of a mobile crisis team, or professional person designated by the county may, upon probable cause, take, or cause to be taken, the person into custody for a period of up to 72 hours for assessment, evaluation, and crisis intervention, or placement for evaluation and treatment in a facility designated by the county for evaluation and treatment and approved by the State Department of Health Care Services. At a minimum, assessment, as defined in Section 5150.4, and evaluation, as defined in subdivision (a) of Section 5008, shall be conducted and provided on an ongoing basis. Crisis intervention, as defined in subdivision (e) of Section 5008, may be provided concurrently with assessment, evaluation, or any other service.

(b) The professional person in charge of a facility designated by the county for evaluation and treatment, member of the attending staff, or professional person designated by the county shall assess the person to determine whether he or she can be properly served without being detained. If in the judgment of the professional person in charge of the facility designated by the county for evaluation and treatment, member of the attending staff, or professional person designated by the county, the person can be properly served without being detained, he or she shall be provided evaluation, crisis intervention, or other inpatient or outpatient services on a voluntary basis. Nothing in this subdivision shall be interpreted to prevent a peace officer from delivering individuals to a designated facility for assessment under this section. Furthermore, the assessment requirement of this subdivision shall not be interpreted to require peace officers to perform any additional duties other than those specified in Sections 5150.1 and 5150.2.

(c) Whenever a person is evaluated by a professional person in charge of a facility designated by the county for evaluation or treatment, member of the attending staff, or professional person designated by the county and is found to be in need of mental health services, but is not admitted to the facility, all available alternative services provided pursuant to subdivision (b) shall be offered as determined by the county mental health director.

(d) If, in the judgment of the professional person in charge of the facility designated by the county for evaluation and treatment, member of the attending staff, or the professional person designated by the county, the person cannot be properly served without being detained, the admitting facility shall require an application in writing stating the circumstances under which the person's condition was called to the attention of the peace officer, professional person in charge of the facility designated by the county for evaluation and treatment, member of the attending staff, or professional person designated by the county, and stating that the peace officer, professional person in charge of the facility designated by the county for evaluation and treatment, member of the attending staff, or professional person designated by the county has probable cause to believe that the person is, as a result of a mental health disorder, a danger to others, or to himself or herself, or gravely disabled. If the probable cause is based on the statement of a person other than the peace officer, professional person in charge of the facility designated by the county for evaluation and treatment, member of the attending staff, or professional person designated by the county, the person shall be liable in a civil action for intentionally giving a statement which he or she knows to be false.

(e) At the time a person is taken into custody for evaluation, or within a reasonable time thereafter, unless a responsible relative or the guardian or conservator of the person is in possession of the person's personal property, the person taking him or her into custody shall take reasonable precautions to preserve and safeguard the personal property in the possession of or on the premises occupied by the person. The person taking him or her into custody shall then furnish to the court a report generally describing the person's property so preserved and safeguarded and its disposition, in substantially the form set forth in Section 5211, except that if a responsible relative or the guardian or conservator of the person is in possession of the person's property, the report shall include only the name of the relative or guardian or conservator and the location of the property, whereupon responsibility of the person taking him or her into custody for that property shall terminate. As used in this section, "responsible relative" includes the spouse, parent, adult child, domestic partner, grandparent, grandchild, or adult brother or sister of the person.

(f) (1) Each person, at the time he or she is first taken into custody under this section, shall be provided, by the person who takes him or her into custody, the following information orally in a language or modality accessible to the person. If the person cannot understand an oral advisement, the information shall be provided in writing. The information shall be in substantially the following form:
My name is _____. I am a _____(peace officer/mental health _____ .professional) with _____ . (name of agency). You are not under criminal arrest, but I am taking you for an examination by mental health professionals at _____ (name of facility). You will be told your rights by the mental health staff.

    (2) If taken into custody at his or her own residence, the person shall also be provided the following information: You may bring a few personal items with you, which I will have to approve. Please inform me if you need assistance turning off any appliance or water. You may make a phone call and leave a note to tell your friends or family where you have been taken.

(g) The designated facility shall keep, for each patient evaluated, a record of the advisement given pursuant to subdivision (f) which shall include all of the following: (1) The name of the person detained for evaluation. (2) The name and position of the peace officer or mental health professional taking the person into custody. (3) The date the advisement was completed. (4) Whether the advisement was completed. (5) The language or modality used to give the advisement. (6) If the advisement was not completed, a statement of good cause, as defined by regulations of the State Department of Health Care Services.

(h) (1) Each person admitted to a facility designated by the county for evaluation and treatment shall be given the following information by admission staff of the facility. The information shall be given orally and in writing and in a language or modality accessible to the person. The written information shall be available to the person in English and in the language that is the person's primary means of communication. Accommodations for other disabilities that may affect communication shall also be provided. The information shall be in substantially the following form:
My name is _____. My position here is_____. You are being placed into this psychiatric facility because it is our professional opinion that, as a result of a mental health disorder, you are likely to (check applicable):
( ) Harm yourself.
( ) Harm someone else.
( ) Be unable to take care of your own food, clothing, and housing needs.

We believe this is true because _____
(list of the facts upon which the allegation of dangerous or gravely disabled due to mental health   disorder is based, including pertinent facts arising from the admission interview).

You will be held for a period up to 72 hours.   During the 72 hours you may also be transferred to another facility. You may request to be evaluated or treated at a facility of your choice. You may request to be evaluated or treated by a mental health professional of your choice. We cannot guarantee the facility or mental health professional you choose will be available, but we will honor your choice if we can. During these 72 hours you will be evaluated by the facility staff, and you may be given treatment, including medications. It is possible for you to be released before the end of the 72 hours. But if the staff decides that you need continued treatment you can be held for a longer period of time. If you are held longer than 72 hours, you have the right to a lawyer and a qualified interpreter and a hearing before a judge. If you are unable to pay for the lawyer, then one will be provided to you free of charge. If you have questions about your legal rights, you may contact the county Patients' Rights Advocate at _____(phone   number   for   the   county _____.   Patients' Rights Advocacy office). Your 72-hour period began _____.   (date/time)
 (2) If the notice is given in a county where weekends and holidays are excluded from the 72-hour period, the patient shall be informed of this fact.

(i) For each patient admitted for evaluation and treatment, the facility shall keep with the patient's medical record a record of the advisement given pursuant to subdivision (h), which shall include all of the following:
(1) The name of the person performing the advisement.
(2) The date of the advisement.
(3) Whether the advisement was completed.
(4) The language or modality used to communicate the advisement.
(5) If the advisement was not completed, a statement of good cause.

5150.05.
(a) When determining if probable cause exists to take a person into custody, or cause a person to be taken into custody, pursuant to Section 5150, any person who is authorized to take that person, or cause that person to be taken, into custody pursuant to that section shall consider available relevant information about the historical course of the person's mental disorder if the authorized person determines that the information has a reasonable bearing on the determination as to whether the person is a danger to others, or to himself or herself, or is gravely disabled as a result of the mental disorder.

(b) For purposes of this section, "information about the historical course of the person's mental disorder" includes evidence presented by the person who has provided or is providing mental health or related support services to the person subject to a determination described in subdivision (a), evidence presented by one or more members of the family of that person, and evidence presented by the person subject to a determination described in subdivision (a) or anyone designated by that person.

(c) If the probable cause in subdivision (a) is based on the statement of a person other than the one authorized to take the person into custody pursuant to Section 5150, a member of the attending staff, or a professional person, the person making the statement shall be liable in a civil action for intentionally giving any statement that he or she knows to be false.

(d) This section shall not be applied to limit the application of Section 5328.

5150.1.
No peace officer seeking to transport, or having transported, a person to a designated facility for assessment under Section 5150, shall be instructed by mental health personnel to take the person to, or keep the person at, a jail solely because of the unavailability of an acute bed, nor shall the peace officer be forbidden to transport the person directly to the designated facility. No mental health employee from any county, state, city, or any private agency providing Short-Doyle psychiatric emergency services shall interfere with a peace officer performing duties under Section 5150 by preventing the peace officer from entering a designated facility with the person to be assessed, nor shall any employee of such an agency require the peace officer to remove the person without assessment as a condition of allowing the peace officer to depart.

"Peace officer" for the purposes of this section also means a jailer seeking to transport or transporting a person in custody to a designated facility for assessment consistent with Section 4011.6 or 4011.8 of the Penal Code and Section 5150.

5150.2.
In each county whenever a peace officer has transported a person to a designated facility for assessment under Section 5150, that officer shall be detained no longer than the time necessary to complete documentation of the factual basis of the detention under Section 5150 and a safe and orderly transfer of physical custody of the person. The documentation shall include detailed information regarding the factual circumstances and observations constituting probable cause for the peace officer to believe that the individual required psychiatric evaluation under the standards of Section 5105.

Each county shall establish disposition procedures and guidelines with local law enforcement agencies as necessary to relate to persons not admitted for evaluation and treatment and who decline alternative mental health services and to relate to the safe and orderly transfer of physical custody of persons under Section 5150, including those who have a criminal detention pending.

5150.4.

"Assessment" for the purposes of this article, means the determination of whether a person shall be evaluated and treated pursuant to Section 5150.

5151.

If the facility designated by the county for evaluation and treatment admits the person, it may detain him or her for evaluation and treatment for a period not to exceed 72 hours. Saturdays, Sundays, and holidays may be excluded from the period if the State Department of Health Care Services certifies for each facility that evaluation and treatment services cannot reasonably be made available on those days. The certification by the department is subject to renewal every two years. The department shall adopt regulations defining criteria for determining whether a facility can reasonably be expected to make evaluation and treatment services available on Saturdays, Sundays, and holidays.   Prior to admitting a person to the facility for treatment and evaluation pursuant to Section 5150, the professional person in charge of the facility or his or her designee shall assess the individual in person to determine the appropriateness of the involuntary detention.

5152.

(a) Each person admitted to a facility for 72-hour treatment and evaluation under the provisions of this article shall receive an evaluation as soon as possible after he or she is admitted and shall receive whatever treatment and care his or her condition requires for the full period that he or she is held. The person shall be released before 72 hours have elapsed only if the psychiatrist directly responsible for the person's treatment believes, as a result of the psychiatrist's personal observations, that the person no longer requires evaluation or treatment. However, in those situations in which both a psychiatrist and psychologist have personally evaluated or examined a person who is placed under a 72-hour hold and there is a collaborative treatment relationship between the psychiatrist and psychologist, either the psychiatrist or psychologist may authorize the release of the person from the hold, but only after they have consulted with one another. In the event of a clinical or professional disagreement regarding the early release of a person who has been placed under a 72-hour hold, the hold shall be maintained unless the facility's medical director overrules the decision of the psychiatrist or psychologist opposing the release. Both the psychiatrist and psychologist shall enter their findings, concerns, or objections into the person's medical record. If any other professional person who is authorized to release the person believes the person should be released before 72 hours have elapsed, and the psychiatrist directly responsible for the person's treatment objects, the matter shall be referred to the medical director of the facility for the final decision. However, if the medical director is not a psychiatrist, he or she shall appoint a designee who is a psychiatrist. If the matter is referred, the person shall be released before 72 hours have elapsed only if the psychiatrist making the final decision believes, as a result of the psychiatrist's personal observations, that the person no longer requires evaluation or treatment.

(b) Any person who has been detained for evaluation and treatment shall be released, referred for further care and treatment on a voluntary basis, or certified for intensive treatment, or a conservator or temporary conservator shall be appointed pursuant to this part as required.

(c) A person designated by the mental health facility shall give to any person who has been detained at that facility for evaluation and treatment and who is receiving medication as a result of his or her mental illness, as soon as possible after detention, written and oral information about the probable effects and possible side effects of the medication. The State Department of Health Care Services shall develop and promulgate written materials on the effects of medications, for use by county mental health programs as disseminated or as modified by the county mental health program, addressing the probable effects and the possible side effects of the medication. The following information shall be given orally to the patient:
(1) The nature of the mental illness, or behavior, that is the reason the medication is being given or recommended.
(2) The likelihood of improving or not improving without the medication.
(3) Reasonable alternative treatments available.
(4) The name and type, frequency, amount, and method of dispensing the medication, and the probable length of time the medication will be taken. The fact that the information has or has not been given shall be indicated in the patient's chart. If the information has not been given, the designated person shall document in the patient's chart the justification for not providing the information. A failure to give information about the probable effects and possible side effects of the medication shall not constitute new grounds for release.

(d) The amendments to this section made by Assembly Bill 348 of the 2003-04 Regular Session shall not be construed to revise or expand the scope of practice of psychologists, as defined in Chapter 6.6 (commencing with Section 2900) of Division 2 of the Business and Professions Code.

5152.1.
The professional person in charge of the facility providing 72-hour

evaluation and treatment, or his or her designee, shall notify the county mental health director or the director's designee and the peace officer who makes the written application pursuant to Section 5150 or a person who is designated by the law enforcement agency that employs the peace officer, when the person has been released after 72-hour detention, when the person is not detained, or when the person is released before the full period of allowable 72-hour detention if all of the following conditions apply:

(a) The peace officer requests such notification at the time he or she makes the application and the peace officer certifies at that time in writing that the person has been referred to the facility under circumstances which, based upon an allegation of facts regarding actions witnessed by the officer or another person, would support the filing of a criminal complaint.

(b) The notice is limited to the person's name, address, date of admission for 72-hour evaluation and treatment, and date of release.   If a police officer, law enforcement agency, or designee of the law enforcement agency, possesses any record of information obtained pursuant to the notification requirements of this section, the officer, agency, or designee shall destroy that record two years after receipt of notification.

5250 – 14 days

Welfare and Institutions Code
5250.

If a person is detained for 72 hours under the provisions of Article 1 (commencing with Section 5150), or under court order for evaluation pursuant to Article 2 (commencing with Section 5200) or Article 3 (commencing with Section 5225) and has received an evaluation, he or she may be certified for not more than 14 days of intensive treatment related to the mental health disorder or impairment by chronic alcoholism, under the following conditions:

(a) The professional staff of the agency or facility providing evaluation services has analyzed the person's condition and has found the person is, as a result of a mental health disorder or impairment by chronic alcoholism, a danger to others, or to himself or herself, or gravely disabled.

(b) The facility providing intensive treatment is designated by the county to provide intensive treatment, and agrees to admit the person. No facility shall be designated to provide intensive treatment unless it complies with the certification review hearing required by this article. The procedures shall be described in the county Short-Doyle plan as required by Section 5651.3.

(c) The person has been advised of the need for, but has not been willing or able to accept, treatment on a voluntary basis.

(d) (1) Notwithstanding paragraph (1) of subdivision (h) of Section 5008, a person is not "gravely disabled" if that person can survive safely without involuntary detention with the help of responsible family, friends, or others who are both willing and able to help provide for the person's basic personal needs for food, clothing, or shelter. (2) However, unless they specifically indicate in writing their willingness and ability to help, family, friends, or others shall not be considered willing or able to provide this help. (3) The purpose of this subdivision is to avoid the necessity for, and the harmful effects of, requiring family, friends, and others to publicly state, and requiring the certification review officer to publicly find, that no one is willing or able to assist a person with a mental health disorder in providing for the person's basic needs for food, clothing, or shelter.

5250.1.

The professional person in charge of a facility providing intensive treatment, pursuant to Section 5250 or 5270.15, or that person's designee, shall notify the county mental health director, or the director's designee, and the peace officer who made the original written application for 72-hour evaluation pursuant to Section 5150 or a person who is designated by the law enforcement agency that employs the peace officer, that the person admitted pursuant to the application has been released unconditionally if all of the following conditions apply: (a) The peace officer has requested notification at the time he or she makes the application for 72-hour evaluation.

(b) The peace officer has certified in writing at the time he or she made the application that the person has been referred to the facility under circumstances which, based upon an allegation of facts regarding actions witnessed by the officer or another person, would support the filing of a criminal complaint.

(c) The notice is limited to the person's name, address, date of admission for 72-hour evaluation, date of certification for intensive treatment, and date of release.   If a police officer, law enforcement agency, or designee of the law enforcement agency, possesses any record of information obtained pursuant to the notification requirements of this section, the officer, agency, or designee shall destroy that record two years after receipt of notification.

5251.

For a person to be certified under this article, a notice of certification shall be signed by two people. The first person shall be the professional person, or his or her designee, in charge of the agency or facility providing evaluation services. A designee of the professional person in charge of the agency or facility shall be a physician or a licensed psychologist who has a doctoral degree in psychology and at least five years of postgraduate experience in the diagnosis and treatment of emotional and mental disorders.

The second person shall be a physician or psychologist who participated in the evaluation. The physician shall be, if possible, a board certified psychiatrist. The psychologist shall be licensed and have at least five years of postgraduate experience in the diagnosis and treatment of emotional and mental disorders.

If the professional person in charge, or his or her designee, is the physician who performed the medical evaluation or a psychologist, the second person to sign may be another physician or psychologist unless one is not available, in which case a licensed clinical social worker or a registered nurse who participated in the evaluation shall sign the notice of certification.

5252.
A notice of certification is required for all persons certified for intensive treatment pursuant to Section 5250 or 5270.15, and shall be in substantially the following form (strike out inapplicable section): The authorized agency providing evaluation services in the County of_____has evaluated the condition of:

Name _____

Address _____

Age _____

Sex _____

Marital status _____

We the undersigned allege that the above-named person is, as a result of mental disorder or impairment by chronic alcoholism:
(1) A danger to others.
(2) A danger to himself or herself.
(3) Gravely disabled as defined in paragraph (1) of subdivision (h) or subdivision (l) of Section 5008 of the Welfare and Institutions Code. The specific facts which form the basis for our opinion that the above-named person meets one or more of the classifications indicated above are as follows:
(certifying persons to fill in blanks)

_____

_____ (Strike out all inapplicable classifications.) The above-named person has been informed of this evaluation, and has been advised of the need for, but has not been able or willing to accept treatment on a voluntary basis, or to accept referral to, the following services:

_____

_____

_____

_____

_____

We, therefore, certify the above-named person to receive intensive treatment related to the mental disorder or impairment by chronic alcoholism beginning this ____ day of _____ , 19__, in (Month) the intensive treatment facility herein named_____. _____(Date)

Signed _____

Signed_____

Countersigned _____ (Representing facility).

I hereby state that I delivered a copy of this notice this day to the above-named person and that I informed him or her that unless judicial review is requested a certification review hearing will be held within four days of the date on which the person is certified for a period of intensive treatment and that an attorney or advocate will visit him or her to provide assistance in preparing for the hearing or to answer questions regarding his or her commitment or to provide other assistance. The court has been notified of this certification on this day.

_____Signed

5253.

A copy of the certification notice shall be personally delivered to the person certified, the person's attorney, or the attorney or advocate designated in Section 5252. The person certified shall also be asked to designate any person who is to be sent a copy of the certification notice. If the person certified is incapable of making this designation at the time of certification, he or she shall be asked to designate a person as soon as he or she is capable.

5254.

The person delivering the copy of the notice of certification to the person certified shall, at the time of delivery, inform the person certified that he or she is entitled to a certification review hearing, to be held within four days of the date on which the person is certified for a period of intensive treatment in accordance with Section 5256 unless judicial review is requested, to determine whether or not probable cause exists to detain the person for intensive treatment related to the mental disorder or impairment by chronic alcoholism. The person certified shall be informed of his or her rights with respect to the hearing, including the right to the assistance of another person to prepare for the hearing or to answer other questions and concerns regarding his or her involuntary detention or both.

5254.1.

The person delivering the copy of the notice of certification to the person certified shall, at the time of delivery, inform the person certified of his or her legal right to a judicial review by habeas corpus, and shall explain that term to the person certified, and inform the person of his or her right to counsel, including court-appointed counsel pursuant to Section 5276.

5255.

As soon after the certification as practicable, an attorney or patient advocate shall meet with the person certified to discuss the commitment process and to assist the person in preparing for the certification review hearing or to answer questions or otherwise assist the person as is appropriate.

5256.

When a person is certified for intensive treatment pursuant to Sections 5250 and 5270.15, a certification review hearing shall be held unless judicial review has been requested as provided in Sections 5275 and 5276. The certification review hearing shall be within four days of the date on which the person is certified for a period of intensive treatment unless postponed by request of the person or his or her attorney or advocate. Hearings may be postponed for 48 hours or, in counties with a population of 100,000 or less, until the next regularly scheduled hearing date.

5256.1.

The certification review hearing shall be conducted by either a court-appointed commissioner or a referee, or a certification review hearing officer. The certification review hearing officer shall be either a state qualified administrative law hearing officer, a physician and surgeon, a licensed psychologist, a registered nurse, a lawyer, a certified law student, a licensed clinical social worker, a licensed marriage and family therapist, or a licensed professional clinical counselor. Licensed psychologists, licensed clinical social workers, licensed marriage and family therapists, licensed professional clinical counselors, and registered nurses who serve as certification review hearing officers shall have had a minimum of five years' experience in mental health. Certification review hearing officers shall be selected from a list of eligible persons unanimously approved by a panel composed of the local mental health director, the county public defender, and the county counsel or district attorney designated by the county board of supervisors. No employee of the county mental health program or of any facility designated by the county and approved by the State Department of Social Services as a facility for 72-hour treatment and evaluation may serve as a certification review hearing officer.   The location of the certification review hearing shall be compatible with, and least disruptive of, the treatment being provided to the person certified. In addition, hearings conducted by certification review officers shall be conducted at an appropriate place at the facility where the person certified is receiving treatment.

5256.2.

At the certification review hearing, the evidence in support of the certification decision shall be presented by a person designated by the director of the facility. In addition, either the district attorney or the county counsel may, at his or her discretion, elect to present evidence at the certification review hearing.

5256.3.

The person certified shall be present at the certification review hearing unless he or she, with the assistance of his or her attorney or advocate, waives his or her right to be present at a hearing.

5256.4.

(a) At the certification review hearing, the person certified shall have the following rights:

(1) Assistance by an attorney or advocate.

(2) To present evidence on his or her own behalf.

(3) To question persons presenting evidence in support of the certification decision.

(4) To make reasonable requests for the attendance of facility employees who have knowledge of, or participated in, the certification decision.

(5) If the person has received medication within 24 hours or such longer period of time as the person conducting the hearing may designate prior to the beginning of the hearing, the person conducting the hearing shall be informed of that fact and of the probable effects of the medication.

(b) The hearing shall be conducted in an impartial and informal manner in order to encourage free and open discussion by participants. The person conducting the hearing shall not be bound by rules of procedure or evidence applicable in judicial proceedings.

(c) Reasonable attempts shall be made by the mental health facility to notify family members or any other person designated by the patient, of the time and place of the certification hearing, unless the patient requests that this information not be provided. The patient shall be advised by the facility that is treating the patient that he or she has the right to request that this information not be provided.

(d) All evidence which is relevant to establishing that the person certified is or is not as a result of mental disorder or impairment by chronic alcoholism, a danger to others, or to himself or herself, or gravely disabled, shall be admitted at the hearing and considered by the hearing officer.

(e) Although resistance to involuntary commitment may be a product of a mental disorder, this resistance shall not, in itself, imply the presence of a mental disorder or constitute evidence that a person meets the criteria of being dangerous to self or others, or gravely disabled.

5256.5.

If at the conclusion of the certification review hearing the person conducting the hearing finds that there is not probable cause to believe that the person certified is, as a result of a mental disorder or impairment by chronic alcoholism, a danger to others, or to himself or herself, or gravely disabled, then the person certified may no longer be involuntarily detained. Nothing herein shall prohibit the person from remaining at the facility on a voluntary basis or the facility from providing the person with appropriate referral information concerning mental health services.

5256.6.

If at the conclusion of the certification review hearing the person conducting the hearing finds that there is probable cause that the person certified is, as a result of a mental disorder or impairment by chronic alcoholism, a danger to others, or to himself or herself, or gravely disabled, then the person may be detained for involuntary care, protection, and treatment related to the mental disorder or impairment by chronic alcoholism pursuant to Sections 5250 and 5270.15.

5256.7.

The person certified shall be given oral notification of the decision at the conclusion of the certification review hearing. As soon thereafter as is practicable, the attorney or advocate for the person certified and the director of the facility where the person is receiving treatment shall be provided with a written notification of the decision, which shall include a statement of the evidence relied upon and the reasons for the decision. The attorney or advocate shall notify the person certified of the certification review hearing decision and of his or her rights to file a request for release and to have a hearing on the request before the superior court as set forth in Article 5 (commencing with Section 5275). A copy of the decision and the certification made pursuant to Section 5250 or 5270.15 shall be submitted to the superior court.

5256.8.

The requirement that there is a certification review hearing in accordance with this article shall apply only to persons certified for intensive treatment on or after January 1, 1983.

5257.

(a) During the period of intensive treatment pursuant to Section 5250 or 5270.15, the person's involuntary detention shall be terminated and the person shall be released only if the psychiatrist directly responsible for the person's treatment believes, as a result of the psychiatrist's personal observations, that the person certified no longer is, as a result of mental disorder or impairment by chronic alcoholism, a danger to others, or to himself or herself, or gravely disabled. However, in those situations in which both a psychiatrist and psychologist have personally evaluated or examined a person who is undergoing intensive treatment and there is a collaborative treatment relationship between the psychiatrist and the psychologist, either the psychiatrist or psychologist may authorize the release of the person, but only after they have consulted with one another. In the event of a clinical or professional disagreement regarding the early release of a person who is undergoing intensive treatment, the person may not be released unless the facility's medical director overrules the decision of the psychiatrist or psychologist opposing the release. Both the psychiatrist and psychologist shall enter their findings, concerns, or objections into the person's medical record. If any other professional person who is authorized to release the person believes the person should be released during the designated period of intensive treatment, and the psychiatrist directly responsible for the person's treatment objects, the matter shall be referred to the medical director of the facility for the final decision. However, if the medical director is not a psychiatrist, he or she shall appoint a designee who is a psychiatrist. If the matter is referred, the person shall be released during the period of intensive treatment only if the psychiatrist making the final decision believes, as a result of the psychiatrist's personal observations, that the person certified no longer is, as a result of mental disorder or impairment by chronic alcoholism, a danger to others, or to himself or herself, or gravely disabled. Nothing herein shall prohibit the person from remaining at the facility on a voluntary basis or prevent the facility from providing the person with appropriate referral information concerning mental health services.

(b) A person who has been certified for a period of intensive treatment pursuant to Section 5250 shall be released at the end of 14 days unless the patient either: (1) Agrees to receive further treatment on a voluntary basis. (2) Is certified for an additional 14 days of intensive treatment pursuant to Article 4.5 (commencing with Section 5260). (3) Is certified for an additional 30 days of intensive treatment pursuant to Article 4.7 (commencing with Section 5270.10). (4) Is the subject of a conservatorship petition filed pursuant to Chapter 3 (commencing with Section 5350). (5) Is the subject of a petition for postcertification treatment of a dangerous person filed pursuant to Article 6 (commencing with Section 5300).

(c) The amendments to this section made by Assembly Bill 348 of the 2003-04 Regular Session shall not be construed to revise or expand the scope of practice of psychologists, as defined in Chapter 6.6 (commencing with Section 2900) of Division 2 of the Business and Professions Code.

5258.
After the involuntary detention has begun, the total period of detention, including intervening periods of voluntary treatment, shall not exceed the total maximum period during which the person could have been detained,

if the person had been detained continuously on an involuntary basis, from the time of initial involuntary detention.

5259.

Nothing in this article shall prohibit the professional person in charge of a treatment facility, or his or her designee, from permitting a person certified for intensive treatment to leave the facility for short periods during the person's involuntary additional treatment.

5259.1.

Any individual who is knowingly and willfully responsible for detaining a person in violation of the provisions of this article is liable to that person in civil damages.

5259.2.

Whenever a county designates two or more facilities to provide treatment, and the person to be treated, his or her family, conservator, or guardian expresses a preference for one of these facilities, the professional person certifying the person to be treated shall attempt, if administratively possible, to comply with the preference.

5259.3.

(a) Notwithstanding Section 5113, if the provisions of Section 5257 have been met, the professional person in charge of the facility providing intensive treatment, his or her designee, the professional person designated by the county, the medical director of the facility or his or her designee described in Section 5257, the psychiatrist directly responsible for the person's treatment, or the psychologist shall not be held civilly or criminally liable for any action by a person released before the end of 14 days pursuant to this article.

(b) The professional person in charge of the facility providing intensive treatment, his or her designee, the professional person designated by the county, the medical director of the facility or his or her designee described in Section 5257, the psychiatrist directly responsible for the person's treatment, or the psychologist shall not be held civilly or criminally liable for any action by a person released at the end of the 14 days pursuant to this article.

(c) The attorney or advocate representing the person, the court-appointed commissioner or referee, the certification review hearing officer conducting the certification review hearing, and the peace officer responsible for the detainment of the person shall not be civilly or criminally liable for any action by a person released at or before the end of 14 days pursuant to this article.

(d) The amendments to this section made by Assembly Bill 348 of the 2003-

04 Regular Session shall not be construed to revise or expand the scope of practice of psychologists, as defined in Chapter 6.6 (commencing with Section 2900) of Division 2 of the Business and Professions Code.

5270 – 30 day holds

5270.10.

It is the intent of the Legislature to reduce the number of gravely disabled persons for whom conservatorship petitions are filed and who are placed under the extensive powers and authority of a temporary conservator simply to obtain an additional period of treatment without the belief that a conservator is actually needed and without the intention of proceeding to trial on the conservatorship petition. This change will substantially reduce the number of conservatorship petitions filed and temporary conservatorships granted under this part which do not result in either a trial or a conservatorship.

5270.12.

This article shall be operative only in those counties in which the county board of supervisors, by resolution, authorizes its application and, by resolution, makes a finding that any additional costs incurred by the county in the implementation of this article are funded either by new funding sufficient to cover the costs incurred by the county resulting from this article, or funds redirected from cost savings resulting from this article, or a combination thereof, so that no current service reductions will occur as a result of the enactment of this article. Compliance with this section shall be monitored by the State Department of Health Care Services as part of its review and approval of mental health plans and performance contracts.

5270.15.

Upon the completion of a 14-day period of intensive treatment pursuant to Section 5250, the person may be certified for an additional period of not more than 30 days of intensive treatment under both of the following conditions:

(a) The professional staff of the agency or facility treating the person has found that the person remains gravely disabled as a result of a mental disorder or impairment by chronic alcoholism.

(b) The person remains unwilling or unable to accept treatment voluntarily.

Any person certified for an additional 30 days pursuant to this article shall be provided a certification review hearing in accordance with Section 5256 unless a judicial review is requested pursuant to Article 5 (commencing with Section 5275).

The professional staff of the agency or facility providing intensive treatment shall analyze the person's condition at intervals of not to exceed

10 days, to determine whether the person continues to meet the criteria established for certification under this section, and shall daily monitor the person's treatment plan and progress. Termination of this certification prior to the 30th day shall be made pursuant to Section 5270.35.

5270.20.

For a person to be certified under this article, a second notice of certification shall be signed by the professional person in charge of the facility providing intensive treatment to the person and by either a physician who shall, if possible, be a board-qualified psychiatrist, or a licensed psychologist who has a doctoral degree in psychology and at least five years of postgraduate experience in the diagnosis and treatment of emotional and mental disorders. The physician or psychologist who signs shall have participated in the evaluation and finding referred to in subdivision (a) of Section 5270.15.

If the professional person in charge is the physician who performed the medical evaluation and finding, or a psychologist, the second person to sign may be another physician or psychologist, unless one is not available, in which case a social worker or a registered nurse who participated in the evaluation and finding shall sign the notice of certification.

5270.25.

A second notice of certification is required for all involuntary intensive treatment, pursuant to this article, and shall be in substantially the form indicated in Section 5252.

5270.30.

Copies of the second notice of certification as set forth in Section 5270.25, shall be filed with the court and personally delivered to the person certified. A copy shall also be sent to the person's attorney, to the district attorney, to the public defender, if any, and to the facility providing intensive treatment.

The person certified shall also be asked to designate any individual who is to be sent a copy of the certification notice. If the person certified is incapable of making the designation at the time of certification, that person shall be given another opportunity to designate when able to do so.

5270.35.

(a) A certification pursuant to this article shall be for no more than 30 days of intensive treatment, and shall terminate only as soon as the psychiatrist directly responsible for the person's treatment believes, as a result of the psychiatrist's personal observations, that the person no longer meets the criteria for the certification, or is prepared to voluntarily accept treatment on a referral basis or to remain on a voluntary basis in the facility providing intensive treatment. However, in those situations in which both a psychiatrist and psychologist have personally evaluated or examined a person who is undergoing intensive treatment and there is a collaborative treatment relationship between the psychiatrist and the psychologist, either the psychiatrist or psychologist may authorize the release of the person but only after they have consulted with one another. In the event of a clinical or professional disagreement regarding the early release of a person who is undergoing intensive treatment, the person may not be released unless the facility's medical director overrules the decision of the psychiatrist or psychologist opposing the release. Both the psychiatrist and psychologist shall enter their findings, concerns, or objections into the person's medical record. If any other professional person who is authorized to release the person believes the person should be released before 30 days have elapsed, and the psychiatrist directly responsible for the person's treatment objects, the matter shall be referred to the medical director of the facility for the final decision. However, if the medical director is not a psychiatrist, he or she shall appoint a designee who is a psychiatrist. If the matter is referred, the person shall be released before 30 days have elapsed only if the psychiatrist believes, as a result of the psychiatrist's personal observations, that the person no longer meets the criteria for certification, or is prepared to voluntarily accept treatment on referral or to remain on a voluntary basis in the facility providing intensive treatment.

(b) Any person who has been certified for 30 days of intensive treatment under this article, shall be released at the end of 30 days unless one or more of the following is applicable:

(1) The patient agrees to receive further treatment on a voluntary basis.

(2) The patient is the subject of a conservatorship petition filed pursuant to Chapter 3 (commencing with Section 5350).

(3) The patient is the subject of a petition for postcertification treatment of a dangerous person filed pursuant to Article 6 (commencing with Section 5300).

(c) The amendments to this section made by Assembly Bill 348 of the 2003–04 Regular Session shall not be construed to revise or expand the scope of practice of psychologists, as defined in Chapter 6.6 (commencing with Section 2900) of Division 2 of the Business and Professions Code.

5270.40.
Any individual who is knowingly and willfully responsible for detaining a person for more than 30 days in violation of the provisions of Section 5270.35 is liable to that person in civil damages.

5270.45.

Whenever a county designates two or more facilities to provide intensive treatment and the person to be treated, his or her family, conservator, or guardian expresses a preference for one facility, the professional person certifying the person to be treated shall attempt, if administratively possible, to comply with the preference.

5270.50.

Notwithstanding Section 5113, if the provisions of Section 5270.35 have been met, the professional person in charge of the facility providing intensive treatment, his or her designee, and the professional person directly responsible for the person's treatment shall not be held civilly or criminally liable for any action by a person released before or at the end of 30 days pursuant to this article.

5270.55.

(a) Whenever it is contemplated that a gravely disabled person may need to be detained beyond the end of the 14-day period of intensive treatment and prior to proceeding with an additional 30-day certification, the professional person in charge of the facility shall cause an evaluation to be made, based on the patient's current condition and past history, as to whether it appears that the person, even after up to 30 days of additional treatment, is likely to qualify for appointment of a conservator. If the appointment of a conservator appears likely, the conservatorship referral shall be made during the 14-day period of intensive treatment.

(b) If it appears that with up to 30 days additional treatment a person is likely to reconstitute sufficiently to obviate the need for appointment of a conservator, then the person may be certified for the additional 30 days.

(c) Where no conservatorship referral has been made during the 14-day period and where during the 30-day certification it appears that the person is likely to require the appointment of a conservator, then the conservatorship referral shall be made to allow sufficient time for conservatorship investigation and other related procedures. If a temporary conservatorship is obtained, it shall run concurrently with and not consecutively to the 30-day certification period. The conservatorship hearing shall be held by the 30th day of the certification period. The maximum involuntary detention period for gravely disabled persons pursuant to Sections 5150, 5250 and 5270.15 shall be limited to 47 days. Nothing in this section shall prevent a person from exercising his or her right to a hearing as stated in Sections 5275 and 5353.

5270.65.
Nothing in this article shall prohibit the professional person in charge of an intensive treatment facility, or a designee, from permitting a person certified for intensive treatment to leave the facility for short periods during the person's intensive treatment.

CHAPTER 12
Telehealth

The definition of Telehealth is pretty straightforward and listed below in the definitions as provided by Business and Professions Code 2290.5 as the use of technology in practice through means such as video conferencing, audio, and other data connections in real time or synchronous or as near real time.

Therapists must be either licensed, an intern or trainee to provide services via Telehealth (previously called Telemedicine). However, note that therapists may offer Telehealth Services in another 'jurisdiction' under certain requirements. The requirements are found in this chapter under the California Code of Regulations section.

Be aware that without meeting these requirements,
providing therapy to clients in other states is
illegal and unprofessional
and may subject the therapist
to disciplinary actions.

The therapist must inform clients about the use of Telehealth and must obtain verbal or written consent and document this in the clients records.

Note that previously therapist were required to obtain written consent, but this was replaced with AB 415.

As part of the consent, therapist must ensure that they inform the client that services will be delivered by Telehealth. It would be important for a therapist to discuss and provide clients with information regarding potential risks and benefits of Telehealth.

Definitions

Business and Professions Code
2290.5
(a) For purposes of this division, the following definitions shall apply:
(1) "Asynchronous store and forward" means the transmission of a patient's medical information from an originating site to the health care provider at

a distant site without the presence of the patient.

(2) "Distant site" means a site where a health care provider who provides health care services is located while providing these services via a telecommunications system.

(3) "Health care provider" means a person who is licensed under this division.

(4) "Originating site" means a site where a patient is located at the time health care services are provided via a telecommunications system or where the asynchronous store and forward service originates.

(5) "Synchronous interaction" means a real-time interaction between a patient and a health care provider located at a distant site.

(6) "Telehealth" means the mode of delivering health care services and public health via information and communication technologies to facilitate the diagnosis, consultation, treatment, education, care management, and self-management of a patient's health care while the patient is at the originating site and the health care provider is at a distant site. Telehealth facilitates patient self-management and caregiver support for patients and includes synchronous interactions and asynchronous store and forward transfers.

Counselor Requirements

(b) Prior to the delivery of health care via telehealth, the health care provider initiating the use of telehealth shall inform the patient about the use of telehealth and obtain verbal or written consent from the patient for the use of telehealth as an acceptable mode of delivering health care services and public health. The consent shall be documented.

(c) Nothing in this section shall preclude a patient from receiving in-person health care delivery services during a specified course of health care and treatment after agreeing to receive services via telehealth.

(d) The failure of a health care provider to comply with this section shall constitute unprofessional conduct. Section 2314 shall not apply to this section.

(e) This section shall not be construed to alter the scope of practice of any health care provider or authorize the delivery of health care services in a setting, or in a manner, not otherwise authorized by law.

(f) All laws regarding the confidentiality of health care information and a patient's rights to his or her medical information shall apply to telehealth interactions.

(g) This section shall not apply to a patient under the jurisdiction of the Department of Corrections and Rehabilitation or any other correctional facility.

(h) (1) Notwithstanding any other provision of law and for purposes of this section, the governing body of the hospital whose patients are receiving the telehealth services may grant privileges to, and verify and approve credentials for, providers of telehealth services based on its medical staff recommendations that rely on information provided by the distant-site hospital or telehealth entity, as described in Sections 482.12, 482.22, and 485.616 of Title 42 of the Code of Federal Regulations.

(2) By enacting this subdivision, it is the intent of the Legislature to authorize a hospital to grant privileges to, and verify and approve credentials for, providers of telehealth services as described in paragraph (1).

(3) For the purposes of this subdivision, "telehealth" shall include "telemedicine" as the term is referenced in Sections 482.12, 482.22, and 485.616 of Title 42 of the Code of Federal Regulations.

California Code of Regulation Title 16 Section 1815.5: Standards of Practice for Telehealth

(a) All persons engaging in the practice of marriage and family therapy, educational psychology, clinical social work, or professional clinical counseling via telehealth, as defined in Section 2290.5 of the Code, with a client who is physically located in this State must have a valid and current license or registration issued by the Board.

(b) All psychotherapy services offered by board licensees and registrants via telehealth fall within the jurisdiction of the board just as traditional face-to-face services do. Therefore, all psychotherapy services offered via telehealth are subject to the board's statutes and regulations.

(c) Upon initiation of telehealth services, a licensee or registrant shall do the following:

(1) Obtain informed consent from the client consistent with Section 2290.5 of the Code.

(2) Inform the client of the potential risks and limitations of receiving treatment via telehealth.

(3) Provide the client with his or her license or registration number and the type of license or registration.

(4) Document reasonable efforts made to ascertain the contact information of relevant resources, including emergency services, in the patient's geographic area.

(d) Each time a licensee or registrant provides services via telehealth, he or she shall do the following:

(1) Verbally obtain from the client and document the client's full name and address of present location, at the beginning of each telehealth session.

(2) Assess whether the client is appropriate for telehealth, including, but not limited to, consideration of the client's psychosocial situation.

(3) Utilize industry best practices for telehealth to ensure both client confidentiality and the security of the communication medium.

(e) A licensee or registrant of this state may provide telehealth services to clients located in another jurisdiction only if the California licensee or registrant meets the requirements to lawfully provide services in that jurisdiction, and delivery of services via telehealth is allowed by that jurisdiction.

(f) Failure to comply with these provisions shall be considered unprofessional conduct.

CHAPTER 13
Treating Minors

There are times when minors can consent to their own treatment without parental approval or knowledge. California Family Code 6924 list conditions which must be met in order to treat a minor. In these situations, briefly, minors need to be (1) at least 12 years old or older and are requesting be a client on an outpatient basis for counseling, (2) must be mature enough to participate in the treatment and (2) the clinical issues that are allowed to be treated are those due to being a danger to self and/or others, a victim of child abuse or an alleged victim of incest.

It should be noted that Senate Bill 543 approved September 29, 2010, expands California Family Code 6924 in that it does not place a restriction on the presenting problem of the minor. And Senate Bill 543 actually removes those restrictions, the therapist however, would still need to contact the minors parents or guardians to notify them of the services proposed to be offered unless it has been determined after speaking with the minor that would it would be inappropriate to involve them. Therapists must document whether the attempt to contact the parent or guardian was successful or unsuccessful. The parent or guardian would not be responsible for payment unless they indeed participated in the services and would be responsible only for the services that they specifically participated in. As always, the therapist should document such decisions and actions in the clinical records.

So let's look specifically at what the law says in California Family Code 6924, it reads: (a) As used in this section: (1) "Mental health treatment or counseling services" means the provision of mental health treatment or counseling on an outpatient basis by any of the following: (A) A governmental agency. (B) A person or agency having a contract with a governmental agency to provide the services. (C) An agency that receives funding from community united funds. (D) A runaway house or crisis resolution center. (E) A professional person, as defined in paragraph (2).

(2) "Professional person" means any of the following: (A) A person designated as a mental health professional in Sections 622 to 626, inclusive, of Article 8 of Subchapter 3 of Chapter 1 of Title 9 of the California Code of Regulations. (B) A marriage and family therapist as defined in Chapter 13 (commencing with Section 4980) of Division 2 of the Business and Professions Code. (C) A licensed educational psychologist as defined in Article 5 (commencing with Section 4986) of Chapter 13 of Division 2 of the Business and Professions Code. (D) A credentialed school psychologist as described

in Section 49424 of the Education Code. (E) A clinical psychologist as defined in Section 1316.5 of the Health and Safety Code. (F) The chief administrator of an agency referred to in paragraph (1) or (3). (G) A person registered as an associate marriage and family therapist, as defined in Chapter 13 (commencing with Section 4980) of Division 2 of the Business and Professions Code, while working under the supervision of a licensed professional specified in subdivision (g) of Section 4980.03 of the Business and Professions Code. (H) A licensed professional clinical counselor, as defined in Chapter 16 (commencing with Section 4999.10) of Division 2 of the Business and Professions Code. (I) A person registered as an associate professional clinical counselor, as defined in Chapter 16 (commencing with Section 4999.10) of Division 2 of the Business and Professions Code, while working under the supervision of a licensed professional specified in subdivision (h) of Section 4999.12 of the Business and Professions Code.

(3) "Residential shelter services" means any of the following: (A) The provision of residential and other support services to minors on a temporary or emergency basis in a facility that services only minors by a governmental agency, a person or agency having a contract with a governmental agency to provide these services, an agency that receives funding from community funds, or a licensed community care facility or crisis resolution center. (B) The provision of other support services on a temporary or emergency basis by any professional person as defined in paragraph (2). (b) A minor who is 12 years of age or older may consent to mental health treatment or counseling on an outpatient basis, or to residential shelter services, if both of the following requirements are satisfied: (1) The minor, in the opinion of the attending professional person, is mature enough to participate intelligently in the outpatient services or residential shelter services. (2) The minor (A) would present a danger of serious physical or mental harm to self or to others without the mental health treatment or counseling or residential shelter services, or (B) is the alleged victim of incest or child abuse.

(c) A professional person offering residential shelter services, whether as an individual or as a representative of an entity specified in paragraph (3) of subdivision (a), shall make his or her best efforts to notify the parent or guardian of the provision of services. (d) The mental health treatment or counseling of a minor authorized by this section shall include involvement of the minor is parent or guardian unless, in the opinion of the professional person who is treating or counseling the minor, the involvement would be inappropriate. The professional person who is treating or counseling the minor shall state in the client record whether and when the person attempted to contact the minor is parent or guardian, and whether the attempt to contact was successful or unsuccessful, or the reason why, in the professional person's opinion, it would be inappropriate to contact the minor is parent or guardian. (e) The minor is parents or guardian are not liable for payment for mental health treatment or counseling services provided pursuant to this section unless the parent or guardian participates in the mental health treatment or counseling, and then only for services rendered with the participation of the parent or guardian. The minor is parents or guardian are not liable for payment for any residential shelter services provided pursuant to this section unless the parent or guardian consented to the provision of those services. (f) This section does not authorize a minor to receive convulsive therapy or psychosurgery as defined in subdivisions (f) and (g) of Section 5325 of the Welfare and Institutions Code, or psychotropic drugs without the consent of the minor is parent or guardian.

Minors Consent and Records Access

If the minor indeed consented on their own, they are at least 12 years old, and they met the conditions as previously stated, they would have the right to determine what information (confidential) can be shared. If the therapist believes that information needs to be disclosed to another party, then the minor client must sign a release of information. If parents/guardians bring the minor into therapy, California Civil Code 56.11 indicates the parent or the guardian who would need to sign a release of information to share that confidential information. Therefore, the parents or guardians in this instance would be the responsible person for payment as well because they consented to the treatment of the minor. It should be noted that at the beginning of the services, the therapist, the minor and the parent and/or guardians should have a discussion about what information would be shared with them and what information will be kept confidential. This is an important issue for therapists to consider when working with the minors. We want to make sure that the minors know that we try to keep confidentiality as much as possible in these contexts and simultaneously want to develop therapeutic rapport and trust with them while clarifying that parents and guardians have the right to inspect and request the records of the minor that they bring in therapy.

Minors who consent to their own therapy have a right to access their own clinical records, and in this instance, the parents or guardians would not have such access. It should be noted that a therapist can refuse the request from either the minor or the parent/guardian if the therapist determines that allowing access to the clinical records would (1) harm the therapeutic relationship, (2) the client or (3) potentially have negative consequences on the minors physical safety or psychological safety in accordance with California Health and Safety Code 123115 and 123120.

Divorced/Separated Parents

When a parent brings a minor to therapy for services, the therapist needs to consider the legal and custodial status of the parents involved to determine that a parent can authorize those services. If the parents are currently married, then legally, either parent can authorize the treatment, if they are divorced and there is joint legal custody, then either parent has the legal right to authorize treatment. There are some custody orders in which one parent has the right to authorize services for psychotherapy, and the other parent does not, or the custody order may state that both parents must agree and consent to that treatment. Because there are a variety of stipulations that can be imposed in the custody order, it is suggested that the therapists request a copy of that order prior to the commencement of services. This is of course contingent on the treating provider knowing an order exists or that there is a change in custody status.

Caregivers Authorization Affidavit

If for whatever reason a parent or guardian is unable to consent to services for the minor (e.g., out of the country), relative caregivers of the minor may consent when specific requirements are met. The therapists would have that caregiver complete a form called *The Caregivers Authorization Affidavit*. Therapists are immune from any civil or criminal liability if they have received a completed and signed affidavit and acted in good faith. Therapists are not required to do any type of investigation to verify the validity of the caregiver's relationship with the minor, as stated in California Family Code 6550. A template of the Caregivers Authorization Affidavit is found within the code.

Foster Parents

Foster parents typically cannot consent to treatment for a minor unless it has been authorized by the court. In emergency situations, consent is generally not necessary. The therapist should attempt to contact parents/guardian or those who would have authority to consent, but in emergency situations, this is not always possible or necessary.

Custodial vs. Non-Custodial

Let's cover something that is often confusion for some individuals on exams and in life situations. You might hear the term non-custodial parent – this is essentially an individual (typically a biological parent) who does not have physical custody of the minor but often still has legal rights and has the legal ability to make decisions on behalf of the minor. So if you see the term non-custodial on a test or asked about a non-custodial parent, it just typically means the child is not in their physical custody, but they typically are still able to make legal decisions on behalf of the minor child or access records, unless otherwise specified by a court order.

Emancipated Minors

When we look at emancipated minors, these are individuals who before the age of 18 are able to engage in decision-making activities that typically are available only for adults. A minor who becomes emancipated can do several things once they are emancipated without parent/guardian permission. Emancipated minors can receive (1) medical care without parent/guardian consent, (2) they can apply for work permits, (3) they can sign up for school and college, (4) they can live where they want. While these minors would not be required to have parental support, there are still some restrictions the court imposes. Even if a minor becomes emancipated, they still must go to school. In California for some emancipated minors, they cannot enter into a marriage without permission from their parents/guardians. If an emancipated minor violates the law, just because they are emancipated does not mean that they are going to go to jail or prison where adults are, they would instead go to juvenile hall.

In California, consistent with California Family Code beginning with section 7000, there are essentially three ways to be identified as an emancipated minor (1) the minor could get married (need permission of their parents or legal guardians and from the court), they could join the Armed Forces (considering that they got permission again from their parents/guardians and that the Armed Forces accepted them) or (3) they can get a declaration of emancipation from a judge but they would have to prove all of the following: (a) they are at least 14 years old, (2)they do not want to live with their parents, (3) the parents do not mind that they move out, (4) they can handle and manage their own finances, (5) they have a legal way to make the money (need to be able to demonstrate that they can take care of themselves, they have a job, and (6) that having emancipation would actually be a good thing for them.

An emancipated minor who comes to seek therapy and counseling services would, therefore, be able to consent to their own treatment and their information would be kept confidential. Their parents/guardians would have no right to access clinical records. A question that comes up often is if an emancipated minor is a victim of some type of abuse would the therapist call CPS, the answer is yes! if they are a minor, you would still contact Child Protective Services; the individual is still under the age of 18. Just because the individual is emancipated does not mean that other clinical and safety issues may come up that could be a violation. If an emancipated minor engages in sexual intercourse with an adult and you believe that it is coercive sexual activity or there is undue influence, you would make a report to Child Protective Services or law enforcement or the appropriate agency designated to take those reports on behalf of a minor.

Restricting Records Access

Earlier, we briefly mention that therapists can restrict access to records; let's take a closer look at this. California Health and Safety Code 123115 states (a) The representative of a minor shall not be entitled to inspect or obtain copies of the minor's patient records in either of the following circumstances:

(1) With respect to which the minor has a right of inspection under Section 123110. (2) Where the health care provider determines that access to the patient records requested by the representative would have a detrimental effect on the provider's professional relationship with the minor patient or the minor's physical safety or psychological well-being. The decision of the health care provider as to whether or not a minor's records are available for inspection or copying under this section shall not attach any liability to the provider, unless the decision is found to be in bad faith. (b) When a health care provider determines there is a substantial risk of significant adverse or detrimental consequences to a patient in seeing or receiving a copy of mental health records requested by the patient, the provider may decline to permit inspection or provide copies of the records to the patient, subject to the following conditions:

(1) The health care provider shall make a written record, to be included with the mental health records requested, noting the date of the request and explaining the health care provider's reason for refusing to permit inspection or provide copies of the records, including a description of the specific adverse or detrimental consequences to the patient that the provider anticipates would occur if inspection or copying were permitted. (2) (A) The health care provider shall permit inspection by, or provide copies of the mental health records to, a licensed physician and surgeon, licensed psychologist, licensed marriage and family therapist, licensed clinical social worker, or licensed professional clinical counselor, designated by request of the patient. (B) Any person registered as a marriage and family therapist intern, as defined in Chapter 13 (commencing with Section 4980) of Division 2 of the Business and Professions Code, may not inspect the patient's mental health records or obtain copies thereof, except pursuant to the direction or supervision of a licensed professional specified in subdivision (g) of Section 4980.03 of the Business and Professions Code. Prior to providing copies of mental health records to a registered marriage and family therapist intern, a receipt for those records shall be signed by the supervising licensed professional.

(C) Any person registered as a clinical counselor intern, as defined in Chapter 16 (commencing with Section 4999.10) of Division 2 of the Business and Professions Code, may not inspect the patient's mental health records or obtain copies thereof, except pursuant to the direction or supervision of a licensed professional specified in subdivision (h) of Section 4999.12 of the Business and Professions Code. Prior to providing copies of mental health records to a person registered as a clinical counselor intern, a receipt for those records shall be signed by the supervising licensed professional. (D) A licensed physician and surgeon, licensed psychologist, licensed marriage and family therapist, licensed clinical social worker, licensed professional clinical counselor, registered marriage and family therapist intern, or person registered as a clinical counselor intern to whom the records are provided for inspection or copying shall not permit inspection or copying by the patient. (3) The health care provider shall inform the patient of the provider's refusal to permit him or her to inspect or obtain copies of the requested records, and inform the patient of the right to require the provider to permit inspection by, or provide copies to, a licensed physician and surgeon, licensed psychologist, licensed marriage and family therapist, licensed clinical social worker, or licensed professional clinical counselor designated by written authorization of the patient. (4) The health care provider shall indicate in the mental health records of the patient whether the request was made under paragraph (2).

Minor Consent in Law

California Family Code
6920.
Subject to the limitations provided in this chapter, notwithstanding any other provision of law, a minor may consent to the matters provided in this chapter, and the consent of the minor's parent or guardian is not necessary.

6924.
(a) As used in this section:
(1) "Mental health treatment or counseling services" means the provision of mental health treatment or counseling on an outpatient basis by any of the

following:
    (A) A governmental agency.
    (B) A person or agency having a contract with a governmental agency to provide the services.
    (C) An agency that receives funding from community united funds.
    (D) A runaway house or crisis resolution center.
    (E) A professional person, as defined in paragraph (2).

(2) "Professional person" means any of the following:
    (A) A person designated as a mental health professional in Sections 622 to 626, inclusive, of Article 8 of Subchapter 3 of Chapter 1 of Title 9 of the California Code of Regulations.

(B) A marriage and family therapist as defined in Chapter 13 (commencing with Section 4980) of Division 2 of the Business and Professions Code.

(C) A licensed educational psychologist as defined in Article 5 (commencing with Section 4986) of Chapter 13 of Division 2 of the Business and Professions Code.

(D) A credentialed school psychologist as described in Section 49424 of the Education Code.

(E) A clinical psychologist as defined in Section 1316.5 of the Health and Safety Code.   (F) The chief administrator of an agency referred to in paragraph (1) or (3).

(G) A person registered as a marriage and family therapist intern, as defined in Chapter 13 (commencing with Section 4980) of Division 2 of the Business and Professions Code, while working under the supervision of a licensed professional specified in subdivision (g) of Section 4980.03 of the Business and Professions Code.

(H) A licensed professional clinical counselor, as defined in Chapter 16 (commencing with Section 4999.10) of Division 2 of the Business and Professions Code.

(I) A person registered as a clinical counselor intern, as defined in Chapter 16 (commencing with Section 4999.10) of Division 2 of the Business and Professions Code, while working under the supervision of a licensed professional specified in subdivision (h) of Section 4999.12 of the Business and Professions Code.

(3) "Residential shelter services" means any of the following:

    (A) The provision of residential and other support services to minors on a temporary or emergency basis in a facility that services only minors by a governmental agency, a person or agency having a contract with a governmental agency to provide these services, an agency that receives funding from community funds, or a licensed community care facility or crisis resolution center.

    (B) The provision of other support services on a temporary or emergency basis by any professional person as defined in paragraph (2).

(b) A minor who is 12 years of age or older may consent to mental health treatment or counseling on an outpatient basis, or to residential shelter services, if both of the following requirements are satisfied:

(1) The minor, in the opinion of the attending professional person, is mature enough to participate intelligently in the outpatient services or residential shelter services.

(2) The minor (A) would present a danger of serious physical or mental harm to self or to others without the mental health treatment or

counseling or residential shelter services, or (B) is the alleged victim of incest or child abuse.

(c) A professional person offering residential shelter services, whether as an individual or as a representative of an entity specified in paragraph (3) of subdivision (a), shall make his or her best efforts to notify the parent or guardian of the provision of services.

(d) The mental health treatment or counseling of a minor authorized by this section shall include involvement of the minor's parent or guardian unless, in the opinion of the professional person who is treating or counseling the minor, the involvement would be inappropriate. The professional person who is treating or counseling the minor shall state in the client record whether and when the person attempted to contact the minor's parent or guardian, and whether the attempt to contact was successful or unsuccessful, or the reason why, in the professional person's opinion, it would be inappropriate to contact the minor's parent or guardian.

(e) The minor's parents or guardian are not liable for payment for mental health treatment or counseling services provided pursuant to this section unless the parent or guardian participates in the mental health treatment or counseling, and then only for services rendered with the participation of the parent or guardian. The minor's parents or guardian are not liable for payment for any residential shelter services provided pursuant to this section unless the parent or guardian consented to the provision of those services.

(f) This section does not authorize a minor to receive convulsive therapy or psychosurgery as defined in subdivisions (f) and (g) of Section 5325 of the Welfare and Institutions Code, or psychotropic drugs without the consent of the minor's parent or guardian.

California Family Code
6928.

(a) "Sexually assaulted" as used in this section includes, but is not limited to, conduct coming within Section 261, 286, or 288a of the Penal Code.

(b) A minor who is alleged to have been sexually assaulted may consent to medical care related to the diagnosis and treatment of the condition, and the collection of medical evidence with regard to the alleged sexual assault.

(c) The professional person providing medical treatment shall attempt to contact the minor's parent or guardian and shall note in the minor's treatment record the date and time the professional person attempted to contact the parent or guardian and whether the attempt was successful or unsuccessful. This subdivision does not apply if the professional person reasonably believes that the minor's parent or guardian committed the sexual assault on the minor.

Definitions & Payment

6929.

6929. (a) As used in this section:

(1) "Counseling" means the provision of counseling services by a provider under a contract with the state or a county to provide alcohol or drug abuse counseling services pursuant to Part 2 (commencing with Section 5600) of Division 5 of the Welfare and Institutions Code or pursuant to Division 10.5 (commencing with Section 11750) of the Health and Safety Code.

(2) "Drug or alcohol" includes, but is not limited to, any substance listed in any of the following: (A) Section 380 or 381 of the Penal Code.   (B) Division 10 (commencing with Section 11000) of the Health and Safety Code.   (C) Subdivision (f) of Section 647 of the Penal Code.

(3) "LAAM" means levoalphacetylmethadol as specified in paragraph (10) of subdivision (c) of Section 11055 of the Health and Safety Code.

(4) "Professional person" means a physician and surgeon, registered nurse, psychologist, clinical social worker, professional clinical counselor, marriage and family therapist, registered marriage and family therapist intern when appropriately employed and supervised pursuant to Section 4980.43 of the Business and Professions Code, psychological assistant when appropriately employed and supervised pursuant to Section 2913 of the Business and Professions Code, associate clinical social worker when appropriately employed and supervised pursuant to Section 4996.18 of the Business and Professions Code, or registered clinical counselor intern when appropriately employed and supervised pursuant to Section 4999.42 of the Business and Professions Code.

(b) A minor who is 12 years of age or older may consent to medical care and counseling relating to the diagnosis and treatment of a drug- or alcohol-related problem.

(c) The treatment plan of a minor authorized by this section shall include the involvement of the minor's parent or guardian, if appropriate, as determined by the professional person or treatment facility treating the minor. The professional person providing medical care or counseling to a minor shall state in the minor's treatment record whether and when the professional person attempted to contact the minor's parent or guardian, and whether the attempt to contact the parent or guardian was successful or unsuccessful, or the reason why, in the opinion of the professional person, it would not be appropriate to contact the minor's parent or guardian.

(d) The minor's parent or guardian is not liable for payment for any care provided to a minor pursuant to this section, except that if the minor's parent or guardian participates in a counseling program pursuant to this section, the parent or guardian is liable for the cost of the services provided to the minor and the parent or guardian.

(e) This section does not authorize a minor to receive replacement narcotic abuse treatment, in a program licensed pursuant to Article 3 (commencing with Section 11875) of Chapter 1 of Part 3 of Division 10.5 of the Health and Safety Code, without the consent of the minor' s parent or guardian.

(f) It is the intent of the Legislature that the state shall respect the right of a parent or legal guardian to seek medical care and counseling for a drug- or alcohol-related problem of a minor child when the child does not consent to the medical care and counseling, and nothing in this section shall be construed to restrict or eliminate this right.

(g) Notwithstanding any other provision of law, in cases where a parent or legal guardian has sought the medical care and counseling for a drug- or alcohol-related problem of a minor child, the physician and surgeon shall disclose medical information concerning the care to the minor's parent or legal guardian upon his or her request, even if the minor child does not consent to disclosure, without liability for the disclosure.

Caregiver's Authorization Affidavit

California Family Code
6550.
(a) A caregiver's authorization affidavit that meets the requirements of this part authorizes a caregiver 18 years of age or older who completes items 1 to 4, inclusive, of the affidavit provided in Section 6552 and signs the affidavit to enroll a minor in school and consent to school-related medical care on behalf of the minor. A caregiver who is a relative and who completes items 1 to 8, inclusive, of the affidavit provided in Section 6552 and signs the affidavit shall have the same rights to authorize medical care and dental care for the minor that are given to guardians under Section 2353 of the Probate Code. The medical care authorized by this caregiver who is a relative may include mental health treatment subject to the limitations of Section 2356 of the Probate Code.

(b) The decision of a caregiver to consent to or to refuse medical or dental care for a minor shall be superseded by any contravening decision of the parent or other person having legal custody of the minor, provided the decision of the parent or other person having legal custody of the minor does not jeopardize the life, health, or safety of the minor.

(c) A person who acts in good faith reliance on a caregiver's authorization affidavit to provide medical or dental care, without actual knowledge of facts contrary to those stated on the affidavit, is not subject to criminal liability or to civil liability to any person, and is not subject to professional disciplinary action, for that reliance if the applicable portions of the affidavit are completed. This subdivision applies even if medical or dental care is provided to a minor in contravention of the wishes of the parent or other person having legal custody of the minor as long as the person providing the medical or dental care has no actual knowledge of the wishes of the parent or other person having legal custody of the minor.

(d) A person who relies on the affidavit has no obligation to make any further inquiry or investigation.

(e) Nothing in this section relieves any individual from liability for violations of other provisions of law.

(f) If the minor stops living with the caregiver, the caregiver shall notify any school, health care provider, or health care service plan that has been given the affidavit. The affidavit is invalid after the school, health care provider, or health care service plan receives notice that the minor is no longer living with the caregiver.

(g) A caregiver's authorization affidavit shall be invalid, unless it substantially contains, in not less than 10-point boldface type or a reasonable equivalent thereof, the warning statement beginning with the word "warning" specified in Section 6552. The warning statement shall be enclosed in a box with 3-point rule lines.

(h) For purposes of this part, the following terms have the following meanings:
  (1) "Person" includes an individual, corporation, partnership, association, the state, or any city, county, city and county, or other public entity or governmental subdivision or agency, or any other legal entity.
  (2) "Relative" means a spouse, parent, stepparent, brother, sister, stepbrother, stepsister, half brother, half sister, uncle, aunt, niece, nephew, first cousin, or any person denoted by the prefix "grand" or "great," or the spouse of any of the persons specified in this definition, even after the marriage has been terminated by death or dissolution.
  (3) "School-related medical care" means medical care that is required by state or local governmental authority as a condition for school enrollment, including immunizations, physical examinations, and medical examinations conducted in schools for pupils.

6552.
The caregiver's authorization affidavit shall be in substantially the following form: Caregiver's Authorization Affidavit
Use of this affidavit is authorized by Part 1.5 (commencing with Section 6550) of Division 11 of the California Family Code. Instructions: Completion of items 1-4 and the   signing of the affidavit is sufficient to   authorize enrollment of a minor in school and   authorize school-related medical care.

Completion of items 5-8 is additionally   required to authorize any other medical care. Print clearly. The minor named below lives in my home and I am 18 years of age or older.

1. Name of minor: _____.

2. Minor's birth date: _____.

3. My name (adult giving authorization): _____.

4. My home address: _____   _____.

_____

5. ( ) I am a grandparent, aunt, uncle, or   other qualified relative of the minor (see   back of this form for a definition of "qualified relative).

6. Check one or both (for example, if one   parent was advised and the other cannot be   located):

( ) I have advised the parent(s) or other   person(s) having legal custody of the minor of   my intent to authorize medical care, and have   received no objection.

( ) I am unable to contact the parent(s) or   other person(s) having legal custody of the   minor at this time, to notify them of my   intended authorization.

7. My date of birth: _____.

8. My California driver's license or   identification card   number: _____.

+--+
|Warning: Do not sign this form if any of the statements above are incorrect, or you will be   committing a crime punishable by a fine, imprisonment, or both.
+--+

I declare under penalty of perjury under the laws   of the   State   of California that the foregoing is true and   correct.
Dated: _____ Signed: _____

Notices:
1. This declaration does not affect the rights of the minor's parents or legal guardian regarding the care, custody, and control of the minor, and does

not mean that the caregiver has legal custody of the minor.

2. A person who relies on this affidavit has no obligation to make any further inquiry or investigation.

Additional Information:

TO CAREGIVERS:
1. "Qualified relative," for purposes of item 5, means a spouse, parent, stepparent, brother, sister, stepbrother, stepsister, half brother, half sister, uncle, aunt, niece, nephew, first cousin, or any person denoted by the prefix "grand" or "great," or the spouse of any of the persons specified in this definition, even after the marriage has been terminated by death or dissolution.

2. The law may require you, if you are not a relative or a currently licensed foster parent, to obtain a foster home license in order to care for a minor. If you have any questions, please contact your local department of social services.

3. If the minor stops living with you, you are required to notify any school, health care provider, or health care service plan to which you have given this affidavit. The affidavit is invalid after the school, health care provider, or health care service plan receives notice that the minor no longer lives with you.

4. If you do not have the information requested in item 8 (California driver's license or I.D.), provide another form of identification such as your social security number or Medi-Cal number.

TO SCHOOL OFFICIALS:
1. Section 48204 of the Education Code provides that this affidavit constitutes a sufficient basis for a determination of residency of the minor, without the requirement of a guardianship or other custody order, unless the school district determines from actual facts that the minor is not living with the caregiver.

2. The school district may require additional reasonable evidence that the caregiver lives at the address provided in item 4.

TO HEALTH CARE PROVIDERS AND HEALTH CARE SERVICE PLANS:
1. A person who acts in good faith reliance upon a caregiver's authorization affidavit to provide medical or dental care, without actual knowledge of facts contrary to those stated on the affidavit, is not subject

to criminal liability or to civil liability to any person, and is not subject to professional disciplinary action, for that reliance if the applicable portions of the form are completed.

2. This affidavit does not confer dependency for health care coverage purposes.

CHAPTER 14
Subpoena, Search Warrants, Depositions & Witness Testimony

In chapter 8 we covered issues of confidentiality, privilege and applicable exceptions and briefly covered issues on subpoenas and warrants. After the final review of this book, we received feedback from practitioners in the community hoping we would expand the discussion on these issues. So, we decided to do just that. In this *bonus* chapter we have provided a brief discussion on some special topics that are not always covered so clearly in graduate school or training programs. As stated multiple times in this book, none of the information provided is meant to offer legal advice and readers are responsible for obtaining such advice and guidance from their professions regulatory board, professional organization or contact an attorney as appropriate.

Subpoenas

A therapist may receive a subpoena from the courts or from an attorney who represents a client or an opposing party. The subpoena typically requests a therapist to (1) either show up and provide testimony or to (2) show up and provide requested documentation such as clinical records or just to provide (certify mail or fax) the requested documentation. These requests are typically identified as subpoena ad testificandum (testify) or subpoena duces tecum (bring documents). Subpoena duces tecum (Latin) is a command to produce the written evidence or the records as required by the court and subpoena ad testificandum simply asks you to show up and provide testimony. This may be an oral or written form depending on the instructions. Knowing the source of the subpoena is important because it may dictate how you respond. If the subpoena comes from the court and it is approved and signed by the judge, then it is a court-ordered subpoena, it cannot be ignored, and you must comply with the subpoena.

If the subpoena comes from the attorney, you typically have several ways to respond: (1) you can assert privilege on the clients behalf and that's something that you should do, (2) you can contact the client and determine if the client would like to have that information shared which means the client is then waiving their privilege, (3) the therapist could obtain a release of information to speak to the clients attorney for clarification purposes to determine what information they are actually looking for or (4) the therapist can speak with the client and the client can then have their attorney requests for a motion to quash the subpoena. As there are a variety of factors involved, it may be important for therapists who have received a subpoena to speak to their own attorney to determine what specific actions they may need to take. Remember you cannot just ignore a subpoena, you must respond to it, and again, there are several ways to respond to a subpoena depending on the source. Failure to respond to them may result in you being found in contempt of court, you might be fined, and ultimately you could be jailed.

In most cases, subpoenas give the recipient therapists approximately five days' notice to provide the documentation. If the request is to come to court, the date and time would be listed. If a therapist receives a subpoena from out of state, it would be prudent for the therapist to speak to their own attorney about whether that particular subpoena is valid as certain requirements must be met in order for the subpoena to be valid in the State of California. Again, if the subpoena is from the court, essentially it is a court order, and therapists must comply with the court order.

Search Warrants

As a clinical therapist, you may be provided a search warrant, and how you respond is important. There are two reasons that you would be receiving a search warrant (1) it may be because you are identified as someone being suspected of criminal activity or perhaps (2) one of your clients is being suspected of criminal activity. If you are provided a search warrant in which *you* are identified as the individual suspected of criminal activity, any records requested must be provided and surrendered. If however, you are not being suspected of criminal activity and the person who is the subject of a search warrant is a *client* then several things have to happen: (1) the warrant has to be issued in conjunction with section 1524 of the California Penal Code. This section of the penal code requires that a special master be appointed by the court to conduct the search. This is vitally important if the individual that is the subject of the suspected criminal activity is a client or a previous client, then a regular search warrant will not be valid.

The search warrant needs to be executed in conjunction and consistent with California Penal Code 1524, and a special master must be *present* and appointed to provide the search. The Special Master is typically identified as a lawyer, and they are appointed by the court, and they are identified by paperwork that certifies their status with the Superior Court of California. If that search warrant does not accompany this special master as identified in Section 1524 of the California Penal Code, then the therapist needs to assert privilege, and again you are asserting privilege on behalf of your client, consistent with California Evidence Code 1015. As a therapist, you will want to consult with an attorney about these particular issues so you do not want to put yourself in a situation in which you are not complying with an officer of the law. If the officer proceeds without the special master, you want to at least assert privilege in these particular situations, ask the officer to document that you have asserted privilege and ask the officer to put the documents in a sealed envelope (or sealed folder) so that it can be taken directly to the courts due to the privileged and confidential information. Therapists should also document these actions to illustrate attempts to assert privilege on the client's behalf.

Depositions

There may be times when a therapist is asked to give testimony outside of a courtroom, and these are typically called depositions. While the testimony may be outside of the courtroom, it is still part of a judicial proceeding. It is important that therapists know that they can only discuss information regarding a case or regarding a client when the client themselves have signed a release of information, and therefore, a waiver of privilege. The only other time that a therapist can disclose this type of information in a deposition is if the court has compelled and court ordered that testimony. It would be prudent for therapists to obtain an attorney to assist in defending in that deposition and to ensure that that therapist only responds and answers questions consistent with the requirement. The therapist can obtain legal representation in several ways: (1) it may be from their malpractice carrier (2) it could be through reimbursement (they obtained the legal counsel and get reimbursed) (3) it may be from their professional organization that they are members of or (4) it may be that the clients attorney who is willing to defend the deposition on behalf of the therapist. Additionally, the therapist needs to ensure that the attorney who subpoenaed them is informed that they will have legal representation.

Fact & Expert Witness

Offering testimony in a legal proceeding takes time away from other clients in your practice, so considering who will pay for your time is important. Typically, the individual that has subpoenaed the therapist will be the one that pays; therefore it is important to determine whether the individual that subpoenaed the therapist is asking for the therapist to be an expert witness or to be a fact witness. A fact witness is a therapist who provides testimony based upon the information that they know (facts).

A fact witness responds to things that they heard or saw as it relates to a client-therapist relationship. The therapist would not be providing opinions about the client's treatment or about the client in general, but simply information that the therapist knows and perhaps even documented during sessions. The therapist would then be paid and/or reimbursed for their time based upon Government Code 68093.

An expert witness is someone that provides opinions, they "opine" and according to Assembly Bill 1204, it states that the expert witness testimony regarding a client is information about their prognosis, about their diagnosis, about their treatment and it is considered to be "opined evidence" or opinion-based. Therefore, if a therapist is asked to be an expert witness in these particular situations, it is because they are asked to provide opinions about the client, their behavior, and their diagnosis amongst other things. The ability for a therapist to be an Expert Witness is based upon the therapist's knowledge, skills, training and education and their opinions are usually based upon literature (the research that's out there) that is consistent with the profession. Unlike a fact witness that is paid directly by the courts for their testimony, here an expert witness would be reimbursed for their time by the individual requiring the testimony.

Laws, Regulations and Codes presented in this book were compiled from Official Legislative Information for the State of California and other available information from the California Board of Behavioral Sciences.

Index

Scope of Practice

Education & Licensure

Practice Requirements

Unprofessional Conduct & Enforcement

General BBS Disciplinary Actions

General Training Requirements

Mandated Reporting – Children / Definitions

Duty to Report & Timeline

Required Information in Reports

Minor Consensual Sexual Activity

Mandated Reports – Adults / Legislative Findings

Duty to Report & Timeline

Mental Health Psychiatric Holds – Gravely Disabled

Mental Health Psychiatric Holds – 5150 72 hours

Mental Health Psychiatric Holds – 5250 14 days

Mental Health Psychiatric Holds – 5270 30 days

Telehealth

Treating Minors

Caregiver's Authorization Affidavit

ABOUT THE AUTHORS

Daniel Stewart, PhD, is a Counselor Educator in the College of Education, at California State University, San Bernardino where he teaches educational and clinical counseling. After completing a Master of Science in Counseling, and a Master of Social Work, he went on to complete a Doctorate of Philosophy (PhD) from the University of Louisiana, Monroe. Dr. Stewart has completed additional training in counseling psychology internationally. He is a Licensed Marriage and Family Therapist, a Licensed Professional Clinical Counselor and Licensed Clinical Psychologist while additionally possessing a Pupil Personnel Services (PPS) Credential to provide services in the K12 school setting. Dr. Stewart is a State Program Assessment Reviewer for accreditation of Counseling Programs in California (CTC). His work focuses on the use of ethically sound principles within clinical practice, centered on cultural sensitivity while examining issue of power. He consults, teaches and trains associate, trainees, licensed therapists and organizations. He is a member of the editorial board for the *Wisdom in Education Journal and* also serves as a Legislative and Ethics Committee Member for the California Association for Professional Clinical Counselors. He is currently a member of the American Psychological Association, American Counseling Association, California Association for Licensed Professional Counselors, and California Association of Marriage and Family Therapists.

Ashlee N. Fisher, MA, is an advocate, responder, and clinician who specializes in trauma, relationships and resiliency. She obtained her Master of Arts at Pepperdine University, Graduate School of Education and Psychology in Clinical Psychology with an emphasis in Marriage and Family Therapy. She is a Licensed Marriage and Family Therapist and is a Certified Clinical Trauma Professional. She is currently completing her PhD in Counseling Psychology at the University of Texas at Austin where she studies trauma and resiliency in families of public safety officers, as well as clinician best practices in ethical decision making. She is an active member in the American Psychological Association Division 18, Psychologists in Public Service. Ashlee has served as a consultant in areas of domestic violence and trauma informed practices in development of mental health public policy. She facilitates trainings for law enforcement agencies in trauma-informed techniques, peer support and cultural competencies. She also promotes improved relationships between marginalized populations and law enforcement through skill building, training, and advocacy. She currently serves as a clinician on the Traumatic Incident and Event Response (TIER) Team, National Resiliency Task Force covering Customs and Border Protection agencies. She served as a member of the Crisis Intervention Team with the San Diego Police Department and is a member of the Disaster Mental Health Services team with the American Red Cross.

Made in the USA
Las Vegas, NV
24 August 2024

94369234R10197